ENGLISH

高等学校英语专业文化通识教育基础教程

A Brief History of European Civilization
—From Antiquity to Early Modernity

欧洲文明简史
——从上古时代到现代初期

主　编　宋晓堃
副主编　尚劝余　张华鸿　詹俊峰　梅园

广东高等教育出版社
Guangdong Higher Education Press
广州

图书在版编目（CIP）数据

欧洲文明简史——从上古时代到现代初期 = A Brief History of European Civilization—From Antiquity to Early Modernity. 英文／宋晓堃主编. —广州：广东高等教育出版社，2011. 11（2021. 3 重印）
ISBN 978 - 7 - 5361 - 4177 - 3

Ⅰ. ①欧…　Ⅱ. ①宋…　Ⅲ. ①英语 - 高等学校 - 教材 ②文化史 - 欧洲　Ⅳ. ①H31

中国版本图书馆 CIP 数据核字（2011）第 229730 号

广东高等教育出版社出版发行
地址：广州市天河区林和西横路
邮编：510500　电话：（020）87557232
网址：http://www. gdgjs. com. cn
广州市穗彩印务有限公司印刷
787 毫米 ×1092 毫米　16 开本　22. 5 印张　576 千字
2011 年 11 月第 1 版　2021 年 3 月第 4 次印刷
印数：6 001 ~ 8 000 册
定价：40. 00 元

前　言

本书是根据我国大学英语专业《欧洲文化入门》或《西方文明入门》课程的教学需要而编写的一部教科书。

2000年，教育部颁布《高等学校英语专业英语教学大纲》，对我国21世纪的英语教育提出了新的要求。新教学大纲规定，英语专业学生培养方案需在文化通识教育、博雅教育的基础上发展学生听、说、读、写四大核心语言技能。《欧洲文化入门》或《西方文明入门》课程体现了新教学大纲精神，成为英语专业文化通识教育的基础课程。

自2001年以来，在张华鸿老师的带领下，华南师范大学外国语言文化学院为英语专业全日制本科、成人夜大、网络学院、辅修专业和非英语专业等不同层次学生开设了《欧洲文明入门》文化通识教育课程，迄今已有10余年，选课学生累计达5 000余人。在此期间，本课程教师团队结合国内外现有教材和网络资源，自行编写讲义，并不断修改、完善。

2007年，《欧洲文明简史》纳入了华南师范大学“十一五”重点教材规划项目。教材编写组由宋晓堃、尚劝余、张华鸿、詹俊峰、梅园五位老师组成，宋晓堃任组长，具体主持和协调教材编写。经过四年的通力合作和辛勤笔耕，《欧洲文明简史——从上古时代到现代初期》终于编写完成并由广东高等教育出版社出版。

与目前国内为数不多的相关教材相比，本教材具有如下几个特点。

1. 目前国内学者编写的相关英文教材，在内容上侧重于狭义的文化层面的介绍，即宗教、文学、艺术等上层建筑领域的主要成就的介绍，缺乏对欧洲文明或文化的历时性与共时性相结合的全面揭示，使学生只知其然而不知其所以然。本教材旨在从历时性与共时性相结合的角度，对各时期经济—社会—政治基础和不同领域重大文化或文明成就进行综合梳理，避免以条目形式简单罗列各项史实，以期帮助学生了解西方文明或文化的内在历史逻辑和联系，建立动态的立体的文明史观，既知其然，亦知其所以然。

2. 目前国内也引进了一些国外学者撰写的有关欧洲文明史或西方文明史的大学原版教材，但这些原版教材对我国大多数学生来说，存在语言难度较大、内容与原有的中学知识无法顺利衔接等问题。本教材针对我国大多数学生的实际情况，在语言方面尽可能避繁就简，通俗易懂，在句法上尽量使用简单句式，在词汇上尽量选用大学英语四、六级词汇表范围内的词汇，在内容上以中学世界历史、世界地理和国际政治三门课程所覆盖的知识为基础，注重与中学人文知识的衔接。

3. 目前国内外有关欧洲文明史教材的编写都是上起古代下至20世纪，但国内许多大学通识教育基础课程一般都在一个学期完成教学，因此教学内容偏多，至少需要一个学年以上才能完成。本教材上起古代近东地区文明的发轫，下至16世纪西欧宗教改革运动，经本教材编写组成员多年的实际教学检验，正好上满一个学期。此外，到16世纪，欧洲文明各基本要素已然显现并相互杂糅，形成独具一格的欧洲文明风貌，其后西欧各国在世界范围扩张，欧洲文明陆续在美洲、大洋洲出现变异体，需另书介绍。

4. 与目前国内相关教材相比，本教材在编写体例上别具一格。为了帮助学生掌握课文的组织结构和中心要点，本教材每章开篇设有章节提纲（Chapter Outline）和重点问题（Focus Questions）；为了帮助学生理解课文，附有旁注和脚注，对重大事件、地名、人名、语言难点或学生不容易理解的地方做出注释。同时，每章后都结合课文重点，设计名词解释题、判断正误题及多项选择题，这些练习题不仅可以帮助学生记忆各种信息，巩固和提高文化和语言知识，还可以帮助学者复习、归纳所学内容，便于自学。

总之，本教材不仅适用于我国大学英语专业学生，而且也适用于非英语专业学生、自学者和高中学生。

本教材编写具体分工如下：

宋晓堃：第一章、第四章、第五章、第九章；尚劝余：第六章、第七章；张华鸿：第八章；詹俊峰：第二章；梅园：第三章。宋晓堃负责全书的统稿，并对一些章节进行了修改或重写。高级汉—英—法同传专家 William White 先生，资深英语外籍教师 Peter Gordon 和 Thomas Ackerman 先生对书稿进行了耐心细致地审读，编写组对他们的辛劳表示衷心感谢。

编写组抱着认真负责的态度开展编写工作，在编写过程中尽量考虑到我国英语专业基础阶段学生的语言能力、文化知识储备情况和学生常用的学习策略，但是百密一疏，教材中一定还会有诸多疏漏，我们恳请广大教师和学生提出宝贵的批评意见，以便有机会再版时改进。

宋晓堃
2011 年 9 月
于华南师范大学

Contents

Part Ⅰ Ancient World

Part II The Medieval World

Chapter 9 Reformation (1500–1600)

Part I Ancient World

Civilization began along major river valleys in the eastern hemisphere and along coastal areas in the western hemisphere. The major early civilizations in ancient world are Mesopotamian Civilization around the Tigris-Euphrates River in the West Asia, Egyptian Civilization around the Nile River in North Africa, Indian Civilization around the Indus River in South Asia, Chinese Civilization around the Yellow River in East Asia, Greo-Roman Civilization around the Aegean Sea and Mediterranean Sea in Western Europe, Native American Civilization along coastal areas in America.

Among these early civilizations, some are closely linked with European civilization. It is widely accepted that the Ancient Near East Civilization (i. e. Mesopotamian Civilization and Egyptian Civilization) is the cradle of human civilization; but it is only recently established that the ancient Near East is also the source of European civilization. To understand the birth of European civilization, we need to go back to the ancient Near East, where people in Mesopotamia and Egypt developed organized societies and created the ideas and institutions that we associate with civilization. The ancient Greeks and Romans, who created Greo-Roman Civilization and played such a crucial role in the development of Western civilization, were themselves nourished and influenced by these older societies in the ancient Near East.

The Greo-Roman Civilization which has been influencing the West broadly and profoundly up to today is considered the fountain-head of European civilization. The Greo-Roman Civilization is also called Classical Civilization. It starts from Minoan Civilization and ends with the fall of Western Roman Empire. It includes Hellenic (or Greek) Civilization (29th—4th century BC), Hellenistic Civilization (4th—1st century BC) and Roman Civilization (753 BC—476 AD). Classical Civilization emphasized matters concerning mankind and the making of this world into a better place; hence the classical tradition stresses rational and secular knowledge, liberty, freedom of inquiry, the nobility of human achievement, and the worth of the individual. These values form the core of Western civilization.

Chapter 1
Civilizations in the Ancient Near East

CHAPTER OUTLINE

1. Introduction
2. Civilization in **Mesopotamia**
3. Ancient Egyptian Civilization
4. The **Hebrews**: History and Religion
5. Conclusion

Mesopotamia *n.* 美索不达米亚，两河流域

Hebrew *n.* 希伯来人（的）

FOCUS QUESTIONS

1. In what ways did geography influence the historical development of civilizations in Mesopotamia and Egypt?
2. What were the similarities and differences in the religious belief of the Sumerians, Egyptians, and Hebrews?
3. In what ways did civilizations and cultures in the ancient Near East influence the development of European civilization?

The Abduction of Europa（欧罗巴的掳掠）

In Greek mythology（神话）, Europa was the beautiful daughter of the Phoenician king, Agenor. One day, Zeus, the King of the Olympian gods, saw Europa as she was gathering flowers by the sea and immediately fell in love with her.

Driven by his love for Europa, Zeus transformed himself into a magnificent white bull（公牛）and appeared on the sea shore where Europa was playing with her maidens. The great bull walked gently over to Europa and knelt at her feet. The great animal looked so gentle and friendly that Europa had no fear of it. She hung flowers about the bul's neck and even climbed upon its back.

But suddenly, the bull jumped into the Mediterranean Sea（地中海）, carrying Europa away. When it finally reached the island of Crete（克里特岛）Zeus transformed back into his human form and made Europa his lover beneath a tree. Europa became the first queen of Crete and had three sons by Zeus. The land was later named after Europa (Europe) and the people living there were called Europeans.

1. Introduction

cradle *n.* 摇篮
Cornell University 康奈尔大学
origins *n.* 起源
stir up *v. pr.* 激起
controversy *n.* 争议
approximately *adv.* 大约
corresponding to *v. pr.* 相当于
Armenia 亚美尼亚
Cyprus 塞浦路斯
Iran 以色列
Lebanon 黎巴嫩
Archeological *adj.* 考古学的
relics *n.* 遗物，遗迹
Mesopotamian *adj.* 美索不达米亚的，两河流域的
Hebrew *adj.* 希伯来的

People traditionally regard ancient Greece as the **cradle** of European civilization. However, in recent years, questions have been raised about the truth of this general understanding. In 1987 Professor Martin Bernal at **Cornell University** published a book entitled *Black Athena: The Afro-Asiatic Roots of Classical Civilization.* In this book, he puts forward a new theory of Greek cultural **origins**. Based on large amounts of historical evidence, Professor Bernal argues that the emergence and development of ancient Greek culture was influenced much more greatly by civilizations in the ancient Near East than had previously been acknowledged. Bernal's new account of the origins of ancient Greek culture has **stirred up** heated discussions. Was ancient Greek culture created in Europe and by Europeans only? Or was its development a result of cultural exchanges and interactions between people in ancient Greece and their neighbors outside of Europe? To find an answer to this **controversy**, this chapter will examine the development of early cultures and civilizations in the ancient Near East.

The term "ancient Near East" refers to a historical region **approximately corresponding to** much of the modern Middle East; **Armenia**, **Cyprus**, Iran, Iraq, **Israel**, Jordan, **Lebanon**, Palestine, Syria, and a major part of Egypt. But the region was no longer called "ancient Near East" after it was conquered by Alexander the Great (356—323 BC) conquered the region in the 4th century BC. **Archeological** evidence suggests that this is the area that gave birth to the earliest human civilizations. Different peoples living in this region created many amazing cultures; **relics** and traditions of which survive to the present day. As it is impossible to cover them all in one chapter, we will focus on the development of two civilizations and one culture in the region, namely, the **Mesopotamian** civilization, the Egyptian civilization, and the **Hebrew** culture.

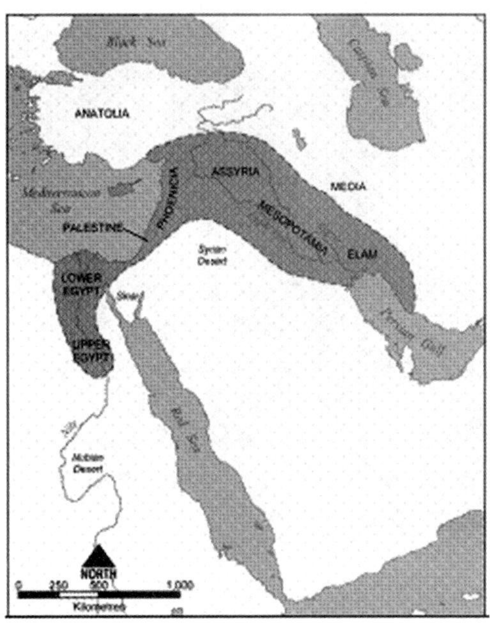

Map 1 Ancient Near East

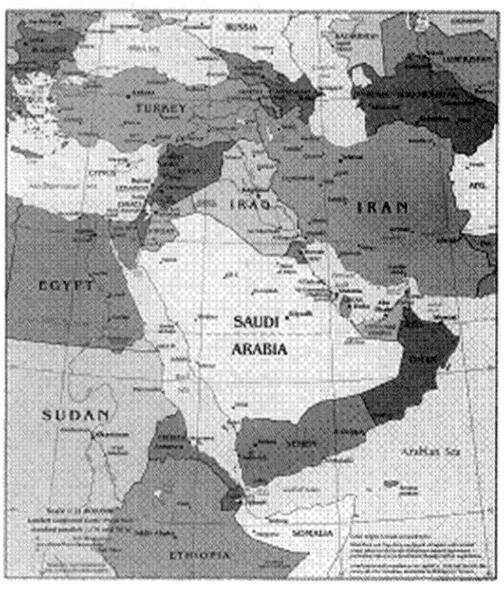

Map 2 Modern Middle East

2. Civilization in Mesopotamia

From the mountains in today's **Turkey** two great rivers—the **Tigris** and **Euphrates**—separately start their long journeys. On their way, the two rivers grow bigger as many smaller rivers join them. These rivers create many small plains and lowlands. Towards the end of their journeys, the two rivers meet each other and flow into the **Persian Gulf**. Ancient Greek people called the land between the Tigris and Euphrates "Mesopotamia", meaning "the land between the two rivers". To the north of Mesopotamia lies the mountainous **Iranian plateau** and to its south the **Syrian desert**, both areas dry and hot. The climate in Mesopotamia is also hot but humid, thanks to the rivers.

Every year in late spring or early summer, snow in the Turkish mountains melted. Melting snow caused the flooding of the Tigris and Euphrates which would wash **silt** down from the mountains adding new layers of rich soil to the plains. The rich soil and humid climate provided a wonderful environment for early agriculture. According to **legends**, this is where the **Garden of Eden**—the garden created by God for the first man, Adam—was situated. And the Tree of Life grew right on the spot where the Tigris meets the Euphrates. When seen on a map, the green plains in Mesopotamian form the shape of a new moon. This is why this area is also called "**the fertile crescent**".

Turkey 土耳其
the Tigris 底格里斯河
the Euphrates 幼发拉底河
Persian Gulf 波斯湾
Iranian plateau 伊朗高原
Syrian desert 叙利亚沙漠
silt *n.* 沉积土
legend *n.* 传说
Garden of Eden 伊甸园
the fertile crescent 富饶的新月地

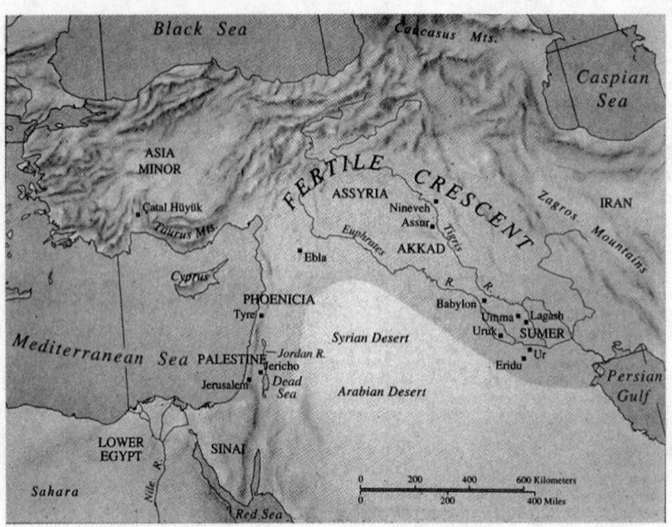

Map 3 A bird-view of the Mesopotamian plain

Around 8000 BC, people in Mesopotamia started producing food by farming. Although the two rivers provided a plentiful water supply, and the soil in the river plains was very rich, farming was not easy. The Mesopotamian people were faced with two natural challenges. First, the annual floods between April and June were **irregular**. It was very difficult for people to predict and control the flooding. Often the floods caused great damage. Second, in such a hot region, the tremendous heat would cause rapid **evaporation** of the river water. When the water evaporated, large amounts of salt from the water would be left in the soil, making farming impossible.

irregular *adj.* 不规则的

evaporation *n.* 蒸发

One way to solve both problems was to build **irrigation** systems. **Dams** and **canals** were built to control the flooding and to water the land. Farming supported by these irrigation systems required **division of labor** and cooperation. Different people took care of different tasks: some planted the crops, some built the dams, some dug the canals, some supervised the activities, and still some prayed to gods for more rain and few floods. As systematic agriculture began to provide a **consistent** food **surplus**, populations grew and small villages developed into larger towns and cities. More **complex** social structures appeared in these towns and cities. The first human civilization was born.

irrigation *n.* 灌溉
dam *n.* 水坝
canal *n.* 运河
division of labor 分工

consistent *adj.* 持续的
surplus *n.* 剩余
complex *adj.* 复杂的

2.1 Brief history of Mesopotamia

It is important to bear in mind that the so-called Mesopotamian civilization was not one single civilization. It included cultures, customs, ideas and traditions developed by different groups of people over the course of several thousand years. Some of the early civilizations whose ideas were **assimilated** by the Mesopotamians included the **Sumerians**, **Akkadians**, **Babylonians** and **Assyrians**. When different groups lived in the same area without natural boundaries, cultural contacts and exchanges were frequent, but conflicts were also inevitable. One after another, these peoples ruled the region, either through economic or military power. Because of the absence of natural boundaries, neighboring regions also had a great influence on Mesopotamian history. Foreign invasions were frequent. Finally, in 539 BC, the Persians—a group of people from what is now modern day Iran—conquered the region and put an end to the Mesopotamian civilization.

assimilate *v.* 吸收
Sumerians 苏美尔人
Akkadians 阿卡德人
Babylonians 巴比伦人
Assyrians 亚述人

The creators of the Mesopotamian civilization were the Sumerians. Although today we regard the Sumerians as the founders of the first human civilization, we know very little about their origin. We assume that the Sumerians were not native in Mesopotamia. This assumption is mainly based on linguistic evidence. The most widely spoken language in the region was the **Semitic language**. Semitic-speaking populations at the time included **Akkadians**, **Amorites**, **Phoenicians**, **Hebrews**, and Arabs among many others.① But the Sumerians were the only non-Semitic speaking people there. So we assume that the Sumerians arrived in Mesopotamia from somewhere else, but we have no idea where they came from. On foot from today's Iran, **Afghanistan**, or even India? Or by sea from some other region? No one knows. Wherever they came from, the Sumerians arrived in southern Mesopotamia and settled down there. **Archeological** evidence shows that the earliest Sumerian economic and social activities in Mesopotamia dated back to about 5500 BC.

Semitic language 闪语
Akkadians 阿卡特人
Amorites 亚摩利人
Phoenicians 腓尼基人
Hebrews 希伯来人
Afghanistan 阿富汗
archeological *adj.* 考古学的

The Sumerians were the first people to start systematically farming the land. Over time the Sumerians learned to control the Tigris and Euphrates Rivers by constructing irrigation systems. They began intensive, year-round agriculture in southern Mesopotamia which produced a stable food supply. Over time, systematic agriculture and stable food surplus allowed Sumerian villages to **evolve into** self-governing city-states. By 3000 BC a number of Sumerian independent

evolve into *v. pr.* 演变成

① 演化至今，现代闪语主要包括阿拉伯语和希伯来语。

cities, including Eridu, Kish, Nippur, Lagash, Ur, and Uruk exercised economic and political control over the surrounding countryside. Gradually, these cities developed into city-states, forming the basic units of Sumerian civilization which lasted for the next one thousand years.

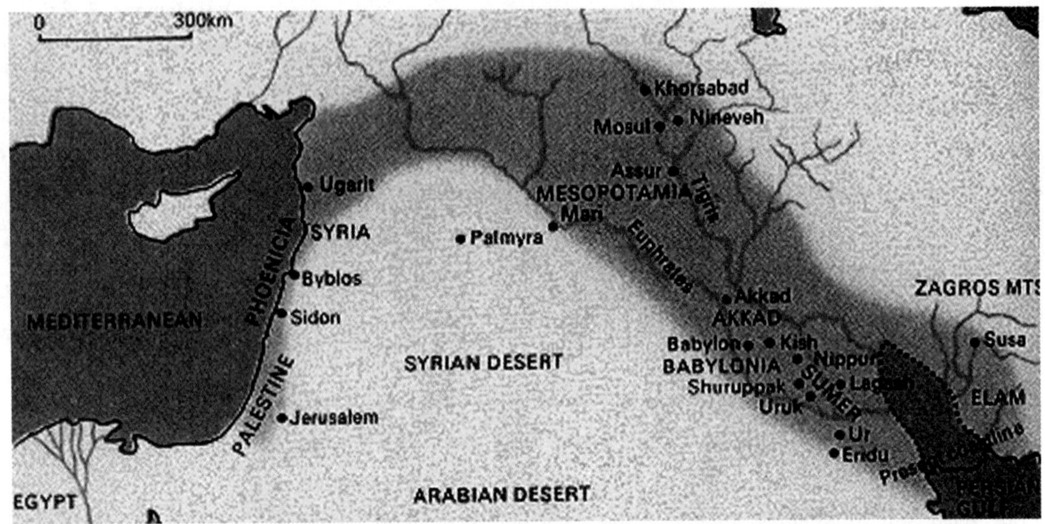

Map 4　The Sumerian city-states along the two rivers

The Sumerian culture was most developed in the lower river region, closest to the Persian Gulf. The main cities included: Eridu. Ur, Lagash, Uruk, Nippur, Shuruppak, Kish. Eridu was the cultural centre in the south, and Nippur the cultural centre in the north.

wheel *n.* 轮子

handicraft *n.* 手工业

pottery *n.* 陶器

Persian Gulf 波斯湾

The main sector of the Sumerian economy was based on agriculture, which used major technological innovations and inventions. A significant invention (one of many by the Sumerians) was the **wheel**, which at first was a round disc made of a piece of solid wood. When food supply was no longer a problem, some Sumerians were freed from farming and took up activities in **handicraft** and trade. Famous for their woolen textiles, **pottery**, and metalwork, Sumerian businessmen traded extensively with their neighbors, leading to the development of a trade network in the **Persian Gulf** region.

Ziggurat *n.* 塔庙

profit *n.* 利润

priest *n.* （男）祭司

At the center of each Sumerian city stood a temple, which was called a **Ziggurat** and built to honor the city's chief protecting god or goddess. All land in Sumer belonged to gods; this included both the land used for agriculture and the land that the great cities were built on. Whoever wanted to farm must rent the land from the temple. All **profits** must go back to the gods through the temple. In reality, it was the **priests** (or priestesses) living in the temples that controlled most of the land in the name of the gods. Priests (or priestesses), therefore, had great economic and political power. In many Sumerian city-states the powerful priests were also the kings of the city-states.

The social structure in the Sumerian city-stated was highly **hierarchical**. At the top was the king who was helped by advisory **councils** of **noblemen**. Most noblemen were family members of the kings. Under the king and his nobles, all members of society fell into one of two basic groups: the free person, and the slave. Most slaves were prisoners of war. But a free person may also be turned into slave if he could not pay his debt. Considered as the **private property** of the owner, slaves could be bought and sold. Compared with ancient Greek and Roman societies, the number of slaves in the Mesopotamian society was much smaller and the role of slaves in the economy much more limited.

hierarchical *adj.* 等级森严的

council *n.* 理事会

nobleman *n.* 贵族(男性)

noblemen *pl.*

private property 私有财产

As the Sumerian city-states grew in number and size, they started to fight over control of land and water. Around 2900 BC Sumerian city-states entered into the "warring period". For the next 500 years, wars destroyed the small Sumerian city—states and weakened the big ones. Then around 2340 BC the Akkadians—a group of Semitic people from the North-defeated the Sumerian city-states and established an empire. But the Empire was never very stable because of constant Sumerian revolts and foreign invasions. In less than 100 years the Empire of Akkad collapsed, almost as fast as it had developed. The Mesopotamian plain was again **ruined** by war. There were short periods of revival for the Sumerian city-states, and at one point, the king of the city-state of Ur, Ur-Nammu (2112—2095 BC) even managed to unify the Sumerian and Mesopotamian states. But eventually in 2004 BC the Sumerian civilization was put to an end by another group of Semitic-speaking people, the **Amorites**.

ruin *v.* 毁坏

Amorites 亚摩利人

Out of the conquered territories of the Sumerians and Akkadians, **Hammurabi** (1792—1750 BC), the great king of the Amorites created a huge empire, which because the capital was located in the city of Babylon, was later known as the Old Babylonian Empire. During his reign, Hammurabi took several measures to **concentrate** power in his own hands. Within the empire, a highly centralized and efficient **bureaucratic** system was created. In this system, the king appointed all the officials and sent supervisors to monitor local affairs. Local officials must report to the king by letter. Common people were encouraged to write to the king to report corruption and injustice, and to

Hammurabi 汉谟拉比

concentrate *v.* 集中

bureaucratic *adj.* 官僚的

compilation *n.* 编集成典
code of laws 法典

help maintain social order. Hammurabi ordered the **compilation** of **code of laws**. He also continued building a strong army for self-defense and further military expansion. For the next 150 years, a highly centralized royal authority, supported by efficient administrative, legal and military networks, brought peace and stability to the Mesopotamian region. This, in turn led to strong economic and cultural developments.

migrant *n.* 移民

With its wealth, the Old Babylonian Empire attracted foreign **migrants** as well as invaders. Once again, the flat Mesopotamia plains left the Empire open to foreign attacks, and in 1595 BC the **Hitties sacked** the city of Babylon.① The Babylonian Empire collapsed, but the Hittites failed to consolidate their rule and in the next few hundred years a number of kingdoms fought for regional dominance. For ordinary people life was chaotic and insecure.

Hittie *n.* 赫梯人
sack *v.* 攻陷
consolidate *v.* 巩固
dominance *n.* 霸主地位
chaotic *adj.* 混乱的

Finally, wars and conflicts among different kingdoms were ended by the rise of the Kingdom of Assyria around 1300 BC. Originated in the northern Mesopotamia, the Semitic-speaking Assyrians were known for their military skills. In creating a strong army, they improved Sumerians' technological invention, most importantly the **wheeled chariots** and iron weapons. Continuous military expansion transformed the kingdom into an empire. Between 800 and 700 BC, the Assyrian Empire covered not only the Mesopotamian area but also Syria, Palestine, and large part of today's Turkey and Egypt. Although the Assyrians tried to imitate the Babylonians to replace military rule with an imperial administrative and legal system, their rule was not welcomed by the non-Assyrian groups. Internally, revolts were frequent; externally, defense of the long borders was difficult. In 612 BC, the empire **collapsed**. There was a brief period of Babylonian revival. Then in 539 BC, the city of Babylon was conquered by Cyrus the Great, the founder of **Persian Empire**. As the political map of the ancient Near East was rearranged, the ancient Mesopotamian civilization ended, but its **legacy** continues to influence us today.

wheeled chariot 有轮战车
collapse *v.* 崩溃
Persian Empire 波斯帝国
legacy *n.* 遗产

① 赫梯是一个位于安纳托利亚（今天土耳其）的亚洲古国。王国最初建立于公元前 19 世纪，随后骁勇善战的赫梯人不断向两河平原地区扩张。公元前 14 世纪，赫梯帝国达到鼎盛时期，国土疆域包括安纳托利亚大部、叙利亚西北部、两河平原上游地区。但两个世纪后，帝国分裂成几个独立小国，最后一个赫梯国于公元前 8 世纪消亡。

2.2 The Cultural Achievements of Mesopotamia

Although today we are far removed from that time, some of our most basic and fundamental knowledge and tools **originated** in ancient Mesopotamia. For example, we cannot imagine leaving our home without locking the door; it was in ancient Mesopotamia that locks and keys were first used; we cannot survive in this world without knowing the time, it was in ancient Mesopotamia that the **sexagesimal system** of keeping time was developed; we cannot imagine going everywhere only on foot, it was in ancient Mesopotamia that the wheel was first invented. The list of innovations and inventions made by the ancient Mesopotamians is very long; the first postal system, the first use of iron, the first **magnifying glass**, the first libraries, the first plumbing and flush toilets, the first guitars, the first **aqueducts**, the first paved roads, and on and on.

originate *v.* 起源

sexagesimal system 六十进制

magnifying glass 放大镜

aqueduct *n.* 导水渠

It is not only things that originated in Mesopotamia, it is also ideas, ideas that would shape the world to come. The Assyrians, for example, developed the idea of **imperial** administration, i. e. dividing the land into territories administered by local governors who reported to the central authority. This fundamental model of administration has survived to this day, and can be seen in America's **federal** system.

imperial *adj.* 帝国的

federal *adj.* 联邦制的

In general terms, civilization created by the Sumerians survived the later Semitic-speaking peoples. The Sumerians determined to a large extent the religious, ethical, and artistic directions of the Mesopotamian civilization. While the Semitic-speaking Akkadians, Amorites, and Assyrians also made important contributions to cultural development in the region, they continued to worship the Sumerian gods, to retell the Sumerian **myths** and **epics**, to use the writing system invented by the Sumerians, and to improve the Sumerian science and technology.

myth *n.* 神话

epic *n.* 史诗

2.2.1 Religion

Generally speaking, religion is a system of beliefs, **rituals**, and **standards of conduct**. As in all other **primitive** societies, religion played a vital role in ancient Mesopotamia. Religion in Mesopotamia gave the world its first **mythology**. In Sumerian myths and legends we can see some of the questions these people had asked about the world they lived in and of their own lives: Why does it rain? Why do the rivers flood? Who are we? Where are we? How do we get here? Where are we going? What is right? What is wrong? As science and

ritual *n.* 仪式

standard of conduct 行为标准

primitive *adj.* 原始的

mythology *n.* 神话

technologies were not advanced, people provided explanations for these questions by **attributing** them **to** gods, goddess, and spirits.

The Sumerians practiced a **polytheistic** religion, in other words, they believed in many gods and goddess. According to Sumerian mythology, in the beginning water was everywhere, then one day the sky-god An (or Annu) and the earth-goddess Ki created the **universe** out of the water. That is why the Sumerian word for universe is "an-ki". In this universe, the earth was a flat **disc** covered by the heaven. The most powerful god governing the universe was the air-god Enlil, son of An and Ki. **Subordinate to** Enlil there were many lesser gods, goddesses, and spirits. All gods and goddess in the Sumerian mythology had human form, but unlike humans, they remained forever strong, forever young. Gods created human beings in their own image because they needed servants. The living purpose of all men, therefore, was to serve the gods, their creators.

Sumerians believed that man had a soul, but once he died, the soul would **perish**. For them, death was the end of life. The Sumerians' disbelief in life after death can be found in the stories about **Gilgamesh**. The best-known and most popular hero in the mythology of the ancient Near East, Gilgamesh was a Sumerian king who ruled the Kingdom of Uruk somewhere between 2750—2500 BC. Born with superhuman strength, courage, and power, he appears in numerous legends and myths, including the ***Epic of Gilgamesh***. The epic tells of Gilgamesh's adventure in search of **immortality**. Written more than 3 000 years ago, this epic is one of the earliest works of literature in the world. It is an adventure story that explores the nature of human existence. The story deals with values and concerns that are still relevant today.

Because the Sumerians did not believe in life after death, their **funerals** were simple. In a way, it is not hard to understand why people in Mesopotamia did not believe in life after death: in a region with plenty natural destruction (e. g. floods) and human made disasters (e. g. wars), life was **fragile** and often short; when every day was a struggle for survival, who would have the time to think about life after death?

attribute... to... 把……归因于……
polytheistic *adj.* 多神论的
universe *n.* 宇宙
disc *n.* 圆盘
subordinate to *v. pr.* 次于
perish *v.* 消逝
Gilgamesh 吉尔迦美什
Epic of Gilgamesh 《吉尔迦美什史诗》
immortality *n.* 永生
funeral *n.* 葬礼
fragile *adj.* 脆弱的

On his travels, Gilgamesh meets a goddess who tries to persuade him to accept human mortality with these words:

"Gilgamesh, whither rovest thou? "吉尔迦美什哟，你要流浪到哪里?
The life thou pursuest thou shalt not find. 你所探求的生命将无处寻觅。
When the gods created mankind, 自从诸神把人创造，
Death for mankind they set aside, 就把死给人派定无疑，
Life in their own hands retaining. 生命就在人们自己的手里!
Thou, Gilgamesh, let full be thy belly 吉尔迦美什哟，你只管填满你的肚皮，
Make thou merry by day and by night. 不论白天黑夜，尽管寻欢逗趣;
Of each day make thou a feast of rejoicing, 每天摆起盛宴，
Day and night dance thou and play, 白天夜里你尽管跳舞游戏，
Let thy garments be sparkling and fresh, 将你华丽的衣衫穿起;
Thy head be washed, bathe thou in water. 你洗头，沐浴，
Pay heed to the little one that holds thy hand, 爱你那手里领着的儿女;
Let thy spouse delight in thy bosom, 让你怀里的妻子高高兴兴。
For this is the task of mankind." 这才是'做人'的正理。"

2.2.2 Language

Sumerians also created the first known writing system in human history. Their writing system was probably their most important creation. With a writing system, cultural development moved on to a higher stage and civilization emerged. The earliest Sumerian writing system was a simple **pictographic** one. Pen and paper had not yet been invented. The Sumerians would write with a **reed** on a wet **tablet** made out of mud. In the beginning, writing was developed in order to keep records of farming and trade. On the wet **clay** tablet, Sumerians would first draw pictures of the things to be counted and then mark the amount next to the pictures. As economic activities grew in complexity, simple **pictograms** were gradually replaced by more abstract cuneiform scripts. It took centuries for the writing system to evolve from pictograms to **cuneiform**.

pictographic *adj.* 象形的
reed *n.* 芦苇
tablet *n.* 平板
clay *n.* 黏土
pictogram *n.* 象形文字
cuneiform *n.* 楔形文字

The cuneiform script invented by the Sumerians in about 3400 BC, greatly influenced the Mesopotamian region and remained in use throughout the region for more than 30 centuries. While the other Semitic-speaking groups continued using their own spoken language, they all used the **phonetic** system of the cuneiform script to **transcribe** their spoken languages. Although cuneiform was widely used in the region, the number of people who could read and write was small. It

phonetic *adj.* 语音的
transcribe *v.* 抄录

scribe *n.* 书吏
durable *adj.* 耐久的

took many years to learn to read and write. Someone who could read and write was given the title of "**scribe**", which means "reed" in Sumerian. Thanks to the Sumerian invention of a **durable** writing system, a large number of written materials have survived which help us to understand more about Mesopotamian society and culture.

Figure above shows the transformation of the Sumerian writing system from the simple pictographic form to more complex cuneiform.

2.2.3 *Law*

Just as in many other places, rulers in ancient Mesopotamia used religion to justify their rule. They claimed that their right to rule came from the gods. To make sure everything was done in a way that the god's would approve of, laws and rules were necessary. As early as 3000 BC rulers in Mesopotamia started to compile and implement laws. The Code of Ur-Nammu (2100 BC) is the oldest written copy of a system of laws that has been discovered so far. It was written in the Sumerian language on a piece of clay.

Code of Hammurabi 汉谟拉比法典
inscribe *v.* 雕刻
preface *n.* 序言
righteousness *n.* 正义
articles *n.* 条款
retaliation *n.* 一报还一报
severe *adj.* 严厉的
gender *n.* 性别

The most famous set of laws, however, was **Code of Hammurabi**. It was created around 1750 BC by the great Babylonian king Hammurabi (1728—1686 BC) after he unified Mesopotamia. The code was **inscribed** on a big piece of stone in the Akkadian language in the cuneiform script. In the **preface** to the law code, Hammurabi stated that he was ordered by the gods "to bring about the rule of **righteousness** in the land". The code contains 282 **articles**, each with no more than two sentences and with the same syntactic structure "If... then...". The system was based on the principle of **retaliation** ("an eye for an eye, a tooth for a tooth"), but often punishments for crimes were, by present standards, unnecessarily **severe**, for example, one may be put to death for stealing. Besides, punishments vary according to the social status and **gender** of the criminal. The Code of Hammurabi reveals to us a society with a system of strict justice, but in this society individuals were not equal.

Despite its many drawbacks, the Code of Hammurabi helped to regulate relationships in various domains such as the family and business. It also contributed to political and cultural unification in the

Babylonian Empire. The Code of Hammurabi and other sets of laws have thus remained an important part of the cultural heritage from the Mesopotamian civilization. For centuries these laws had been used as textbooks for the training of scribes.

The Code of Hammurabi emphasizes the principle of retaliation ("an eye for an eye") but punishment vary according to social status and gender. The following examples illustrates these differences.

196. If a free man had destroyed the eye of a member of the aristocracy, then he shall have his eye destroyed.

198. If he has destroyed the eye of a free man's slave or broken the bone of a free man's slave, then he shall pay one-half his value.

3. Ancient Egyptian Civilization

Around 3150 BC, when the Sumerians were busy building cities along the Tigris and Euphrates, another ancient civilization emerged along the lower area of the River Nile in northern Africa. This was the ancient Egyptian civilization. For the next 3 000 years the Egyptians would make amazing contributions to mankind's development. Just as with the Mesopotamian civilization, the long-lasting Egyptian civilization was also brought to an end by foreign invasion. In 332 BC Egypt was conquered by **Alexander the Great** (356—323 BC). Then, in 31 BC the expanding Roman Empire took over Egypt from the Greeks, turning it into a Roman province and renaming it "Africa". Known as one of the four ancient civilizations, Egyptian civilization equals the Mesopotamian civilization in its glory and pride. Like the Mesopotamian civilization, it was also a "river valley" civilization; however, the two civilizations had very different political histories and patterns of development, mainly due to the differences in their natural environment.

Alexander the Great 亚历山大大帝

3.1 Egypt: "The Gift of the Nile"

By calling Egypt "the gift of the Nile", Greek historian **Herodotus** (484—425 BC) nicely summed up the importance of the Nile to ancient the Egyptian civilization. The Nile, the longest river in the world (6 670 km), was the lifeline of the ancient Egyptian civilization. Without it, Egyptian civilization could not have existed. In contrast to Mesopotamia, the climate in Egypt is hot but dry. Land in Egypt

Herodotus 希罗多德

moisture *n.* 水分

annual *adj.* 一年一度的

Ethiopian *adj.* 埃塞俄比亚的

receives little rainfall. In this area short of rainfall, the Nile was the only source of **moisture**. Without the River Nile, the area would be entirely deserts. Apart from water supply, the Nile's **annual** floods also created a fertile green valley across the desert. Every June, heavy summer rain in the **Ethiopian** highlands caused flooding that overflowed the banks of the Nile. When the floods went down they left rich black mud which was ideal to grow healthy crops. As early as 7000 BC, the ancient Egyptian people started agricultural activities along the river banks and in the north river delta, using the rich soil and water provided by the Nile to produce food for themselves and their animals. Today almost 95% of Egypt's population still lives in the Nile valley.

Map 5 Ancient Egypt

pharaoh *n.* 法老

plough *v.* 耕犁

Because of the importance of the Nile, Egyptian farmers divided their year into three seasons, based on the cycles of the Nile River. Between June and September was the Flooding Season (*Akhet*). No farming was done at this time, as all the fields were flooded. Instead, farmers would repair tools or make new ones, and many would be called upon to work for their king, the **pharaoh**, building pyramids or temples. From October to February was the Growing Season (Peret). This was the time when farmers **ploughed** the fertile soil left behind by the floods and **seeded**. Then in March, April and May the fully grown crops had to be cut down and removed before the Nile flooded again. This was the Harvesting Season (Shemu). It was also the time to repair the canals ready for the next flood.

seed *v.* 播种

All Egypt depended, in some way, on the Nile for water, food and transportation. In the Flooding Season, farmers used spears and nets to catch fish. They would also use the nets to catch birds that flew close to the surface of the water. Another way the Nile helped the ancient Egyptians was in trade. The Nile was the quickest and easiest way to travel from place to place. And then there were reeds, called **papyrus**, waving in plenty alongside the Nile. Papyrus was the primary material from which the Egyptians made paper, boats, and building materials.

papyrus *n.* 纸莎草

3.2 A Brief History of Ancient Egypt

In sharp contrast to the frequent political **upheavals** and constant foreign invasions that took place in Mesopotamia, peace and stability featured the long history of ancient Egypt. Egypt's unique natural environment played an important role in its political history. As we have mentioned earlier, the Nile flooded every year, creating fertile land along the river banks. What was unique about the Nile was that its annual flooding was regular and **predictable**, unlike the flooding of the Tigris and Euphrates. It was, therefore, easier for people to control the floods. Farming on the rich soil along the river banks was much less labor-intensive, that is to say, to produce enough food for all did not require everyone to work in the fields. Sufficient food surplus provided the economic basis for internal stability. It allowed people to work on magnificent monuments such as the pyramids and temples or to take up new professions such as **artisan** and trader.

upheaval *n.* 动乱

predictable *adj.* 可预测的

artisan *n.* 工匠，手艺人

Another natural factor contributing to stability in the political development of ancient Egypt was the environment in the neighboring areas of the Nile Valley. The Nile Valley is surrounded by deserts and seas—the Sahara desert to the west, the Mediterranean to its north, and the Red Sea to the east, all served as excellent natural defenses, making foreign invasions less frequent than in Mesopotamia. Before Greek expansion into the region during the 4th century BC, Egypt had experienced few massive foreign invasions. A healthy and strong agricultural economy, internal stability, and external security, all ensured great continuity in Egyptian civilization.

The history of ancient Egypt spans from the early settlements in the northern Nile Valley 5 000 years ago to the Roman conquest in 30 BC. In

King Menes 美尼斯法老

Pharaonic Period 法老时代

millennium *n.* 一千年

millennia *pl.*

dynasty *n.* 朝代

around 3150 BC, **King Menes** from Upper Egypt in the north conquered Lower Egypt in the south and unified the Nile Valley. The unification marked the beginning of the **Pharaonic Period** which was to last for the next three **millennia**. In total, there were thirty one **dynasties**. The Pharaonic Period ended in 332 BC when Alexander the Great conquered Egypt. Later, in 31 BC, the Romans took over the Greek rule of Egypt and turned it into a Roman province renaming it "Africa".

3.3 Ancient Egyptian Culture and Society

Cairo *n.* 开罗

aesthetics *n.* 美学

Most people associate Egypt with its pyramids. For thousands of years, more than 100 pyramids stood solid and strong on the west bank of the Nile, against the shifting sand of the Sahara desert. Most pyramids are grouped around or near **Cairo** and were built in the periods called "the Old Kingdom" (2686—2125 BC) and "Middle Kingdom" (2055—1650 BC). Many questions have been raised about the pyramids. What was their function? Or, in other words, why did ancient Egyptians build them? Why are all the pyramids located on the west bank of the Nile? Why did they all have the same pyramidal shape? What was inside the pyramids? Exactly who built the pyramids? How and why could they afford their time and energy to build the pyramids? How did they build the pyramids? Answers to these questions will reveal to us almost some important aspects of Egyptian civilization, its economy, social structure, political system, religion, language, science, technology, and **aesthetics**.

3.3.1 Religion in Egyptian Society

polytheistic *adj.* 多神论的

hawk *n.* 鹰

jackal *n.* 豺狗

Religion is the key to our understanding of ancient Egyptian civilization for it guided every aspect of Egyptian life. Like most peoples in the ancient Near East, Egyptians were **polytheistic**. The Egyptians had as many as 2000 gods and goddesses. Because of their strong belief in gods, the ancient Egyptians built temples everywhere in the country. Each city had a temple built for the protecting god (or goddess) of that city. Temples were not only places for gods to live; they were also the places for men to communicate with their gods. The ancient Egyptians believed that the gods were the creators and rulers of the universe and man. Some of these gods were worshipped throughout the whole country, while others had only a local following. Egyptian gods and goddesses often had a human body and an animal head. For example, Horus, the sky god, had the head of a **hawk**, and body of a human; and Anubis, the god of afterlife, had the head of a **jackal**. The only exceptions were the two most powerful gods, Amon-Ra and Osiris.

Amon-Ra was believed to be the sun god and the lord of the universe. Osiris was the god of the underworld. Both of them were depicted in human form.

For a short period of time, some kind of monotheistic trend also developed in Egyptian religious belief. This happened under the rule of the Pharaoh Akhenaten (1353—1336 BC) in the New Kingdom period. Akhenaten started a new worship of the god Aten who represented the force of light. He wanted people to believe that Aten was the only real god, the only god worth worshipping. But since the new monotheistic trend was more the idea of the king instead of the people, after Akhenaten died, ordinary Egyptians went back to worshipping other gods again, as they had before.

A main feature of the Egyptian religion was their belief in life after death. Similar to the Mesopotamian people, the ancient Egyptians believed in the existence of human souls; but different from Mesopotamians, they believed that some time after death a person's spirit might come back to his body and the person would live again. For them, every human being was made up of his body and his spiritual parts. The ancient Egyptians also believed that a person's thoughts and emotions were located in the heart instead of the brain. When a person died, his spiritual parts would leave the body. His heart would be judged by Anubis, the god of the afterlife, to see what kind of person he had been when alive. If this person was bad and immoral, his spiritual parts would be destroyed; if he was good and moral, his spiritual parts would continue to exist. Then, one day the spiritual parts may return to the person's body and this person would live forever. Some modern scholars think that Christianity might have borrowed their ideas of final judgment and **resurrection** from the ancient Egyptians.

resurrection *n.* 复活

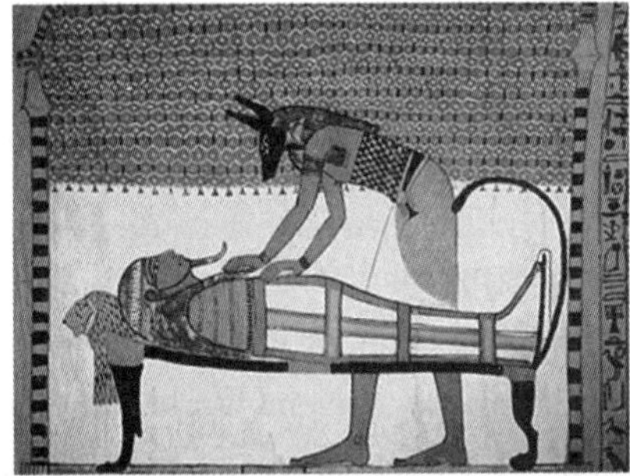

Anubis was the ancient Egyptian god in charge of mummification and burial. On the left, he attends to a mummy; on the right, he weighs the heart of a dead person to judge whether he can have a life after death.

preservation *n.* 保存
mummification *n.* 制作木乃伊
mummy *n.* 木乃伊

Given their firm belief in life-after-death, the ancient Egyptians tried their best to prevent the bodies of the dead from rotting. They developed a complicated method of **preservation**, called **mummification**. It took more than 70 days to turn the body of a person into a **mummy**. The ancient Egyptians' practice of mummification has revealed to us the advanced level of their medical knowledge and techniques. However, very few Egyptians could afford to pay for the expensive process of mummification. In the early days, only the bodies of pharaohs' could be mummified. Pharaohs also ordered the design and construction of huge stone tombs, such as the pyramids, to protect their bodies. When a Pharaoh died, his body would be buried in the pyramid. The most important thing inside the pyramid was naturally the mummy of the Pharaoh. But, to make sure that the Pharaoh had a good after-life, treasures would also be put inside. There would also be paintings and drawings showing what the Pharaoh had done in his lifetime so that the gods would know how important or good he was.

Why, then, did ancient Egyptians choose the pyramidal shape for their Pharaoh's tomb? Again, the answer is to be found in their religious beliefs. In the ancient Egyptian mythology, in the beginning the universe was a lifeless dark ocean. Then one day the first land emerged from this ocean. It was a pyramidal hill. Together with the hill the sun god Ra rose above the sea. He brought light into the darkness and created all things. The shape of pyramid was thus closely linked with the idea of new life. The reason why all pyramids are on the West bank of the Nile is also religious. This was the side of the sunset. For the ancient Egyptians, sunrise meant the beginning of life and sunset the end of life. When looked at from a distance, the pyramids along the Nile look like the rays of the Sun. As we have mentioned earlier, the ancient Egyptians believed their Pharaoh to be the son of Ra, the sun god. Pharaohs buried in the huge pyramids continued to overlook the whole country even after death. The pyramids were an important symbol of royal power. They reminded people of the glory and power of the Pharaoh, a living god on earth.

King Khufu 胡夫国王

The largest and the most famous pyramid is the Great Pyramid at Giza built for **King Khufu** (2613—2563 BC) It is not only the oldest and the largest of the Seven Wonders of the Ancient World but also the only one surviving for us to visit today. The Great Pyramid is 140 meters high and each of its sides 230 meters long. It takes about twenty minutes to walk all the way around the pyramid. For over 3 800 years, the Great Pyramid was the tallest man-made structure in the world. In total, over 2.3 million blocks of solid stone were used to build the Great Pyramid. An average stone block used to build the structure weighs two and a half tones, the weight of a large car. Some larger ones used in the construction weigh fifteen tones. The total mass of the pyramid is estimated at 5.9 million tones. Most of the blocks came from the east bank of the Nile, and they were taken across the river by boat. Without machinery, the ancient Egyptians cut, lifted and moved these stones all by hand. It took more than 100 000 men twenty years to build the Great Pyramid. Inside, the body of Khufu rested in a great stone **coffin**. His body was preserved to last forever, and many treasures were buried with him. As a saying goes, "Man fears Time, but Time fears the pyramids."

coffin *n.* 棺材

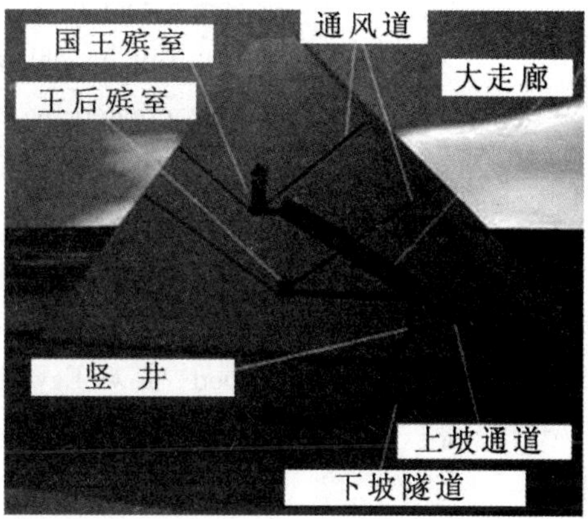

The Great Pyramids at Giza Located some 25 kilometers southward of the Cairo city center, the three pyramids at Giza are the oldest of the Seven Wonders of the World and the only one still in existence.

3.3.2 Social Structure in Ancient Egypt

In a way, the structure of ancient Egyptian society also had the shape of a pyramid. At the very top of the structure was the Pharaoh, at the bottom the ordinary farmers and slaves. Pharaoh was the owner of all Egypt, the most important and powerful person in the kingdom. As the head of the government and high priest of every temple, he was both the political and the spiritual leader of the land. Ancient Egyptians believed that their pharaoh was the son of Ra, the sun god. When a pharaoh died he was believed to be united with the sun and then a new pharaoh would rule on earth. The pharaoh was semi-god. Most pharaohs were men but some well-known pharaohs, such as Nefertiti and Cleopatra, were women. The pharaonic rule was **hereditary**, though occasionally it might be interrupted or even replaced by **domestic**

hereditary *adj.* 世袭的

domestic *adj.* 国内的

rival *n.* 竞争对手

rivals or foreign power.

absolute *adj.* 绝对的
divine *adj.* 神圣的

Since Pharaoh received his power from god, his words were laws. Under the Pharaoh's **absolute** and **divine** rule, the legal system in ancient Egypt was underdeveloped. All activities were controlled by the strong central government. Second only to the Pharaoh were the priests living in the temples. The priests were servants of the gods. Their duty was to care for the gods and to attend to their needs. They also served as go-betweens in communications between men and gods. Other duties of the priests included **funeral rites**, education, supervising the artists and works, and advising people on problems. As they were the ones that could best understand the gods' will, priests occupied a very important place in society. Together with the large number of **bureaucrats**, priests helped the Pharaoh maintain order and structure in the society.

funeral rites 葬礼仪式
bureaucrat *n.* 官僚

But in reality, ancient Egypt's economic and cultural developments were created by millions of skilled workers and general laborers. These laborers were mainly farmers, not slaves. Slavery as a system hardly existed in ancient Egypt, although there were slaves in ancient Egypt, their number was limited and they were mainly prisoners of war from foreign **tribes**. As the Nile provided the ancient Egyptians with plenty of food, few Egyptian farmers were enslaved. When the fields were flooded between July and November and farming was made impossible, famers were called upon to build the pyramids for their king. They were paid in food and clothing and were normally well treated.

tribe *n.* 部落

Generations of ancient Egyptians worked hard for their Pharaohs and achieved many remarkable feats of engineering and construction all by hand! The Egyptians had no iron tools or machinery to help them. They probably used **sledges** to drag the massive blocks of stone on specially built slopes, as they did not have the wheel. These **gigantic** tombs show that the Egyptians were very skillful architects and builders. In building the pyramids, the Egyptians developed their scientific knowledge and technology, such as architecture, **arithmetic**, **geometry**, and **surveying**. For ordinary people in ancient Egypt, their ruler was a god and everyone followed the Pharaoh's orders unquestioningly.

sledge *n.* 滑橇
gigantic *adj.* 巨大的
arithmetic *n.* 算术
geometry *n.* 几何
surveying *n.* 土地丈量

3.3.3 Ancient Egyptian Writing System: Hieroglyphics

The Egyptian language has the longest history of any language. Its writing system, **hieroglyphs** were developed as early as 3400 BC and remained in use for nearly 4 000 years. For the ancient Egyptians, the

hieroglyphics *n.* 象形文字
hieroglyph *n.* 象形字，象形符号

written language was a gift from their gods, and man was given the gift to record "the words of god". In this view, the written language was not a simple representation of the material world as linguistic signs had **divine** and magic powers. For example, they believed that a person's name was part of his spirit; they also believed that the name was closely connected with the person's life in this world and his life after death. It was therefore very important to **erect** a solid tombstone with the person's name and title. Because of this belief in the divine nature of the writing system, only priests could learn to write. The priests' control of the written language contributed to the stability of the centralized political system and also helps to explain why the ancient Egyptian language had such a long history. However, when Egypt was conquered by the Greeks in the 4th century BC, the fall of the Egyptian ruling class also led to the disappearance of their written language.

divine *adj.* 神的

erect *v.* 矗立

The Egyptian writing system contained more than 2 000 hieroglyphic characters. Originally, each hieroglyph represented a common object in ancient Egypt, and over time, they were used to represent the sound of the object or an idea associated with the object. We all know the ancient Chinese used different **calligraphic styles** to write Chinese characters. There are four styles in Chinese calligraphy: **the official script**, **the regular script**, **the running script**, and **the cursive script**. Similarly, Egyptian hieroglyphs are divided into three types according to their calligraphic style: hieroglyphic, hieratic, and demotic. Hieroglyphic was the formal writing system used for important official and religious documents. Because it was almost always inscribed on stones in large size monuments such as pyramids and **obelisks**, it was also called "sacred carving". Most ancient Egyptian texts that we can still see today are written on stone in the hieroglyphic script. Because many religious texts were written in this style, it was also called the "**priestly script**". Different from the sacred carving, hieratic was written in ink with a reed brush on papyrus, allowing scribes to write quickly. It was just a more cursive form of monumental hieroglyphics. From 600 BC onward an even more cursive script, the **demotics** replaced hieratic as the script for everyday use.

calligraphic style 书法风格

the official script 隶书

the regular script 楷书

the running script 行书

the cursive script 草书

obelisk *n.* 方尖碑

priestly script 僧侣体

demotics 通俗体

3.3.4 Art for Eternity

eternity *n.* 永恒

There are many paintings on the walls of the tombs inside the pyramids. They are the most important source for our study of art in ancient Egypt. A main feature of all ancient Egyptian arts is the combination of geometric regularity and keen observation of nature.

Clear and simple lines combined with simple shapes and flat areas of color helped to create a sense of order and balance in the art of ancient Egypt. The style of Egyptian art used in all statues, paintings, jewelry and **pottery** obeyed one law: Everything had to be represented from its most characteristic angle. No one wanted anything different, and no one asked an artist to be "**original**". It was more important for an artist to complete his work according to the rules than to create his own style. The best artist was the one who could make his artistic work most like the admired crafts of the past. Everything that was considered good and beautiful in the age of the pyramids was held to be just as excellent a thousand years later. With little outside influence, for more than 3 000 years some basic elements of Egyptian art remained remarkably stable.

pottery *n.* 陶器

original *adj.* 具原创性

Much of the ancient Egyptian art that we see today comes from tombs and monuments. From these works of art we can see a strong emphasis on life after death and a sense of order. In fact, for the ancient Egyptians, art works were not intended to be enjoyed, they, too, were meant to "keep alive" the soul. A key **function** of the paintings, jewelry and pottery in the tombs was to provide the soul with company and comfort in the other world. It was therefore very important for an artist to preserve everything of the present time as clearly and permanently as possible. In both its form and color, works of art must follow some basic rules. For example, in paintings, colors were more symbolic than natural: red skin implied healthy youth; yellow skin was used for women or middle-aged men who worked indoors; blue or gold indicated **divinity**; black was used for royal figures to express the fertility of the Nile; all male figures were darker than the female ones. In order to clearly define the social **hierarchy** in a painting, sizes of the figures were based not on their distance from the painter's point of view but on their relative social importance. For instance, the Pharaoh would be drawn as the largest figure in a painting no matter where he was situated, and a greater god would be drawn larger than a lesser god.

function *n.* 功能

divinity *n.* 神性

hierarchy *n.* 等级

4. The Hebrews: History and Religion

Of all the peoples that lived in the Mesopotamian region, the ancient Hebrews are the only ones that survive today. Nowadays, they are known as **Jews**. Although the ancient Hebrews never achieved

Jew *n.* 犹太人

political dominance in the region, their culture, especially their religion, had perhaps the greatest influence on western society as well as the western intellectual tradition. Our knowledge of the ancient Hebrews mainly comes from their Bible (Tanakh) which **corresponds to** the **Old Testament** in the **Christian** Holy Bible. It represents an oral history of the ancient Hebrews and was written between 1250 and 150 BC. Because the nameless authors wrote the Hebrew Bible mainly for religious purposes, the Bible can only give us the broad outlines of Hebrew history. Some historical facts and dates in the book are **imprecise** or even **erroneous**.

correspond to *v. ph.* 相当于
Old Testament 旧约
Christian *adj.* 基督教的
imprecise *adj.* 不精确
erroneous *adj.* 错误的

4.1 "The Children of Israel": A Brief History

It is possible that in the early days, the Semitic-speaking Hebrews were a **nomadic** people living in the Sumerian city of Ur. Then, possibly around 2285 BC these people decided to leave **Sumer** to find a place of their own. According to their Bible, God showed Himself to the Hebrew leader, Abraham. God then promised to give Abraham and his **descendants** a land of their own if they worshipped only Him. After 40 years of wandering in the desert, Abraham finally led his people to settle down in the land of **Canaan**, which was "flowing with milk and honey." Canaan, "the Promised Land," given to the Jewish people by God, includes modern Israel and the **Palestinian** Territories. Abraham was thus the founder of the Hebrew race.

nomadic *adj.* 游牧的
Sumer *n.* 苏美尔
descendent *n.* 后裔
Canaan *n.* 迦南地
Palestinian *adj.* 巴勒斯坦的

Years later, Abraham's grandson, Jacob was renamed "Israel" by an angel, the name after which the modern nation of Israel is named. The offspring of Jacob's twelve sons became the twelve tribes of Israel, and they were called Israelites or Children of Israel. According to the Bible, because of severe **famine** in Canaan, Israel took his whole family to Egypt. At the time, Joseph, the 11th son of Israel, was the Pharaoh's **vizier**, the highest official in Egypt. The family was therefore well treated by the Pharaoh. Joseph's period as vizier in Egypt is thought to have been around the year 1720 BC, but after his death, a new Pharaoh was worried that the Israelites might help Egypt's enemies to take over the land; he then turned them into slaves and made them build his cities.

famine *n.* 饥荒
vizer *n.* 维奇尔(首席大臣)

The **Israelites** suffered for a long time in Egypt. Finally, God showed himself to Moses and commanded him to lead the Children of Israel out of Egypt to return to their Promised Land (Canaan). With God's help Moses confronted Pharaoh and his magicians and led the Israelites out of Egypt to seek once more their land of freedom and of

Israelite *n.* 以色列人

exodus *n.* 出埃及

commandment *n.* 戒律

Jerusalem *n.* 耶路撒冷

Islamic *adj.* （信）伊斯兰教的

Ottoman Turk 奥斯曼土耳其人

exile *n.* 流亡，流亡者

Judaism *n.* 犹太教

peace. The **exodus** (meaning departure from Egypt) under Moses may have occurred about 1300 BC. Moses then received from God the Ten **Commandments** and other moral laws, first orally, and later inscribed on two stone tablets.

For centuries, the Israelites wandered from one place to another. Through contacts and conflicts with other peoples, they gradually developed a "we" group identity. This identity helped transform the nomadic tribe into a nation. According to the Hebrew Bible, the Israelites created a united kingdom under the king Saul around 1050 BC. The son of Saul, David, made **Jerusalem** the national capital. This united kingdom lasted until 920 BC. But later because of internal disagreement and conflict, it was divided into two kingdoms, the Kingdom of Israel in the north, and the Kingdom of Judah in the South. These two states developed separately. Although the Kingdom of Israel in the north was more advanced in both economic and cultural affairs than the Kingdom of Judah, politically, it seemed to be much less stable than its southern neighbor.

In 721 BC the kingdom of Israel was occupied by the Assyrians and then in 587 BC the kingdom of Judah was conquered by the Babylonians. Since then, one after another, foreign rulers controlled this area, the Greeks, the Romans, the Arabs, the **Islamic** Egyptians, the **Ottoman Turks**, and the British. The Children of Israel either lived under foreign rules or left their homeland to live as **exiles** in foreign lands. It was not until 1948 that the Israelites regained political independence with the creation of the modern State of Israel. Despite their more than two-thousand-year-long history of foreign conquest and exile, the Hebrews survived as one people and they never gave up their faith or their religion. The strength of their nation could only be explained from their religion, **Judaism**.

The 10 Commandments were given by God to the people of Israel on Mount Sinai after He had delivered them from slavery in Egypt (Old Testament, Exodus, Chapter 20)（旧约，出埃及记，第20章）。

"And God spoke all these words, saying: 'I am the LORD your God... 上帝吩咐这一切的话说："我是耶和华——你的上帝……

ONE: "You shall have no other gods before Me." 除了我以外，你不可有别的神。

TWO: "You shall not make for yourself a carved image—any likeness of anything that is in heaven above, or that is in the earth beneath, or that is in the water under the earth." 不可为自己雕刻偶像，也不可做什么形象仿佛上天、下地，和地底下、水中的百物。
THREE: "You shall not take the name of the LORD your God in vain." 不可妄称耶和华——你上帝的名。
FOUR: "Remember the Sabbath day, to keep it holy." 当记念安息日，守为圣日。
FIVE: "Honor your father and your mother." 当孝敬父母。
SIX: "You shall not murder." 不可杀人。
SEVEN: "You shall not commit adultery." 不可奸淫。
EIGHT: "You shall not steal." 不可偷盗。
NINE: "You shall not bear false witness against your neighbor." 不可作假见证陷害人。
TEN: "You shall not covet your neighbor's house; you shall not covet your neighbor's wife, nor his male servant, nor his female servant, nor his ox, nor his donkey, nor anything that is your neighbor's." 不可贪恋人的房屋；也不可贪恋人的妻子、仆婢、牛驴，并他一切所有的。

4.2 Israelite Religion: Judaism

In the ancient Near East, the Hebrew religion was very unique: while all the other peoples (Sumerians, Babylonians, or Egyptians) worshiped many gods and goddess, the Hebrews believed in only one God. For the Jews, their God was the only real God: He was the creator and ruler of the universe and mankind. This monotheistic religion practiced by the ancient Hebrews and modern Jews is Judaism. It is based on moral principles and rules in the Hebrew Bible, the Tanakh. According to Jewish belief, Judaism began with the **Covenant** between God and Abraham and developed further when God gave Moses a set of moral laws.

covenant *n.* 盟约

Essentially, the Tanakh tells the history of the Israelites' relationship with God. The most important part of the Tanakh is the first three sections, the Torah (meaning "teaching"). The Torah is the founding religious document of Judaism and the most holy text in Judaism. Because the Jews believed that these texts were written by Moses with inspiration from God, the Torah is also known as the **Five Books of Moses**. Later, it is accepted by **Christianity** as part of the Bible, comprising the first five books of the Old Testament. Apart from the Ten Commandments, the Torah contains more than 600 rules and restrictions.

Five Books of Moses《摩西五书》

Christianity *n.* 基督教

Unlike other ancient Near Eastern gods, Jehovah, the only real God for the Hebrews, was not created. He is **eternal** and the source

eternal *adj.* 永恒的

handiwork *n.* 手工创造物
demystify *v.* 去神秘化
self-conscious *adj.* 有自我意识
autonomy *n.* 自主权
worth *n.* 价值
righteous *adj.* 正直的
violate *v.* 违背
prevail *v.* 盛行
eradicate *v.* 消灭

of all creation in the universe. He is above nature and not part of nature. In this sort of religion, there is no place for a sun god or moon god. The Hebrews saw nature as an example of God's **handiwork**. Nature was thus **demystified**—it was no longer supernatural, but natural. This is very important because once nature was demystified scientific thought could begin.

This monotheism also created a new awareness of the individual. In God, the Hebrews developed an awareness of the Self or the "I" —the individual was **self-conscious** and aware of his own moral **autonomy** and **worth**. The Hebrews believed that man had the freedom and capacity to choose between good and evil. Although God was all powerful, He was also just and merciful. He did not want His followers to be slaves. God does not control mankind—rather, men must have the freedom to choose. Freedom did not mean, "do as you please", instead, it meant voluntary obedience to those moral commands which God had given to the Hebrews through Moses. Men and women could make the right choice if they learnt to know their God. To know God, one just had to be **righteous**, moral, loving, merciful and just. When men and women loved God, they were improved.

One of the central religious principles of the Hebrew faith is that God had made a special agreement with his people. This agreement is called the Covenant. The Hebrews, then, considered themselves as God's chosen people. They did not believe they were better than anyone else-instead, they believed that God had rescued them from Egyptian slavery and selected them to receive His laws. This was quite heavy a responsibility. If the Hebrews **violate** the laws of God written down by Moses, they would be breaking the covenant—their special agreement with God. It could lead to national disaster and the destruction of the Hebrew nation. The bottom line is this: Hebrew society had the moral obligation to make justice **prevail**—at the same time, evil had to be **eradicated**. This sense of moral obligation was written into Hebrew law. The poor, widows, children and the sick were all protected by law; the rich and poor were to be treated under the same laws, something unheard of in the Code of Hammurabi.

5. Conclusion

Now, let us go back to the question raised at the beginning of this chapter. If we all agree that ancient Greece was the origin of European civilization, what, then, was the origin of ancient Greek civilization? Was the ancient Greek civilization created by people in Greece all by themselves? Or was the cultural emergence and development of ancient Greece influenced in some important ways by cultures and civilizations outside of Greece?

Our overview of the early civilizations and cultures in the ancient Near East has shown a clear connection between ancient Near Eastern civilizations and ancient Greek civilization. The former had undoubtedly influenced the development of ancient Greek society and culture. The Mesopotamians and Egyptians were the founders of human civilizations. They were the first to develop systematic agricultural production. They were the first to create city-states, kingdoms and empires. They were the first to organize complex political, military, social and religious structures. They were the first to raise basic questions about human existence: the relationship between human and nature, between man and man, between man and himself, and between life and death. They were the first to develop different systems of religious belief to answer these questions. And then they were the first to create writing systems to keep records of their activities and ideas. Through trade, military conquest and personal travels, ideas, knowledge, skills and techniques developed in the ancient Near East were brought to ancient Greece and contributed to cultural progress in the entire Mediterranean region.

Exercises

Ⅰ. Terminology: choose the suitable terms to fill in the blanks.

A. polytheist B. monotheism C. scribe
D. Hammurabi's code E. epic F. hieroglyph
G. covenant H. irrigation I. Ziggurat J. cuneiform

- In both ancient Sumer and Egypt, someone who could read and write was called a __1__.
- When you believe in many gods, you are a __2__; but if you believe in only one god, then you are practising __3__.
- __4__ is a system to bring water into the fields. This system may include dams, ditches, dikes and canals.
- __5__ is the temple built by the Sumerians for their gods and goddesses.
- __6__ was the most famous set of Mesopotamian laws based on the principle of retaliation.
- The writing system created by the Sumerians was the __7__ whereas the one created by the Egyptians was the __8__.
- The legendary stories of Gilgamesh is written in the form of __9__.
- According to Jewish belief, the Hebrews became God's chosen people after God had signed a __10__ with Abraham.

Ⅱ. Decide whether the following statements are true (T) or false (F).

1. Mesopotamian civilization was based on the tradition, culture and custom of one single group of ancient people living in the region. ( )
2. Legends have it that the Garden of Eden was situated on the Mesopotamian plain. ( )
3. It was the Sumerians who first started systematic agriculture. ( )
4. The basic units of the first human civilization were city-states. ( )
5. The Hammurabi Code is the oldest known legal document in human history. ( )
6. Similar to all ancient agricultural societies, ancient Egyptians also divided a year into four seasons. ( )
7. Judaism instilled a sense of individualism and equality into the Hebrew society. ( )
8. The Hammurabi Code ensured that every one is equal before the law. ( )
9. In the ancient Egyptian society there were only male pharaohs. ( )
10. All Egyptian gods have a human body and an animal head. ( )

Ⅲ. Multiple choices: choose the answer that best completes the statement or answers the question.

1. According to Professor Martin Bernal, the origin of the Greek culture could be traced back to ________.

A. the Persians B. the Aryan settlers

C. the Ancient Near Easters D. the Indians

2. Which one of the countries below was not part of the ancient Near East?

A. Armenia. B. Turkey. C. Israel. D. Iraq.

3. The so-called Mesopotamia civilization included cultures developed by the following groups of people EXCEPT ________.

A. Babylonians B. Persians

C. Sumerians D. Assyrians

4. ________ is the longest river in the world.

A. The Tigris B. The Amazon

C. The Mississippi D. The Nile

5. The Sumerian civilization had ________ cultural center (s).

A. 1 B. 2 C. 3 D. 4

6. The wheel was invented by ancient ________.

A. Egyptians B. Indians

C. Greeks D. Sumerians

7. All land in Sumer belonged to ________.

A. the kings B. gods C. the nobles D. free farmers

8. Which one of the following statements about the Sumerian economy is NOT true?

A. The economy was mainly based on agriculture.

B. The annual flood of the Tigris and the Euphrates played a vital role in its economy.

C. The land was owned by the kings and the nobles.

D. Sumerian businessmen helped develop an extensive trade network in the Persian Gulf region.

9. Which one of the following groups of people did not speak the Semitic language?

A. Hebrews. B. Arabs. C. Sumerians. D. Babylonians.

10. Which one of the following statements about the Code of Hammurabi was NOT true?

A. The Code helped Hammurabi consolidate his rule in the Mesopotamia.

B. The Code was based on the principle of retaliation.

C. Everyone received equal punishment for the same crime committed.

D. The Code was written in the Akkadian language.

11. Which one of the following peoples first practiced monotheism?

A. Ancient Egyptians. B. Ancient Hebrews.

C. Ancient Greeks. D. Ancient Sumerians.

12. The Tigris and Euphrates are originated from which country?

A. Iraq. B. Armenia. C. Turkey. D. Iran.

13. Which one of the following items was NOT invented by the ancient Mesopotamians?

A. guitar. B. magnifying glass. C. lock and key. D. gunpowder.

14. Egypt was conquered by ________ in 31 BC and renamed "Africa".

A. Greeks B. Arabs C. Romans D. Persians

15. Which one of the following statements about Judaism is NOT true?
A. Judaism was the earliest monotheism in the ancient Near East.
B. Judaism began with the covenant between God and Abraham.
C. The Ten Commandants are a set of moral laws given to Israel by God.
D. The Hebrew Bible is the base of the Old Testament of the Christian Holy Bible.
16. In ancient Egypt, only ________ could learn to write.
A. priests B. pharaohs C. nobles D. men
17. Which one of the following statements about ancient Egyptian religious belief is NOT true?
A. The ancient Egyptians practised polytheism.
B. All Egyptian gods had an animal head and a human body.
C. Ancient Egyptians built temples to communicate with their gods.
D. Egyptians believed in final judgement and resurrection.
18. The ancient Egyptians divided a year into ________ seasons.
A. 2 B. 3 C. 4 D. 5
19. The founder of the Hebrew race was ________.
A. Jacob B. Moses C. Abraham D. Joseph
20. Which one of the following statements about the ancient Egyptian art is NOT true?
A. The more important a person or a god, the larger his size on a painting.
B. Ancient Egyptians artists created a variety of individual styles.
C. Wall paintings inside the pyramids were meant to keep the dead company.
D. Colors in the paintings have symbolic meanings.

Chapter 2
Greek Civilization

CHAPTER OUTLINE

1. Introduction
2. History of the Ancient Greeks
3. Cultural Achievements of the Ancient Greeks
4. Conclusion

FOCUS QUESTIONS

1. What was the Greek polis and how did it develop in Athens and Sparta in the Archaic period?

2. What effect did the Greco-Persian Wars and the Peloponnesian War have on Greek civilization?

3. What are the differences between the Hellenic and Hellenistic cultures?

4. Why is ancient Greece considered as the cradle of Western civilization?

1. Introduction

An influential theory proposed by German scholar Walter Burkert in 1984 suggests that in the formative period of Greek civilization between approximately 750 and 650 BC, the **migration** of Near Eastern **craftsmen** not only brought eastern skills and images to ancient Greece, but also influenced Greek religion and literature by the eastern models to a significant degree. ① This theory points to the fact that ancient Greek civilization is by no means an **isolated** or **self-sufficient** civilization that has "accidentally" or "**miraculously**" evolved from a local cultural phenomenon into a western and global cultural heritage. Instead, as a sea-based culture originating in the Mediterranean, ancient Greek

migration *n.* 迁徙
craftsman *n.* 手工艺者
isolated *adj.* 孤立的
self-sufficient *adj.* 自给自足的
miraculously *adv.* 奇迹般地

① 1984年，德国学者华尔特·布尔科特（Walter Burkert）在其出版的德文著作《古希腊宗教和文学中的东方化时期》（Die Orientalisierende Epoche in der Griechischen Religion und Literatur）中提出了该学说。

enlighten *v.* 启蒙
interaction *n.* 互动
enormous *adj.* 巨大的

civilization was **enlightened** by the ancient Near East civilizations and fed on the cultural interactions between the east and the west.

Often viewed as the foundation of western civilization, ancient Greek civilization continues to have an **enormous** impact on the world till this day. But who created the ancient Greek civilization? What are the main achievements of ancient Greek civilization? What was the impact of ancient Greek civilization on western civilization? To answer all these questions, this chapter will take a closer look at the historical development and cultural achievements of the ancient Greeks.

2. History of the Ancient Greeks

Map 6 Map of Greece

contract *v.* 收缩
Asia Minor 小亚细亚

The Greek world was called "Hellas" (meaning "the place with a Greek way of life") in ancient times and the word "Greek" originates from the Roman name for them—*Graeci*. Boundaries of the ancient Greece expanded and **contracted** with wars and invasions, but in general, the territory of ancient Greece included the Greek mainland, the west coast of **Asia Minor** (the Asian part of modern Turkey, known as Ionia), the in-between islands such as the Cycladic Islands and the island of Crete, and southern Italy as well as Sicily (known as **Magna Graecia**). The Greek mainland can be further divided into three geographical regions. Northern Greece consisted of countries such as **Macedonia** and **Thrace**, and **Mount Olympus**, which is the highest point in Greece and home of the mythical Greek gods. Central Greece, connected to northern Greece by a narrow pass named **Thermopylae**, contained the countries such as Boeotia (with its chief city of Thebes) and Attica (with its chief city of **Athens**). Forming the southern Greece was the **Peloponnesus Peninsula**, which was connected to central Greece by the narrow **Isthmus of Corinth**. Laconia (with its capital city of **Sparta**) was located in the southern Greece.

Ancient Greek civilization was greatly shaped by its geographical features. On one hand, numerous mountains and hills divided the Greek mainland and islands into small and isolated regions, making it difficult for the people to communicate or travel by land. As a result, different Greek communities followed their own separate paths and developed their own ways of life. On the other hand, as the ancient Greece was surrounded on three sides by water, including the **Aegean Sea** to the east, the **Ionian Sea** to the west and the **Mediterranean** to the south, the ancient Greeks were not only blessed with excellent fishing opportunities, but also efficient travel routes. Already since their early history, the ancient Greeks sailed to other areas around the Mediterranean and Aegean seas to conduct trades, build up settlements and bring back new ideas.

Magna Craecia [拉] 大希腊

Macedonia *n.* 马其顿

Thrace *n.* 色雷斯

Mount Olympus 奥林巴斯山

Thermopylae 温泉关

Athens 雅典

Peloponnesus Peninsula 伯罗本尼撒半岛

Isthmus of Corinth 科林斯地峡

Sparta 斯巴达

Aegean Sea 爱琴海

Ionian Sea 爱奥尼亚海

Mediterranean 地中海

2.1 Early Greece

Early signs of civilization emerged during the **Bronze Age**, when the Cycladic culture (3000—2000 BC), Helladic culture (2800—1650 BC) and Minoan culture (2800—1450 BC) **coexisted** in the Aegean region. These cultures **overlapped** in time and coincided with the three major regions of the ancient Greece, that is, the Cycladic Islands, the Greek mainland and the island of Crete. Developed by the Cyclades people in the Early Bronze Age, Cycladic culture was the earliest of the three, but it, together with the Helladic culture, was **submerged** in the rising influence of the Minoan culture. The Minoan culture developed to such a high level that it is often regarded as the first

Bronze Age 青铜时代

coexist *v.* 并存

overlap *v.* 同时发生

submerge *v.* 淹没

advanced civilization of Europe. ①

2.1.1 *The Minoan Civilization*（*2800—1450 BC*）

Crete 克里特

The Minoan civilization developed on the island of **Crete**. Since the island of Crete is located in the centre of the eastern Mediterranean at the crossroads of Africa, Asia, and Europe, the Minoans had lived in contact for centuries with all of its **contemporary** major civilizations. By doing trade with regions such as ancient Egypt, Cyprus, Syria and Mesopotamia, the Minoans accumulated great wealth, absorbed influences from these regions and developed a high level of civilization.

contemporary *adj.* 同时代的
Cyprus 塞浦路斯
accumulate *v.* 积累

The Minoans enjoyed general peace and prosperity at home and had increasingly frequent contact with the great powers of the Near East. They also developed a strong **naval** power, which enabled them to build their settlements around the Aegean as far as Sicily and extend their cultural influence to neighboring regions such as Egypt, Cyprus and the Middle East. Their art was copied and adapted by the peoples of the Greek mainland and the Cyclades islands.

naval *adj.* 海上的，海军的

The Minoan civilization reached its height between 2000 and 1450 BC. The palace of Knossos, the largest and most **spectacular** palace on Crete, demonstrates the obvious prosperity and power of this civilization. ② The palace was sophisticatedly designed; around a central courtyard, it included numerous living rooms for the royal family, as well as many storerooms and workrooms. Walls in many living rooms were decorated with beautiful **fresco**, vividly depicting plants, animals, and the Minoan social life. The images in the fresco paintings and other decorative objects reveal that the Minoans appreciated the beauty of the nature and **worshipped** female goddesses. Minoan women seemed to be equal in social status with men: both men and women were engaged in boxing and bull-leaping as **leisure** activities.

spectacular *adj.* 壮观
fresco *n.* 壁画
worship *v.* 崇拜
leisure *adj.* 休闲

The centers of the Minoan civilization suffered a sudden and **catastrophic** collapse around 1450 BC. The cause of this destruction has been heatedly debated. Some historians believe that Crete was

catastrophic*adj.* 灾难性的

① “弥诺斯文明（Minoan civilization）”一词是由英国考古学家、克诺索斯古城（Knossos）的发掘者亚瑟·埃文斯（Arthur Evans，1851—1941）所创。希腊神话中，宙斯和欧罗巴（Europa）之子弥诺斯（Minos）是克里特岛之王，死后成为地府的三法官之一。

② 相传此处为古希腊神话中关押弥诺陶洛斯（Minotaur）的克里特岛迷宫。诺陶洛斯为弥诺斯的妻子帕西淮（Pasiphaë）同一头公牛生出半人半牛的怪物。在一场战争中，弥诺斯战胜了雅典，他强迫雅典人以童男童女为牲供弥诺陶洛斯吞食。到第三年献牲的时候，忒修斯（Theseus）自愿前往，并在阿里阿德涅（Ariadne）的帮助下杀死了这个怪物。

devastated by a powerful **volcanic eruption**. Most historians, however, maintain that the destruction was the result of invasion by mainland Greeks known as the **Mycenaeans**. Scholars call the Mycenaeans the "earliest Greeks" and their culture the "first **Hellenic** culture" because they were the first people known to have spoken Greek.

volcanic eruption 火山爆发

Mycenaean 迈锡尼人

Hellenic *adj.* 希腊的

2.1.2 The First Greek Society: The Mycenaean Era (1650—1200 BC)

When the Mycenaeans emerged on the Greek mainland, the **affluent** and peace-loving Minoan civilization was already at its peak. The Mycenaeans had close contact with the Minoans, learning and borrowing the Cretan technology and ideas. For instance, the Mycenaeans adapted the Minoan script to their spoken language (a form of archaic Greek dialect) and developed their own writing system. The Mycenaeans also followed the Minoans' example to engage in international trade and oversea settlements.

affluent *adj.* 富有的

Over time, as the Mycenaeans grew strong, they came to perceive the Minoans as their main economic competitor. In order to improve the trading and **colonizing** opportunities, the Mycenaeans conquered the island of Crete in around 1450 BC and replaced the Minoans as the leader of the Aegean region. They **looted** and destroyed the city of **Troy** in **Asia Minor** in about 1200 BC. From 1450 to 1200 BC, the Mycenaean power reached its highest point, expanding their influence over the Greek mainland, the Aegean and Ionian seas, Crete, and the coast of Asia Minor. They also established further trading contacts with the great Near Eastern kingdoms, including the Hittites, Assyrians, Babylonians and Egyptians.

colonize *v.* 殖民

loot *v.* 洗劫

Troy 特洛伊

Asia Minor 小亚细亚

After the Trojan War, the Mycenaeans went through a period of civil war. At the same time there were frequent invasions by the Dorians, another Greek-speaking people from the north equipped with **superior** iron weapons. Between roughly 1200 and 1100 BC, virtually all major Mycenaean cities were sacked and destroyed and the Mycenaean **refugees** fled to new settlements first in Attica and in its chief city, Athens, and later in Ionia along the west coast of Asia Minor. The outside invasion coupled with the internal conflict caused the downfall of the Mycenaean civilization.

superior *adj.* 精良的

refugee *n.* 难民

Generally speaking, the Mycenaean society was divided into kingdoms, each ruled by a king who was the military, **judicial** and religious leader. The king was assisted by the military command, priests and nobles, whereas the freeman and slaves were obliged to

judicial *adj.* 司法的

perform duties for the court and pay taxes. The Mycenaeans had a warrior culture, which left behind many traces in Greek legends. Also called the "Age of Heroes", the Mycenaean era serves as the source of inspiration of the famous **Homeric epics.**

Homeric epic 荷马史诗

2.2 The Dark Age (1200—750 BC)

After the fall of the Mycenaean civilization, ancient Greek history entered into the so-called Dark Age. This period was thus called for two reasons. First we know little of this era not only because of a lack of written evidence but also because of our inability to understand the Mycenaean writing system; then, from the little we know, the Greek society at this time was largely poor and backward. Greece's economy collapsed and Greek population dropped dramatically. The Greeks no longer lived in cities; instead they formed small **tribal** groups. Agriculture was underdeveloped; the old Greek settlements were abandoned, and the large trading empire beginning with the Minoans and inherited by the Mycenaeans ceased to function. This situation lasted for about 300 years.

tribal *adj.* 部落的

Toward the end of the Dark Age, some significant developments paved the way for the recovery of the Greek society. Advanced technologies of making tools and weapons out of iron were developed in Greece, announcing the approach of the Iron Age. Agriculture and trade were gradually revived and Greeks relearned how to write, not with the Mycenaean script but with a new alphabetic written system adapted from **Phoenician** alphabet. Two renowned epics, ***Iliad*** and ***Odyssey*** appeared at this time, providing us with knowledge of the heroic ideal of Greek society in the Bronze and Iron Ages. For this reason the Greek Dark Age is also called the "Age of Homer." The Greeks also learned from the Phoenicians the artistic and literary traditions of the ancient Near East and incorporated these influences into their own culture and created a brand new Greek civilization. New socio-political **institutions** were gradually established in different parts of Greece.

Phoenician *adj.* 腓尼基的
Iliad《伊利亚特》
Odyssey《奥德赛》

institution *n.* 机构

2.3 The Archaic Period (750—500 BC)

archaic *adj.* 古代的
Archaic Period 古朴时代

The economic recovery around 800 BC led to dramatic growth in population. At the time, most Greeks still lived in small villages based on families or clans. As the population grew, resources and farmland became rather limited and local inhabitants were forced to contact other villages for trade and other purposes. Accordingly, conflicts between different local communities arose. There was an urgent need to form a new political basis to unite these communities with a common set of laws, religion, defense system and territory. Originating in as early as 9th or 10th century BC, the ***polis*** (or city-state) became a preferable choice for the Greeks in need.

polis *n.* 古希腊城邦

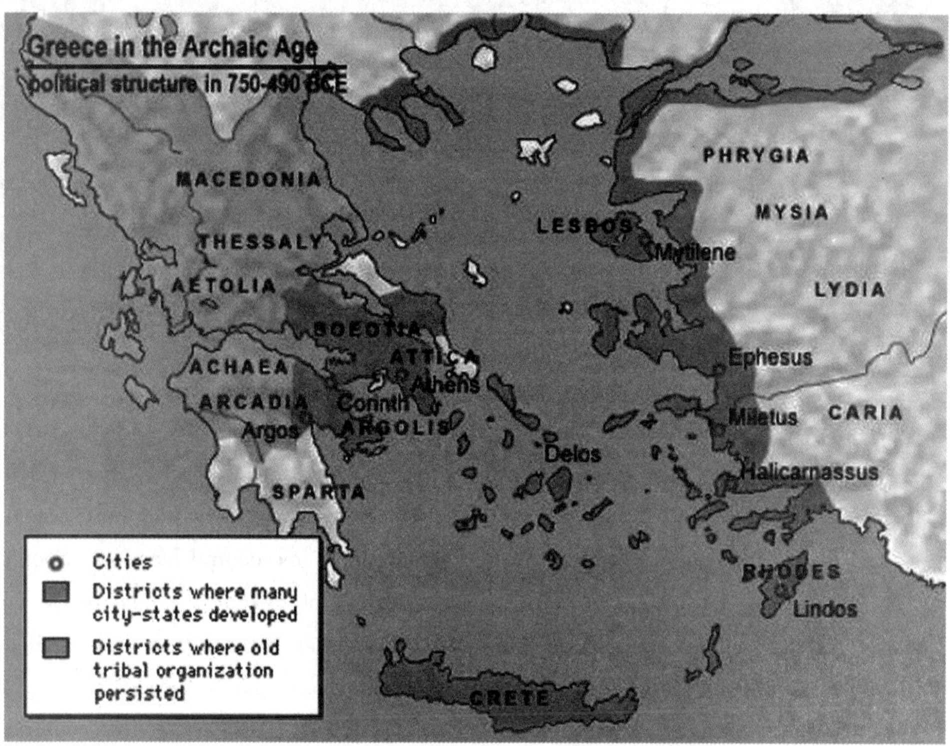

Map 7 Greece in the Archaic Age

Greek polis, Athens

Artist's Reconstruction of the Greek polis, Athens

Politically, a *polis* (or city-state; plural form: *poleis*) is a small but **autonomous** political unit in which all major political, social, and religious activities were carried out at one central location. Socially and culturally, a *polis* is a community of citizens who shared a common identity and common goals. Geographically, a *polis* was made of the ***acropolis*** and the ***agora***. The urban public space comprising the *acropolis* and *agora* was surrounded by the khora [the countryside]. The *khora* provided the necessary food supply while main economic and political activities took place in the agora and acropolis, respectively.

autonomous *adj.* 自治的

acropolis *n.* 卫城

agora *n.* 城邦广场

Greek *Poleis* varied greatly in size and population. In some cases, a *polis* might also contain temples, public areas and entertainment facilities (e. g. theatre, stadium). The inhabitants of a *polis* were generally divided into three categories, adult native males, native women and children, and slaves and resident foreigners. Of the three categories, only the adult native males were citizens with political rights. Since every *polis* was independent, the ancient Greeks were divided in their **loyalty**. Fierce competition among citizens of different poleis prevented the Greeks from forming a stable and unified country and eventually brought about the **ruin** of the world of Greek city-states.

loyalty *n.* 忠诚

ruin *n.* 崩溃

Since around 750 BC, Greek *poleis* had spread throughout the Mediterranean basin **via** vigorous colonization. Greek settlements stretched all the way from the coast of Asia Minor and the Aegean islands, to mainland Greece, Sicily, North Africa, and even Spain.

via *prep.* 通过

Several strong *poleis* emerged as the dominant cultural centers. These *poleis* exhibited considerable variety in their governmental structures, which can best be seen by examining the two most famous and powerful Greek *poleis*, Athens and Sparta.

2.3.1 Athens

Located at the Attica Peninsula in central Greece, Athens was the birthplace of **democracy**, a system of government in which power is either held by elected **representatives** or directly by the people themselves. It took a long time before democracy took form and became established in Athens.

democracy *n.* 民主政体
representative *n.* 代表

Early Athens was ruled by a **monarch**. By 600 BC, Athens had established a unified *polis* on the peninsula of Attica and replaced the **monarchy**, the political system in which a country is ruled by a king, with the **oligarchy**, the political system in which a small group of people hold all the power. The wealthy land-owning nobles called ***Eupatridae***, prominent by wealth and birth, became the ruling-class of Athens. The council of nobles, assisted by a board of nine **magistrates**, possessed nearly all powers of the state, while the **People's Assembly** had little voice in the political and religious life of Athens. Soon, increasing numbers of Athenian farmers fell into debt to the nobles and sold into slavery. The conflicts between the social classes became so severe that Athens was on the brink of civil war.

monarch *n.* 君主
monarchy *n.* 君主制
oligarchy *n.* 寡头政体
Eupatridae *n.* 古希腊世袭贵族
magistrate *n.* 执政官
People's Assembly 公民大会

Recognizing the danger of the situation, in 594 BC, the Athenian aristocrats and **commoners** agreed to appoint **Solon** (638—558 BC) as the sole magistrate for one year and gave him extraordinary powers to reform the Athenian government. Solon forbade the enslavements of indebted farmers and set up a fund to buy back Athenians who were sold into slavery abroad. He encouraged the development of trade, agriculture and industries and changed the qualifications for public offices from birth to wealth. He divided Athenian society into four classes (called tribes) based on wealth. All adult males from the three wealthiest classes had the right to serve on the Council of 400 through election. The fourth and poorest class was allowed to participate in not just the People's Assembly, which was open to all free-born Athenian men over 18 and had the right to elect the magistrates; but also the **People's Court**, where any citizen could be elected as judge to hear appeals from Athenians as to the government affairs. Regarded as too **radical** by the aristocracy and as too mild by the commoners, Solon's reforms did not solve the social crisis of Athens, but they did lay the

commoner *n.* 庶民
Solon 梭伦
People's Court 民众法庭
radical *adj.* 激进

foundation for the Athenian democracy.

Peisistratus 毕西特拉图
tyrant *n.* 僭主
unconstitutionally *adv.* 违宪
tyranny *n.* 僭主政体
derogative *adj.* 贬低的

Around 560 BC, advocates of radical reform established a military leader named **Peisistratus** (607—528 BC) as a **tyrant**, which in ancient Greek context meant a ruler who seized power **unconstitutionally** or the one who inherited such power. It should be noted that the word "**tyranny**" did not have the **derogative** meaning in ancient Greece as today, but signified a step toward democracy, where the citizens took control of the polis for themselves. Many of the tyrants were progressive when they were in power. Peisistratus was a good example. While enforcing most of Solon's reforms, Peisistratus went even further than Solon by weakening the aristocracy and benefiting the unprivileged. He **banished** many nobles, confiscated their lands and redistributed them among the poor. He increased the power of the People's Assembly and the People's Court associated with the poorest classes. He also **patronized** the arts and sponsored state religious festivals, fostering the growth of Athenian culture and national pride. Peisistratus remained a popular tyrant until his death, but his sons were not supported by the people and were eventually overthrown by the aristocratic opponents with some help from Sparta in 510 BC.

banish *v.* 流放
confiscate *v.* 没收充公
patronize *v.* 赞助

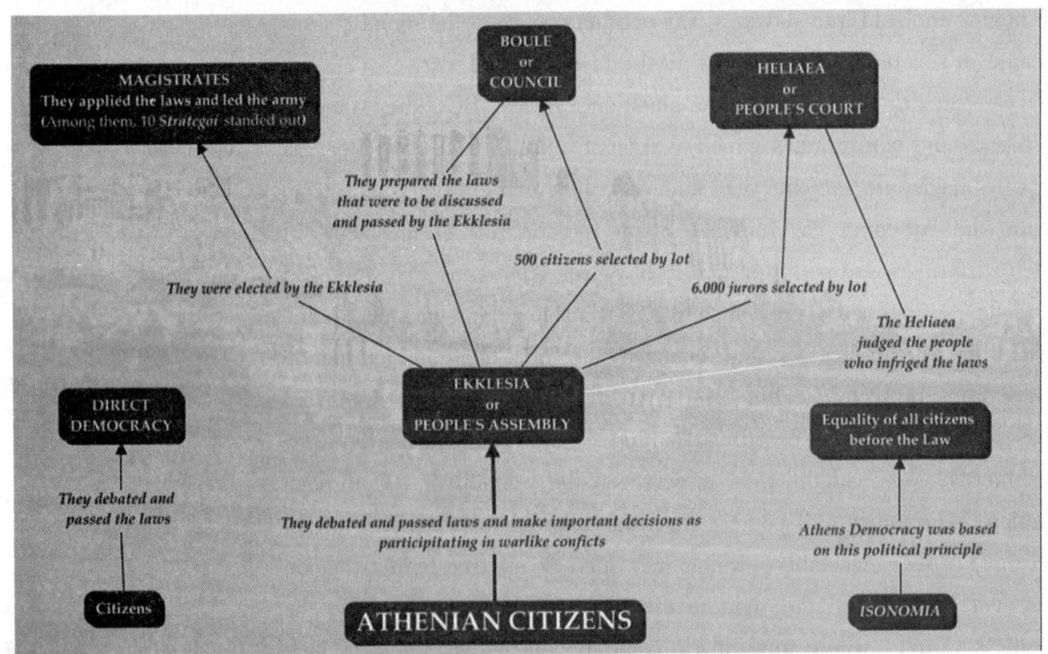

A Chart of Athenian Democracy

There was a short period of aristocratic rule until 508 BC, when a new tyrant named **Cleisthenes** (570—507 BC) seized power. Cleisthenes began a series of reforms that would help build up a governmental system based on political equality and participation of citizens and that would eventually produce Athenian democracy. He **abolished** the four traditional noble-dominated tribes and reorganized Athenian society into ten new tribes, each containing citizens from different classes and areas. Thus he broke down the local power bases of the aristocracy. The Council of 400 designed by Solon based on the traditional four tribes was replaced by a new Council of 500, whose members were chosen by **lot annually** from the ten tribes. The Council of 500 would manage state finances, foreign policy and war, and set the agenda for the People's Assembly, which functioned as the legislative and the supreme court. From each tribe one magistrate was elected, who would manage Athens on a daily basis. With these reforms, the council of nobles became ornamental and the people gradually took place of the tyranny. Cleisthenes also introduced the practice of **ostracism**, whereby the citizens could vote to send anyone considered dangerous to the state in exile for ten years. This practice was designed to remove **factionalism** and discourage **tyrants.**

Cleisthenes 克里斯提尼

abolish *v.* 废除

lot *n.* 抽签

annually *adv.* 每年

ostracism *n.* 陶片放逐法

factionalism *n.* 派系之争

tyrant *n.* 暴君

By 502 BC, Athens had pretty much established its fame as the Hellenic centre of democracy, of trade and commerce, and of art and literature. In the next one hundred years, the ancient Greek world would be politically and culturally dominated by Athens.

It should be noted that early Greek democracy was different from modern democracy. For example, only the free, male adult Greek citizens participated in the running of the *polis*, whereas all women, slaves and foreigners were denied of the political power. So it is safe to say that early Greek democracy began as an expanded version of oligarchy. Despite that, early Greek democracy represented a certain degree of equality between the citizens in the polis, ensured an easier coexistence between the classes and laid the groundwork for the democratic principles that were to be developed in Athens in the next two hundred years.

2. 3. 2 Sparta

While Athens dominated the cultural and intellectual life of ancient Greek world with its brilliant achievements in literature, fine arts, philosophy and democracy, Sparta, a rival polis of Athens, developed a peculiar **militaristic** tradition and prided itself on the brave and

militaristic *adj.* 军事化的

patriotic *adj.* 忠君爱国的
warrior *n.* 武士

patriotic Spartiate **warriors**.

Located in Laconia in the south-central Peloponnesus, Sparta began as several small villages of Dorian Greeks, which combined to form the *polis* of Sparta. In 700 BC, Sparta was in urgent need of more fertile land to support its booming population, so it decided to further expand their territory in the Peloponnesus by conquering Messenia, an agriculturally wealthy region west of Sparta. After twenty years of war, Sparta defeated and enslaved the Messenians. Feeling threatened by the uprising of the Messenian slaves who outnumbered them ten to one, the Spartans began to enact a military government and became the most militarized polis in Greece.

Spartan society was divided into three main classes, the native Spartans, the foreigners, and slaves. Determined by blood, the native Spartans were citizens enjoying full political and legal rights. By contrast, foreign tradesmen and craftsmen living in Sparta had personal freedom but no political rights. Slaves in Sparta were public property and thus had no right to speak of. Owned by the state, slaves were forced to work for the native Spartans.

contemptuous *adj.* 蔑视
suspicious *adj.* 怀疑的
barracks *n.* 兵营
childbearing *n.* 生儿育女

In general, Sparta was a closed military society, **contemptuous** of book learning and **suspicious** of foreigners. The lives of the Spartans were rigidly organized and tightly controlled by the state. Sparta had a unique public education system for the Spartiate citizens. The newborn babies would be inspected by elders. The weak and deformed babies would be abandoned to die. By this practice Sparta hoped to ensure that only those who were physically fit would survive. Boys were removed from their parents' control and began military drill at the age of 7. From age 7 to 18, the boys went through rigorous military training and they slept in **barracks** on hard beds, ate coarse food, wore simple clothing and spent little time learning reading or writing. They learned to endure pain and hardship without complaint and to obey orders strictly without question. At the age of 20 they became competent warriors and began to serve in the army until age 60. Although permitted to marry, they were required to live in barracks until 30. Since Spartan men were busy with military training or warfare, Spartan women enjoyed more rights than the rest of the Greek world. Unlike most Greek girls, Spartan girls received physical and gymnastics training from age 7 to 12, which was supposed to strengthen them for **childbearing** and make them healthy mothers of warrior sons. They continued an education in letters until they were until they were married, usually around age 18. Compared with most ancient Greek women, Spartan women enjoyed more domestic freedom. They controlled farm workers and servants, were free to move about and could even **inherit** property.

inherit *v.* 继承

The Spartan government was a unique **blend** of monarchy, oligarchy and democracy. It was headed by two kings who ruled jointly. They served as high priests and military commanders of Sparta and each king acted as a **check** on the other. A council comprising 28 elders over age 60 as well as the two kings was the main policy-making body and the supreme court of Sparta. Below the council was an assembly of all the Spartiate males over the age of 30. The assembly elected the council members and approved or vetoed council proposals. But the true power resided in the ***ephors*** ["overseers"], a group of five officials also elected by the assembly on an annual base. The overseers were given the civil authority in leading the council, supervising the military, educational system and the infant selection system, as well as having the power to veto any ruling made by the council or the assembly and even to depose the king.

blend *n.* 混合

check *n.* 牵制

ephor *n.* 监理官

Due to its military power, Sparta was recognized as the leader of the united Greek forces during the Greco-Persian Wars and became the principal enemy of Athens during the Peloponnesian War. Sparta's defeat by Thebes in 371 BC ended Sparta's prominent role in Greece. However, it maintained its political independence until 146 BC, when the Romans conquered Greece.

2.4 The Classical Period (500—338 BC)

classical *adj.* 古典的

The Classical period, which lasted from about 500 to 338 BC is the most famous period of ancient Greek civilization. During this period, ancient Greeks reached their highest prosperity and produced amazing cultural accomplishments. This is the age of the brilliant philosopher Socrates, the great dramatists like Sophocles, Euripides and Aeschylus, and the great historians Herodotus and Thucydides. Amazing monuments to human achievement were constructed in Athens and other Hellenic poleis. It is an age of human discovery and achievement—an age which proudly bears the name classical. Unfortunately, the Classical period was also an era of war and conflict, first between the Greeks and the Persians, then between the Athenians and the Spartans. While the defeat of the Persians ensured the Athenian political, economic, and cultural dominance, the Peloponnesian War

decline *n.* 衰败

led to the end of the Athenian empire and the **decline** of Greek city-states.

2. 4. 1 The Greco-Persian Wars (*492—479 BC*)

Darius Ⅰ 大流士一世

Thrace 色雷斯

Macedonia 马其顿

As the Greeks spread throughout the Mediterranean, they came into contact with the Persian Empire to the east. The Ionian Greek cities in western Asia Minor had been under Persian control since 544 BC. In 521 BC **Darius** Ⅰ (550—486 BC) became king of the Persian Empire and it was under his reign that the empire reached its greatest extent, stretching from western India to Eastern Europe. In 513 BC Darius I, for the first time, conquered **Thrace** and **Macedonia** and posed threat to Greece. Between 499 and 494 BC, the Ionian Greek cities, assisted by the city-states of Athens and Eretria, rebelled against Persia. Despite initial victories, the revolt was crushed by Persian forces. To punish Athens and Eretria for supporting the Ionian revolt, Darius I launched an attack on the Greek mainland.

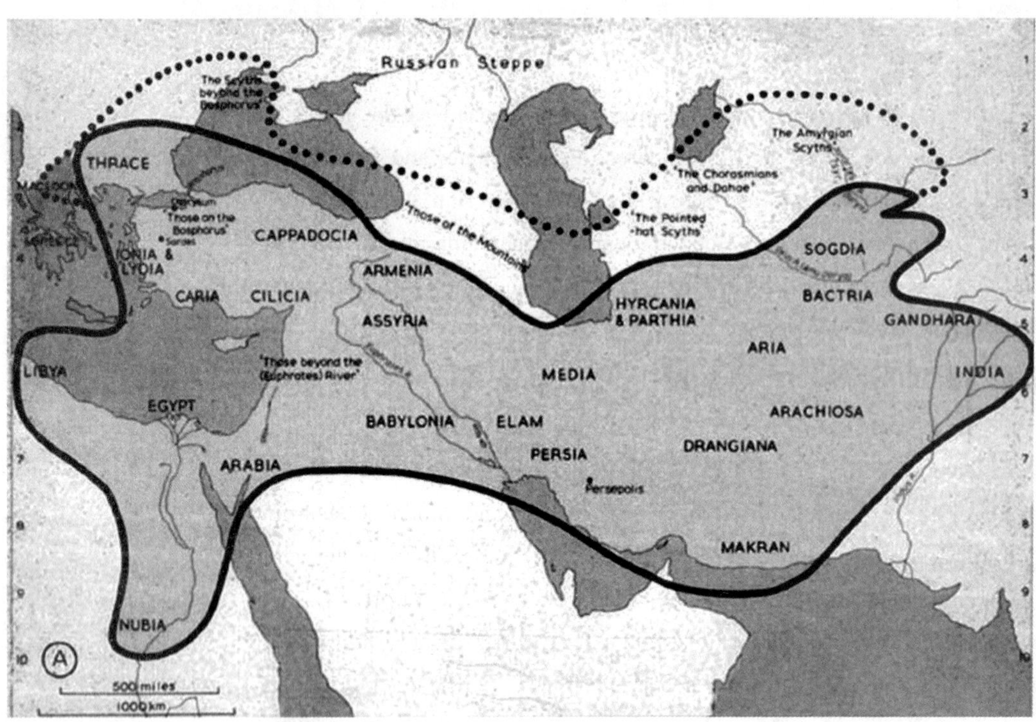

Map 8 The Persian Empire under Darius I (**490 BC**)

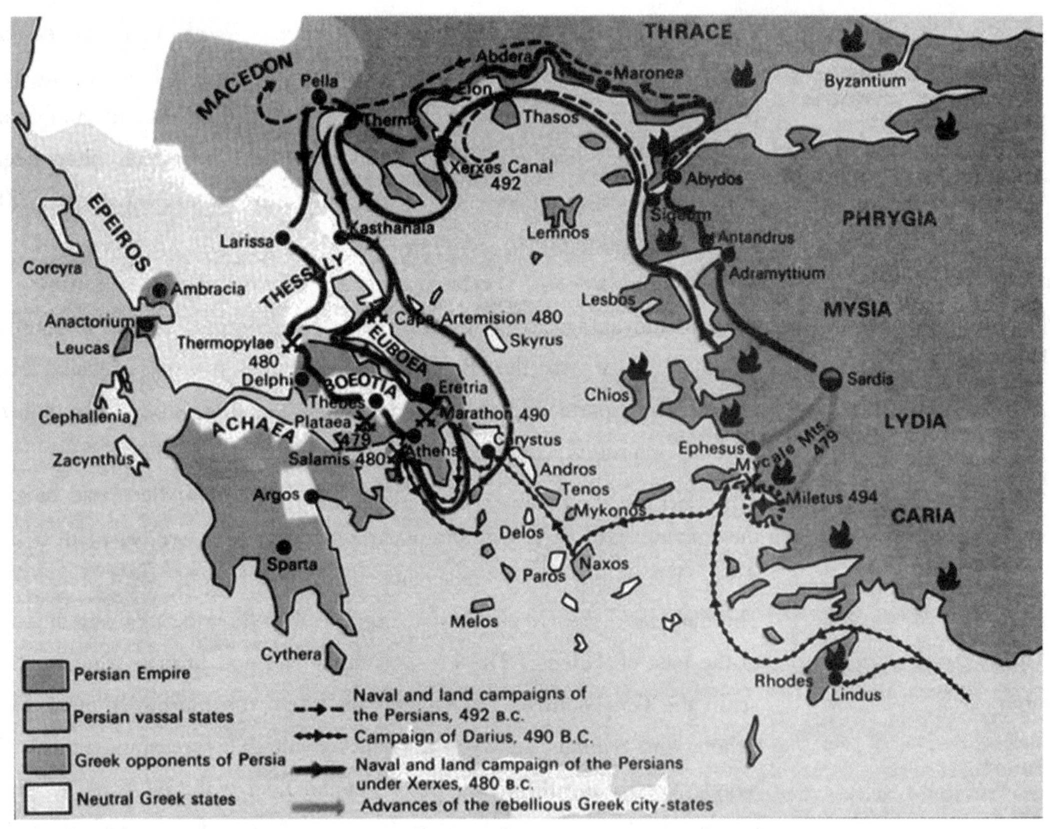

Map 9 The Greco-Persian Wars

After re-conquering Thrace and Macedonia in 492 BC, Darius I sent a large naval **expeditionary force** to destroy Eretria in 490 BC. When the Persian army landed on the northeast coast of Attica, Athens sent a messenger to the Spartans for help, but the Spartans were delayed by an important religious festival. Athens had to rely on its own force for defense. Though heavily outnumbered by the Persians, the Athenian army crushed the Persian forces and won a smashing victory in the battle of **Marathon** by their superior training, tactics and armor.① Herodotus recorded that 6 400 Persians died in the battle, compared with only 192 Athenians. The victory over the world's greatest empire gave Athens a burst of confidence and pushed it towards power and glory.

expeditionary force 远征军

Marathon 马拉松

In 480 BC Darius's son and successor **Xerxes Ⅰ** (519—465 BC) launched an even larger attack on Greece with a force of hundreds of

Xerxes Ⅰ 薛西斯一世

① 马拉松（Marathon）：希腊地名，在雅典东北30公里。公元前490年，雅典军在此打败波斯军队，史称马拉松之战。为了把胜利消息迅速告诉雅典人，希腊派遣长跑优胜者斐迪庇第斯（Phidippides）从马拉松跑至雅典中央广场（全程42.195公里）。斐迪庇第斯在报捷后即倒地牺牲。为了纪念此事，1896年雅典举行第一届奥林匹克运动会时设立了“马拉松长跑”项目。

ships and several hundred thousand soldiers. While many Greek city-states remained neutral or even cooperated with the Persians to avoid being destroyed, a number of city-states including Athens and Sparta formed a Greek league, with Spartan generals as supreme commanders, to counter Xerxes' attack. The Greek league had over 300 ships, 200 of which were prepared by Athens, and about 50 000 soldiers. Obviously outnumbered by the Persians, the Greeks decided to **minimize** the Persians' advantage in numbers by meeting them only at narrow routes at Thermopylae where the Persian troops could not pass easily. King Leonidas of Sparta and his 300 Spartans, together with a few thousand soldiers recruited from other Greek city-states, fought fiercely at Thermopylae till death. At the same time the Greek fleet was blocking the Persian navy at the Straits of Artemisium. The war lasted over three days. When the news came that the Greek troops were defeated at Thermopylae, the Greek navy decided to withdraw to Salamis, an island to the east of Athens. The Persians advanced and burned Athens. Once again the Greeks **lured** the Persian fleet into the narrow straits between Athens and Salamis and won a decisive victory by crushing the Persian navy. Xerxes and the remnants of Persian fleet withdrew to Asia Minor, leaving the land force in northern Greece. In 479 BC, Greek troops led by the Spartans destroyed the Persian army in central Greece and a Greek fleet commanded by the king of Sparta destroyed the remaining Persian fleet in the battle of Mycale in Asia Minor. The Greco-Persian Wars ended and the Greek army liberated the Ionian Greek cities.

minimize *v.* 使……最小化
Thermopylae 温泉关
lure *v.* 引诱

Victory over the Persians ensured the Greek *poleis* of the freedom essential to economic and cultural prosperity in the 5th century BC and **engendered** a consciousness of Greek unity and a common culture. In 478 BC, Athens and its allies formed the **Delian League** on the island of Delos to create and fund a **standing navy** to defend Greek independence against the Persians. Athens, the largest member of the League and the major Greek naval power, became permanent head of the League. Athens became Greece's leading naval power and Sparta remained the superior land power. Until the middle of the 5th BC, the two leading powers **coexisted** peacefully. Athens advanced further its process of **democratization** and reached the highest point in its cultural achievements.

engender *v.* 使……形成
Delian League 提洛同盟
standing navy 常备海军
coexist *v.* 并存
democratization *n.* 民主化进程

2.4.2 The Age of Pericles (460—429 BC)

In Athens, the period from 460 BC to 429 BC was dominated by a statesman named **Pericles** (495—429 BC), so the era was also called

Pericles 伯利克里

the "Age of Pericles". It is the "Golden Age" of classical Greece, because this period witnessed the greatest achievements of Greek culture and the flowering of Athenian democracy. It was in this period that Athens became the undisputed capital of Greek civilization.

Though a member of the aristocracy, Pericles further developed the democracy devised by his **predecessors** and offered many benefits to the common people of Athens. In Pericles' time the People's Assembly, the Council of 500 and the People's Court shared the political power. The People's Assembly, having the final authority, could make laws, elect or **depose** generals. The executive power resided in a board of 10 generals, whose duties were to administer financial, diplomatic and military affairs. Pericles gave every Athenian citizen the right to propose and **amend** laws and made it easier for poorer citizens to participate in the People's Assembly and Court by paying them a wage for attendance. Through these measures, the common free citizens of Athens became a major force in politics and they rewarded Pericles by re-electing him as general for the next thirty years.

predecessor *n.* 前任

depose *v.* 罢黜

amend *v.* 修订

During the Age of Pericles, the political developments in Athens were matched not only by economic growth, but also by the intellectual and artistic creations. As a generous **patron** of the arts, literature and sciences, Pericles encouraged the development of Greek culture by both public policy and personal example. He not only befriended many great artists and thinkers of his time and sponsored the production of Athenian dramas, but also ordered to rebuild the city of Athens, a city seriously damaged in Greco-Persian Wars and to construct several masterpieces of 5th century Greek architecture, including the **Parthenon**①, one of the most nearly perfect temples ever erected, and the **Propylaea**. In the Age of Pericles, the Athenian citizens not only actively participated in politics of the state, but enjoyed dramas, discussed philosophy and took pleasures in physical exercises in their leisure time. It was a time of prosperity, exuberance and freedom.

patron *n.* 赞助人

Parthenon 帕特农神庙

Propylaea 雅典卫城山门

2.4.3 Peloponnesian War (431—404 BC)

The glorious achievements of the Age of Pericles were made possible by the surplus wealth and resources flowing into Athens from Athens' allies in the Delian League. Although the danger from Persia was already over, Athens continued to demand ships, labor and money

① 帕特农神庙（Parthenon）：女神雅典娜的主要神庙，位于雅典卫城上，建于公元前 447 年和公元前 432 年之间，被认为是多利安式建筑的杰出代表。

subject *n.* 子民

from the member states of the Delian League. As the originally voluntary members of the League turned into unwilling **subjects**, the League was transformed into the Athenian Empire. Beginning in 465 BC, many members of the League resenting the imperialistic policy of the Athenian empire rebelled against the rule of Athens, but Athens crushed each rebellion ruthlessly.

Map 10 Greek poleis in the Peloponnesian War

besiege *v.* 围困

fortification *n.* 防御工事

hoplite *n.* 重甲步兵

The growth of Athenian power greatly disturbed Sparta and its allies. After a series of Athenian actions against the interests of the allies of Sparta, Sparta declared war on Athens in 431 BC and set out to invade Attica, the productive land surrounding Athens and to **besiege** Athens. Following Pericles' order, the population of Attica moved inside the **fortifications** of Athens and the defensive walls connecting Athens and Piraeus, a city of east-central Greece. Pericles advised the Athenians to avoid open battle with the superior Spartan **hoplites** and to rely on the strong Athenian fleet to give them food supplies from the sea and attack Spartan coasts. Dependent on its large empire, strong navy and rich treasury, the Athenians did not suffer much at first. But in 429 BC, the crowded condition inside the walls of Athens gave rise to a

plague that killed a third of the Athenian population, including Pericles. After his death, the leadership of the Athenian government passed to some **demagogues** far inferior to Pericles in wisdom and morality. Among them was Cleon, who managed some successes in the wars against Spartans and turned down the opportunity of concluding a peace with Sparta in 425 BC. Then Cleon was killed in battle in 421 BC, the Athenians and Spartans signed a **truce**, which lasted for only six years.

plague *n.* 瘟疫

demagogue *n.* 蛊惑民心的政客

truce *n.* 休战协议

In 415 BC, an aristocrat named Alcibiades convinced the Athenians to send the finest Greek fleet to attack the powerful city of Syracuse in southeastern Sicily and add Sicily to the Athenian empire. The **ill-advised** expedition failed, with thousands of Athenians killed or **enslaved** and the entire Athenian fleet destroyed. Though Athens managed to build another navy, its force was greatly reduced. Seizing this opportunity, the Spartans turned to the Persians for money and help to create a powerful Spartan fleet. In 405 BC, the Spartans destroyed the poorly led Athenian fleet. Besieged by land and sea, Athens **surrendered** in 404 BC, giving up control of its empire. Sparta refused Corinth and Thebes' call for the destruction of Athens, but imposed harsh terms on Athens such as stripping it of its fleet, tearing down its defensive walls and installing an oligarchic government.

ill-advised *adj.* 不明智的

enslave *v.* 使……沦为奴隶

surrender *v.* 投降

The Peloponnesian Wars were a disaster for all Greek poleis. After the war, the Greek city-states went into **decline**. In Athens, democracy collapsed and the empire crumbled. In Sparta, class **polarization** became ever more serious and old Spartan virtues were corrupted by wealth and power. As Sparta weakened from within, other city-states rose to challenge its **predominance**. Eventually in 371 BC, Sparta was defeated by Thebes and lost all claim to power and influence. Now that both Athens and Sparta lost their positions of leadership, the remaining Greek *poleis* continued fighting with each other. The constant clashes and warfare in the world of Greek city-states provided left the door open for invasion from a rising political power from the north of Greece, the kingdom of **Macedonia**. In 338 BC the Macedonians conquered the Greek city-states. The Golden Age of Classical Greece gave way to a new era.

decline *n.* 衰亡

polarization *n.* 两极分化

predominance *v.* 霸主地位

Macedonia 马其顿

2.5 The Hellenistic Period (323—31 BC)

The Macedonians had long been regarded by the Greeks as barbarians. The region of Macedonia had remained **insignificant** before **Philip Ⅱ** (382—336 BC) became king in 359 BC. Building up a strong army, Philip II united Macedonia. Under his reign, Macedonia

insignificant *adj.* 无足轻重的

Philip Ⅱ 菲利普二世

diplomacy *n.* 外交
agression *n.* 侵略
assassinate *v.* 暗杀
Alexander the Great 亚历山大大帝
Afghanistan 阿富汗
malaria *n.* 疟疾
Hellenistic *adj.* 希腊化
hybrid *n.* 混合物
cosmopolitan *adj.* 世界性的
oriental *adj.* 东方的
incorporate *v.* 吸收

gradually dominated much of Greece through a combination of **diplomacy** and military **aggression**. Philip defeated the alliance of Athens, Thebes, and a number of smaller *poleis* in 338 BC and formed a new Greek league, the "League of Corinth" in 337 BC, which was intended to provide forces for a war against Persia. It was for the first time in history when all of mainland Greece was under the authority of a single king. But Philip was never able to realize his dream since he was **assassinated** by one of his own guards in 336 BC. The throne was succeeded by his twenty-year-old son, Alexander III, now known as **Alexander the Great** (356—323 BC).

Alexander began his reign by securing his northern frontier and suppressing rebellions in the Greek league. From 334 BC on, Alexander embarked on an expedition to conquer Persia and achieved a series of stunning victories. At last, he not longer managed to conquer Persia, but built up the largest empire in the ancient world. With his conquest, Greek civilization attained its widest reach, expanding to include Asia Minor, Syria, Palestine, Egypt, Persia, and the land further East to the Western parts of India, and as far north as today's **Afghanistan**. In northwest India, due to the rebellion of his now weary and homesick soldiers, Alexander had to withdraw to Babylon, where he died of **malaria** in 323 BC.

Alexander the Great's conquests laid the foundations for the **Hellenistic** civilization in all the lands of the eastern Mediterranean and western Asia. The term *Hellenistic* means "Greek-like", and stands in contrast to *Hellenic*, or purely Greek. Hellenistic civilization was "Greek-like" because it was a **hybrid** composed of Greek and Asian elements. Alexander himself spoke Greek and had been educated by the great Greek philosopher Aristotle. Many aspects of the Hellenistic world were influenced by the Greek culture. Greek became the language of government; Greek philosophy and literature spread throughout western Asia. At the same time, the Hellenistic civilization was more than the localized, purely Greek Hellenic civilization; it was a **cosmopolitan** civilization based upon a mixture of Greek and **Oriental** cultures. While learning and popularizing Greek culture, the Hellenistic world also **incorporated** features from a number of different cultures such as Persian and Indian.

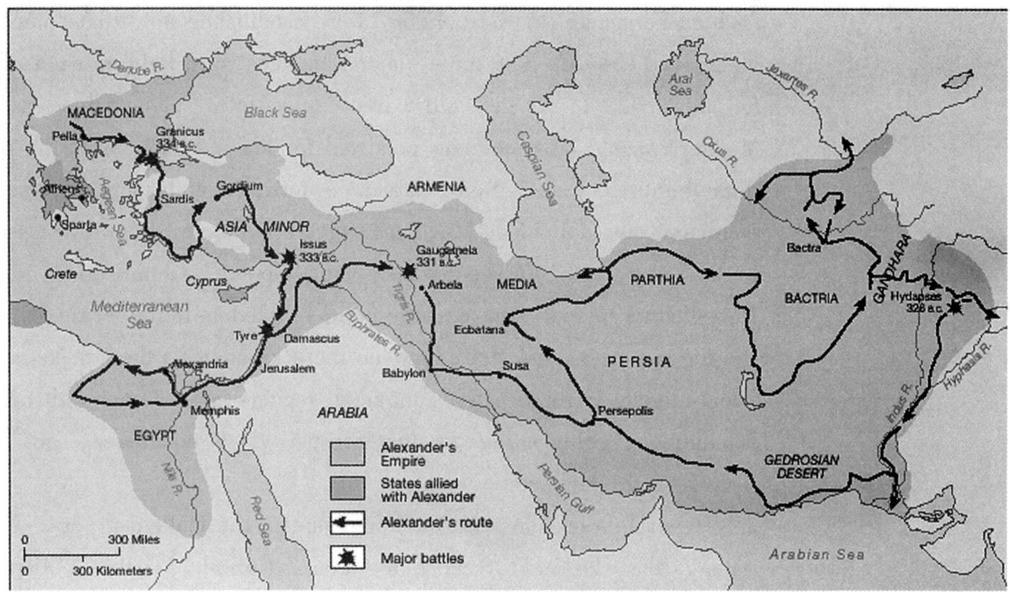

Map 11 Alexander's Empire

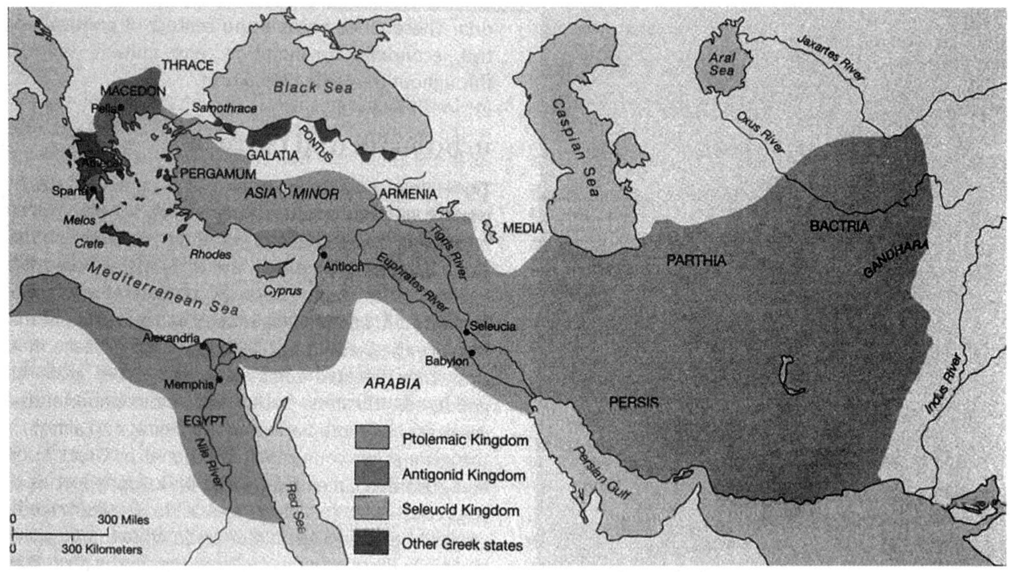

Map 12 The Hellenistic Kingdoms

After Alexander's death, his generals fought for the various portions of his empire and by 275 BC, three major Hellenistic kingdoms emerged. **Ptolemy** ruled Egypt and parts of the Middle East. **Seleucus** controlled Syria and the remnants of the Persian Empire and **Antigonus** dominated Macedonia, Thrace, and parts of northern Asia Minor. Among them, Ptolemaic Egypt was the most prosperous, sophisticated and longest-lasting Hellenistic kingdom. Several smaller kingdoms,

Ptolemy 托勒密
Seleucus 塞琉古
Antigonus 安提柯

such as Pergamum in Asia Minor, were established at various times in Hellenistic Greece. The three major kingdoms were fighting each other for the control of the old Greek city-states along the eastern Mediterranean. This situation persisted for the most part over the next three hundred years. Being larger in territory and more diverse in ethnicity, the Hellenistic kingdoms were very different from the classical Greek city-states. Macedonians and Greeks administered these Hellenistic kingdoms and left little political freedom to the local citizens. Despite the occasional **strife** between these kingdoms, the Greeks could freely migrate to these newly conquered regions and interact with native populations, contributing to the prosperity of commerce, art and science in the Hellenistic world.

strife *n.* 纷争

Several Greek cities became dominant in the Hellenistic era. City-states of the Classical Greece like Athens, Corinth, Thebes, Miletus, and Syracuse continued to flourish, while others, such as Antioch in Syria, Pergamum in Anatolia, Seleucia in Mesopotamia, emerged as major centers throughout the kingdoms. Alexandria in Egypt was the largest and most famous of all Hellenistic cities. Founded by Alexander the Great in 331 BC, **Alexandria** became the commercial, cultural and intellectual centre of the Hellenistic world under the Ptolemy's. The famous Library of Alexandria stored half a million **scrolls** and aspired to host the entire knowledge of the known world.

Alexandria 亚历山大城

scroll *n.* (羊皮)书卷

At the time of Hellenistic era, Rome had risen to a formidable power. Gradually, large part of the Hellenistic kingdoms disintegrated due to the Roman invasion. In 31 BC **Octavian** (later Augustus) defeated the rulers of Egypt by Anthony and Cleopatra in the naval battle of Actium, and completed the demise of the Hellenistic era. After the battle of Actium, the entire Hellenic world became subject to Rome. Greece in the next two thousand years was to undergo a series of conquests that made its people subjects of numerous powers and did not gain its self-determination until the 19th century.

Octavian 屋大维

3. Cultural Achievements of the Ancient Greeks

Greece in antiquity saw a remarkable intellectual and cultural growth throughout the Hellenic and Hellenistic world and made many influential contributions to western civilization in such areas as philosophy, science, literature, and art.

3.1 Religion and Mythology

Traditional Greek religion was characterized by **polytheism**. All Greek gods were in human forms and each had distinct human-like **personality**. The Greeks believed that the gods differed from human only in their **immortality** and supernatural powers. In Greek belief, the gods lived on top of Mount Olympus in Northern Greece. Among the 12 most important and powerful Olympian gods, Zeus was the chief **deity** and father of many gods. For the ancient Greeks, gods were creators and governors of the universe and mankind. Different gods were in charge of different aspects of human life and activities. While the 12 Olympian gods were **revered** by all Greeks, each Greek polis was under the protection of one particular God. For example, Athena was the God of Athens and Sparta, Apollo was worshipped at Delphi and Delos and Zeus was worshiped at Olympia. ①

polytheism *n.* 多神论

personality *n.* 性格

immortality *n.* 长生不老

deity *n.* 神

revere *v.* 敬慕

Greek Name	Roman Name	**God/Goddess of...**
Zeus	Jupiter	the sky and thunder. King of the gods and ruler of Mount Olympus.
Hera (sister and wife of Zeus)	Juno	marriage and family. Queen of the gods.
Poseidon (brother of Zeus)	Neptune	the seas, earthquakes and horse.
Dionysus (son of Zeus)	Bacchus	wine, celebrations and **ecstasy**. Patron god of the art of theatre.
Apollo (son of Zeus, twin brother of Artemis)	Phebo	light, knowledge, music, poetry, prophecy and **archery**.
Artemis (daughter of Zeus)	Diana	the hunt, **virginity** and all animals.
Hermes (son of Zeus)	Mercury	commerce and thieves. Messenger of the gods.
Athena (daughter of Zeus)	Minerva	wisdom, handicrafts, defense and strategic warfare.
Ares (son of Zeus)	Mars	war, violence.
Aphrodite	Venus	love, beauty, and desire.

ecstasy *n.* 狂欢

archery *n.* 箭术

virginity *n.* 贞洁

① 古希腊宗教和神话中的12主神通常不包括冥王哈德斯（Hades），因为他大部分时间都在地府，而在万神庙中并无席位。罗马神话中的12主神大致相同，只是把狄俄尼索斯（Dionysus，罗马神话中名为巴克斯 Bacchus）换成了赫斯提（Hestia，罗马神话中名为维斯塔 Vesta），这样便刚好有6位男神和6位女神。

Greek Name	Roman Name	**God/Goddess of...**
Hephaestus (son of Zeus)	Vulcan	fire, blacksmith and craftsman.
Demeter (sister of Zeus)	Ceres	**fertility**, agriculture, nature, and the seasons.

Fertility *n.* 繁殖

reciprocal *adj.* 相互的

For the Greeks, mankind and the gods had a **reciprocal** relationship. That is to say, people honored the gods by offering sacrifices, adorning their sanctuaries, offering prayers and holding festivals; and in return, the gods would protect and benefit the people and states that paid them honor. Otherwise, the gods would be angry and punish mankind with either natural disasters or defeat in war.

The worship of Olympian gods led to the development of Greek temple. Each temple was the home of a patron deity of a city-state and the major building of the city's life. The main religious ceremony, namely the sacrificial ritual, took place outside the front of the temple. Worshippers would offer the blood, bones and hides of food animals to the gods and ate the rest as food. **Oracles** also played an important role in the Greek religion and beliefs. In order to know the will of gods, people consulted the oracle, a sacred shrine dedicated to a god or goddess that would reveal the future. The most famous was the oracle of Apollo at Delphi in central Greece, where a priestess who went into a **trance** would relay Apollo's message to the people. There were also some important public festivals held to honor the gods. For instance at Olympia, in the western Peloponnesus, every four years after 776 BC, Olympic games were held to honor Zeus. Greek city-states would even cease fire during the period of Olympic Games. In all, religion played an important role in Greek society and was intricately connected to every aspect of its daily life

oracle *n.* 神示所，神谕

trance *n.* 出神状态

Accompanying the religious believes and rituals of the ancient Greek was the Greek mythology, which contained a large body of myths and legends concerning Greek gods, heroes, monsters and wars. Greek mythology **originated** from the Minoan, Mycenaean, Dorian and Hellenic myths and the oldest recordings of Greek myths could be traced back to Homer and Hesiod's epics. Greek mythology is important primary source for us to learn about ancient Greeks' understanding of the **universe**, the origin of man, as well as the relationship between man and nature, between man and man. These imaginative and beautifully told stories also provide later generations with inspirations for art and literature.

originate *v.* 起源

universe *n.* 宇宙

While Olympian gods were celebrated by poets and artists and worshipped by common people, early philosophers and scientists were searching for non-mythological explanations of the origin of the universe and human beings. During the 6th century BC, a group of Greek thinkers made a radical break with archaic religion and developed speculative philosophy. So the study of philosophy was encouraged in part by questions arising from religious beliefs.

3.2 Philosophy

Ancient Greek philosophy arose in the 6th century BC and continued through the Hellenistic period. Philosophy in Greek means "love of wisdom", and this wisdom refers to the knowledge of the way things really are as opposed to the way things appear to be as **distorted** by senses. Ancient Greeks assumed that one ought to live one's life in **conformity** to the way things really are. Ancient Greek philosophy had three basic categories: **metaphysics**, **epistemology** and **ethics**. Metaphysics dealt with the nature of existence and asked such questions as "what is the world made of?" and "what is the ultimate substance of all reality?" **Materialism** and **idealism** were two basic approaches of metaphysics. Epistemology was concerned with the nature of knowledge and asked such questions as "How do we know about truth and reality?" and "Is our knowledge of truth and reality reliable?" Two basic approaches of epistemology were **empiricism**, which said that all knowledge comes from the senses and rationalism, which said that knowledge comes from reason. Ethics dealt with values related to human conduct, especially its goodness and badness, or rightness and wrongness. **Hedonism**, believed that pleasure or happiness is the highest good and **cynicism**, and that world is essentially evil and we should distance ourselves from it, were the two extremes of ethics.

distort *v.* 扭曲

conformity *n.* 符合，遵照

metaphysics *n.* 形而上学

epistemology *n.* 认识论

ethics *n.* 伦理

materialism *n.* 唯物主义

idealism *n.* 唯心主义

empiricism *n.* 经验主义

rationalism *n.* 理性主义

hedonism *n.* 享乐主义

cynicism *n.* 犬儒主义

3.2.1 The Pre-Socratic Philosophy

Greek philosophy did not begin in Greece proper, but in Miletus, the richest city of Ionia (the west coast of today's Turkey). The earliest Greek philosophers were mainly natural philosophers, who liked to ponder on the questions related to the origin of the universe. **Thales** (636—546 BC), founder of Greek geometry and astronomy and recognized by Aristotle as the first philosopher, held the opinion that everything comes from one basic **substance**, water. His student, **Anaximander** (610—546 BC) argued that everything derives not so much from any specific basic substance as from the "unlimited" or

Thales 泰利斯

substance *n.* 物质

Anaximande 阿纳克西曼德尔

Anaximenes 阿那克西米尼

the Milesian school 米利都学派

whim *n.* 心血来潮

prerequisite *n.* 前提

prerequisite *n.* 前提

Pythagoras 毕达哥拉斯

"undefined" substance. Anaximander's student, **Anaximenes** (585—528 BC), proposed that the "unlimited" substance is actually air. Since these earliest philosophers were all from Miletus, they were called **the Milesian school**. The Milesian school was important because they saw the physical world as being governed by laws of nature, rather than by the **whims** of the gods. This is the **prerequisite** for the development of science and philosophy.

Different from the Miletus school that emphasized the nature of the universe, **Pythagoras** (582—500 BC) was the first philosopher to bring philosophy into connection with practical life. As a mathematician, Pythagoras believed that number gives rise to proportion, and proportion gives rise to harmony. Since the universe is based on number, mankind can lead a harmonious life by pursuing the purity of mathematics.

Heraclitus 赫拉克利特

logos 逻各斯（意为世界普遍规则）

Parmenides 巴门尼德

Some other philosophers continued the Milesian argument as to the origin of the universe. **Heraclitus** (540—475 BC) assumed that fire is the basic substance and he named the principle governing the universe "**logos**". He also declared that change is essential to the entire universe and his famous sayings were "All things change" and "You cannot step into the same river twice". But **Parmenides** (515 BC) argued that change is only an illusion created by senses and that reality is a world of pure and unchanging existence. He was the earliest Western idealistic philosopher to distinguish thinking from being, and senses from reality and this proposition would be taken up and developed by Plato and his followers in later decades. By contrast, **Democritus** (460—370 BC) developed materialist theory of atomism. In his theory, the world was made up of **atoms**. Different in shape, size and arrangement, but similar in quality, atoms were indivisible and imperishable. They moved about constantly and created different objects when combined. Democritus' theory of atomism was the **culmination** of ancient materialism.

Democritus 德谟克利特

atom *n.* 原子

culmination *n.* 巅峰之作

3.2.2 Classical Greek Philosophy

In the latter half of the 5th century BC, Greek philosophers gradually shifted their focus from the material world to the everyday life of mankind. They expected wisdom to be more useful and practical to human life. Representing such a trend was the **Sophists**, who held the view that truth and morality are subjective and relative and it is wise for people to decide on and gain one's own good without regard for morality. The Sophists provided instructions in almost everything of higher learning

sophist *n.* 智者派，诡辩学派

for a fee, and they emphasized the art of rhetoric and logic, which was supposed to provide students with the useful skills to win arguments and persuade audience in public life, even if they wanted to make the worse case appear to be better, and the wrong case to be right. The Sophists' **relativist** and **skeptical** views on truth and morality eventually brought about sharp criticism from Socrates, Plato, and Aristotle.

relativist *adj.* 相对主义的
skeptical *adj.* 怀疑的

Socrates (470—399 BC) left no written works and was known to us mainly through the writings of his pupil Plato. Unlike his Sophist contemporaries, Socrates taught his pupils for free and did not claim to have ready answers to all philosophical questions. He believed that all real knowledge is within each person and philosophers should use questions-and-answer technique, or **dialectic** method, to lead people to see things for themselves by using their own reason. His incessant questioning of authority and exposure of other's ignorance made him many enemies. In 399 BC, shortly after the Peloponnesian War, Socrates was accused by the democratic court of Athens of atheism and corrupting the Athenian youth and sentenced to death. Refusing his friends' offer to save him, Socrates chose to respect the laws of his state and accept his fate calmly. The trail of Socrates is usually considered one of history's great **miscarriages of justice**.

Socrates 苏格拉底
dialectic *adj.* 辩证的
miscarriage of justice 误判

As Socrates' greatest pupil, **Plato** (429—348 BC) set up a famous school in Athens called **the Academy** and wrote a large number of famous dialogues, including ***Phaedo***, ***Symposium***, and ***Republic***, all presenting philosophic conversations between Socrates and his pupils. Besides illustrating the philosophical thought of Socrates, these dialogues also put forward important original concepts of Plato himself, especially his theory of **Ideas** (hence the name **Idealism**). For Plato eternal and unchanging Ideas such as Beauty, Truth, Justice and Goodness are the only proper source of knowledge but they exist only in the mind of God. Only the trained mind can understand these Ideas, which is the goal of philosophy. Plato's philosophy was very influential in religious, especially Christian, teaching and writing.

Plato 柏拉图
the Academy 雅典学园
Phaedo《斐多篇》
Symposium《会饮篇》
Republic《理想国》
idea *n.* 理念
idealism *n.* 唯心主义，唯理论

Aristotle (384—322 BC), Plato's greatest pupil, developed a different philosophical system and set up his own school, the Lyceum. As the tutor of Alexander the Great, whose expansion in the ancient world helped accumulate necessary information and materials for scientific research, Aristotle was a man of **encyclopedic** knowledge and enduring influence. In addition to his interest in logic, metaphysics, ethics, poetics and politics, Aristotle gathered an enormous amount of

Aristotle 亚里士多德
encyclopedic *adj.* 百科全书式的

anatomy *n.* 解剖学

teleological *adj.* 目的论的
organism *n.* 有机体

information on physics, biology, **anatomy**, zoology, and other sciences. Based on his own research and reasoning, Aristotle showed his disagreement with the Platonic idealism and argued that Form (or Idea) and Matter are inseparable and Idea does not exist as a higher reality than the material world. Different from Plato, he valued the **senses** as important guides to truth and he believed change was not an illusion. Aristotle's view of change was teleological, that is, he believed that every organism changes and grows toward a particular end and is an integral and harmonious part of a larger whole. Aristotle's scientific writings not only were the most influential philosophical classics of Greek and Roman civilizations, but also remained significant during the Middle Ages in the Arabic and Latin worlds.

3.2.3 Hellenistic Philosophy

The dramatic political, social, economic and diplomatic changes in the Hellenistic era generated many uncertainties in the minds of the Greeks. Philosophers turned to focus on ethics, the discovery of the best way to live. Most of the Hellenistic philosophers agreed that the peace of mind, or freedom from troubles, is the essence of the good life.

Epicureanism *n.* 伊壁鸠鲁学说
Stoicism *n.* 斯多葛学说
disintegrate *v.* 瓦解

intellectual *adj.* 智识的

Zeno 芝诺

self-discipline *n.* 自律

Two of the most representative philosophical schools of this period were **Epicureanism** and **Stoicism**, both originated in Athens in about 300 BC. Epicureanism featured the escapist arguments of Epicurus (341—270 BC) and his followers, who held that the world is made of nothing but atoms, the soul will **disintegrate** just as the body, so the highest and only good in this life is pleasure. Despite general misunderstandings of later people, the pleasure recommended by Epicurus is actually **intellectual**, including the moderate satisfaction of body appetites, the mental pleasure of contemplating excellence, and above all, serenity of soul. Stoicism had a more lasting influence. The founder of Stoicism, **Zeno** (335—263 BC) believed that the only good is harmony with nature, which is governed by the divine and universal reason, and the truly wise man lives in harmony with this nature by means of human reason and pursuit of wisdom.① Stoicism also emphasized such outwardly directed concepts as duty and **self-discipline**, which made it popular with later Roman rulers.

Epicureanism and Stoicism are similar in several ways. For

① Stoic一词来源于希腊文中Stoa Poikile，为雅典一处著名画廊。因芝诺常在此讲学论道，故该学派得名Stoicism。

example, both were concerned not with the welfare of society but with the good of the individual. They were both materialistic and reliant on reason as the key to the solution of social problems. They both treasured the peace of mind and attracted many followers.

3.3 Science

The insatiable curiosity of the Greeks directed them towards the fervent inquiries into the facts and laws of nature, hence the germination of science. It is no wonder that most of the greatest philosophers of ancient Greece were also men of science. **Thales**, for instance, is regarded by many as the father of science because he was the first Greek philosopher to seek to explain the physical world in terms of natural rather than supernatural causes. In general, ancient Greek science covered a wide range of practices and the boundaries between disciplines were fluid. Contrary hypotheses were discussed and challenged, so that newer and more advanced theories and methodologies would be produced.

Thales 泰利斯

In the field of mathematics, **Euclid** (325—270 BC) compiled a treatise on **plane geometry** named Elements, which was hugely influential in both Western and Islamic civilizations and had remained the basic textbook for the subject until today. But the greatest mathematician of ancient Greece was **Archimedes** (287—212 BC), a Sicilian Greek who calculated the approximate value of π (the ratio of a circle's circumference to its diameter) and invented a terminology for expressing numbers up to any magnitude. **Pythagoras** (580—500 BC) was perhaps the first to explain the universe in abstract mathematical language. He proposed that numbers were the underlying and unchangeable truth of the universe, thus elevating mathematics almost to a religious cult.

Euclid 欧几里得

plane geometry 平面几何

Archimedes 阿基米德

Pythagoras 毕达哥拉斯

Advances in mathematics promoted advances in astronomy. **Eratosthenes** (276—196 BC) was the first person to measure the Earth's **circumference** with amazing accuracy. But the most renowned of the earlier Greek astronomers was **Aristarchus** (310—230 BC), who was famous for his **heliocentric hypothesis** that said the earth revolves around the sun, instead of the sun around the earth. But his theory was rejected by his contemporaries, mainly because the heliocentric hypothesis was in conflict with Aristotle's teachings and lacked exact data due to technological limitations. **Hipparchus** (190—120 BC) attacked the heliocentric theory of the universe as proposed by Aristarchus and his works on **geocentric theory**set the foundation for the

Eratosthenes 埃拉托色尼

circumference *n.* 周长

Aristarchus 阿里斯塔克斯

heliocentric hypothesis 日心说

Hipparchus 喜帕恰斯

geocentric theory 地心说

Ptolemy 托勒密

lever *n.* 杠杆
pulley *n.* 滑轮
screw *n.* 螺旋
Hippocrates 希波克拉底

dissection *n.* 解剖

Herophilus 奚落菲勒斯
anatomist *n.* 解剖学家

ovary *n.* 卵巢
duodenum *n.* 十二指肠
pulse *n.* 脉搏
Erasitratus 埃拉西斯特拉图斯
motor (sensory) nerve 运动(感觉)神经
Iliad《伊利亚特》
Odyssey《奥德赛》

astronomical work of **Ptolemy** (100—170 AD).

Prior to the Hellenistic period, physics had been a branch of philosophy. It was through the efforts of Archimedes that physics was made a separate and experimental science. He not only discovered the law of floating bodies but also formulated the principles of the **lever**, the **pulley**, and the **screw**.

Ancient Greece also witnessed great development in medicine. **Hippocrates** (460—337 BC), the "father of medicine", founded a school of medicine and set forth a code of medical ethics (the "Hippocratic oath") for doctors. His detailed and accurate clinical accounts of diseases are still useful for modern doctors. In Alexandria in the Hellenistic period, **dissection** of human bodies or even living convicts was allowed by King Ptolemy and became the key to medical advance. **Herophilus** (335—280 BC) was the greatest **anatomist** of antiquity and probably the first to practice human dissection. His achievements included the recognition of the brain as the centre of the nervous system, the discovery of the **ovaries** and the **duodenum**, and a detailed theory of the diagnostic value of measuring **pulse** rates. **Erasistratus** (304—250 BC) recognized the importance of the heart and distinguished between **motor** and **sensory nerves.**

3.4 Literature

At the beginning of Greek literature stand the two monumental epics of Homer, the ***Iliad*** and the ***Odyssey***, which were based on the heroic legends of the Trojan War in the Mycenaean era and were written down during the Greek Dark Age.① The two poems are told in simple, direct, and eloquent language and reflect the view prevailing among Greeks in those days that man's acts and fate are controlled by the gods. The legendary author of these epics, Homer, was a professional singer of heroic poetry who probably lived around 800 to 700 BC, centuries after the Trojan War. Although these epics are credited to Homer, there is no doubt that it was the oral tradition passed down from the Mycenaean era that gave Homer knowledge of a society which was long

① 《伊利亚特》主要描写了十年特洛伊战争的最后一年。希腊联军主将阿喀琉斯(Achilles)因喜爱的一个女俘被统帅阿伽门农(Agamemnon)夺走，愤而退出战斗，特洛伊人乘机大破希腊联军。在危急关头，阿喀琉斯的好友穿上阿喀琉斯的盔甲上阵，但却被特洛亚大将赫克托尔(Hector)杀死。阿喀琉斯悔恨已极，重上战场，杀死赫克托尔。特洛伊老国王夜入阿喀琉斯大帐要回儿子尸体。史诗在赫克托尔的葬礼中结束。《奥德赛》连接《伊利亚特》的情节，讲述了希腊英雄奥德修斯(Odysseus)在特洛伊战争中取胜及返航途中的历险故事。

gone by his day. And most of what we know about the heroic ideal of late Dark Age Greece derives from Homer's works.

The other great epicist of Greek antiquity was **Hesiod**, who is thought to have lived and worked around 700 BC. Hesiod spoke of himself in his poetry and referred to himself as a farmer in Boeotia, a region in central Greece. In ***Works and Days***, a faithful depiction of ancient rural life, Hesiod vividly described the five successive ages of mankind: the Golden Age, ruled by Cronus, when human lived happily as gods, free from pain, sorrow and trouble; the Silver Age, ruled by Zeus, when human were made inferior to gods and committed crimes against each other; the Bronze age, an epoch of war when men were violent and warlike; the Heroic age, the time of men as demigods and heroes; and lastly the Iron age, the corrupt present when all manner of evils spread and humans lived in misery. In ***Theogony***, a systematic account of the gods, Hesiod gave us the most detailed presentation of the Greek creation myth. According to this work, the world began with **Chaos**, a primordial void of darkness. Out of the void emerged Gaia (the Earth), who gave birth to Uranus (the Sky). From the union of Gaia and Uranus were born the 12 **Titans**, 3 **Cyclops** and 3 hundred-handed Giants. One of the Titans, Cronus, castrated his father and became ruler of the world until he was overthrown by his own son, Zeus. Then the new pantheon of gods and goddesses was founded on the top of Mount Olympus.

The Archaic Greeks also developed another poetic form, the **lyric**, so called because it was originally sung by individuals or a **chorus** accompanied by a musical instrument called the **lyre**. Unlike epic that is composed to praise the deeds of the great heroes, lyric is a short poem expressing the poet's personal feelings and thoughts. The first of the known lyric poets was **Archilochus** (680—645 BC), who wrote about love and hate, war and travel. The great **poetess Sappho** from the island of Lesbos (625—570 BC) wrote long poems and wedding songs to express her intimately feelings, including her passionate love of women, which produced the word ***lesbian*** (from the island's name, Lesbos).

By the 5th century BC, the age that followed the Greco-Persian Wars, drama became popular in Athens. Drama fulfilled the religious, civic and educational functions in Greek antiquity and became one of the most important contributions of the Greeks to western civilization. There were two major forms of Greek drama in the Classical Period, tragedy

Hesiod 赫西奥德

Works and Days《工作与时日》

Theogony《神谱》

Chaos *n.* 混沌

Titan *n.* 提坦巨人

Cyclop *n.* 独眼巨人

castrate *v.* 阉割

lyric *n.* 抒情诗

chorus *n.* 合唱团

lyre *n.* 里拉琴

Archilochus 阿基罗库斯

poetess *n.* 女诗人

Sappho 萨福

lesbian *n.* 女同性恋

and comedy. Tragedy was usually about the suffering of a hero and it usually ended in disaster. Growing out of simple performances at religious festivals in honor of the god Dionysus, tragedy was presented in the great outdoor theatre on the slopes of the Acropolis, where 3 male actors wearing masks and costumes acted all the parts and a chorus of 12 or 15 singers would interrupt the play by singing or speaking lines that helped explain the play. The drama consisted of set speeches, dialogue between characters, and choral odes. Thousands of people packed the theatre to enjoy the dramas produced by famous playwrights, who, funded by wealthy citizens to pay for the costumes and train the chorus members, would present tragedies in the state-sponsored competition for prizes. They liked to adapt mythological materials for the plots of their dramas and explored in their plays the fierce conflicts between good and evil, law and morality, individual freedom and God's will.

Aeschylus 埃斯库罗斯

Aeschylus (525—456 BC) is often recognized as the "father of Greek tragedy". Prior to Aeschylus, Greek tragedy had only one actor, who interacted with the chorus. Aeschylus made a major improvement by adding a second actor and diminishing the importance of the chorus so that it was possible to present flexible dramatic actions and dialogues. He was also the first Greek dramatist to use complicated **props**, stage machinery, and costumes for dramatic effect. Aeschylus wrote over 80 plays, 7 of which survive. In his dramas, the plots, characters and actions are not so **sophisticated**, but the verses and lyrics are grand, vivid and powerful. His dramas are often concerned with major moral issues. For example, he believed that God would punish human beings for their **transgressions** and it was by this suffering that human eventually learned the God's will. The **trilogy** known as ***Oresteia*** (458 BC) was the finest of his works and also the only complete Greek trilogy that we possess today. Comprising three connected tragedies Agamemnon, The Libation Bearers and The Eumenides, the Oresteia trilogy told the bloody story of the family of Agamemnon, King of Mycenae.①

prop *n.* 舞台道具

sophisticated *adj.* 精妙复杂

transgression *n.* 罪过

trilogy *n.* 三部曲戏剧

Oresteia《奥瑞斯提亚》

Sophocles 索福克勒斯

Another great Athenian tragedian was **Sophocles** (496—406 BC). His works are regarded as the best example of Greek drama for their

① 《奥瑞斯提亚》(Oresteia) 三部曲梗概：特洛伊战争结束后，希腊联军统帅阿伽门农回到家中，被妻子克吕泰尼丝特拉 (Clytemnestra) 所杀。他们的儿子俄瑞斯忒斯 (Orestes) 为了替父报仇，杀害了母亲克吕泰尼丝特拉。从此，俄瑞斯忒斯被复仇女神 (Furies) 所追逐，惶惶不可终日。最后他逃到雅典城，在那里接受了女神雅典娜的审判，最后被判无罪。

controlled and graceful language, *vivid* **characterization** and perfect form. Like Aeschylus, Sophocles was also an innovator of tragedy; he introduced a third actor onstage and expanded the chorus from 12 to 15 members. But unlike Aeschylus's tragedy in which the character's fate was totally governed by God's will, Sophocles' tragedy depicted characters whose fate was influenced more by their own personality. In so doing, Sophocles developed his characters to a greater extent than earlier playwrights. For example, his characters often unwisely and unsuccessfully struggled against their fate. They suffered a lot in that process, but eventually they would manage to overcome their difficulties. Sophocles' most famous play was ***Oedipus the King*** (429 BC),① in which Oedipus suffered the fate determined by the gods and unknowingly killed his own father and married his mother, but at last he still believed in the fact that as a free man he must bear responsibility for his own actions.

characterization *n.* 人物刻画

Oedipus the King《俄狄浦斯王》

The third outstanding Athenian tragedian **Euripides** (485—406 BC) is the most revolutionary Greek dramatist known in modern times. Compared with his predecessors who were only concerned with the aristocracy in their works, Euripides brought tragedy closer to the experience of the ordinary people. His plays paid much more attention to people of low social status like women and slaves and created less heroic and more realistic characters. Euripides viewed the human soul as a place where opposing forces struggle, where strong passions such as hatred and jealousy conflict with reason. Euripides's extant plays are concerned with three basic themes: war, religion and women. ***Medea*** (431 BC) is perhaps Euripides's most famous and most influential play.② It told the story of the jealousy and revenge of a woman, Medea, who was betrayed by her husband Jason. Euripides did not present Medea as simply a **villain**; rather, he brilliantly presented her as a woman with conflicting emotions and sophisticated personality, making the character true to life and worthy of sympathy.

Euripides 欧里庇得斯

Medea《美狄亚》

villain *n.* 反面人物

Greek comedy developed later than tragedy. Since 486 BC, comedies had become an official part of the dramatic competition and

---

① 《俄狄浦斯王》(Oedipus the King) 梗概：俄狄浦斯是底比斯国王莱厄斯 (Laius) 和王后乔卡斯塔 (Jocasta) 之子，在出生时即被抛弃，后在无意中杀害了他父亲尔后娶了他母亲，当后来真相大白时，俄狄浦斯弄瞎了自己的眼睛，自我流放于国外。

② 《美狄亚》(Medea) 梗概：美狄亚是科尔喀斯国 (Colchis) 的公主及女巫，她帮助伊阿宋 (Jason) 取得了金羊毛后，做了伊阿宋的妻子，又因伊阿宋的不忠诚而杀了他们的子女以图报复。

prizes were given to best productions. Like tragedy, comedy arose from the religious ritual in honor of Dionysus, but unlike tragedy usually based on mythology, Old Comedy of the Classical period was set in the present and poke fun at public figures and events. It was strongly **satirical** and full of jokes, puns and **obscenities**. The most famous playwright of the Old Comedy was **Aristophanes** (450—385 BC), who was bold enough to make fun of everyone and criticize every institution and public policy. As most of his plays were produced during the Peloponnesian War, he condemned Athens' imperial policies in *Babylonians* (426 BC), attacked the Peloponnesian War in *The Acharnians* (425 BC), ridiculed Athenian democracy in *The Birds* (414 BC) and imagined Athenian women going on a sex strike to force their men to stop the war in *Lysistrata* (411 BC). In some other plays, he even satirized the philosophy of Socrates and the tragedies of Euripides.

satirical *adj.* 讽刺意味
obscenity *n.* 猥亵语言
Aristophanes 阿里斯多芬

Towards the end of the 4th century BC, the political climate of the Hellenistic Athens dominated by Macedonia made **scathing** political satire impossible, so the political and social commentary of the Old Comedy was given away to the mild satire of ordinary people and their private domestic problems of the New Comedy. The representative of the New Comedy was **Menander** (342—290 BC), whose plays were known for their extremely intricate plots, creative use of love theme and realistic portrayal of characters. Menander's comedy influenced the Roman stage and later Shakespeare's comedy.

scathing *adj.* 尖刻的
Menander 米南德

In the Hellenistic period, Alexandria became the new cultural centre and the Alexandrian writers were known not for their creativity and originality as Hellenic writers were, but for their learned research and extensive knowledge. The forms of poetry chiefly cultivated by the Alexandrians were epic, lyric, **elegy** and **epigram. Callimachus** (305—240 BC) was one of the most influential Hellenistic poets and scholars. His extant works include 64 epigrams and a 120-volume catalogue of all the books in the Alexandrian Library. **Theocritus** (300—260 BC) was perhaps the best poet of the era. He invented **idylls** or pastoral poetry, a new genre portraying country life in a romantic and idealized way. His poems bring alive the timeless pastoral life in the hills of Sicily and south Italy.

elegy *n.* 挽诗
epigram *n.* 诙谐短诗
Callimachus 卡利马科斯
Theocritus 提奥克利图斯
idyll *n.* 田园诗

3.5 Historiography

historiography *n.* 史学

History is the systematic analysis of past events, especially the political, social and economic development of a country, a continent or the world. It was introduced to the Western world by the Greeks and the term history comes from a word used by Herodotus, historia, meaning "inquiries" or "research". In the Archaic Greece, most people regarded the mythic tales of epic poetry as factual records. It was not until the 5th century BC did the Greeks begin to write their history based on critical examination of sources, synthesis of chosen details and rational inquiries into the causes and course of human events.

Herodotus (484—425 BC) is widely known as the "father of history" and his The Histories written between the 450s and 420s is the earliest known critical historical work in Western civilization. *The Histories* recounted the rise of the Persian Empire, the origins of both Athens and Sparta, and the laws and customs of the Egyptians. Herodotus viewed the conflict between Athens and Persia as one between freedom and tyranny and his portrayal of both the Greeks and the Persians was very impartial. For the writing of his works, Herodotus traveled extensively and interviewed many people to obtain his information, and he exhibited a critical attitude toward the materials he used. Despite that, Herodotus sometimes included **tall tales** in his works and made errors in **chronology** and statistics. The overall emphasis of his works laid on the actions of men, but he also stressed the important role of gods in the determination of historical events.

Herodotus 希罗多德

tall tales 荒诞不经的故事

chronology *n.* 年月顺序

Thucydides (460—400 BC) is considered the greatest historian of the ancient world. He wrote a generation later than Herodotus, from whom he differed by his greater concentration on political and military events, his more critical and accurate use of documents and accounts, and his disregard for the divine forces as explanatory causal factors in history. As an Athenian politician and general in the Peloponnesian War, Thucydides saw action in the war until he was exiled for a defeat. It was during the exile that he wrote a notably objective and rationalistic chronicle of the Peloponnesian war in *History of the Peloponnesian War*, which sets a good example for later Western historical writings.

Thucydides 修昔底德

The third important Greek historian was **Xenophon** (430—355 BC), whose historical works are valuable for their depiction of late Classical Greece. His writings were superficial in comparison to those of Thucydides, but he wrote with authority on military matters. In ***Hellenica***, Xenophon took up Greek history where Thucydides' history ended and recounted the last seven years of the Peloponnesian war, as

Xenophon 色诺芬

Hellenica《希腊史》

aftermath *n.* 后果
Anabasis《长征记》
mercenary *n.* 雇佣军

well as its **aftermath**. Xenophon's best and most famous historical work was the ***Anabasis*** ["March up Country"], which is about his adventures as a **mercenary** soldier for the Persians after the Peloponnesian War. He also wrote four works in praise of Socrates, presenting a prudent and practical picture of Socrates in contrast to Plato's philosophical portrait.

Polybius 波利比奥斯

The most profound of the Hellenistic historians was **Polybius** (203—120 BC), who wrote a 40—volume history in Greek on the rise of Rome and attempted to harmonize the Greek and Roman points of view.

3.6 Art

simplicity *n.* 简洁

The art of ancient Greece has lasting influence with its **simplicity** and beauty on the history of Western civilization and on the culture of many countries from ancient times until the present. Though its roots can be traced back to the Bronze Age civilizations, Ancient Greek art as a distinct culture did not begin until 1000 BC. The practice of fine art in Ancient Greece spans three basic eras: the Archaic Period, a period of gradual experimentation; the Classical Period, the golden age of Greek art; and the Hellenistic Period, which saw the export of Greek arts, artists and culture to Rome and beyond. The art of Ancient Greeks is known for three main items: architecture, sculptures and **vase** paintings.

vase *n.* 花瓶

Parthenon

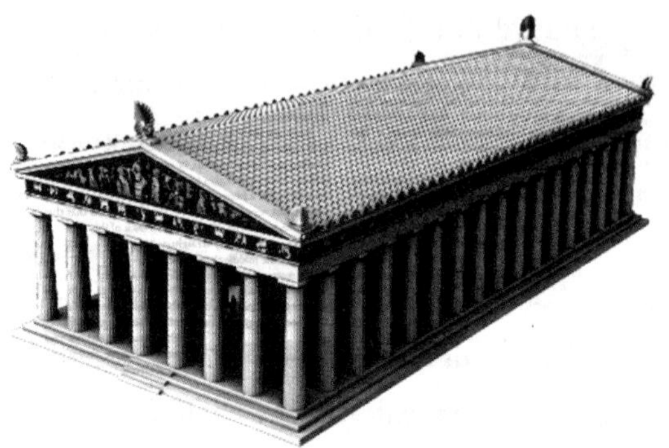

Digital reproduction of the original Parthenon

In architecture, the most important structure was the temple dedicated to a god or goddess. Most Greek buildings in the Archaic and Early Classical periods were made of wood or mud-brick and nothing remained of them. Greek architecture reached its peak in the Classical Period. The finest example of the Greek temple and Doric architecture, the **Parthenon**, was built on the Acropolis of Athens between 447 and 432 BC. With its grand size, many columns, elaborate sculptural decoration and the colossal gold-and-ivory statue of Athena, the Parthenon **typifies** the supreme artistic ability of ancient Greeks and is one of the world's greatest cultural monuments.

Parthenon 帕台农神庙

typify *v.* 是……的典型

In the Hellenistic period, the Greeks continued to build temples, but they also began to build many other types of large public buildings, such as theatres and gymnasia. Two great examples of Hellenistic architecture were the Library of Alexandria and Lighthouse of Alexandria, neither of which has survived. Over the centuries, the Greeks developed three principal styles (order) of **columns**: the more formal and dignified Doric order, used in mainland Greece and especially in the Parthenon; the more relaxed and decorative Ionic order, used in the cities of Ionia and some of the Aegean islands; and the more ornate Corinthian order, popular in the Hellenistic age and used by the Roman in their massive public buildings in later ages.

column *n.* 柱子

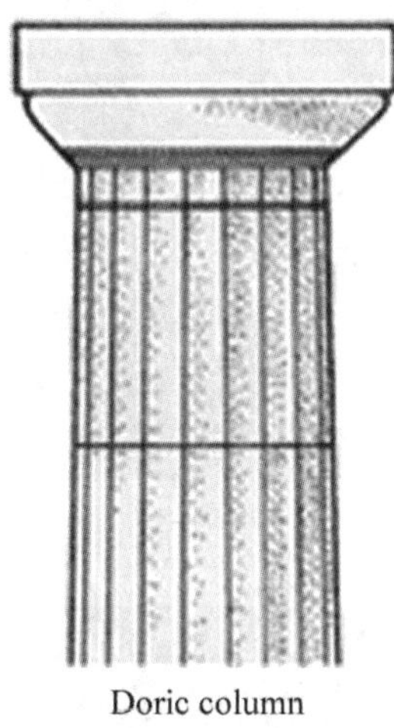
Doric column

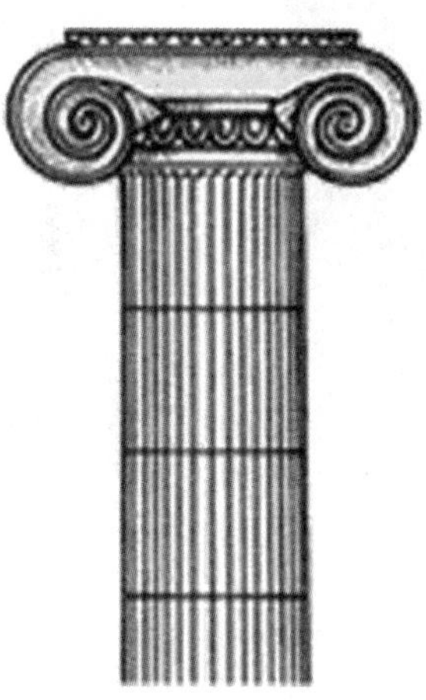
Ionic column

Corinthian column

Three principal Greek styles of column

In the art of sculpture, the beauty of human form was the most important subject for Athenian sculptors, which reflects Greek belief in the nobility of man. Influenced by the Egyptian and Mesopotamian monumental stone sculptures, Archaic Greek artists created two sculptural forms of standing and smiling humans: the kouros (**nude** young men) and the kore (clothed young women.) Though appearing rigid and unnatural, these original statues paved the way for the artistic peak of sculpture of the next era. In the Classical period, Greeks

nude *adj.* 裸体的

rigid *adj.* 僵硬

sculptors had learned to represent human body in a more natural and relaxed style, either in motion or at rest. Proportion became the main **preoccupation** of sculptors and the human figure became understood as a universe of opposing forces which created a perfect aesthetic entity the moment they achieved balance. The best of these sculptures achieved almost godlike perfection in their ideal proportions, balance, calm and ordered beauty.

preoccupation *n.* 全神贯注的事物

The Hellenistic period saw dramatic changes in the sculptural style. While earlier Greek sculpture had sought to idealize humanity and express Greek ideals of balance and restraint, Hellenistic sculpture emphasized extreme realism and liked to represent extreme emotion in the human face and figure. Representative sculptures from this period all show a more **sensuous** and emotional taste.

sensuous *adj.* 悦目的

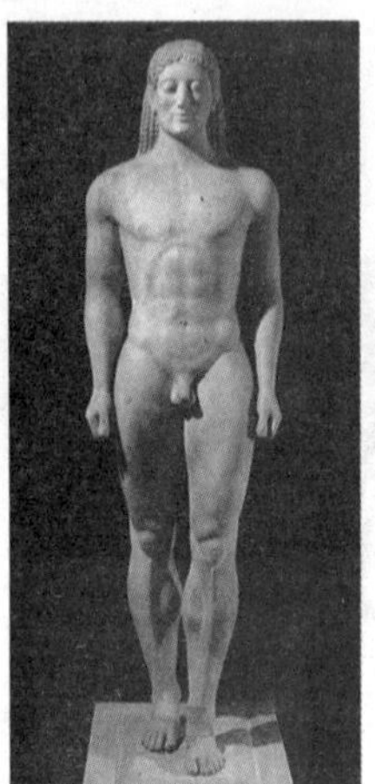
Kouros (600 BC)

Kore (600 BC)

Myron's *Discobolus* (460—450 BC)

Praxiteles' *Aphrodite of Knidos* (350 BC)

Venus of Melos (200 BC)

Winged Victory of Samothrace (200 BC)

Laocön (100 BC)

Thousands of ancient Greek vases have survived and it has been discovered on their surface the paintings of great variety and extraordinary beauty. These vase paintings show an evolution from black-figure style in the Archaic Period to red-figure style in the Classical Period. The black-figure technique painted figures in black on the natural red clay vase. This technique originated in Corinth in around 700 BC and had been perfected by Athenians by 550 BC. Gradually the black-figure style was replaced by the red-figure technique in about 530 BC. In red-figure technique, the background and the outline details on the figures were painted in black, but the rest of each figure was unpainted and so kept the red color of the natural vase. With the red-figure technique, painters could add tiny details that made their pictures come alive. These vase paintings reflect the importance of strength, athletic competition and battles in ancient Greece.

Black-figure painting (40 BC)

Black-figure painting (540 BC)

Red-figure painting (520—510 BC)

Red-figure painting (440 BC)

4. Conclusion

Ancient Greek achievements in the areas of politics, philosophy, science, history, literature and art are of the highest order. Among their numerous accomplishments, the ancient Greeks are credited with inventing democracy, oratory, rhetoric, biology, zoology, atomic theory, competitive athletics, drama, and so on, and all ways of thinking and acting that had enriched human life immeasurably and influenced Western civilization immensely.

humanism *n.* 人本主义
rationalism *n.* 理性主义
superstition *n.* 封建迷信

Underlying the Greek achievement was **humanism** and **rationalism**. The ancient Greeks expressed a belief in the worth, freedom and dignity of the individual and encouraged the fullest development of human potential. Free of Near Eastern **superstitions** and traditions, the Greeks were the first to define man as an individual with the capacity for reason. In the western world, it was the Greeks who first examined each problem in a spirit of critical inquiry and discovered the means to give rational order to nature and to human society.

Byzantine *adj.* 拜占庭的
Slav *n.* 斯拉夫人

Romans, who conquered the Greeks in war, were themselves overcome by admiration for Greek cultural achievements. The Byzantine Empire inherited classical Greek culture directly, and the preservation of classical Greek learning in medieval **Byzantine** tradition further exerted strong influence on the **Slavs** and later on the Islamic Golden Age. The study of Greek classics was a key element of the Western European Renaissance from 14th to 16th century. In 18th and 19th century, Europe and the Americas witnessed a renewed interest in ancient Greek learning in the Neoclassicism movement. In general, ancient Greek culture is the foundation of Western civilization.

Exercises

Ⅰ. Terminology: choose the suitable terms to fill in the blanks.

A. polis B. monarchy C. oligarchy D. tyranny E. democracy
F. oracle G. idealism H. tragedy I. historiography J. Parthenon

- A Greek __1__ was a form of theatre that grew out of religious performances in honor of Dionysus and depicted the suffering and ruin of a hero.
- Platonic __2__ refers to Plato's theory that the reality we perceive through our senses is only an imperfect copy of the abstract, eternal and unchanging Ideas.
- In ancient Greece, a __3__ was an independent state that consists of a city and the surrounding country area.
- __4__ is the narrative presentation of history based on a critical examination, evaluation, and selection of material from primary and secondary sources and subject to scholarly criteria.
- __5__ is the finest example of the Greek temple and Doric architecture built on the Acropolis of Athens between 447 and 432 BC.
- In ancient Greece, a (n) __6__ was a place where people could go to ask the gods for advice or information about the future.
- There were four government forms in ancient Greece: __7__ means the rule of a king; __8__ means the rule of a few; __9__ means the rule of one man; and __10__ means the rule of the people.

Ⅱ. Decide whether the following statements are true (T) or false (F).

1. Mount Olympus is the highest point in Greece and home of the mythical Greek gods. ( )
2. The Minoan civilization is often regarded as the first advanced civilization of Europe. ( )
3. Though the idea of democracy originated in Athens, the practice was very different from today's western countries. ( )
4. Acropolis is an open space or plaza that served both as a market and as a place where citizens could assemble. ( )
5. The word "tyranny" was just as derogative in ancient Greece as today. ( )
6. The Greek city-states varied greatly in their governmental structures. ( )
7. Athenian magistrate Solon devised the Council of 500 as a check to the power of the nobles. ( )
8. Among the Olympian gods, Zeus was the chief deity and he was mainly worshipped at Olympia. ( )
9. According to Aristotle, Form (or Idea) exists as a higher reality than the material world. ( )
10. Lyric is a poetic form so called because it was originally sung by individuals or a chorus accompanied by a musical instrument called the lyre. ( )

Ⅲ. Multiple choices: choose the answer that best completes the statement or answers the question.

1. Which one does not belong to the Bronze Age civilizations of ancient Greece?

A. Cycladic civilization. B. Helladic civilization.
C. Hellenistic civilization. D. Minoan civilization.

2. The following descriptions of the Mycenaean culture are true EXCEPT for ________.

A. The Mycenaeans were the first people known to have spoken Greek
B. The Mycenaeans regarded the Minoans as their potential enemies
C. The Mycenaean raid on Crete was recorded in Homer's epics
D. The Mycenaean era is also called the "Age of Heroes"

3. Which description of Greek democracy of the Archaic Period is not true?

A. It began as an expanded version of oligarchy.
B. It is the same with modern democracy.
C. It ensured an easier coexistence between different classes.
D. Solon's reforms laid the foundation for the Athenian democracy.

4. Who replaced the Council of 400 with the Council of 500?

A. Solon. B. Persistratus. C. Cleisthenes. D. Pericles.

5. Whose power was gradually reduced in the process of Athenian political reforms?

A. People's Assembly. B. People's Court.
C. Council of citizens. D. Council of nobles.

6. Which of the following group of people did not constitute a class in Sparta?

A. The native Spartans. B. Foreigners.
C. Slaves. D. Nobles.

7. Which description of Spartan women is incorrect?

A. They enjoyed more political rights and domestic freedom that the rest of the Greek world.
B. They received physical training instead of literacy education.
C. They could inherit property.
D. They usually got married at 18.

8. In the first Greco-Persian War, Greek army defeated the Persian forces and won a smashing victory in the battle of ________.

A. Thermopylae B. Marathon C. Salamis D. Plataea

9. The following descriptions of the second Greco-Persian War are true EXCEPT for ______.

A. The Persian army was led by Xerxes I, who was Darius son
B. All Greek city-states united to counter the Persian invasion
C. The Greek army was greatly outnumbered by the Persian army
D. The Greek army won a decisive victory in the straits between Athens and Salamis

10. Which description of the Age of Pericles is NOT true?

A. It is the Golden Age of classical Greece.
B. It was when Athens secured its status as the capital of Hellenic civilization.

C. It witnessed great developments in democracy, economy, art and science.

D. It was when the nobles became a major force in politics.

11. Which one is NOT the aftermath of the Peloponnesian Wars?

A. In Athens, democracies collapsed and the empire crumbled.

B. Many city-states rebelled against the imperialistic rule of the Athens.

C. In Sparta, class conflict became severer and traditional virtues were corrupted.

D. There were constant clashes between different city-states.

12. Which Hellenistic kingdom ruled Egypt and parts of the Middle East?

A. Ptolemaic Kingdom. B. Antigonid Kingdom.

C. Seleucid Kingdom. D. Pergamum Kingdom.

13. Which description of the Hellenistic civilization is incorrect?

A. It was a cosmopolitan and open culture.

B. It was a mixture of Greek and Oriental cultures.

C. It helped to popularize Greek thinking and life styles.

D. Its commercial, cultural and intellectual centre was Athens.

14. The largest and most famous of all Hellenistic cities is ________.

A. Athens B. Sparta C. Alexandria D. Thebes

15. Which description of the traditional Greek religion is incorrect?

A. Ancient Greeks believed that the gods have human forms and human personality.

B. For the Greeks, the gods only favored those people and states that honored them.

C. In ancient Greece, the main religious ceremony took place inside the temple.

D. Oracles also played an important part in the Greek religion and beliefs.

16. Epicureanism and Stoicism are similar in the following ways except for ________.

A. Both were concerned with the good of the individual

B. Both were idealistic in world view

C. Both believed that reason is the key to solution of social problems

D. Both thought highly of the peace of mind

17. Which one does NOT indicate that Euripides was the most revolutionary dramatist in ancient Greece?

A. His creation of less heroic and more realistic characters.

B. His sharp criticism of conventional values.

C. His view of the human soul as a place where opposing forces struggle.

D. His use of graceful language and perfect form.

18. Who is usually regarded as the "father of history"?

A. Herodotus. B. Thucydides. C. Xenophon. D. Polybius.

19. Of the following orders of columns, which one is more formal and dignified and mainly used in mainland Greece?

A. Doric. B. Ionic. C. Corinthian. D. Composite.

20. Which of the following statements about ancient Greek sculpture is NOT true?

A. The beauty of human form was the most important subject.

B. The archaic Greek artists created two sculptural human forms, the kouros and kore.

C. The classical Greek sculptors represented human body in a less natural style.

D. The Hellenistic Greek sculptors liked to represent extreme emotions in the human face and figure.

Chapter 3
Roman Civilization: from A City to An Empire

CHAPTER OUTLINE

1. Introduction
2. Rome: from Republic to Empire
3. Roman culture
4. Conclusion

FOCUS QUESTIONS

1. What social, political, and military practices made it possible for Rome to expand from a collection of villages to a Mediterranean power?

2. Why did the Roman Republic collapse?

3. What were the features of pax Romana ? What made it possible?

4. In what ways was Roman civilization a continuation of Greek civilization? In what ways was it unique?

1. Introduction

While the Greeks were struggling against the Persians and later fighting among themselves, a new civilization started to emerge in central Italy. As early as the reign of Alexander the Great, Rome was the dominant city among those of the Italian peninsula. Over the next five centuries Rome's power continued to increase, first across Italy and then **swallowing up** the Hellenistic world and the empire of Carthage. By the end of the first century BC, Rome had grown from a city-state into one of the largest empires in history. Its territories embraced all the coastal lands of southern Europe, North Africa, western Asia, and considerable parts of northern Europe too. By conquest and assimilation, Rome made the **Mediterranean** a "Roman lake."

swallow up *ph. v.* 吞食

Mediterranean *n.* 地中海

As the saying goes, all roads lead to Rome. Our exploration of European culture has now brought us to Rome, to Italy, and to the history of ancient Roman civilization. In tracing Rome's rise from a city-state to an empire, this chapter will focus on the transformation of the Roman political institutions. This will help us understand Rome's strength and stability. The efficient political institutions created by the Romans have continued to inspire later generations. Much of the modern vocabulary of politics, from president to forum, can be traced back to Rome. We will then look at various aspects of ancient Roman life and culture.

2. Rome: from Republic to Empire

Alps *n.* 阿尔卑斯山

agrarian *adj.* 农业的

Italy is a long peninsula in the shape of a boot. It extends about 1 200 kilometers from the **Alps** into the Mediterranean. The land of the Italian peninsula contributed significantly to the course of Roman history. Italy was (and still is) rich in fertile land. The amount of arable land in Italy is greater than that of Greece. As a result, the Romans remained a predominantly **agrarian** people during most of their history. Italy's long coastline has both advantages and disadvantages: it leaves Italy open to opportunities through overseas trade and expansion, but also the threat of invasion by sea.

Map 13 Map of Italy today

The native population in Italy spoke a version of Latin. They probably entered the peninsula over the Alps from the north around 2000 BC. These people were named "Italic" by the Greeks. One group of the Italic people settled down in small villages on the plain of Latium near the **Tiber River**, which would later become the centre of the city of Rome. Rome's location in Italy was central and protected. Located 24 kilometers inland on the banks of the Tiber, Rome enjoyed access to the sea but was still far enough from it to be safe. The seven hills surrounding Rome offered it a natural defense both from humans and from nature (the Tiber often flooded its banks).

Tiber River 台伯河

Around the 8th century BC the small villages on the Latium plain began to merge. By the 6th century BC, the newly-formed city of Rome had streets, walls, drains, and temples. What caused the transformation? Perhaps the key factor was the Romans' contact with their neighbors, the Greeks and the **Etruscans**.

Etruscan 伊特拉斯坎人

2.1 The First Romans and Their Neighbors

The Founders of Rome

The bronze sculpture above shows the legendary she-wolf suckling Romulus and Remus.

Like many other ancient cities, Rome has a number of legends about its birth. According to the most popular one, after the fall of Troy, Aeneas, a Trojan prince, led his followers to Italy and founded the city of Rome. The poet **Virgil** (70—19 BC) retells this legend in his ***Aeneid***, the classical epic of the Roman Empire, borrowing much of the story from Homer. In a similar way, Rome borrowed extensively from the older Greek and Near Eastern civilizations. The myth of Aeneas symbolizes the flow of Greeks and Near-Easterners into Italy as well as Rome's debt to the Greco-Oriental world.

Virgil 维吉尔

Aeneid《埃涅阿斯纪》

Modern scholars do not tell such colorful tales, but they do agree that two groups of people contributed significantly to the early development of civilization in Italy, namely the Etruscans and the

Greeks. Around the 8th century BC the Greek cities began to establish colonies far from their native lands. Many of them chose locations in southern Italy and Sicily. The new Greek settlers planted **olive** trees and grapevines which they had brought from home. They built temples and houses in Greek styles. They introduced the Greek alphabet, which was later re-adapted into the Roman (Latin) alphabetic system. Many Greek words also found their way into Latin. The Greek settlers set up their own religious and political institutions. Overall, a truly Greek culture was able to flourish in Italy.

olive *n.* 橄榄

The initial politics of Rome was however most influenced by the Etruscans, a non-Indo-European speaking people who migrated to Italy around 1000 BC. We do not know where the Etruscans came from and why they migrated, but it is most likely that they came from Asia Minor or Anatolia (today's Turkey). The Etruscans mostly settled down in the area north of the Tiber river and on the west side of the Italian peninsula. Successful, wealthy, and fierce, the Etruscans then started expanding their control to much of Central Italy. Some time before 800 BC, the Etruscans crossed the Tiber River and conquered many small Latin towns (in Latium), including Rome. By the 6th century, under their influence, Rome had started to become an actual city.

Rome's political system began as a **monarchy** under a line of Etruscan kings. The king possessed absolute power over his people. He alone could make laws. The king was assisted by a "**senate**" —this word is derived from the Latin word "senex" meaning "old man". The senate was a council made up of leading (old) men from different tribes or clans. Its main function was to implement the wishes of the king. Sometimes the senate would debate a proposed law or even vote on it. However, the king was free to ignore the results of any senate vote. The senate's power was thus limited during this period. Later during the Roman republic, however, it became an extremely powerful **institution.**

monarchy *n.* 君主制

senate *n.* 元老院

institution *n.* 机构

Under its Etruscan kings, Rome prospered during the 6th century BC. But the native population resented "foreign" rule. The Romans felt that government should serve everyone. But the monarchical system only answered to the king. Worse still, the king was of a "foreign" race. This eventually drove the Romans to join forces with other Latin tribes in a large-scale rebellion. In 509 BC they overthrew the Etruscan king and founded an independent Roman city-state.

2.2 The Roman Republic (509—31 BC)

The Romans now had the chance to put their political ideas into practice by setting up a republican form of government. The English word 'republic' derives from the Latin *res publica*, literally meaning "public things". Although the Romans continued to use this word to describe their state well into the imperial period, we now only apply it to the state of Rome between the late 6th century BC, when the monarchy ended, and the late first century BC, when a new imperial monarchy was established by **Octavian**. The newly established Republic promised liberty, which for the Romans meant both freedom from "foreign" rule and freedom to participate in public affairs. The Republic was intended as a **commonwealth** which belonged to the Roman people.

Octavian 屋大维

commonwealth *n.* 共同体

In theory the ultimate source of power in this ancient republic, as in modern republics, was the *demos* (people). But which people? The Roman state had historically had a number of class categories. Each class had a different level of legal and political rights. At the bottom of Roman society was the large number of slaves. Although their hard work created enormous amounts of wealth for the republic, slaves were considered property and were essentially at the mercy of their owners. The killing of a slave was not considered murder, but **property** damage. Slaves were not considered Roman citizens and had no political rights. As for women, although they enjoyed a certain degree of freedom and respect, they had no political rights. Thus, when we discuss political life in the Roman republic, we need to bear in mind that we are only concerned with free male adults.

property *n.* 财产

2.2.1 Government of the Republic

The transition from a monarchy to a republican form of government was not easy. The young republic faced threats both from within and from without. In the process of responding to these threats the Roman Republic developed a **sophisticated constitution**. The constitution was never a written document, but rather a set of guidelines and principles which constantly evolved. Roman political institutions creatively drew inspiration from both the Greeks and Etruscans. Rome was also pragmatic and changed its political institutions in response to problems. The result was a strong and stable state.

sophisticated *adj.* 复杂的

constitution*n.* 宪法

The government of the Roman Republic was divided into three branches: **executive**, **deliberative**, and **legislative**. The executive branch was made up of **magistrates**, that is, elected public officials;

executive *adj.* 行政

deliberative *adj.* 审议

legislative *adj.* 立法

magistrates *n.* 行政官员

separation of power 三权分立
checks and balances 制衡
tyranny *n.* 暴政
judicial *adj.* 司法的
campaign *n.* 竞选运动
consul *n.* 行政长官
dictator *n.* 独裁官
decree *n.* 政令

the deliberative branch was the Roman Senate; and the legislative branch was composed of four different assemblies of the people. This division can be called the **separation of powers**. There was also a complex set of **checks and balances** between these three branches, so as to reduce the risk of **tyranny** and corruption. Many centuries later the same principles were adopted by the newly-founded United States of America, but they combined the legislative and deliberative functions, while also adding a separate **judicial** branch. In Rome, on the other hand, justice was not a separate power, but controlled by the executive branch.

Executive power lay in the hands of Rome's powerful magistrates. They were elected, not chosen by lottery as in the Greek poleis. Winning an election required **campaigning**, which in turn required money and connections. The magistrates had a very heavy workload but received no salary, unlike in the Greek poleis. As a result, only a wealthy few could afford to hold public office in Rome. Two of the magistrates were elected as the chief civil and military officers of Rome. They were called **consuls**. Like the former king, the consuls had the power to issue orders and punishments.

To prevent officials from becoming too powerful, the Romans put a one-year term limit on all magistrates' posts. They also required every magistrate to make decisions together with one or more colleagues. As for the two consuls, each had the power to block the other's actions. In case of disagreement between the two consuls, the Senate would step in to mediate. In times of emergency, however, the Republic would give the executive power to one single magistrate. The **dictator**, as he was called, made binding decisions, but could stay in office for only six months.

The Senate as a political institution survived from the monarchy into the republic. During most of the Republic, the Senate consisted of three hundred men. All senators were former magistrates and each served for life. In theory, the Roman Senate only guided and advised the magistrates, but because its members were former officials, it was respected as the guardian of Roman wisdom and traditions. The Senate became the dominant force in the areas of religion, foreign policy, and public finance. The Senate did not pass laws, but its **decrees** were treated with the greatest respect. On all important issues magistrates would consult the Senate.

This painting shows a vivid debate in the Roman enate. The outfit worn by the Senators is called the toga. Only Roman citizens could wear a toga.

The legislative branch of the Roman Republic included four assemblies of the people-the Assembly of Curiae, the Assembly of Century, the Tribal Assembly, and the **Plebeian Council**. These assemblies were created at different times and according to different criteria. The Assembly of Curiae was the oldest of the four. It already existed under the monarchy and was kept in place by **conservative** Romans after the foundation of the Republic. Family background determined its membership: only adult males from noble families could join. These people, called **Patricians** (in Latin meaning "well-fathered") made up less than 10 percent of the total population.

plebeian Council 庶民委员会

conservative *adj.* 保守的

patrician *n.* 古罗马贵族

The Assembly of Century was also called the Army Assembly, as its members represented Roman soldiers. The whole army was divided into 193 (later 373) voting blocks on the basis of wealth, each block having a single vote. It was therefore possible to find one voting block (century) with only ten rich land-owners as members, while another included several thousand landless poor soldiers. Members of this assembly were called **centurions**, an important military rank.

centurion *n.* 百人团团长

The Plebeian Council (also called "Council of the People") was created in 471 BC. Members of this assembly were drawn from among the common Roman citizens, known as plebeians. The plebeians were a diverse group. Some had grown wealthy through trade or agriculture, but most were small-holding famers, merchants, or poor urban residents. The assembly was subdivided into different "tribal" groups. These were not ethnic or kinship groups, but rather geographical divisions according to the citizens' places of residence. Patricians were forbidden to take part in this Council's meetings.

Then there was the Tribal Assembly, the assembly of all Roman citizens. It included both patricians and plebeians. During the years of the Roman Republic, citizens were organized into thirty-five tribes, each tribe having one vote. Membership in a tribe was also determined by a man's residence. Each year, the Tribal Assembly elected magistrates who did not command troops. Then from these elected magistrates the Century Assembly elected two as the consuls.

In the early years of the young republic, the Assembly of Curiae was the most important lawmaking body. It also elected Consuls (the only elected officials at the time) and **tried** judicial cases. But as the army grew more and more powerful, over time, the Assembly of Century gradually replaced the Assembly of Curiae as the most important legislative branch. It elected consuls, voted on laws and treaties, and approved declarations of war and peace. However, voting in this assembly was structured in such a way that the wealthiest citizens would always have a majority. The Plebeian Council and the Tribal Assembly only became Rome's main legislative bodies in the third century BC.

try *v.* 审理

Roman assemblies had both democratic and undemocratic features. On the one hand, all decisions were made by majority vote, and only after a **succession** of speeches and campaigns. Everyone, even slaves, could attend their lively public debates. On the other hand, not everyone enjoyed equal rights. Slaves and women, for example, could not participate in political life. The republic placed a strong emphasis on liberty, but much less on another principle which is now seen as equally important: equality. The common people's fight for equality took place in the legislative branch, in a series of class conflicts that took place in Rome during the fifth to the third century BC. Let us now take a closer look at how these class conflicts occurred.

succession *n.* 系列

2.2.2 *Conflict of the Orders* (*494—287 BC*)

Conflict of the Orders 等级斗争

Right from the beginnings of the republic, there were severe divisions and conflicts between the patricians and plebeians. In 509 BC, there were only 136 patrician families, but they dominated the Republic through their control of the Assembly of Curiae. The plebeians, on the other hand, did not have their own assembly at the beginning. Although they could sit in the Assembly of Curiae, they had no voting rights. They did not even know what legal rights they did have, as laws were unwritten and the patricians had the power to interpret them. To maintain their **privileges**, the patricians passed laws

privilege *n.* 特权

to forbid intermarriage between the two classes. At times of war, the plebeians were forced to join the army, but they had no right to hold office. All magistrates came from the patrician class. When their terms ended, they entered the senate. Plebeians could not rise in status, but they could fall: if they owed debts and failed to pay them, they would be sold into slavery.

Quite understandably, the plebeians resented such inequality. In the early 5th century BC this resentment erupted into an open rebellion. This started a two-century political struggle, known as the Conflict of the Orders. The patricians were unable to exist without the plebeians; not only did the plebeians provide the food and labor that kept the Roman economy going, they also supplied soldiers for the Roman army. If the plebeians acted together as a group, they could shut down the Roman economy and armed forces. The latter was an especially important bargaining chip, as Rome was almost always in military conflict during the age of the Republic.

In 494 BC, with Rome at war with two neighboring tribes, the plebeians all left the city, refusing join the battle. They declared the formation of the Plebeian Council and elected their own officers—the ***tribunes***. The patricians were forced to agree to these new institutions. At first there were two tribunes, but their number rapidly increased to ten.

tribune *n.* 保民官

Elected annually, the tribunes offered protections to the plebeians: within the city of Rome, a tribune had the right to veto any act of the magistrates, assembly, or senate. The tribunes also presided over meetings of the Plebeian Council, which passed laws. In other words, the plebeians won the power to make their own legislation. At the time, however, their laws did not have any force over patricians.

This victory was followed by a successful demand for the formalization and codification of Roman law and the constitution. The codified law became the famous **Law of the Twelve Tables**. This written law gave all citizens a clear idea of their legal and political rights. In 445 BC, plebeians acquired the right to marry a patrician, and in 367 BC they made it legally required that at least one consul should be a plebeian. After the completion of his term of office, this consul would become a member of the Senate, so the patrician hold on the Senate was also gradually broken. The final victory was achieved in 287 BC: all decisions and laws made by the Council of Plebeians had force over the entire Roman citizenry, including the patricians.

Law of the Twelve Tables 十二铜表法

adaptability *n.* 适应性
flexibility *n.* 灵活性

The result of these political struggles again demonstrated the Romans' **adaptability** and **flexibility**. They reformed their institutions as the need arose, rather than holding stubbornly to tradition or blindly pursuing some idealistic vision. Conflicts of interest were managed by making political compromises instead of through civil war. This political wisdom not only consolidated the young republic but also expanded it from a city-state into an empire.

2.3 Roman Expansion

In 509 BC the newly founded independent city-state of Rome was much smaller than Athens or Sparta, yet in less than 400 years it would enjoy dominance over the entire Mediterranean region. The Roman Empire was built in three stages: the conquest of Italy, the conflict with Carthage and expansion into the western Mediterranean, and the intervention in and gradual domination of the Hellenistic kingdoms in the eastern Mediterranean. How and why could Rome develop from a small city-state into such a large world power?

2.3.1 The Conquest of Italy (*509—264 BC*)

Right from its independence, Rome was engaged in continuous warfare with its neighbors. The number one enemy was the Etruscan city-states to Rome's north and west. Instead of fighting alone, the Romans formed a military alliance, the Latin League, with other city-states in the same region (Latium). The League quickly drove the Etruscans out of the Italian peninsula and steadily conquered all the Etruscan territory during the fifth and fourth centuries BC.

Rome was the leading power in the Latin League. When its key role in military victories against the Etruscans further strengthened Rome's position, its Latin allies began to feel fearful. A number of Latin city-states demanded to withdraw from the League. When Rome turned them down flat, these city-states rose up against Rome to demand independence in 340 BC. However, it only took Rome two years to defeat the Latins in this uprising. In 338 BC, Rome dismantled the Latin League and took control of the entire region of Latium.

In 295 BC, Rome began a war with a tough Latin people living in the **Apennine** mountains, the **Samnites**. The Samnites were joined by

Apennine 亚平宁山脉
Samnite 萨莫奈人
Gallic 高卢人（的）

the remaining Etruscan cities, by **Gallic** tribes,[①] and some rebellious Italian cities. Again, the Romans emerged **victorious** from this war in 280 BC and took control of all of central Italy. Rome then turned southwards and conquered the Greek colonies in Southern Italy. Thus by about 275 BC Rome had become master of the entire Italian peninsula.

victorious *adj.* 胜利的

In the process of conquest, the Romans took a **pragmatic** approach in order to hold on to their new territories. Rome did not destroy the cities it conquered, but instead granted them certain rights. Some cities were allowed full Roman **citizenship** for their residents, particularly those near to Rome. Others were allowed a more limited status. Some cities were allowed complete autonomy. Some were allowed the status of allies. All, however, were required to send Rome taxes and troops. In addition, Rome settled soldiers on the captured lands; for the soldiers, this was a reward for their service, while for Rome they became permanent military settlers in the conquered lands. In order to **reinforce** these settlements, the Romans began an ambitious road-building project. Their roads were of the highest quality and went in straight lines so that soldiers and supplies could be quickly moved into rebellious territories. The response to any revolt was swift and harsh. The combination of rights and citizenship for the conquered territories (or at least the promise of future rights and citizenship) and the rapid response to rebellions produced a lasting peace on the Italian Peninsula.

pragmatic *adj.* 务实的

citizenship *n.* 公民身份

reinforce *v.* 进一步强化

2.3.2 Rome versus Carthage: the Punic Wars (264—146 BC)

After the conquest of Italy, Rome became one of two great powers in the Mediterranean region. The other was Carthage. It was not only the most prosperous trading nation but also had the strongest **navy**. Originally the city of Carthage had been a colony founded by the Phoenicians in around 750 BC. After Phoenicia was conquered by the Persians, Carthage became an independent city-state and over time expanded into an empire covering North Africa, southern Spain, Sardinia, Corsica, and western Sicily.[②] When Rome's territory reached the southern tip of Italy, the two great powers came into direct contact. **Mutual suspicion** drove the two into a lengthy struggle for control of the western Mediterranean.

navy *n.* 海军

mutual *adj.* 相互的

suspicion *n.* 猜疑

---

① 古罗马时代高卢人（Gauls）为凯尔特族的一个分支，居住在法国和意大利北部的平原。以游牧为生的高卢人骁勇善战，是年轻的罗马共和国遇上的最彪悍的劲敌。公元前387年，意大利北部平原的高卢人翻过阿尔卑斯山，大败罗马兵团，攻陷罗马城，烧杀一空。罗马人答应交纳赎金后，高卢人撤兵。罗马人在废墟上重建家园。

② 在拉丁文中Phoenician的形容词为Punicus，因此迦太基人又被称为布匿人（Punic）。

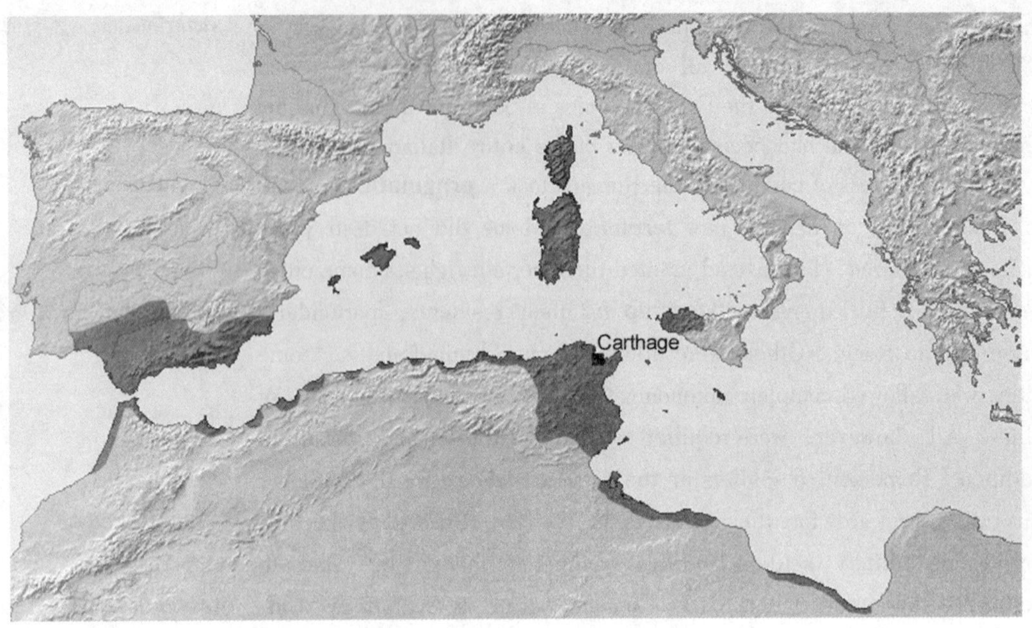

Map 14 The Carthage Empire

intervene *v.* 干涉

indemnity *n.* 赔款

mine *n.* 矿藏

Hannibal Barca 汉尼拔将军

In 264 BC Rome decided to **intervene** in a conflict between two Sicilian cities, and sent an army to Sicily. The Carthaginians protested against this Roman intervention, and the First Punic War broke out. At the start of the war, Rome had no navy, but the adaptable Romans quickly built a navy strong enough to fight against the Carthaginians for 23 years. Fought entirely off the island of Sicily, the war ended in 241 BC with the Romans defeating the Carthaginian navy. The two powers signed a treaty. Carthage agreed to give up Sicily and pay an indemnity for the war. By gaining Sicily, Rome drove the Carthaginians out of its backyard. Taking advantage of the Carthaginians' weakness, Rome then seized Sardinia and Corsica and demanded an additional **indemnity**.

Forced to give in to Rome's demands, Carthage decided to expand in Spain instead, under the leadership of the Barca family. With Spain's rich silver and copper **mines**, Carthage grew wealthy and mighty. The brilliant young general Hannibal Barca (248—183 or 182 BC) crossed the Alps with his army and entered Italy in a war of revenge in 218 BC. This marked the beginning of the Second Punic War.

Hannibal crushed the Roman armies in northern Italy. This was the largest defeat Rome ever suffered. Roman allies in southern Italy and Sicily opportunistically chose to side with the Carthaginians. In addition, the king of Macedon, Philip V allied himself with Hannibal and began his own war against Rome in 215 BC.① The situation was nearly hopeless for the Romans.

The Romans, however, decided to invade Spain and cut off Hannibal's supply lines. The **tactic** worked: Hannibal was forced to retreat. One of the greatest generals in history, Hannibal won almost every single battle against the Romans but still lost the war. By 202 BC Rome had reduced Carthage to a dependent state and taken over much of its territory. The Second Punic War turned Rome from a regional power into an international empire: it had gained control over most of northern Africa, Spain, and the major islands in the western Mediterranean.

tactic *n.* 策略

Determined to bring the Carthaginians to their knees, Rome moved inland into North Africa and attacked the city of Carthage itself, starting the third and last Punic war (149—146 BC). This time Carthage was no match for the Romans. The Romans captured and destroyed the capital city in 146 BC. The Carthaginians were either killed or sold into slavery. The territory was later turned into a Roman province called Africa.

2.3.3 The Conquest of the Hellenistic East (200—133 BC)

During the Second Punic War, the Macedonian king Philip V made an **opportunistic** alliance with Hannibal against Rome. He soon moved aggressively into Greece and made plans to conquer Egypt. His ambition naturally made the Romans suspicious. Now Carthage was destroyed, the Romans decided to take action to prevent any threat from Greece and Macedon. Rome demanded that Philip V stop taking over Greek territory. When he refused, Rome started a war, defeating him in just three years. Upon its victory, Rome declared all the Greek cities free; it did not colonize Greece but chose to play the role of its protector.

opportunistic *adj.* 机会主义的

Philip V died in 179 BC. His successor Persus started to challenge Rome's **hegemony** in Greece. Rome responded by invading Greece again (172—168 BC). Victorious, Rome took independence away from the Greeks and Macedonians. Their experience told them that an **iron-fisted** approach was a better **guarantee** of security. Only two Hellenistic kingdoms were left independent: the Seleucid kingdom (today's Syria) and Ptolemaic Egypt. Even here, Roman ambassadors and generals frequently interfered in their affairs, and it was no surprise

hegemony *n.* 霸权

iron-fisted *adj.* 铁腕的

guarantee *n.* 保障

① 第二次布匿战争中，由于罗马人同时也与马其顿国王菲利普五世交战，故此次战争又被称为第一次马其顿战争（the First Macedonian War）。

annex *v.* 吞并

when they were finally **annexed** by Rome in the 1st century BC.

2.4 The Collapse of the Roman Republic (133—31 BC)

After the Third Punic War, the Roman Republic entered into a period of conflict. The relationship between different social classes grew tense. A series of rivalries, assassinations, and civil wars took place. These conflicts only ended when Octavian came to power in 33 BC, by which time the constitution of the Roman Republic was destroyed. What caused the social and political struggles of the late republic? Why and how did the Republic collapse?

unintended *adj.* 预想不到的

Expansion led to enormous and **unintended** changes in Rome's society, economy, and morals. The vast amount of wealth generated by expansion went to the hands of the generals, diplomats, magistrates, tax collectors, and businessmen who followed in the wake of Rome's armies. Ordinary Romans did not share in these profits. Small farmers suffered the most. For most of the Republican period, the Roman army was not a purely volunteer army; ownership of some land was required in order to serve as a soldier.① Small farmers were thus the main force of the army; however, this often meant they had to leave for years to fight abroad, and it was hard for their wives and children to keep the family farm running in their absence. Often their land was bought up by the wealthy. In addition, much of the farmland on the Italian peninsula was ruined by numerous battles.

Neither did common people have a share in the vast newly-conquered lands. Known as public land, these lands belonged to the state of Rome. In theory all Roman citizens had the right to use them; a tax was however required in order to have the right to farm it, payable in the form of a percentage of the **crops** or animals raised on the land. Naturally small farmers could not afford this. Public land, too, ended up in the hands of the large landowners.

crop *n.* 农作物

Expansion also transformed the labor force. Large numbers of prisoners of war were brought back to Italy as slaves. By the end of the second century BC they were the majority of the population of Italy, and the economy was dependent on them. Slaves were often purchased by

---

① 直到公元前2世纪的最后几年，罗马大体上实行传统的兵农合一的公民兵制度，所有的士兵都必须符合严格条件的财产条件并能够自行购置所属兵种等级对应的武器装备。公元前107年马里乌斯当选执政官后，对罗马进行了一系列军事改革。其中关键的一项改革就是放弃财产资格限制，规定凡是自愿且符合条件的罗马公民，包括无财产者都可以应募入伍。

large landowners to work the land. This further reduced small farmers' **competitiveness**. Landless and unemployed, many former small farmers flooded into the city of Rome.

competitiveness *n.* 竞争力

The expanded use of slave labor also provoked conflict. Treated brutally, slaves often tried to escape or revolt. Their most famous rebellion was led by the **gladiator Spartacus** in 73—71 BC.

gladiator *n.* 角斗士
Spartacus 斯巴达克斯

As the rich grew richer and the poor poorer, the Roman society became increasingly unstable. Attempts were made to deal with this inequality. Between 133 and 122 BC the two Gracchus brothers, both elected tribunes, attempted reforms. They proposed a limit on the amount of land a person could have, and **distribution** of the public land to landless free citizens. This clearly went against the nobility's interests, and was opposed by the Senate. The reforms of the Gracchus brothers failed: the elder of the two, Tiberius was **assassinated** and the younger Gaius was killed by a mob. Of their economic ideas, only the proposal to sell Roman citizens cheap **grain** was adopted.

distribution *n.* 分配
assassinate *v.* 暗杀
mob *n.* 暴民
grain *n.* 粮食

The murders of the Gracchus brothers marked a new political trend: debate and **compromise** were replaced by more violent solutions. Roman leaders increasingly relied on military power. The army's increasing importance in domestic politics started with the military reforms launched by **Gaius Marius** (157—86 BC). During his years as consul, Marius **relaxed recruitment** policies. The old requirements of land ownership and self-purchased equipment were removed; the state provided equipment, and professional soldiers replaced the former citizen-soldiers. The reformed army was made up of mainly volunteers from the bottom of Roman society. They were provided with food and shelter, and also promised land and a share of the spoils of war as payment for their service. A new bond of personal loyalty was created between Marius and soldiers. Backed by his new army, Marius was elected consul seven times.

compromise *n.* 妥协
Marius 马里乌斯
relax *v.* 放松
recruitment *n.* 征兵

Rome's politics in the first century BC was dominated by powerful generals. Rivalry between them often led to civil war, where rival generals tried capturing Rome with their personal armies, and thousands of people on either side were killed. The first such civil war broke out between Marius and **Sulla** (138—78 BC) in 88 BC and ended in a complete victory for Sulla, who assumed the office of dictator.

Sulla 苏拉

After the death of Sulla, three powerful individuals came to dominate Roman army and political life—**Crassus** (115—53 BC), **Pompey** (106—48 BC), and **Julius Caesar** (100—44 BC).

Crassus 克拉苏
Pompey 庞贝
Caesar 恺撒

Crassus, the richest man in Rome, had successfully put down the slave rebellion led by Spartacus. Pompey won fame as a military hero for his conquest of Syria and Palestine. Caesar, on the other hand, started out as a spokesman for the *populares*, a group of senators siding with the general public. Despite his initial lack of military influence, Caesar was to outlast Crassus and Pompey and play a critical role in the transformation of Republic into Empire.

coalition *n.* 同盟
Triumvirate *n.* 三雄执政
subvert *v.* 颠覆

In 60 BC, these three powerful figures formed an informal **coalition**. Known as the First **Triumvirate** (three-man group), this coalition was designed to **subvert** the existing government. Their combination of wealth and power allowed them to dominate Roman politics and fulfill their ambitions: Pompey received a command in Spain, Crassus was given a command in Syria, and Caesar was granted a special military command in Gaul (today's France). Caesar conquered all of Gaul and gained fame, wealth, and military experience as well as a large army loyal to him. The First Triumvirate was the beginning of the end of the Republic, for these ambitious men intended to control the government for their own advantage.

When Crassus died in battle in 53 BC, the balance of power was disrupted. Rivalry between Pompey and Caesar led to the second civil war. Caesar marched into Italy with his army in 49 BC and defeated Pompey's forces. In 46 BC. Caesar had the Senate appoint him dictator for ten years. He was given power over the entire Roman territory, and was above the law and constitution. Two years later, he pushed to have his position of dictator extended for life. Caesar's absolute power made him effectively a monarch, which was **controversial** for the Romans, proud of their republican tradition. In 44 BC a group of senators assassinated Caesar as he entered the Senate.

controversial *adj.* 有争议的

The dream of a revival of the Republic, however, disappeared after yet another power struggle. After Caesar's death, two men divided the Roman world between them—Octavian, Caesar's grandnephew and chosen heir, taking the west, and Mark Antony, Caesar's former ally and assistant, the east. The two could not live with each other, however, and a brutal and lengthy civil war followed. Defeated in 31 BC, Mark Antony committed **suicide**. Octavian's **triumph** marked the end of the Roman Republic and the beginning of a new era.

suicide *n.* 自杀
triumph *n.* 胜利

2.5 The Early Empire (31 BC—180 AD)

After the victory of Octavian, peace finally settled. Despite some internal conflicts from time to time, the new state experienced remarkable stability for two hundred years. This peaceful environment saw the first successful exercise of real central control. The vast empire was ruled by a common legal and political system. The same language, Latin, was used for administration and legal matters throughout the empire. Ideas travelled from people to people, and advanced knowledge and technology spread to all four corners of the empire. This was a golden age in Roman history. The transition to the Roman Empire was successful in large part because of Octavian's reforms.

statue of Augustus

(1st century BC) On his deathbed, Augustus prided himself on having found Rome "a city of brick" and having left it "a city of marble".

2.5.1 Pax Augustus (31 BC—14 AD)

Octavian ruled over Italy and the provinces for forty-four years. At the beginning of the period he governed through military power, but later Octavian quickly proved himself a talented statesman. In 27 BC, Octavian **proclaimed** "the restoration of the Republic." He understood that only traditional republican forms would satisfy the aristocracy. At the same time, Octavian was aware that the Republic could not be fully restored. A compromise was worked out. A good example of this compromise between old and new was his choice of title: in 27 BC the Senate awarded him the titles of "**Augustus**" and "**imperator**", but he preferred the modest title ***princeps***, meaning "first citizen". The system of rule that Augustus (Octavian) established was similarly called the **principate**. While in reality power was heavily concentrated in his hands, Augustus skillfully created the impression that the princeps and the Senate were co-rulers, and that his **constitutional** power came legitimately from the Senate.

Pax Augustus 奥古斯都治下的和平
proclaim *v.* 宣布
augustus *n.* 奥古斯都（受人敬仰者）
imperator *n.* 最高统帅
princeps *n.* 元首
principate *n.* 元首制
constitutional *adj.* 宪法的

Augustus was especially eager to stabilize the structure of the army. Peace depended on Rome's military forces, as did the power of the princeps. He maintained a standing army of twenty-eight **legions**, in total about 150 000 men. Roman legionaries were recruited largely from the citizenry in Italy. The army was responsible for guarding the frontiers of the empire as well as for maintaining domestic order within the provinces. The state made a cash payment to soldiers who had served for twenty years. To keep his troops happy, Augustus also rewarded loyal **veterans** with land, often in new overseas colonies. Both measures secured the loyalty of the legions to the state, not to their generals. He also formed a force of some nine thousand men as Rome's police force and as his personal bodyguard.

legion *n.* 罗马军团

veteran *n.* 退役军人

Augustus also created a new system for governing the provinces.

Under the Republic, the senate had appointed the provincial governors. Now the provinces were divided between Augustus and the senate. To prevent any potential rivals from emerging, Augustus kept for himself the frontier provinces as well as wealthy Egypt. Most of the other provinces continued to be ruled as before, by senators serving as governors. This new system helped Augustus gain further support from the senate.

coinage *n.* 货币

Augustus introduced a new **coinage** system across the Empire. In the city of Rome he set up a range of public services, including police, a fire department, and a postal service. Poor people living in Rome received grain for free. Augustus also set up many public works programs, which provided jobs for the poor. He skillfully influenced public opinion via every available channel. Poets and historians were encouraged to write patriotic works. Monumental art and architecture celebrated Roman civic pride. The state funded a large number of public sports and entertainments. Presenting himself as a defender of traditional Roman morality, Augustus revived the old Roman religion, rebuilt temples, and **prohibited** Romans from worshiping other gods.

prohibit *v.* 禁止

For forty-four years, Rome under Augustus enjoyed a new order while maintaining some traditional values. When he died in 14 AD, his new order was so well established that Rome continued to enjoy peace, prosperity, and stability for another two hundred years.

Pax Romana 罗马治下的和平

2. 5. 2 The Pax Romana

Augustus was followed by four of his descendants, the Julio-Claudians, who ruled from 14 to 68 AD. Of the four rulers, Tiberius (rule 14—37) and Claudius (rule 41—54) were generally efficient and devoted. In Claudius' reign Rome invaded and occupied Britain in 43 AD. The other two rulers were **notorious**. Caligula (rule 37—41) acted like a madman; on one occasion he made his favorite horse a senator. Nero (rule 54—68) was **infamous** for his immorality, the murder of his wife and his mother, and his **persecution** of **Christians**.

notorious *adj.* 臭名昭彰

infamous *adj.* 恶名远扬

persecution *n.* 迫害

Christian *n.* 基督徒

The Julio-Claudian line ended with Nero's suicide in 68 AD. The resulting power struggle was won one year later by Flavius Vespasianus, who restored order and founded the Flavian dynasty. For the next thirty years (69—96) the Flavian emperors ruled well. By the time of the last Flavian emperor, all Romans recognized that their rule, good or bad, was provided by the emperor. Faith in the republican spirit gave way to loyalty to the monarch.

In the period of the "Five Good Emperors" (96—180), the Roman Empire reached the height of its prosperity and power. The so-called Five Good Emperors are Nerva (rule 96—98), Trajan (rule 98—117), Hadrian (rule 117—138), Antoninus Pius (rule 138—161), and Marcus Aurelius (rule 161—180). They were examples of the principle of **merit**. Trajan, a Roman citizen born in Spain, was Rome's first emperor from outside Italy. Hadrian and Marcus Aurelius also came from Spain, and Antoninus Pius from Gaul.

merit *n.* 德行

Devoted to public service, the Five Good Emperors were **humane** and generous. Trajan, for example, founded a program of financial aid for poor children in Italy. Hadrian travelled extensively through the empire and answered petitions from individuals in far-off provinces. He also made regulations for the humane treatment of slaves. No longer was it legal for a master to put a slave to death or sell him for immoral purposes. Antoninus was surnamed "Pius" (meaning "dutiful") because he was devoted to his country, the gods, and his adoptive father, Hadrian. The last of the "good emperors", Marcus Aurelius resembled Plato's ideal of the "philosopher king". While fighting against the Germans on the **Danube** frontier, he wrote ***Meditations***, a philosophical work notable for its idealism and love of **humanity**.

humane *adj.* 仁爱

Danube *n.* 多瑙河

Meditations《沉思录》

humanity *n.* 人类

This was the finest period of the empire. It was later called Pax Romana, meaning "Roman peace". The vast imperial territory stretched from Britain to the river Euphrates and from the North Sea to the Sahara desert. The empire had a large population; by the reign of Hadrian, it comprised more than one hundred million people—Italians, Greeks, Egyptians, Germans, Celts, and others. Commerce flourished as the government imposed a uniform currency system and fought against naval piracy. Textiles, foodstuffs, metal (gold, silver, copper, tin, lead, and iron), manufactured goods (glass, pottery, jewelry, paper) and **luxury** items (silk, **ivory**, precious **gems**, **spices**) from all parts of the Mediterranean world were traded in the markets of big cities. The government built and maintained roads, harbors, and ports. The transport links between the cities of the empire, both by land and by sea, ensured greater speed of transport and security for travelers. This **accelerated** cultural interaction.

luxury *n.* 奢侈

ivory *n.* 象牙

gem *n.* 宝石

spice *n.* 香料

accelerate *v.* 加速

3. Roman Culture

Roman civilization was born in central Italy, and then expanded westwards as well as eastwards to include the entire Mediterranean region. In the process of this expansion, the Romans came into contact with different cultures. Greek culture had the strongest impact, and the Romans adopted many of the Greeks' institutions and ideas. They brought elements of Greek culture not only to the western half of the Mediterranean region, but also to Britain, France, Spain, and Romania. Rome thus connected Europe to the cultural **heritage** of the ancient Greece. This is why people now group ancient Rome together with ancient Greece and talk about the Greco-Roman tradition.

heritage *n.* 传承

Yet Rome did not achieve greatness through borrowed ideas alone; Roman civilization was also **distinctive** in its own right. Compared with the Greeks, the Romans valued order and tradition much more highly. They were also far more **practical**, and had a natural talent for both structural and social **engineering**. They were good builders, generals, administrators, and legislators. While they remained interested in Greek philosophy, the Romans were more concerned with law and government. While their art was heavily inspired by the Greeks, the Romans were better known for buildings than sculpture. All in all, Rome's greatness was based on a combination of different traditions.

distinctive *adj.* 与众不同的

practical *adj.* 务实

engineering *n.* 工程

In the early imperial period, Roman culture came into full bloom, not only in the "high" art forms—literature, art, architecture—but also in the improvements of daily life through technology and engineering. Spiritual life also flourished as important new religious trends emerged. This section examines the cultural achievements of the Romans.

3.1 Government

Many ideas and concepts developed by Roman political thinkers during the Republic period remain influential today, for example: **the social contract theory** (that government started off as a voluntary agreement among citizens); the idea of **popular sovereignty** (that all power ultimately resides with the people); the principle of separation of powers (that the legislative, executive, and judicial branches of the government should be kept apart); and the concept that law must have **paramount** status in public life. Although the republican system was replaced by a monarchy after Augustus, in spirit if not in name, these ideas and concepts were never abandoned. They were handed down to

social contract theory 社会契约论

popular sovereignty 主权在民

paramount *adj.* 至高无上的

early modern times to form the theoretical basis of constitutional government in the West.

The Romans also laid the political foundations of modern Europe in other ways. Many current administrative divisions, such as 'county' and 'province' came from Roman practice. In some places European boundaries are almost **identical** to those established by the Roman Empire. The Church in the middle ages also modeled its organization, administrative units, and much of its law after that of the empire. In addition, both the eastern Roman emperors who ruled at Constantinople until 1453 and the German kings of Western Europe made use of Roman imperial titles and symbols of authority, a Roman system of public finance, and Roman law. The legacy of Rome is further illustrated by such modern-day terms as ***fiscal***, *senate*, *consul*, *citizens*, ***municipal***, and ***census.***

identical *adj.* 完全相同的

fiscal *adj.* 财政的

municipal *adj.* 市政的

census *n.* 人口普查

3.2 Evolution of Roman Law

Of the contributions made by the Romans in government and politics, Roman law is the most outstanding. Plenty of evidence can still be seen today. Together with the English common law, Roman law is the foundation of the legal system in most of the West. Roman law is the direct basis for the legal codes of Italy, France, Spain, Scotland, and most Latin American countries. In countries where English common law is used, such as the United States, major legal principles developed by the great Roman jurists are still followed. In addition, Roman legal principles have strongly influenced Muslim law and the **canon law** of the Catholic Church. International law has borrowed many principles from the Roman system.

cannon law 基督教教会法

Roman law evolved over about one thousand years. At first, when Rome was a struggling city-state, laws were unwritten and mixed with religious customs. In the 5th century BC, laws were written down for the first time in the Laws of the Twelve Tables. As Rome grew more prosperous and society became more complex, law was **secularized** (separated from religion). This became known as the **civil law** (law of the city).

secularize *v.* 世俗化

civil law 民法

The next step was the division of law into two systems—one for Roman citizens and the other for conquered peoples who did not have citizenship rights. As the republic grew, Rome acquired a diverse population with different customs and traditions. The conquered peoples had different ideas of justice. It became necessary for Roman and non-Roman citizens to be **tried** separately. Around the 4th century BC a special department was established to conduct **trials** in which non-Roman citizens were involved. As a result, a new kind of law, the law of

try *v.* 审判

trial *n.* 审判

nations, developed so that it could be applied to all foreigners. The law of nations in turn further enriched the development of the civil law. It formed the basis of international law in the modern days.

accumulate *v.* 积累

By the 4th century AD, a great body of law had **accumulated** and was becoming increasingly hard to apply. The logical answer was work out a systematic code of basic principles applicable to all people. The Romans got this idea from **Stoic** philosophy (see "Greek philosophy") which believed in the existence of a rational law applicable to all mankind. All law should be "what a man of common sense and good faith would **deem** to be right." Some efforts to form such a systemized code were made under Caesar, Augustus, and Hadrian. Between 528 and 534 AD, experts appointed by the emperor **Justinian** (rule 527—565) compiled the Roman law from all sources into a few volumes. The primitive and narrow law of a small city-state had evolved into a humane and comprehensive legal system that filled the needs of a global empire.

Stoic *adj.* 斯多葛主义的

deem *v.* 视为

Justinian 查士丁尼一世

3.3 Roman Engineering and Architecture

The empire's administrative needs required a communication system of roads and bridges. The expansion of cities led to the construction of huge public buildings and **aqueducts**. A series of magnificent monuments was built, symbols of Rome's **dignity** and **might**.

aqueduct *n.* 引水渠
dignity *n.* 尊贵
might *n.* 威力

As road builders, the Romans had no equal. Their roads were made to be used by armies and messengers. All roads were constructed of **layers** of stone according to sound engineering principles and were kept in constant repair. Some say that the speed of travel on Roman highways was not **surpassed** until the early 19th century.

layer *n.* 层

surpass *v.* 超越

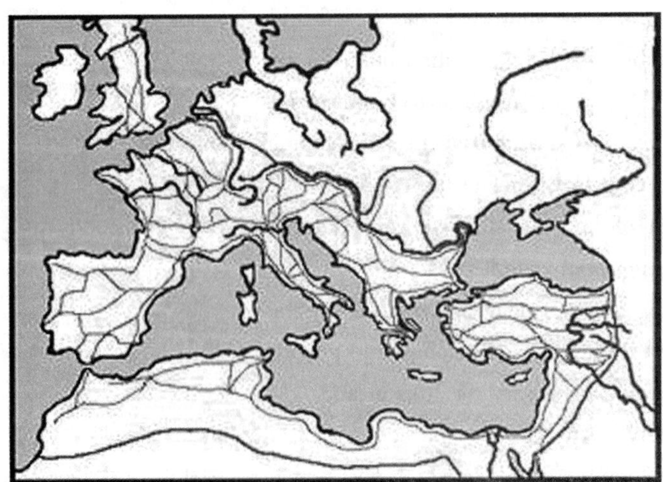

Roman Road System All Roman provinces and cities were connected with each other, and with the capital, by the public highways. All public highways started from the heart of Rome, traversed Italy, pervaded the provinces, and were terminated only by the frontiers of the empire. The construction of the Roman highways was so solid that many of them are still in use today. Although the primary function of these straight highways had been to help the march of the rmies, they helped romote commerce and unite people living in four corners of the vast empire.

The practical nature of the Romans and their skill in engineering were demonstrated also in the many **aqueducts**, bridges, and dams which they constructed. In designing their bridges, the Romans placed a series of **arches** next to one another to provide mutual support. The aqueducts consisted of several tiers of arches providing a tall base for a water channel. Fourteen aqueducts supplied plentiful fresh water for the residents of Rome.

aqueduct *n.* 引水渠

arch *n.* 拱形

Aqueduct of Segovia, Spain.

At first the Romans copied Greek structural models, but later they combined basic Greek elements with their own design. The **post** and **lintel** system of the Greeks was replaced with the more flexible system of the arch and **vault**. The arch was used extensively to provide openings in walls, and the basic Greek **concept** of columns was used as part of the wall to support the arch. The Romans were also famous for their large **domes**. Domes were frequently used to shape large **interior** spaces in temples and public buildings. The largest of these domed structures was a Roman temple, **the Pantheon**, which still stands today in Rome. Perhaps the most famous Roman building is the **Colosseum**. Here we also see a clear combination of Greek and Roman elements.

post *n.* 柱子
lintel *n.* 横梁
vault *n.* 拱顶
concept *n.* 概念

dome *n.* 穹顶
interior *n.* 内部
the Pantheon 万神殿
the Colosseum 竞技场

The dome of the Pantheon remained the largest in the world for more than 1 700 years. It is still the largest unreinforced solid concrete dome in the world today. Here we see the interior of the Pantheon in an 18th century paintin.

The Colosseum was the largest elliptical amphitheatre built during the Roman Empire. Located in the centre of Rome, it is considered one of the greatest works of Roman engineering. Its construction started between 70 and 72 AD and was completed in 80 AD. Capable of seating 50 000 spectators, the Colosseum was used for gladiatorial contests and public spectacles such as animal hunts, executions, and dramas.

3.4 Literature

In literature, the Romans again turned to the Greeks for their basic models. Latin epic, drama, and lyric poetry was usually imitative of the Greek masterpieces, although more moralistic and less imaginative. But it remains one of world's great literatures, largely because of its

innovations in **didactic** poetry, historical writing, and **satire.**

The most important innovation was in drama. Like in Athens, plays were performed during religious and civil festivals, and female roles were played by men. Yet unlike in Athens, tragedy was not popular; Romans preferred comedies, many of them adapted from Greek originals.

It was in the first century BC that Latin literature entered its first great period. The first half of this Golden Age was called the **Ciceronian** period, named after the greatest **orator** and prose writer at the time, **Marcus Tullius Cicero** (106—43 BC). Cicero was a great lawyer and politician; he was elected **Consul** in 63 AD. He wrote extensively on philosophy, political theory, **rhetoric**, and literary criticism, and was considered the first master of Latin language and style. About nine hundred of his letters still exist today. They give us insight into Cicero as a person as well as the problems and manners of republican Rome. Cicero also left numerous other writings. He also recorded much of Greek thought for later generations—especially that of Plato and the Stoics—while reinterpreting them from the standpoint of a Roman intellectual and politician. He did more than any other Roman to make Latin a great literary language.

Julius Caesar was also a man of letters. His speeches were considered second only to Cicero's in quality. It is a pity that most of his writings are lost. But we do have the *Commentaries*, an **autobiography** describing the many wars he fought. Like nearly every politician-autobiographer, Caesar sometimes **exaggerated** his successes and hid his failures. He consistently portrayed himself as a loyal patriot and his opponents as small-minded and unpatriotic. Despite this **bias**, Caesar wrote about his role in history as brilliantly as he acted it. Napoleon later said the education of every general should include a careful reading of Caesar.

The second half of the Golden Age was the Augustan Age. Its political stability created an excellent climate for literature, and in particular for poetry. **Virgil** (70—19 BC) was the greatest of all Roman poets. His masterpiece, a great national epic called the ***Aeneid***, glorifies the family of Augustus and asserts Rome's destiny to conquer and rule the world. Using Homer's Iliad and *Odyssey* as his models, Virgil recounts the journey of Aeneas, the legendary founder of the Latin people, from his home of Troy to Italy. The Aeneid shows Virgil's **enthusiastic patriotism** and is a masterpiece of imperial

innovation *n.* 创新
didactic *adj.* 说教式
satire *n.* 讽刺诗
Ciceronian *adj.* 西塞罗的
orator *n.* 演说家
Cicero 西塞罗
consul *n.* 行政长官
rhetoric *n.* 修辞学
Julius Caesar 恺撒
autobiography *n.* 自传
exaggerate *v.* 夸张
bias *n.* 偏颇
Virgil 维吉尔
Aeneid《埃涅阿斯纪》
enthusiastic *adj.* 热情的
patriotism *n.* 爱国主义

symbolism.

Horace 贺拉斯
lyrical ode 田园颂歌
satirical verse 讽刺诗
brevity *n.* 短暂

Another famous poet of the Augustan period was **Horace** (65—8 BC), who was famous for both **lyrical odes** and satirical verse. Modeling himself on Aristotle, Horace wrote on love, pleasure, the **brevity** of life, and art and nature. His poems show an extremely high linguistic and rhythmical quality. They are filled with memorable phrases like *carpe diem* ("seize the day") and with patriotic sentiments ("it is sweet and fitting to die for one's country"). Horace was translated into Italian, French, German, and English as early as the 16th century and was admired and imitated by such poets as William Wordsworth, Robert Browning, and Alfred Tennyson. ①

Ovid 奥维德
seduction *n.* 引诱
exile *v.* 流放

Not all Roman writers focused on patriotism. **Ovid** (43 BC—17 AD), for example, chose erotic love as his main subject. A collection of his poems in *The Art of Love* was essentially a handbook for **seduction**. Perhaps because of his frankly sexual subject matter, Ovid was **exiled** by Augustus to a distant town in the Black Sea region: a reminder that the peace and order of the Empire did not guarantee personal freedom.

majestic *adj.* 雄壮的
epigrammatic *adj.* 简练幽默的

The period following Augustus' death in 14 AD was one of continued prosperity and stability. Interest in literature remained high, the theatre flourished, and poets and writers both in Rome and the provinces produced a large volume of original work. Although the quality of literature did not measure up to the high standards of the Augustan period, it was still good enough to be titled "the Silver Age of Latin Literature". Whereas the Augustan period was known for its lyrical odes and a **majestic** epic, the Silver Age produced brilliant satirical poetry. It saw a more critical and confident spirit than the Golden Age. The satirical poet Juvenal [55 (?) —130 AD] portrayed the shortcomings of contemporary Roman society. His brilliant **epigrammatic** phrases influenced the writings of the Neoclassical English satirists John Dryden, Jonathan Swift, and Alexander Pope. ②

---

① 华兹华斯（William Wordsworth，1770—1850），英国浪漫主义诗人，与雪莱、拜伦齐名。曾当上桂冠诗人，湖畔诗人之一，文艺复兴以来最重要的英语诗人之一。勃朗宁（Robert Browning，1812—1889），英国维多利亚时代著名诗人。丁尼生（Alfred Tennyson，1809—1892），英国维多利亚时期桂冠诗人。

② 德莱顿（John Dryden，1631—1700），英国著名诗人、文学批评家、翻译家。德莱顿创立了英雄偶句诗，它成为后来英国诗歌的标准形式之一。乔纳森·斯威夫特（Jonathan Swift，1667—1745）英国－爱尔兰作家。讽刺文学大师，以《格列佛游记》和《一只桶的故事》等作品闻名于世。亚历山大·蒲柏（Alexander Pope，1688—1744）是18世纪英国最伟大的诗人。

Latin literature had a major influence on the development of **vernacular languages** and literature in Europe. Out of the Latin spoken by common people in the Roman empire, the Romance family of languages gradually evolved during the Middle Ages, including Italian, Spanish, Portuguese, French, and Romanian. English is a **hybrid** of the Germanic and Romance families, and around half its words are of Latin origin. Even today **Ciceronian** Latin remains a regular part of many school curriculums, while the Latin used by Christian writers of the late Empire is still employed by the Roman Catholic Church to this day.

vernacular language 本国语言

hybrid *n.* 混合物

Cieronian *adj.* 西塞罗式的

3.5 Historiography

During the Golden and Silver Ages, historians produced notable works. **Livy** (59 BC—18 AD) was a contemporary of Virgil. While Virgil's Aeneid is a poetic epic, Livy's **immense** History of Rome is a prose epic; filled with patriotism and admiration for the great Roman leaders, both works glorify Rome's conquests and achievements. In recording early Roman history, Livy brought together the various traditions to produce a single continuous **narrative**. This new approach inspired many later historians. Livy nevertheless drew on the myths that had clouded the history of the early Republic; thus his writing sometimes lacks **objectivity**.

Livy 李维

immense *adj.* 宏大的

narrative *n.* 叙述

objectivity *n.* 客观性

In the Silver Age, historians limited themselves to writing about shorter and more contemporary periods. The leading historian here was **Tacitus** (55—117 AD). He used his writing to improve society. In ***Germania***, Tacitus **contrasts** the idealized and simple life of the German tribes with the corrupt and immoral Roman upper classes. In Histories, he writes about the Flavian dynasty (69—96 AD) and its governing class, portraying its main members as selfish and corrupt. In the ***Annals***, covering Rome from the death of Augustus to that of Nero, he uses vivid prose to depict the shortcomings of the emperors and their courts. Tacitus probably came from southern Gaul and later became a senator and even rose to the office of consul. To some extent, his critical viewpoint was that of an outsider from a province, who later rose to the centre of power. Tacitus sets a high standard of **accuracy**, but his quest for accuracy sometimes conflicts with his desire to criticize the imperial government.

Tacitus 塔西佗

Germania《日耳曼尼亚志》

contrast *v.* 比照

Annals《罗马编年史》

accuracy *n.* 精确

3.6 Sculpture and Painting

After the conquest of Greece, thousands of sculptures and other works of art were brought to Rome. Greek art became fashionable, and thousands of exact reproductions of its famous works were also made locally in Italy.

Although they were strongly influenced by Greek styles, the Romans developed their own distinctive art. They had a different understanding of art's nature and functions; for them it primarily served the function of **commemoration**, and was also effective **propaganda** for glorifying particular emperors. Perhaps the earlier Etruscan art influenced the Romans in this regard. Whereas the Greeks idealized their subject matter, the Romans sought realistic representation of form; whereas the Greeks portrayed types rather than individuals, the Romans produced lifelike **busts** of administrators, soldiers, and emperors.

commemoration *n.* 纪念
propaganda *n.* 宣传
bust *n.* 半身塑像

In painting, the Romans were technically far more advanced than the Greeks. Although they again followed the Greek style, they adapted it to their own tastes. The Romans were particularly skilled in wall painting. In the paintings still to be seen in **Pompeii** and elsewhere, the artist drew the human figure accurately and showed objects in clear (though imperfect) **perspective.**

Pompeii 庞贝古城
perspective *n.* 透视效果

Paintings on the wall of Pompeii houses From left to right, portrait of a young lady, portrait of a married couple, a temple viewed from the inside of a house.

3.7 Science

The Romans had little scientific curiosity. They preferred to adapt the findings of Greek science for their own practical uses. They became masters of medicine, public health, engineering, and map making.

The Romans created the first real hospitals and medical schools and developed the extensive practice of **hydrotherapy**—the use of mineral baths for healing. One of the first public health systems was established in the early Roman Empire, and a large number of doctors were

hydrotherapy *n.* 水疗法

employed by the state to give free care to the poor. The Roman concern for public health was evident in the great aqueducts that supplied plenty of fresh water to Rome daily and in the admirable **drainage** system.

If the Romans themselves were seldom interested in scientific investigation, others in the empire were engaged in serious research. During the Pax Romana, the Greeks at Alexandria continued their mathematical and geographical studies. Roman armies and Greek traders travelling to distant lands provided geographers with important data for new maps of the world. The most famous geographer and astronomer was an Alexandrian scholar named **Ptolemy** (90—168 AD). Despite his high reputation, Ptolemy is often remembered today for some of his serious errors. As the Continent of America and Australia were not yet discovered, the Ptolemy map of the world included only the Old World, This error influenced Columbus's decision to start sailing from Spain in search of Asia. In astronomy Ptolemy was right in following the Hellenistic theory that the world is round, but at the same time he accepted that the Earth is at the centre of the universe. In ***Almagest***, Ptolemy used **geometrical** methods and observed data to argue that all heavenly bodies revolve around the earth. Because of Ptolemy's authority, the **geocentric theory** was generally accepted in Western Europe until the 16th century.

Galen [139 (?) —200 (?)], a **physician** born in Asia Minor, made major breakthroughs in **physiology** and anatomy. Through experiments on animals, Galen demonstrated that a heart can continue to beat even if removed from the body, and that injuries to one side of the brain produce disorders on the opposite side of the body. In his medical **encyclopedia** he summarized the medical knowledge of his time. This encyclopedia remained one of the main doctors' reference books until well into the Renaissance.

drainage *n.* 排水系统

Ptolemy 托勒密

Almagest《大综合论》

geometrical *adj.* 几何的

geocentric theory 地心论

physician *n.* 内科医生

physiology *n.* 生理学

encyclopedia *n.* 百科全书

4. Conclusion

The story of how Rome rose from a **muddy** village along the banks of the Tiber River to the mighty ruler of the Mediterranean will always remain one of the most **fascinating** in world history. Two themes are dominant in the four hundred years of Roman history after 509 BC: the gradual **democratization** of the government and the conquest of the

muddy *adj.* 泥泞的

fascinating *adj.* 引人入胜的

democratization *n.* 民主化

Mediterranean.

During the first two centuries, the plebeians struggled with the privileged patricians. Gradually they gained recognition of their fundamental rights as citizens and acquired more political power. The birth of today's democratic tradition can be seen in the Roman legal and political systems. The Romans left us the concepts of the **supremacy** of the law, the social contract, the sovereignty of the people, and the separation of powers. However, the significant progress of the republican period was lost when Rome was transformed into the **principate**, a monarchy in **disguise**.

supremacy *n.* 至高无上

principate *n.* 元首制

disguise *n.* 伪装

The other major event in early Rome was the conquest of the Mediterranean. Between 509 and 270 BC, the Romans crushed all resistance in Italy. They then turned their attention to Carthage, which surrendered in 201 BC after a series of wars. Having conquered the west, the Romans toward the East and defeated the successors of Alexander the Great. But as the Mediterranean world **succumbed** to the Roman legions, Rome itself faced civil war and decline.

succumb *v.* 屈服

Several reformers, such as the Gracchus brothers, tried but failed to persuade the Senate to conduct reforms. Amidst political disorder, strong men such as Marius, Pompey, Crassus, and Julius Caesar rose to power with military support. The emergence of a one-man dictatorship marked the end of the republic. Augustus, the **heir** of Caesar, ruled wisely and well. On the surface the old republican institutions, such as the Senate, were kept, but Augustus held real power in the new arrangement, called the principate. For two hundred years, millions of people in Italy and the empire's provinces enjoyed peace and prosperity.

heir *n.* 继承人

In the process of conquest and expansion, the Romans borrowed from the cultures of the various conquered peoples. The influence of the Greeks was particularly strong. At the same time, the Romans were able to adapt foreign cultures according to their own ideas. Although they lacked the intellectual brilliance of the Greeks, they **excelled** in human and civil engineering. The Romans made great advances in political theory, governmental administration, and legal systems. They built a network of highways, government buildings, public baths, and stadiums throughout the empire. The Romans also produced realistic painting and sculpture. In literature the Romans developed few new forms but produced a number of masterpieces, and their prose set a standard for later generations. The Latin language remained the ***lingua***

excel *v.* 擅长

franca for law, the Church, and much literature in the Middle Ages. Later it served as the foundation of modern languages spoken by hundred of millions of people today. In a word, the realistic and practical nature of the Roman mind made up for its lack of creativity. Without Rome, European civilization as we know it would not exist. The history of Rome continues to have a major influence on the world today.

lingua franca 通用语

Exercises

Ⅰ. Terminology: choose the suitable term to fill in the blanks.

A. patrician B. plebian C. assembly(ies)
D. republicanism E. monarchy F. tribune G. senate
H. magistrate (s) I. consul J. dictator K. decree

When the Etruscans migrated to Italy, they created a number of __1__. Based on their tribal tradition, the Etruscan king received advice from the __2__, however, the final power to decide remained in the hands of the king. In 509 BC the Romans rose up to overthrow the foreign rule by the Etruscans. Seeing the state as public property, the Romans replaced the monarchical system with __3__. The government of the Roman republic was based on the principle of separations of power. The executive branch was made up of elected officers called __4__. Among the officials, two were elected as the chief civil and military officers. They were called __5__. In times of emergency, however, the Republic would have only one top officer to manage the executive matters. This officer was called __6__. The legislative branch of the Republic consisted of four __7__, each representing one particular group of citizens. In the early days of the Republic, the power to make laws was mainly in the hands of the __8__. The common Roman citizens, called __9__, continuously fought for their rights. Eventually they gained more legislative power and could also elect their own officers, called __10__. Although the senate could only issue __11__ instead of laws, it still had a strong influence on the political life in the Republic.

Ⅱ. Decide whether the following statements are true (T) or false (F).

1. It was the Romans who created the name "Africa" after they conquered the Carthage Empire. ( )
2. In the Roman Republic, citizenship was determined by blood only. In other words, only when both parents were native Romans could a person become Roman citizen. ( )
3. The term "dictator" did not have its present day's derogatory meaning in the period of the Roman Republic. ( )
4. Out of great respect for traditions, the Romans were reluctant to make reforms. ( )
5. The institution of the senate in the Roman Republic could be traced to the Etruscan tradition. ( )
6. The Laws of the Twelve Tables was the first written law in Rome. ( )
7. Officers in the Roman Republic were produced by drawing lots. ( )
8. Octavian kept the republican system in name in order to gain support. ( )
9. The Americans learnt from the ancient Rome in creating their federal government. ( )
10. During the period of the Five Good Emperors, smooth hereditary succession guaranteed political stability. ( )
11. Ptolemy's geocentric theory remained very popular in Europe for centuries. ( )

Ⅲ. Multiple choices: choose the answer that best completes the statement or answers the question.

1. What is the limit of term for the members of the Senate of the Roman Republic?

A. 2 years. B. 4 years. C. 5 years. D. Life.

2. Of the following philosophical schools, which one had perhaps the greatest influence on Roman laws and government?

A. Epicureanism. B. Stoicism.

C. Cynicism. D. Neo-Platonism.

3. It was during the ____ that the Romans were defeated by the famous Carthaginian general Hannibal.

A. the 1st Punic War B. the 2nd Punic War

C. the 3rd Punic War D. the 4th Punic War

4. That Aeneid, the legendary founder of the city of Rome, was the prince of ____ suggests a certain link between the Roman civilization and ancient Near East.

A. Etruria B. Greece C. Troy D. Phoenicia

5. The Roman Republic was founded in ________.

A. 509 BC B. 471 BC C. 445 BC D. 367 BC

6. Olive trees and grapevine were introduced into Italy by ________.

A. Etruscans B. Greeks C. Latins D. Egyptians

7. The government of the Roman Republic included all of the following branches EXCEPT ________.

A. the executive branch B. the deliberative branch

C. the legislative branch D. the judicial branch

8. The first city-builders in Italy were ________.

A. the Greeks B. the Latins C. the Etruscans D. the Italians

9. Which one of the following groups of the people could vote in the Roman assemblies?

A. Roman generals and adult male plebians.

B. Anyone whose parents were Romans.

C. Adult Roman males and females.

D. Literate Greek slaves.

10. Which one of the following was NOT a member of the First Triumvirate?

A. Crassus. B. Sulla. C. Pompey. D. Caesar.

11. Britain was turned into a Roman province in ________.

A. the 1st century BC B. the 1st century

C. the 2nd century D. the 3rd century.

12. Which one of the Roman Emperors resembles the "philosopher king" praised by Plato?

A. Trajan (r. 98—117 AD). B. Hadrian (r. 117—138 AD).

C. Antoninus Pius (r. 138—161 AD). D. Marcus Aurelius (r. 161—180 AD).

13. All of the following political ideas can be accredited to the Romans EXCEPT ________.

A. popular sovereignty B. social contract theory

C. democracy D. separations of power

14. All of the following Roman officers were produced by election EXCEPT ________.

A. consul B. dictator C. tribune D. magistrate

15. In the early days of the Roman Republic, ________ was the most important law making power.

A. the Assembly of Century B. the Plebian Council

C. the Assembly of Curiae D. the Tribal Assembly

16. Which one of the following architectural constructions was not typical Roman?

A. Dome. B. Vault. C. Arch. D. Column.

17. Which of the following reform measures resulted in the moral decline of the Romans?

A. limiting the amount of land owned by individual citizens.

B. selling grain at a low price to citizens.

C. distributing public land to landless citizens.

D. cutting down land taxes or rent.

18. The Roman expansion had many consequences EXCEPT ________.

A. Rome became the hegemony in the Mediterranean region

B. economic gains for all Romans

C. social conflicts and slave uprisings

D. increased political power for military commanders

19. The prose writing of ____ had the greatest influence on Latin literature in the Middle Ages.

A. Livy (59 BC—18 AD) B. Cicero (106—43 BC)

C. Caesar (100—44 BC) D. Tacitus (55—117 AD)

20. The poetic creation of ____ glorifies Rome's conquests and achievements.

A. Virgil (70—19 BC) B. Horace (65—8 BC)

C. Ovid (43 BC—17 AD) D. Juvenal (55—130 AD)

Chapter 4
Decline of the Roman Empire and Rise of Christianity

CHAPTER OUTLINE

1. Introduction
2. The Crisis of the Empire
3. The Empire Reorganized
4. Transformation of the Roman World: the Development of Christianity
5. Transformation of the Roman World: the **Germanic** Invasion
6. Conclusion

Germanic *adj.* 日耳曼人(的)

FOCUS QUESTIONS

1. What internal factors caused the decline of the Roman Empire?
2. What measures were taken by the political leaders to meet these challenges?
3. Why and how did Christianity become the majority religion within the Roman Empire?
4. Why did the Germanic invasions succeed?
5. Did Rome fall? Why or why not?

1. Introduction

Roman expansion began in the days of the Republic and reached its **zenith** under Emperor Trajan (rule 98—117). At this territorial peak, the Roman Empire measured approximately 6 500 000 km^2. All the lands that bordered the Mediterranean Sea were Roman provinces. The Romans proudly called the Mediterranean Sea "our sea". The Empire stretched from the Persian Gulf to the Atlantic coasts of present-day Spain and France, and from the Maghreb (northern Africa) to Hadrian's Wall (between England and Scotland). The area under Rome's rule included parts of more than thirty modern nations. It contained more than 100 million people. It was the largest empire the

zenith *n.* 巅峰

world had ever seen, the first true superpower in human history.

"Diversity in Unity" was perhaps the best description of the Empire in its full glory. All types of topography and climate could be found in the Empire: snow-capped mountains, low green plains, dry and hot deserts, **temperate** and pleasant coastal regions. All provinces were linked to the capital of Rome by laws, trade, social customs, and fine stone roads. People of different skin colors travelled and settled freely across the entire Empire. Everyone used the same **currency**: gold, silver or bronze coins with the image of the Roman emperors. Everyone was subject to the protection or punishment of Roman law. Although people from different regions spoke different mother tongues, they could always communicate with strangers either in Latin or in Greek. Latin was the official language of the Empire, the ***lingua franca*** in the Western Provinces. In the Eastern Provinces, Greek was more widely spoken, mainly due to the strong Hellenistic influence. Provincial governors, whether elected or appointed, all reported to the Senate in Rome. The Senate, in turn, followed the leadership of the emperor, or the "first citizen" of Rome. The strong and well-organized Roman armies brought stability and order to the four corners of the Empire. It seemed that the Roman Empire would last forever.

temperate *adj.* 温润的

currency *n.* 货币

lingua franca 通用语言

Map 15 The changing boundaries of the Roman Empire

The empire's size remained quite stable after Augustus' time. Nature seemed to have set permanent boundaries for the empire: on the west the Atlantic Ocean; the Rhine and Danube on the north; the Euphrates on the east; and towards the south the sandy desert of Arabia and Africa. The only expansion beyond these stable boundaries took place during Trajan's reign (98—117 AD).

But the Empire was not to last. Its glory and power started to decline after 180 AD. There were many **indications** that the Empire was in deep trouble. For example, after the late 2nd century, no more new cities were created in the Empire, and in the existing cities, there was no money for new buildings, except for Christian churches and **monasteries**.

Although the Empire's decline started in 180 AD, it did not collapse immediately. Various reforms were attempted in response to the crisis. In 286 AD, the emperor **Diocletian** divided the vast empire into two parts. A few years later, in 323, the emperor **Constantine** moved the capital from Rome to the city of Byzantium (today's **Istanbul**), which was renamed after him as **Constantinople**. Both emperors took various other measures to **resuscitate** the Empire. Because of strong leaders like them, the declining Roman Empire did not instantly fall apart. But once there was no strong leader, there was no stopping its collapse. This is precisely what happened after the death of Constantine. Less than one hundred years after his death, **Germanic** tribes (the **Goths**) flooded into the Roman Empire. The once-powerful Roman army was unable to stop their invasion. The **barbarians** sacked the city of Rome several times. Finally, in 476, a Germanic military leader named Odoacer overthrew the Western Roman emperor Romulus Augustulus. Nine hundred years of Roman rule had come to an end.

How did this happen? How could these barbarians defeat the Romans? How could such a large and powerful Empire fall? Or, maybe we should ask, how did the Empire survive so long? Historians have struggled to answer these questions. In this chapter we will explore this great mystery. We will first examine the general economic, political and social changes that led to the decline and eventual fall of the Empire. We will pay special attention to the emergence of two factors, namely, the rise of Christianity and the Germanic invasion. These two forces not only played a decisive role in the downfall of the Roman Empire, but also continued to shape the political and cultural landscapes of Western Europe in the Middle Ages.

indication *n.* 迹象

monastery *n.* 修道院

Diocletian 戴克里先

Constantine 君士坦丁大帝

Istanbul 伊斯坦布尔

Constantinople 君士坦丁堡

resuscitate *v.* 恢复

Germanic *adj.* 日耳曼人(的)

Goth *n.* 哥特人

barbarian *n.* 野蛮人

2. The Crisis of the Empire

More has been written on the decline and fall of Rome than on the death of any other civilization. Scholars have suggested many theories to explain the decline of Rome. One of the simplest explanations is that Rome fell because of the Germanic attacks. But from the 4th century onwards, Germanic "barbarians" were already attempting to attack Rome. They did not succeed until the 5th century. So the answer must be found elsewhere. Another explanation is that the decline of the Empire had its roots in the decay of Roman citizens' health. A Canadian environmental scientist even argues that the Romans had been poisoned by **lead** used in their household items such as pans and spoons. But the Romans had been using lead for centuries, how come they had survived for so long?

lead *n.* 铅

Just as Rome was not built in a day, it was not lost in one. The collapse of such a huge empire cannot be explained by one single reason. It is best for us to look inside the empire before it was brought down by the barbarians. In this section we will first focus on Rome's most serious internal problems. Some of these were political, some economic, and some **psychological.**

psychological *adj.* 心理的

2.1 The Flawed Imperial Political System

When the Romans began to expand their empire, they lived under one type of government, republicanism. When they lost their empire, they lived under a different type of government, imperial monarchy. Did the change of the system of government cause the empire to fall? Some historians including Edward Gibbon① believe that it did. To understand the relationship between the Empire's decline and its political system, we must first observe the changes in its form of government over several centuries and their impact on the Empire's health.

In 509 BC, the Romans overthrew the last Etruscan king and founded the Republic. In the early days of the Republic, power was concentrated in the Senate, which was made up of patricians, members of the upper class. For more than 200 years, common Roman citizens struggled by means of many legal and political reforms for equal legal status and political rights. When they finally succeeded, citizenship replaced birth as the only **criterion** to determine a person's social status and political rights. All Roman citizens were protected by Roman law and enjoyed the right to run for civil offices. This long process of reforms and struggles cultivated a strong sense of unity among the citizens of Rome. In this same period, the Romans gradually gained

criterion *n.* 标准
criteria (*pl.*)

① 爱德华·吉本(Edward Gibbon, 1737—1794),英国历史学家。代表作《罗马帝国衰亡史》(The History of the Decline and Fall of the Roman Empire)于1776至1788年间出版,共6册。

control of most of the Italian peninsula. By the mid-second century BC, the Roman Republic had begun its overseas expansion.

Some historians believe the institution of citizenship itself played an important role in Rome's successful expansion. In such a Republican system, soldiers in the Roman army were not fighting for a king. In many respects, they were fighting for themselves: each soldier in the Roman army was given a piece of land after he retired. If a soldier was not a Roman citizen, he could earn citizenship through his military service. In theory, any Roman citizen could **aspire** to be the leader of Rome.

aspire *v.* 渴望

However, the Republican spirit was damaged when Octavian put an end to a long-running civil war in 27 BC. To honor his contribution to peace, the Senate declared that Octavian would be re-elected every year for the rest of his life. The Senate also made him ruler over all the armies of all the provinces. With this power, no one in the empire could challenge him, and he renamed himself Augustus. Grateful for the peace brought by Augustus, known as the Pax Augusta or Pax Romana, few Romans **objected** to the change. Although Octavian called himself princeps (meaning "first citizen") of Rome, he became, in fact, the first king of the Roman Empire. The republican system existed only in name.

object *v.* 反对

What really made Octavian a monarch was the manner in which his successor was to be chosen. In a monarchy, **succession** is determined by birth: the **crown** is passed from parents to their children or to other close relations. Before he died, Octavian told the Senate that he wanted his stepson to succeed him as the *princeps*.① The Senate agreed to this arrangement. Now that the leadership of the empire was determined by birth rather than by election, Octavian had created a monarchy. The Roman political system had departed from the spirit of republicanism.

succession *n.* 继位

crown *n.* 皇冠

The biggest weakness of a monarchy is the **hereditary** system. When leadership is determined by birth alone, the happiness of the people depends on the character and **capability** of one single ruler. An incapable or evil heir to the throne can do great damage to the empire. But when an emperor has no heir, an even bigger problem may appear; with succession uncertain, the way to the **throne** is generally paved by having control of the army. After the death of the great Octavian, the Romans were fortunate to have a few more capable and successful emperors. Quite exceptionally, between 96 and 180 AD, four

hereditary *adj.* 世袭的

capability *n.* 才干

throne *n.* 王位

① 屋大维将帝位传给他的继子兼女婿 Tiberius。

emperors did not pass the throne to their sons or close relatives. Instead, they chose and adopted talented young men to be their successors. The period was called the era of the "Five Good Emperors". In this period, the Empire expanded to its full size.

But the last of the Five Good Emperors, Marcus Aurelius,① left the throne to his selfish and cruel son, Commodus in 180 AD. The twenty-year-old Commodus had little interest in politics, nor had he much respect for the Senate. He often neglected his political responsibilities and focused more on his personal pleasures. His favorite hobby was to fight in gladiators' contests. Although he considered himself a god, his reign greatly disappointed the people of Rome. Some claim that Commodus was the worst emperor in the history of Rome, especially compared to his popular and successful father. Commodus was murdered by **strangling** in 192 AD, but this only led to more problems because Commodus had no designated successor. The armies of different provinces proposed and supported their own candidates. The ensuing power struggles among military leaders resulted in civil war. After a series of battles, Septimius Severus used his troops to seize power in 193. The Severan Dynasty (193—235) was a military monarchy. The army was expanded, soldiers' pay was increased, and military officers occupied important government positions.

strangle *v.* 绞刑

As "**might makes right**" became the rule of the game, the Roman Empire in the 3rd century experienced one crisis after another and nearly collapsed. In less than one hundred years, more than seventy rulers fought for control of the throne. Most of them were powerful generals in the Roman army. Some ruled for only a few months. Some less fortunate stayed in power for merely days or weeks. The civil wars and internal struggles weakened the Empire. Many cities and provinces declared their independence from Rome. The army's **loyalties** were divided between different powerful generals and rulers. Meanwhile, barbarian tribes began to move into the territory of the Empire. With no unified army to fight off the invaders, many cities were sacked.

Might makes right 强权就是真理

loyalty *n.* 忠诚

2.2 Crisis of the Slave Economy

Political unrest, civil war and foreign invasions affected every

① Marcus Aurelius（奥列里乌斯）罗马帝国最伟大的皇帝之一，于161年至180年在位。他不但是一个很有智慧的君主，同时也是一个很有成就的思想家，有以希腊文写成的著作《沉思录》（Meditations）传世。在整个西方文明之中，奥列里乌斯算是一个少见的贤君。可惜他贤能一世，到临死时却未能延续先帝任贤举能的优良传统，而是把帝位传给他品行恶劣的儿子康茂德。

aspect of the Roman economy. As a series of ambitious rulers fought their way to the throne, they needed funds with which to pay the army. One way was to collect taxes. But this was never an easy solution. When the economy did poorly, tax revenue suffered. Apart from taxes, the easiest and fastest solution was to reduce the silver content in coins and add less valuable metals instead. But when some emperors chose to do this, a new problem resulted: **devaluation** of the currency and inflation. In the third century, rising prices everywhere in the Empire made life much harder for common people.

devaluation *n.* 贬值
inflation *n.* 通货膨胀

Military unrest also greatly damaged the Empire's extensive internal trade network. The volume of imports also went down. Large landowners could no longer export their products, and began to produce for the local market instead. This self-sufficient "house economy" ultimately evolved into **manorialism** in the Middle Ages. Inflation and insecurity drove many free city residents to the countryside in search of food and protection. These people, as well as small farmers had to give up basic rights in return for protection from large landholders. They became a new half-free class of citizen. They were tied to the land, and in later Imperial law their status was made hereditary. This provided an early model for **serfdom**, which would form the basis of the medieval feudal society.

manorialism *n.* 农庄制度

serfdom *n.* 农奴制度
medieval *adj.* 中世纪的
feudal *adj.* 封建制度的

But Rome's worst economic problem came from its slave system and from labor shortages. Though slavery was found in nearly all ancient societies, the Romans had more slaves and depended more on them than any other people. Roman civilization was centered around cities, and Roman cities existed largely thanks to the surplus of food produced by slaves. We have no idea of the exact number of slaves owned by Romans at any given time, but we do know that the largest numbers were in Italy and especially in the capital, Rome. By the end of the 2nd century BC, there were probably one million slaves in Italy alone. The number of slaves increased dramatically during the reign of Augustus and continued to increase for almost two centuries. In Augustus' empire, approximately one in every three persons in Italy was a slave. Outside of Italy, the number of slaves in different provinces was lower and it varied from one province to another. The highest average percentage of slaves in the entire Empire might have been 20%, that is to say, one in every five. Large landowners would have thousands of slaves. Most middle-income free citizens had at least a few slaves.

Where did these slaves come from? Roman law gives a general answer: *servi aut nascuntur, aut fiunt* ("slaves are either born or made"). By law, the sons and daughters of a slave would be slaves. But often slaves were forced to work so hard that many died young. The average **life expectancy** of a slave in the Empire was no longer than 30 year. Their birth rate was far lower than their death rate.

life expectancy 预期寿命

To keep the system running, new slaves had to be found. There were several sources. The first was self-sale. When a Roman citizen was unable to repay his debts, he could be "given up" to his creditors. Second, abandonment of infants was also widespread in the Roman world and was only made illegal in 374. Abandoned children usually either died or were made slaves. Some fathers would also sell any or all of their children into slavery. This often happened in hard times as a way for parents to ease their financial and household burdens. A third method was **penal** enslavement: slavery would be imposed as a punishment for grave crimes. Criminals would often be sentenced to **forfeit** their personal rights and be forced to work as slaves in **quarries** or mines or as gladiators. And then there were also many who were kidnapped and sold into slavery, coming from both inside and outside the Empire.

penal *adj.* 惩罚性的
forfeit *v.* 丧失
quarry *n.* 采石场

By far the most important source of slaves was prisoners of war. Frequent Roman conquests provided fresh supplies of slaves to keep the system going. For example, the Roman expansion in Britain continued to supply British slaves for the market. And when the Roman army crushed a **Jewish** rebellion between 67 and 70 AD nearly 100 000 Jews were taken as slaves. However, as the Empire entered into a period of peace and stability, the emperors stopped its **aggressive** military expansion and tried to maintain the current frontiers of the empire. As a result, the number of slaves from this source, i. e. prisoners of war, greatly decreased.

Jewish *adj.* 犹太人的
aggressive *adj.* 侵略的

Slavery, as an economic institution, is **efficient**. The Romans built their entire economy around slavery. But in the late years of the Empire, the number of slaves declined, and the economy began to run out of manpower. Military unrest in the third century AD also meant that many men had to leave their jobs and serve in the army. Major **plagues** in the second and third centuries also wiped out a large part of the population. It has been estimated that by the late third century, disease, **warfare** and a low birth rate had combined to reduce the Empire's population by one third. As a result there were neither sufficient farm laborers to work the land nor enough soldiers to fight Rome's enemies. Labor shortages are thus one possible cause of Rome's decline.

efficient *adj.* 高成效的

plague *n.* 瘟疫

warfare *n.* 战争

2.3 The Culture of Bread and the Circus

circus *n.* 马戏团

Many scholars, including even some Roman writers at the time, have argued that the Empire was weakened by changes in moral values. In other words, success spoiled the Romans. As they accumulated wealth through conquests, the Romans gradually lost many of the good moral qualities that had helped to build the Empire. They feasted all day long, stopped caring about honor, abandoned the pursuit of justice, and neglected faith and self-discipline. In the famous phrase of the Roman writer Juvenal, the people only cared about "bread and circuses." In many ways, the Roman state itself was responsible for this moral **decay.**

decay *n.* 腐败

The trouble began during the Roman Republic from 124 to 122 BC. By this time, thousands of poor people had migrated to Rome from the Italian countryside, hoping for a better life in the capital. Most were disappointed. The poor lived in very dirty conditions and had little food. Famine swept through the city several times. To prevent starvation, the government provided free grain to the needy. By the second century BC, it had become common for many city governments to guarantee the food supply to prevent famine. Laws were made to allow poor Romans to buy grain from the government at a low price. Supporters of this policy believed that the poor, when fed by the state, would be less likely to riot or steal. They would also feel greater loyalty to the government. At first, this policy helped unite the Roman people. It reinforced the idea that in the republic, all people—including the plebeians-shared in the state's success. As Rome became richer, it would only seem proper to use its wealth to **banish** hunger from its streets.

banish *v.* 驱除

counter-productive *adj.* 起反作用的

Although well-intended, the policy became **counter-productive.** Once people knew that cheap grain was available in Rome, more poor people flooded into the city from the countryside. As a result, the city of Rome's population increased rapidly. Instead of reducing the number of poor and hungry people in the city, free provision of grain actually increased it. By the second century AD, half a million Romans were receiving grain handouts. The financial burden on the government increased over the years.

guarantee *v.* 保证

Free grain not only cost the government money but also weakened the work ethic of the people. With access to free or cheap grain **guaranteed**, people had less desire or drive to work. They knew they could survive even without working. Over time it began to feel natural for these people to live on free food provided by the state. Children raised on free food never learned the value or purpose of work as they had never seen their parents working. When free food was **unavailable** or **suspended**, crime increased. The government then had to spend more to maintain order among the lazy poor.

unavailable *adj.* 得不到的

suspend *v.* 暂停

abolish *v.* 废除

popularity *n.* 受欢迎度

Why was the free food policy not **abolished**? One possible explanation: for some politicians the policy could help strengthen their power. By feeding the masses, they would win the support of poor plebeians. The process of managing the food supply also created many new jobs for unemployed Romans. This would further their **popularity** among the poor. As the number of lazy poor grew, some Romans began to question the wisdom of their leaders. The middle and upper classes became angry that their taxes were spent to feed lazy people. The wealthy blamed the poor for the empire's troubles. Social unity started to fall apart.

idle *adj.* 无所事事的

sponsor *v.* 赞助

inaugurate *v.* 举行落成典礼

To find something for the **idle** poor to do, the state also sponsored games and contests known generally as circuses. The state financed the construction of many large stadiums for circuses and sponsored four permanent chariot-racing teams. Funds to support public entertainment came from the state treasury. Ancient Romans loved to watch horse and chariot races. But as Rome grew, the Romans added other, even more brutal sports to their circus events. Human hunters would attack all kinds of wild beasts in the ring with nothing but their bare hands. Sometimes they were killed by the beasts. At moments like this, the crowds would get even more excited. It was reported that when the emperor Titus **inaugurated** the Colosseum in 80 AD, five thousand beasts were killed in one day of games.

The Gladiatorial Games Although some gladiators were free men attracted by the rewards or the excitement, most were slaves, prisoners of war, or condemned criminals. They were trained in special schools. Consistent success could win a gladiator his freedom. This painting shows the bloody nature of the games. The standing combatant is looking to the crowds to see if his opponent should live or die. If the crowd mostly pointed their thumbs downwards, it meant that the loser must be killed. Typically only those fallen gladiators who had fought especially well were spared.

Left: remains of the Colosseum by night Right: a computerized reconstruction of the Colosseum

The gladiatorial shows took place in amphitheatres. The first permanent one was built in Rome in 29 BC, but the most famous one is the Colosseum which could seat fifty thousand spectators and was constructed between 79 and 80 AD. Similar amphitheatres were built throughout the empire, with capacities ranging from a few thousand to tens of thousands. In most cities, the amphitheatre was the biggest single building. Given the central importance of the amphitheatres and gladiatorial shows in Roman cities, it is fair to say that public slaughter was an important part of ancient Roman culture.

To make the circuses more entertaining, the Romans invented the gladiatorial show, one where human fought against human. Most **gladiators** were slaves, criminals and captured soldiers from foreign lands. They were trained to fight in special gladiatorial schools. If they won, they might be freed. If they failed, they would die. The circuses became a brutal extension of the Roman justice system. Criminals were often **sentenced** to fight in the ring. So for even a small crime, death might become the final sentence.

gladiator *n.* 角斗士

sentence *v.* 宣判

In the early days of the republic, games were held during holidays, but by the first century AD, they had become almost daily events. More than one hundred days a year were made public holidays. The emperors and other state officials provided great festivals for the public. People watched the **parades** of gladiators and condemned prisoners in the

parade *n.* 游行

streets, then flooded into the stadiums to cheer each killer blow. Cheers from stadiums could be heard across the capital. The gladiator shows were the most popular topic of conversation. How did this daily **exposure** to human torture and death affect the viewer? What effect did this state-sponsored **bloodshed** have on the minds of the Roman people? What lessons did it teach about the value of human life? The circuses hardened Romans' hearts and corrupted their morals. Such a culture, many historians believe, was doomed to fall apart, as it would lead people to use violence without a second thought. Instead of protecting its citizens from harm, the government encouraged and popularized a culture of violence. The gladiatorial games were more than just public entertainment. They also served a political and social need: **distracted** by these games, the idle masses would worry less about political and social problems. As the emperor Trajan saw it, while the distribution of grain and money satisfied the individual's needs, such spectacles were necessary for the "contentment of the masses." One effect of these brutal spectacles was the decline in public morality which greatly weakened the Roman state.

exposure *n.* 观看
bloodshed *n.* 杀戮
distract *v.* 分散注意力

3. The Empire Reorganized

The **chaos** of the 3rd century AD nearly destroyed the Roman Empire. That it did not was largely due to the limited reforms of two powerful emperors, Diocletian and Constantine. Their efforts to reorganize the Empire gave it a new lease of life. Throughout the 4th century the Roman state continued to **encompass** the entire Mediterranean world.

chaos *n.* 乱象
encompass *v.* 包括

3.1 Dividing the Empire

A high army officer, Diocletian seized the imperial throne in 284 AD. Though strong-willed, Diocletian realized that the Empire was too large to be governed by one person. He divided the Empire into two parts-an eastern half and a western half. The ruler of each half held the **title** of *Augustus*. Diocletian kept for himself the wealthier eastern half and asked a reliable colleague named Maximian to rule the western half. Then each of these two Augusti (Diocletian and Maximian, in the beginning) chose a **lieutenant** to assist them. These two lieutenants were called Caesars and they governed a subsection of the empire. When the two Augusti retired, the Caesars would take their places, and

title *n.* 封号
lieutenant *n.* 中尉

appoint new Caesars in turn to assist them. This system became known as a **tetrarchy**, meaning "rule by four leaders." Diocletian hoped that this system would end the disputes over **succession** and increase governmental efficiency.

tetrarchy *n.* 四雄执政
succession *n.* 继位

Diocletian also introduced administrative reforms. While keeping control over the army, he started to separate military and civil affairs. He also strengthened and enlarged the administrative bureaucracies. These reforms helped reduce the Roman armies' influence on politics. Diocletian also made some economic reforms but they were not very effective. For example, to fight **inflation** in 301 he issued a price **edict** to set maximum wages and prices for the entire empire. But despite severe penalties, this policy was **unenforceable** and failed to work. Diocletian also passed laws to make some jobs, such as those of farmers, bakers and shippers **hereditary**, so that the basic labor necessary to keep the Empire going would continue to be done. But with the collapse of the slave system and the labor shortages, none of these reforms could save the economy.

inflation *n.* 通货膨胀
edit *n.* 诏令
unenforceable *adj.* 无法执行
hereditary *adj.* 世袭的

As Diocletian ruled the eastern half of the empire, he also moved its administrative capital from Rome to Nicomedia in modern-day Turkey. Rome remained the spiritual and symbolic capital of the empire. The Senate continued to meet in Rome, but Diocletian had little need for its members' advice. At first, Diocletian's plan helped hold the Empire together, but later the two halves **drifted** apart. The eastern half grew increasingly wealthier than the western half. In 305 AD. Diocletian built himself a palace in today's Croatia and retired to grow cabbages (the first Roman emperor to retire voluntarily!). To make the new system of succession work, Diocletian also asked his colleague Maximian to retire. But things did not work out as he had planned. Shortly after his retirement, Diocletian's system of shared rule broke down and war broke out among his successors. The son of one of these successors, Constantine, marched on Rome in 312 and defeated his **rivals**. Constantine made himself Emperor of the West. Then, eleven years later, he attacked and defeated the Emperor of the East. Unlike Diocletian, Constantine had no interest in power-sharing. The empire once again had a single ruler.

drift *v.* 漂移
rival *n.* 对手

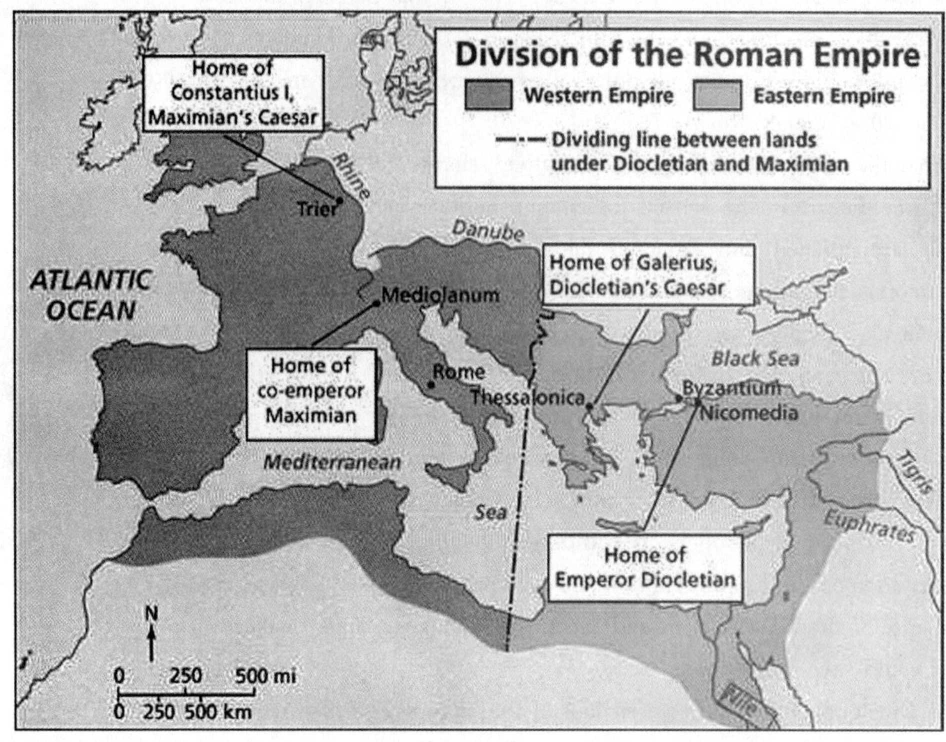

Map 16 Division of the Roman Empire

Diocletian divided the Roman Empire into four regions, each ruled by either an "Augustus" or a "Caesar". But he retained supreme power.

3.2 The Reign of Constantine (312—395)

decree *n.* 政令

tetrarchy *n.* 四雄执政

Constantine followed most of Diocletian's administrative practices. Both men ruled by **decrees**, and both relied on a vast network of spies to control the empire. To maintain a large army, Diocletian had already made military service hereditary. Constantine made even more occupations hereditary, such as those of farmers and craftsmen. The economic reforms of both emperors were based on tight military control. In the short run, they might show some results, but in the long run these policies would only erode the vitality of the imperial economy. And in one crucial matter Constantine did depart from Diocletian's plans: to plan the imperial succession, he abandoned Diocletian's **tetrarchy** system. Instead of appointing a capable outsider, he chose to pass the throne to his family members. The empire returned to being a dynastic monarchy.

Considering himself a great emperor, Constantine started to build a new capital in 324 AD and named it New Rome, but everyone called it Constantinople, or "Constantine's city". One reason for the move was military. Constantinople was surrounded on three sides by water and protected by walls, making it easy to defend. Situated at the mouth of the Black Sea, on the border between Europe and Asia, it had advantages as a gateway for communications and trade. Moving the capital from Rome to Constantinople further shifted the centre of the Roman civilization towards the east. Constantinople would remain the political and economic center of the Roman Empire until 1453, when the city was finally conquered by the **Ottoman Turks.**

Ottoman Turk 奥斯曼土耳其

Constantine played an important role in restoring order and stability to the Roman Empire at the beginning of the fourth century. This marble head of Constantine was part of an enormous seated statue of the emperor in Rome. It is 12 meters high and weighs nine tons. The enlarged eyes emphasize the emperor's spiritual vision. Constantine put these impressive statues throughout the empire for people to worship.

Before he died, Constantine divided the empire between his three sons, which resulted in civil war. Succession conflicts among Constantine's **descendants** would continue for most of the 4th century. Sometimes the empire was divided, other times it was reunited. The last emperor to rule over a unified Roman empire was Theodosius. Before he died in 395 AD, he followed the family's tradition by dividing the empire between his two sons. This was the final division of the empire, because in 476 AD Germanic (Goth) invaders put an end to the Western Roman Empire.

descendant *n.* 后裔

4. Transformation of the Roman World: the Development of Christianity

When the Romans were building their empire, they practiced one religion; when the empire was collapsing, they practiced another. Between the first and fifth centuries, Christianity grew from being a little-known religion in Judea to the official state religion of the Roman world. Thereafter, it became a key (perhaps the key) force in transforming the Roman world and in shaping the civilizations of the Western world up to the present day. For Christians, their religion's extraordinary growth and impact are proofs of its truth. For historians, the **triumph** of Christianity was closely linked to the fate of the Empire, but they disagree on the exact historical role Christianity played. Some believe that the rise of Christianity weakened the Empire, while others argue that it strengthened it. Whether it was the cause or the result of the fall of the Empire, the rise of Christianity marks a **fundamental** break with the dominant values of the Greco-Roman world. Christian views of God(s), human beings, and the world were very different from those of the Greeks and Romans. To understand the emergence of Christianity, we must first examine both the religious environment of the Roman world and the Jewish background from which Christianity emerged.

triumph *n.* 胜利

fundamental *adj.* 彻底的

4.1 Imperial Roman Religious Beliefs

The earliest Romans believed that natural objects had spirits. Invisible and shapeless spirits lived in every river, spring, lake and tree. Every spirit had its unique power. By using their power, the spirits caused natural events such as storms, lightning, wind, rainbows, flood, drought, disease, and healing. This belief is known as animism, from the Latin word anima, meaning "soul". The Romans respected and worshipped these spirits. They believed they had to ask permission of the spirits before taking anything from nature. For example, Romans would leave a small **offering**, usually food, before taking water from a lake or river. If a person wanted to cut down a tree, he was required to give a **sacrifice**. The Romans believed that if a person did not follow the proper ritual, something bad would happen to that person. For example, the water might make the drinker ill, or the woodcutter might get cut by his own axe.

offering *n.* 供品

sacrifice *n.* 牺牲，祭品

ritual *n.* 仪式

Contact with the Greeks and Etruscans changed Roman religious beliefs. The Romans began to give their spirits names and personalities. They started to call them "gods" and began to tell stories about their gods and goddesses. Most of these stories, known as myths, were borrowed from the Greeks and Etruscans. For example, the Romans adopted the Greek belief that the world was ruled by twelve mighty gods. Although new Roman names were given to these gods, they kept the Greek stories about their personalities and powers. For example, Zeus in Greek mythology became Jupiter for the Romans, but remained king of the gods and ruler of the heavens. Hero, wife of Zeus and queen of the gods for the Greeks, was called Juno by the Romans. With the exception of Apollo, eleven principal Olympian gods were renamed by the Romans. In addition to the major gods, the Romans also worshipped many minor gods, goddesses, and spirits.

As the Romans conquered the Mediterranean world, they took their beliefs with them. They expected the people they conquered to honor Roman holidays and rituals. They did not, however, require conquered peoples to give up their own religious beliefs or practices. Since the Romans already believed in many gods, they had no reason to fear or hate new gods in foreign lands. Romans would only object to a local religion if it threatened people's loyalty to the empire. As the empire expanded, the Romans learned about many new religions. Sometimes they adopted foreign beliefs as their own. For example, many Romans started to believe in the Egyptian goddess Isis, the goddess of life, death, and love. Viewed as the ideal combination of three female roles, Isis was especially popular among Roman women.

The Romans influenced religious thought in the lands they conquered as well. During the second century BC, some Greeks began to worship the goddess Roma as the **personification** of the Roman state. In some Greek cities, people had long regarded their kings as gods. It was natural for them to worship their Roman conquerors in the same way. People started to see Julius Caesar, Mark Antony, and other Roman statesmen and generals as gods. The worship of kings was also common in Asia. During the reign of Augustus, temples to Augustus began to appear in the eastern part of the empire. Augustus did not discourage such practices. He knew such worship would help unite the empire. For this reason, the emperors who succeeded Augustus encouraged people to worship them. The worship of Roman leaders became known as the **Cult** of the Living Emperors, or the Imperial Cult.

personification *n.* 化身

cult *n.* 膜拜

imperial cult 皇帝崇拜

The Romans considered the worship of their emperors an important element in their success. A typical Roman place of worship would be a small temple located in the commercial centre of a town. The temple pictured here was built in Vienna in the first century BC. It was dedicated to Augustus.

However, not all of the people conquered by Rome were willing to accept Roman religious beliefs or the Imperial Cult. The greatest resistance came from the Jews living in Judea. For thousands of years, the Jews had worshipped only one god, Yahweh. Their fundamental laws, also known as the Law of Moses, forbade the worship of any other god. Honoring and worshipping a living emperor also went against these laws, so the Jews refused to follow the Roman custom. The Romans considered these views unreasonable and even **treasonous**.

treasonous *adj.* 谋反的

4.2 Jews under Roman Rule

The religion of the Jews, Judaism, was much more than a spiritual faith. It was a legal system, political system, and way of life. When Pompey conquered Judea and turned it into a Roman province in 64 BC, the Romans respected the Jews' religion. Instead of placing a governor in charge of the province, Pompey handpicked a Jewish high priest to head the local government. Although the Jews had to pay taxes, they enjoyed limited self-rule. In 37 BC, the Romans even made Herod, a Jew loyal to Rome, King of Judea. Herod ruled wisely and rebuilt the temple of Jerusalem. People called him Herod the Great out of respect.

However, the Romans changed their policy in Judea in 6 AD. A Roman governor was again appointed as the **supreme** official in Judea, reporting directly to the emperor. At the same time, the Romans required the Jews to pay higher taxes. Tensions rose in Judea. The Jews refused to honor the Cult of the Living Emperors. A group of **devout** Jews known as the **Zealots** began to protest Roman rule. They refused to pay any taxes except for those required by Jewish law. The Romans responded with force. Roman soldiers attacked the Zealots. The Jewish Temple in Jerusalem was destroyed.

supreme *adj.* 最高的

devout *adj.* 虔诚的

Zealots 奋进党

While the Zealots battled Roman troops, a second movement arose in Judea. Known as the **Messianic movement**, this uprising also called for the end of Roman rule. Its members believed that a leader called the Messiah would unite the Jews and destroy their enemies, ushering in an era of peace and harmony. Ancient Jewish scriptures had promised that such a leader would appear during a time of suffering. To many Jews, the era of Roman rule seemed to be the time for the Messiah to save them. At this point a Jewish holy man appeared in a region of Judea called Galilee. His name was Yeshua, or Jesus. It was with the teachings of Jesus that Christianity began to develop.

messianic *adj.* 弥赛亚的，复国

Messiah *n.* （犹太教）弥赛亚、先知、救世主

4.3 The Career of Jesus

There is no doubt that Jesus was a real historical figure; but it is difficult to find out very much about him. When he was still alive, little was written about him. The earliest available materials are the letters and stories written by his followers many years after his death. All these works are included in the New Testament, spreading to the world the "good news" —the **gospels**—about Jesus. ①

gospel *n.* 福音

Jesus grew up in Galilee, an important centre of the Zealots. Although he was not trained as a religious leader or teacher, Jesus was allowed to speak and teach in the temple. He **preached** change. He told his listeners to turn from worldly desires and seek inner peace through **prayer** and **meditation**. He urged his followers to love one another and to show kindness to all people, not only to Jews, but also to non-Jews. Jesus himself had made friends with all kinds of **outcasts**; he even shared meals with the tax collectors hated by many people. Jesus told his followers: "Love the Lord your God with all your heart and with all your soul and with all your mind and with all your strength... Love your neighbor as yourself... in everything, do to others what you would have them do to you."

preach *v.* 宣讲
prayer *n.* 祷告
meditation *n.* 冥想

outcast *n.* (被家庭、社会)遗弃的人

Christian Ideals: The Sermon on the Mount

Christianity was one of many religions competing for attention in the Roman Empire during the first and second centuries. As can be seen from the excerpts below, Christians emphasized humility, charity, brotherly love, and a belief in the inner being and a spiritual kingdom superior to this material world. These values and principles were different from those of classical Greco-Roman civilization.

① 基督教的圣经由《旧约》和《新约》两部分所构成的,而其《旧约》来源于《希伯来圣经》,二者内容大致相同。

The Gospel According to Matthew

Now when he saw the crowds, he went up on a mountainside and sat down. His disciples came to him, and he began to teach them saying:

Blessed are the poor in spirit: for theirs is the kingdom of heaven.

Blessed are those who mourn: for they will be comforted.

Blessed are the meek: for they will inherit the earth.

Blessed are those who hunger and thirst for righteousness: for they will be filled.

Blessed are the merciful: for they will be shown mercy.

Blessed are the pure in heart: for they will see God.

Blessed are the peacemakers: for they will be called sons of God.

Blessed are those who are persecuted because of righteousness for theirs is the kingdom of heaven...

You have heard that it was said: "Eye for eye, and tooth for tooth." But I tell you, Do not resist an evil person. If someone strikes you on the right cheek, turn to him the other also...

You have heard that it was said: "Love your neighbor, and hate your enemy." But I tell you, Love your enemies and pray for those who persecute you...

Do not store up for yourselves treasures on earth, where moth and rust destroy, and where thieves break in and steal. But store up for yourselves treasures in heaven, where moth and rust do not destroy, and where thieves do not break in and steal. For where your treasure is, there your heart will be also...

No one can serve two masters. Either he will hate the one and love the other, or he will be devoted to the one and despise the other. You cannot serve both God and Money.

Therefore I tell you, do not worry about your life, what you will eat or drink; or about your body, what you will wear. Is not life more important than food, and the body more important than clothes? Look at the birds of the air, they do not sow or reap to store away in barns, and yet your heavenly Father feeds them. Are you not much more valuable than they? ... So do not worry, saying, What shall we eat? or What shall we drink? or What shall we wear? For the pagans run after all these things, and your heavenly Father knows that you need them. But seek first his kingdom and his righteousness, and all these things will be given to you as well.

earthly *adj.* 人间的

Jesus declared that a new kingdom was being established in Judea. Some Zealots and members of the Messianic movement thought that this meant Jesus would help them drive the Romans from their homeland. But they were wrong. Jesus said that his kingdom was a spiritual kingdom, not an **earthly** one. When Jews asked him how they should behave towards their Roman rulers, Jesus spoke of peace and cooperation. "Give Caesar what is Caesar's," he said, "but give God what is God's."

Many Jews found comfort in the words of Jesus. They were also impressed by stories of miracles he performed. As his fame grew, thousands came to see and hear him. When he entered Jerusalem before the feast of the **Passover** in 29 AD, he was greeted like a king. People put down **palm** branches before the donkey on which he rode. Some called out, "Messiah! Messiah!"

Passover *n.* (犹太教) 逾越节

palm *n.* 棕榈

Once in Jerusalem, Jesus was captured by the Romans. He was accused of the crime of **blasphemy**, that is, the belief that one is god-like. He was sentenced to death by the Roman governor, Pontius Pilate. Jesus was nailed to a **crucifix**, a wooden cross, with his limbs outstretched. In this position, his lungs slowly filled with **fluid**, causing a slow and painful death.

blasphemy *n.* 渎神

crucifix *n.* 木质十字架

fluid *n.* 液体

When Jesus died, it seemed that his mission had failed. His followers lost hope and many gave up their faith. But something happened in the early Christian community that turned the group around. It was reported that around dawn on the Sunday after Jesus' death, some of his female followers went to put **spices** on his body. The body was put in a cave, its entrance sealed up with a large stone. But when the women returned, they saw that the stone had been rolled away and found that Jesus' body had disappeared. They then saw one or two young men in shining clothing who told them that Jesus had risen from the dead. This rising from the dead is called the **Resurrection**. The New Testament indicates that the resurrected Jesus continued to appear in different places for forty days before he was finally "carried up into heaven." Before his **ascension** into heaven, Jesus promised that he would return again.

spice *n.* 香料

resurrection *n.* 复活

ascension *n.* 升天

Debate about the nature of the Resurrection began very early in the church. Some denied that Jesus' body was physically raised from the dead. Others argued that his resurrection was essential to the Christian faith. Non-Christians denied the story, claiming that Jesus' followers had stolen his body from the tomb. This debate has continued over the centuries. Whatever the nature of the Resurrection, two things are **undeniable**. First, a belief in Jesus' physical resurrection became one of the most important teachings of Christianity. The Resurrection became the key to understanding the life, teachings, mission, and person of Jesus. It transformed a dead Jewish preacher into a Christian living Lord who was God in the flesh. Second, this strong belief in

undeniable *adj.* 不可否认的

Jesus' resurrection greatly transformed his early followers. It helped strengthen their faith. After Jesus' death, his followers started travelling around the Roman Empire, preaching stories about his life, death, and resurrection, and spreading his teachings. They claimed that their teacher had risen from the dead. Many of them fearlessly faced rejection, imprisonment, and death to proclaim that Jesus was the Messiah.

4.4 The Rise of Christianity

From the life of Jesus Christ himself, we can see that Christianity developed from Judaism. In the early days Christianity was actually a **sub-branch** of Judaism: the earliest Christian Church was in Jerusalem, and the Christians saw themselves as a Jewish group. At first, the number of Jesus' followers in Judea was small. Like Jesus, they were devout Jews. Although they remembered Jesus in a ritual of breaking bread and sharing wine, they continued to observe the laws, holidays and rituals of Judaism. But the Jewish leaders regarded Christians as rebels who claimed Jesus had been the Messiah. The Jewish leaders started to **persecute** the young church. Many Christians fled from Judea, spreading Christianity to other parts of the Empire, to Samaria, to Cyprus, and to Syria.

sub-branch *n.* 分支

persecute *v.* 迫害

The settlement of a number of important disagreements in the early Christian community also pushed the development of Christianity onto a different path from that of Judaism. The most important debate in the early Christian community concerned the **universality** of the gospel, namely, who can hear the gospel? The church had to decide if the gospel was intended for Jews alone or for all people.

universality *n.* 普世性

In the beginning, the Christian leader, Peter, took the traditional position that the message of Jesus was for Jews alone. His view was challenged by Paul of Tarsus. For Paul, Jesus' message was for all people, Jews and non-Jews alike. It was Paul's ideas, not Peter's, that directed the future of the young church. Paul was the most important figure in shaping the ways in which Christians understood and explained their faith. In fact, Paul is second in importance only to Jesus in the history of Christianity. The New Testament reports that Paul undertook three **missionary** trips, with amazing success. By the time Paul died around 67 AD, he had founded many churches throughout the eastern half of the Roman Empire; small groups of Christians were meeting on a regular basis throughout the empire. Paul wrote a number of letters to these early churches and some of these became an important

missionary *n.* 传道

part of New Testament.

Over time, the close links between Christianity and Judaism gave way to a complete break, in part because of their conflict over whether Jesus was the Messiah. In the beginning, Christians worshipped at Jewish gatherings. Eventually they either **withdrew** of their own will, or were barred by the others (Jews) from attending. This separation from Judaism had several results. One was that majority of the Christians stopped following the Jewish Law. Christians also began to hold worship services on Sunday (the day of the Resurrection) instead of Saturday (the Jewish **Sabbath**) to emphasize the break with Judaism.

withdraw *v.* 退出
bar *v.* 禁止
Sabbath *n.* （犹太教）安息日

Although, towards the end of the first century, Christianity and Judaism developed into two different religions, their histories remain **intertwined**, and their faiths have similar views of God, **revelation**, creation, man's duty to God and other men, sin, **salvation**, and the final judgment. In fact, they are so closely related that scholars sometimes refer to the Judaeo-Christian tradition.

intertwine *v.* 交织
revelation *n.* 神的启示
salvation *n.* 救赎

The Christians' belief in one God led them to reject the Greco-Roman gods and the Cult of the Living Emperors, just as the Jews did. For this reason, many Romans viewed Christians with suspicion. They doubted the Christians' loyalty to the state, since honoring the gods and the Imperial Cult was an important element of Roman society. The Christians also spoke of a day when Jesus would return to earth and establish a new kingdom. Many Romans took this as a direct threat to the empire. In the eyes of most Romans, **innovation** in religion was not a good thing.

innovation *n.* 创新

At the beginning, the Roman state was indifferent toward this newly emerging religion. During the first and second centuries, Christians were tolerated by Roman authorities. Occasionally, local governments **persecuted** Christians for refusing to worship the official state gods. The first persecution of Christians in Rome happened after a fire broke out in the city. The emperor, Nero, declared that the fire had been started by Christians. Many Christians were dragged from their homes and put to death. During the third century there were some centrally organized persecutions. The last wave of Christian persecution occurred under the emperor Diocletian. A firm believer in traditional Roman religion, Diocletian had ordered Christian churches destroyed and books burned. He then ordered that all Christian clergy should be arrested. If they refused to worship the state gods, they would be executed. But these persecutions were too short-lived to do much

persecute *v.* 迫害

damage. By the early 4th century, the number of Christians had increased. It was no longer possible to wipe them out through persecution.

Still, the number of Christians was not large. No reliable statistics exist, but most scholars now believe that in the year 300 only 1 to 5 percent of the empire's total population was Christian. Even in the more Christianized eastern half of the empire, no more than 10 percent of the population was Christian. Its numbers were growing, but it seemed unlikely Christianity would ever become the main religion of the empire.

The fate of the Christians changed drastically during the next ten years. Galerius, one of the leaders in Diocletian's four-man rule, issued a **decree** from his deathbed in 311 AD. He declared that Christians could rebuild their churches and **reclaim** their property. He also stated that as long as the Christians respected law and order, they were free to practice their religion. This order was known as the **Edict of Toleration.**

decree *n.* 政令
reclaim *v.* 要求收回
Edit of Toleration 宽容诏令

A more important event for Christians happened one year later on a battlefield near Rome. Constantine was fighting over control of the western empire. Before the battle, Constantine said that he had a vision (or a dream). He saw a huge cross in the sky. At the same time, he heard a voice saying, "By this sign, you shall conquer." Constantine made a promise: if he won the battle, he would become a Christian. The next day, Constantine's army defeated the enemy. Although Constantine was not **baptized** until the end of his life, he issued the famous **Edict of Milan** in 313 AD officially tolerating Christian belief. After being appointed as Augustus by the Senate, Constantine gave Christians complete freedom of worship in the provinces he ruled—Italy, Spain, and North Africa. Once he defeated his rivals and united the empire in 324, Constantine extended these freedoms across the empire. Constantine used his power to raise the status of Christianity. He declared Sundays to be a Christian holiday. He used state funds to build Christian churches. He had the Christian cross **inscribed** on Roman coins. He appointed Christians to important positions in government. Although Constantine did not ask the non-Christians to change their religion, many Romans did **convert** to Christianity. Many did so out of sincere religious feelings, but others became Christians in order to further their careers in Constantine's government.

baptize *v.* 洗礼
Edit of Milan 米兰诏令
inscribe *v.* 雕刻
convert *v.* 皈依

In 380, Theodosius I made Christianity the official state religion. During his reign, the Christian emperor ordered the building of several magnificent churches and monuments in Constantinople. Theodosius tried to unify the empire's religion. He made all non-Christian worship illegal. Although Theodosius' successors were more tolerant of other religions, no other religion could compete with Christianity in importance.

Growing slowly in the first century, Christianity took root in the second, and had spread quickly and widely by the third century. Why was Christianity able to attract so many followers? First of all, the Christian message offered hope to the Roman world. In Christian belief, Jesus' death and resurrection offered mankind salvation, that is to say, if one believes in Jesus and follows the teachings of the Bible, his soul will be saved and he will rise up from the dead when Jesus returns from heaven to this world. In the declining Roman world full of injustice and suffering, such a prospect offered people meaning and purpose for their lives. It gave them a personal relationship with God and a link to higher worlds. People found hope and comfort in the spiritual kingdom, beyond the simple material pursuits of their everyday lives.

Second, the Romans were used to multiple religious practices and they could accept Christianity as simply another mysterious eastern religion. At the same time, they could accept Christianity even more easily, as Jesus had been a human figure, not a mythological one. Moreover, Christianity was not restricted to men or to any specific group of people. It was open to everyone, regardless of age, sex, skin color or social class.

Finally, Christianity satisfied the human need to belong. Christians formed communities and groups. Members of the Christian community met regularly to worship God together and to assist each other as well as non-members. The vast, **impersonal** and remote Roman state could never offer such daily contact and such a deep sense of belonging.

impersonal *adj.* 缺乏人性的

4.5 The New Contours of Fourth-Century Christianity

contour *n.* 轮廓

From their earliest days onwards, Christians disagreed on things, including on the **interpretation** of the Bible. Different regions of the empire also tried to preserve a sense of their separate identities by preferring different **theological** formulas. When Christianity was still a minority religion, Christians managed to control their religious and regional divisions in order to present a united front against non-believers. But once Christianity became the official religion of the

interpretation *n.* 诠释

doctrinal *adj.* 教义的

Roman Empire, unity gave away to bitter doctrinal disputes. These disputes and splits greatly transformed the doctrine, organization and outlook of Christianity. In the late 4th century Christianity was a very different religion from the one persecuted by the early Roman emperors.

Arians 阿里乌斯教派
Athanasians 阿塔纳休斯教派
Trinity *n.* 三位一体

One early bitter dispute was between the **Arians** and **Athanasians** over the nature of the **Trinity**. The Arians were followers of a priest named Arius (280—336) and were the more intellectual group. Under the influence of Greek philosophy, they argued that Jesus as the Son was created by God, and therefore the Son could not be equal with the Father. For them, Jesus Christ (the Son) was not of the same **substance** as God and was therefore not coeternal (existing together for ever) with Him. In sharp contrast, the followers of St. Athanasius argued that even though Christ was the Son, he was fully God. For them, Father, Son, and Holy Ghost were all absolutely equal and composed of an identical substance. After long struggles Athanasius's side won out and the Athanasian doctrine became the Christian **dogma** of the Trinity, as it continues to exist today.

substance *n.* 物质

dogma *n.* 教条

The debate over the Trinity was followed by other doctrinal quarrels during the next few centuries. These are too numerous to explain in detail here. The results of these quarrels were significant. For one thing, they gradually fixed the dogmas of the Catholic faith. The faith began to take on a clearly defined form which was **unprecedented** in the history of human religion. For another, the gradual **accumulation** of mainstream dogmas and doctrines suppressed differences in opinion. Anyone who differed from a certain mainstream position would be excluded from the community and often persecuted as a **heretic**. In the subsequent history of Christianity this concern for doctrinal **uniformity** was both the strength and a weakness of the Church.

unprecedented *adj.* 前所未有的
accumulation *n.* 积累

heretic *n.* 异端
uniformity *n.* 统一性

hostility *n.* 敌对

The doctrinal disputes also deepened regional **hostilities**. In the 4th century Christians in the West and in the East grew further apart from each other. Religion widened what were originally regional economic and administrative differences. Generally speaking, the imperial government had stronger control over the East, and after 476 AD there were no Roman emperor in the West at all. The result was that in the East the emperor had considerable religious authority and control, while in the West the future of relations between State and Church was more open.

Within the Church itself, its organization became more and more complex and hierarchical. At the time of St. Paul there was only one distinction, between **clergy** and **laity**. As Christianity gained popularity

clergy *n.* 神职人员
laity *n.* 一般信徒

and expanded within the Roman Empire, a hierarchical organization developed within the ranks of the clergy. As Christian organization was centered in cities, over time one **bishop** in each important city gained authority over all clergy in its region. Bishops who were based in the largest cities, such as Rome, Jerusalem, Constantinople, and Alexandria would enjoy even higher rank. They became known as the **archbishops**.

bishop *n.* 主教

archbishop *n.* 大主教

The city of Rome was of central importance for Christians. Peter was the first bishop of Rome; Paul also spent years preaching there. The bishop of Rome gradually became recognized as overall leader of the Christian church, not only in the Western Roman Empire but throughout the growing Christian community. This seemed natural; according to the New Testament (Matthew 16: 18—19), Peter had been chosen by Christ as the **shepherd** and rock of the Church. As Christ gave him the keys of the kingdom of heaven, Peter had the power to punish people for their sins and even to **absolve** them from guilt. Christian believers could thus accept that all bishops of Rome were successors of Peter and enjoyed the same authority and prestige.

shepherd *n.* 牧羊人

absolve *v.* 宣布……无罪

In the 4th century, successive bishops of Rome claimed authority over the Church. The political situation of the Empire also strengthened their claim. After the capital was moved to Constantinople there was seldom any effective imperial control over the West. In 445, Emperor Valentinian III issued a decree commanding all Western bishops to submit to the **jurisdiction** of the bishop of Rome.

jurisdiction *n.* 管辖范围

The Church's hierarchical organization helped it to conquer the Roman world. Its influence massively increased as the Western Roman Empire declined and finally collapsed in the 5th century. In every Western city, there was a bishop supervising and answering the practical and spiritual needs of the large number of followers. The well-organized Church was able to take over many functions of government in the West, and help preserve order in an age of chaos. But the new emphasis on administration also had negative effects: as the Church developed its own administrative structure it inevitably became more concerned with worldly affairs, and distant in spirit from the simple Christianity of the early days.

Not everyone was pleased with the changes in the Church. The clearest reaction to the **secularization** of the Church was the spread of **monasticism**. Monks seek to live pure Christian lives by withdrawing from society in favor of a **secluded** existence. The Monastic movement

secularization *n.* 世俗化

monasticism *n.* 隐修生活方式

secluded *adj.* 与世隔绝的

emerged in the third century and became popular in the fourth. More and more Christians took refuge from the increasingly organized and hierarchical Church. The males who did this were called **monks** and females were called **nuns**. Today we often think of monks as groups of priests who live in a community, but in the early days, monks were not priests but **laymen**; monks customarily became priests only later during the Middle Ages.

monk *n.* 修道士
nun *n.* 修女
layman *n.* 平信徒

Although the word monk means "alone", most monks and nuns lived in communities. At first many lived in desert caves. They tried to completely control their flesh so they could dedicate themselves to God. They practiced **celibacy** (refusal of marriage and all sexual intercourse), lived in simple rooms with few comforts, and possessed only enough clothing to protect themselves from the weather. They spent hours and days fasting (going without food), praying, and worshiping. To control the flesh some took drastic measures, such as starving or **castrating** themselves. They often felt they were involved in a life and death struggle with the devil. Living a simple and often tough life away from mainstream society, they eagerly awaited the return of Christ and his establishment of the kingdom of God on earth.

celibacy *n.* 立誓不婚，禁欲
castrate *v.* 阉割

5. Transformation of the Roman World: the Germanic Invasion

In 410, the **Visigoths** (a Germanic tribe) sacked Rome. These invaders looted gold and jewelry from the temples and palaces, stole precious artworks, and took goods from the shops. In 455, another Germanic tribe, the **Vandals**, also sacked Rome. Finally, in 475 a Germanic military leader named Odoacer led his tribesmen to Rome and defeated the Roman army. Odoacer now controlled the armed forces of Italy; the western Roman Emperor was arguably nothing but a **puppet**. Historians today usually regard 476 as the end of Roman self-rule in Western Europe, after nine hundred years. Who were the Germanic peoples? Why did they move into the Roman world? What was their relationship with the Romans? What role did they play in the fall of Rome?

Visigoth *n.* 西哥特人
Vandal *n.* 旺达人
puppet *n.* 傀儡

5.1 Early German-Roman Relationship

Most Romans saw the Visigoths, and the other Germanic tribes that overran the Roman Empire, as barbarians, stupid and crude. But they were not. Admittedly, they had a very different society to that of

Rome. They did not build great cities, as the Romans did. Instead, they lived in small groups scattered about the land. They raised crops and **livestock**. Each tribe had rules and **taboos** that were passed down from one generation to the next, but they lacked the body of written laws that held Roman society together. Disputes were settled by councils of elders, not courts. These peoples did not have plays or literature as the Roman did, but they enjoyed story-telling and poetry. In many ways, their culture was not very different from that of the early Romans.

livestock *n.* 家畜
taboo *n.* 禁忌

The greatest strength of the Germanic tribes lay in their attitude towards battle and heroism. They cherished combat, considering it nearly **divine**. Germanic boys were raised to be warriors, not merchants or government officials. They competed in numerous hunting and battle skill contests. The strongest warriors usually became the tribe's leaders. Few leaders were physically weak; most were men of strength, courage and strong will. Their people were not paid soldiers, but blood relatives, unshakably loyal to their tribe and leader.

divine *adj.* 神圣的

Germanic peoples had been known to the Romans since the 2nd century BC. Despite their many social differences, the two groups had co-existed relatively peacefully. Many Germans had been allowed to cross the border and settle on Roman soil as farmers or slaves. Some even became paid soldiers in the imperial army. The Germans admired what was worthy in Roman civilization and the Romans admired the physical strength and the simplicity of values of the Germans.

Toward the end of the 3rd century this peaceful co-existence changed. The starting-point was the arrival of a nomadic Asian people, the **Huns**. Defeated by the Chinese imperial army, the Huns swept across the plains of Russia into Eastern Europe. These people were as **fierce** as the Germanic tribes, and even more numerous. As the Huns migrated westward toward present-day Romania, the territory of the Visigoths (a Germanic tribe), the Visigoths were forced to flee into the Eastern Roman Empire. The Germanic peoples put increased pressure on the northern **Rhine** and **Danube**, the frontiers of the Roman Empire.

Hun *n.* 匈奴人
fierce *adj.* 凶猛好斗
Rhine *n.* 莱茵河
Danube *n.* 多瑙河

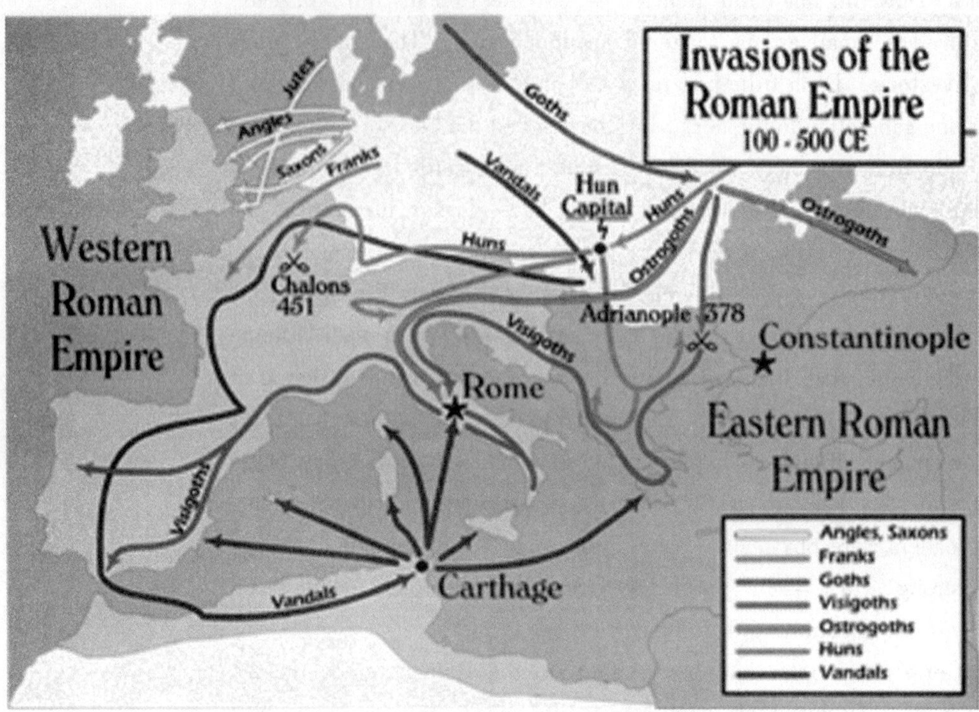

Map 17 Germanic invasions of the Roman Empire

At first, the Visigoth leaders asked the Romans directly for help. They offered to help the Romans fight the approaching Huns if the Romans would allow them to cross the Danube and settle in Roman territory. The Roman soldiers at the border knew the Visigoth offer was a valuable one. They immediately reported it to the Eastern Roman emperor, Valens, who was a former soldier. Valens considered it a wise move to get help to fight the Huns, so he granted the Visigoths permission to settle within the empire in return for their military service. Little did Valens know that this decision would set off a series of events, leading directly to the collapse of the western half of the Roman Empire.

Unlike other peoples who had been absorbed into the Roman Empire, the Visigoths did not accept Roman laws or customs. Their alliance with Rome was purely military. They did not participate in the Roman state nor did they expect the Romans to **interfere** with their lives. The Romans also treated them badly after their arrival. The new settlers were forced to live on small pieces of poor-quality land and pay very high prices for food. This **discrimination** turned the Visigoths from potential friends of the Romans into their enemies. In 378, the Visigoths rebelled against Roman rule. In a battle near Adrianople,

interfere *v.* 干涉

discrimination *n.* 差别对待，歧视

they defeated the Roman army. The emperor Valens died in the battle.

Emperor Valens' successor, Theodosius, made peace with the Visigoths. He allowed them self-rule and strengthened the military alliance. Theodosius used the Visigoths not only to resist the Huns, but also to fight the Persians and other Germanic tribes. When civil war broke out in 383, Theodosius enrolled even more Visigoths to fight the army of Maximus, who had taken control of the western half of the empire. With the Visigoths' help, Theodosius won. By the time he died in 395, however, more than half of the Roman army was made up of Germanic tribesmen. Future emperors would soon find out that the Germans were an army within an army; they were more loyal to their tribal leaders than to the Roman state.

After Theodosius died, the Visigoths elected one of their nobles, Alaric, as their king. By uniting behind one **representative**, the Visigoths believed that they could force Rome to give them more and better land. This demand was ignored by the Romans, so Alaric used his army to start a rebellion. However, this time the Visigoths were not lucky. Each time the two forces clashed, the Visigoths were defeated. Finally, the Roman commander Stilicho, who was himself a member of another Germanic tribe, allowed the Visigoths to **retreat**.

representative *n.* 代表

retreat *v.* 撤退

At the same time, Stilico was fighting another war with the east Roman emperor over control of the **Balkans**. Worse still, in 406 four Germanic tribes started to cross the Rhine into Gaul. With two wars already on his hands, Stilicho was unable to stop their invasion. Once the Rhine border was broken, new Germanic tribes poured into Gaul, including the **Franks** and the **Burgundians**. As these tribes settled in Gaul, they pushed the Visigoths further south. Angry with Rome, Alaric of the Visigoths led his people to the capital for **revenge**. There was nothing anyone could do. The warlike Visigoths defeated the Roman army and entered the capital in 410.

Balkans *n.* 巴尔干地区

Frank *n.* 法兰克人

Burgundian *n.* 勃艮第人

revenge *n.* 报复

After this, the western Roman army was so weak that the emperor had no choice but to include more Germanic tribes in it. When the Huns led by Attila invaded Gaul in 451, the Visigoths and the Franks helped the Romans to defend it. By the middle of the 5th century, the armies of Gaul, Spain, and Italy were under the control of Germanic soldiers.

In 475, a Roman general named Romulus Augustus **deposed** the western Roman emperor Nepo. The emperor in the east had no choice but to ask the barbarian forces to help him. A German military leader

depose *v.* 废黜

named Odoacer led his tribesmen to Rome and defeated the forces of Romulus Augustus. In 476, Nepo was restored to the throne, but only in name. Odoacer actually controlled the armed forces of Italy. Historians usually take the year 476 as the end of the Western Roman Empire.

5.2 The Rise of German Kingdoms and the Fall of the Western Roman Empire

Over time, a number of Germanic kingdoms were created within the Western Roman Empire. The Visigoths were the first to establish a Germanic kingdom on Roman territory. As mentioned above, in the beginning they were only granted permission to settle as rewards for military service. But when the Romans treated them poorly, the Visigoths rebelled and crushed their Roman rulers. In 378, they killed Valens, the emperor of the Eastern Roman Empire. They then attacked Italy and sacked Rome in 410. Later, the Visigoths moved across Gaul and created the first kingdom in **Aquitaine** in 418. They then moved into Spain, where they founded a second kingdom that lasted until the Muslim invasions of the 8th century.

Aquitaine 阿基坦（今法国西南部，南接西班牙）

As the Visigoths approached Italy in the early 5th century, the Western Empire responded by moving troops to Italy from Britain and from the Rhine and Danube frontiers. With frontier defenses weakened, further political disasters followed. In 407, England fell to the **Angles**, **Saxons** and **Jutes**, and these three Germanic tribes created a dozen small kingdoms there. The Vandals, **Sueves** and **Alans** also crossed the Rhine. Moving westward, they swept into **Gaul** (roughly modern France and Belgium) and made their way southwards into Spain. The Vandals arrived in Spain in 411 and their settlement, although short-lived, gave the region of **Andalusia** (from Vandalusia) its name. The Vandals then entered North Africa where they established their capital and built a naval fleet, with which they **raided** Sicily and Italy. The word ***vandalism*** **commemorates** their **atrocities**. Another Germanic tribe, the Burgundians moved into south eastern Gaul (today's **Provence**).

Angle 安格鲁人
Saxon 撒克逊人
Jute 朱特人
Sueve 苏维汇人
Alan 阿兰人
Gaul 高卢地区

Andalusia 安达卢西亚（位于西班牙最南端）
raid *v.* 侵袭
vandalism *n.* 打砸抢
commemorate *v.* 纪念
atrocity *n.* 暴行
Provence 普罗旺斯

Another Germanic people, the Franks migrated in a very different way to the other Germanic tribes, and as a result created a greater and longer-lasting kingdom. They did not abandon their homeland when they set out for new territory. From the lower Rhine, they gradually expanded into northern Gaul late in the 5th century. Under the leadership of Clovis (rule 481—511), the various Frankish tribes were united, which gave them the military strength to depose the last Roman governor in Gaul, drive the Visigoths from Aquitaine into Spain, absorb the Burgundian Kingdom and eventually conquer most of Gaul. Within the next three centuries, other Franks continued conquering all of Gaul and reunited Western Europe.

By the end of the 5th century, the Roman imperial government had come to an end in the West. That half of the Roman Empire was thoroughly overrun by Germanic peoples, who seized political power and established independent kingdoms throughout Western Europe. The Visigoths occupied Spain, the Burgundians held Provence, the Ostrogoths ruled Italy, and the Franks held Gaul, which would become the longest-lasting state established by any of the Germanic tribes: France.

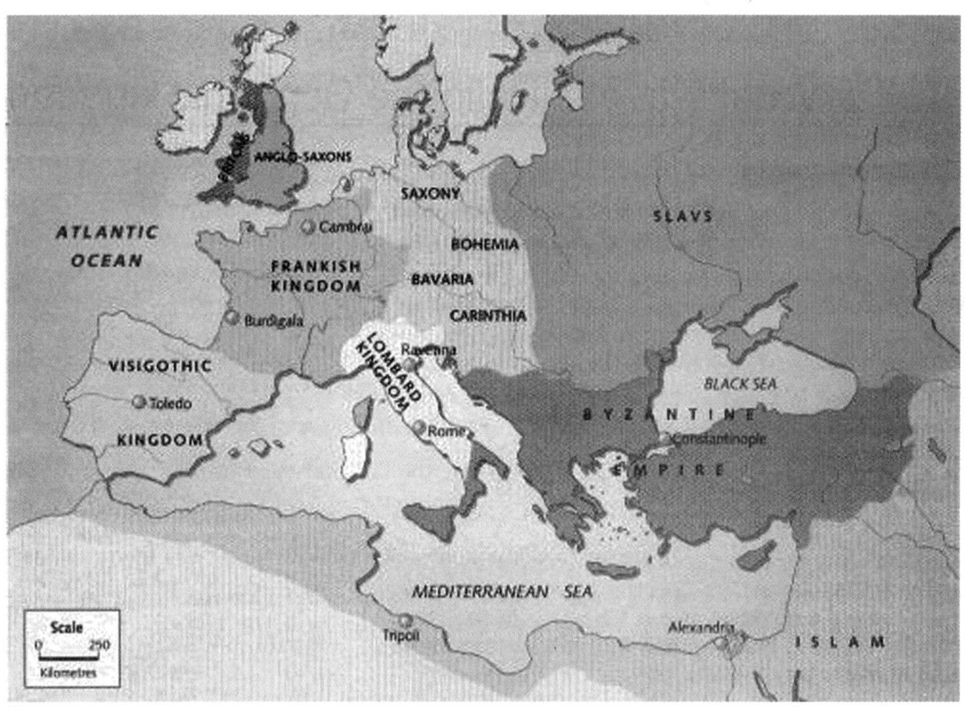

Map 18　Main Germanic kingdoms

Although the Germanic tribes sped up the breakup of the Roman state in the West, the imperial government survived in the Greek-speaking Eastern half. In 527, the Eastern Emperor Justinian (rule 527—565) launched an **offensive** from Constantinople to re-conquer the most important western territories which had been lost to the Germanic peoples. His armies conquered the Vandals in North Africa in 533.

offensive *n.* 进攻

From there, they invaded Italy where, after almost twenty years of warfare, they **dethroned** the Ostrogothic king. Justinian succeeded in restoring imperial rule but the revival was short-lived. In 568, a new Germanic tribe, the Lombards, entered Italy and conquered the northern plain that still bears their name, Lombardy.

dethrone *v.* 废黜

The largest Germanic tribe probably numbered no more than 100 000. Despite their relatively small numbers, the invaders were able to invade Western Europe because they were militarily superior to the Roman army, the frontiers were poorly defended, and because they likely met with little opposition from the Roman population. In 440, a Christian priest wrote that the "Romans were far worse enemies than their enemies outside, for although the barbarians had already broken them, they were being destroyed even more by themselves."

Despite their history of success in handling relations between the many other ethnic groups within the empire, the Romans made some serious mistakes when dealing with the Germanic peoples. The greatest strength of the Empire had been its ability to make people living within its borders feel as though they belonged to the world's first superpower. The ancient Roman poet Claudian wrote:

> "Rome alone has taken the conquered to her **bosom** as a mother, not a ruler, and she has cherished the whole human race under one name. She has called the conquered her citizens and gathered them in the **wide-flung** net of her devotion. To her way as peacemaker we all owe the fact that the newcomer may live as in his own land, that a man may change his home, that men may go to **Thule** for pleasure and penetrate what once was fearful wilderness, that we may think of the Rhine or the **Orontes**, that we are all one people."

bosom *n.* 怀抱

wide-flung *adj.* 撒开的

Thule *n.* 极北地区

Orontes 奥伦特斯河（经黎巴嫩、叙利亚和土耳其南部进入地中海）

The leaders of Rome failed to convince Germanic invaders that they were part of "one people." The Germans were never **assimilated** by the Romans. Instead, they kept their own social structures and values. As military allies or paid soldiers of the Empire, the Germanic warriors were never required to serve directly in the imperial army. They only obeyed their own leaders on the battlefield. As a result, Germanic tribes never felt any real loyalty to Rome. Nor were they required to pay the usual taxes to the state treasury. Therefore, Spain and Gaul, which had once contributed to Roman wealth, simply stopped doing so. The lack of tax income from these lands greatly weakened the empire. It was

assimilate *v.* 同化

Romans' inability to create a bond with the invaders that led to the ruin of the Western Roman Empire. The fall of Rome into the hands of the barbarians was a political, not a military, failure.

6. Conclusion

The ancient Romans had created one of the largest empires in history. From its early days, Romans had shown a remarkable capacity to assimilate different cultures within the lands they conquered. The Empire's expansion was both a process of Romanization of the foreign lands and a transformation of the Roman world itself. The rise and development of Christianity was the best **illustration** of such a two-way interaction. Although historians use the year 476 to mark the end of the western Roman Empire, few people at the time even noticed what happened to the last western Roman emperor. Roman culture in fact continued to influence the rise and fall of the Germanic kingdoms in Western Europe. The new Germanic rulers continued to use many Roman laws and traditions. Many of the invading Germanic tribes were Christianized. In the eastern Roman Empire, the mixture of Roman and Greek elements created the magnificent Byzantine civilization.

exert *v.* 发挥

Undoubtedly, the civilization of Rome exerted a great influence on latter-day European and "Western" culture. The styles and techniques of Roman buildings were kept in the Middle Ages and are still used for many governmental buildings in the West. The legal systems of nearly all continental European countries still **incorporate** most of the basic elements of Roman law. Throughout the Middle Ages, Latin was used as a *lingua franca* among many nations. As a language Latin never really disappeared. It survives to this day in its "purer" form as the language of the **Catholic** Church. When combined with neighboring Germanic and Celtic languages, it gave rise to many modern Romance languages: Italian, French, Spanish, Portuguese, and Romanian. Latin also influences modern Germanic languages: German, **Dutch**, **Afrikaans**, Norwegian, Swedish, Danish and Icelandic. English can be seen as a **hybrid** of the Germanic and Romance families, and shows strong influences from Latin.

incorporate *v.* 吸收

Catholic *adj.* 天主教

Dutch *n.* 荷兰语

Afrikaans *n.* 南非荷兰语

hybrid *n.* 混杂物

Rome's history of conquest, at least in Europe and around the Mediterranean, was imitated, but never matched, by later leaders from **Charlemagne** to **Napoleon**. Today many people in the West still believe that they share cultural similarities with the Romans. Roman

Charlemagne 查理曼大帝

Napoleon 拿破仑

history is often compared to the history of Great Britain in the 19th century or the United States in the 20th. The dream that one can not only conquer, but in doing so create a *Pax Romana*—a vast area of peace, prosperity and common ideas—continues to **inspire** successive generations of Europeans. It is impossible to understand modern Europe with its Union without knowing about the Roman Empire.

Exercises

Ⅰ. Terminology: choose the suitable term to fill in the blanks.

A. ressurection	B. gladiator	C. decree	D. Imperial Cult
E. monasticism	F. Trinity	G. celibacy	
H. lingua franca	I. tetrarchy	J. Messiah	
K. sacrifice	L. Colosseum		

- Both Constantine and Diocletian ruled by official commands called __1__, and both relied on a vast network of spies to control the empire.
- The worship of Roman leaders became known as the __2__.
- After the Roman conquest, the Jews believed that a leader called __3__ would unite the Jews and destroy their enemies, leading to an era of peace and harmony.
- The Romans believed they had to ask permission of the spirits before taking anything from nature. For example, if a person wanted to cut down a tree, he was required to leave an offering of an animal by killing it in a ceremony. This offering is called a __4__.
- The way monks in the Middle Ages sought to live pure Christian lives by withdrawing from society in favor of a secluded existence is called __5__.
- All Catholic nuns practise __6__ by seeing themselves as brides of Christ.
- Although Latin was the official language of the Roman Empire, in the eastern part of the Empire Greek remained the __7__.
- __8__ was the most spectacular stadium built for gladiator contest by the Roman state.
- For Catholic Christians, the __9__ comprises the Holy Father, the Holy Son, and the Holy Spirit.
- The miracle of __10__ convinced Jesus' followers that He was indeed the Son of God.
- In the __11__ designed by emperor Diocletian, he co-ruled the Roman Empire with his three colleagues.
- To entertain themselves, the Romans forced prisoners of war or criminals to fight as __12__.

Ⅱ. Decide whether the following statements are true (T) or false (F).

1. Although people from different regions in the Roman Empire spoke different mother tongues, they could always communicate with strangers either in Latin or in Greek, the official languages of the Empire. (　　)

2. In the Roman Empire, a foreign soldier could earn citizenship through his military service. (　　)

3. The Roman government offered free food to the poor people to achieve greater harmony. (　　)

4. Earlier Christian leaders all agreed that the gospel was intended for Jews and non-Jews as well to hear. (　　)

5. Roman state financed gladiator shows to make people forget social and economic problems. (　　)

6. The Romans were extremely intolerate of foreign religions. (　　)

7. At the age of 30, Jesus started to preach; but he had no intention to create a new religion. (　　)

8. That the early Christians suffered systematical persecution by the Roman authorities was a myth. (　　)

9. After Christianity became the state religion of the Roman Empire in the 4th century, all other religious beliefs disappeared. (　　)

10. Like the Jews, the Christians rejected the Greco-Roman gods and the Cult of the Living Emperors. (　　)

11. When creating their own kingdoms, the Germanic tribes rejected all Roman institutions. (　　)

12. Since the 3rd century the eastern half of the Roman Empire was more prosperous than the western half. (　　)

13. The Roman Empire was the first true superpower in human history. (　　)

Ⅲ. Multiple choices: choose the answer that best completes the statement or answers the question.

1. Roman religion is ________.

A. borrowed entirely from the Greeks

B. not purely Roman

C. invented by Romans

D. borrowed from the Egyptians

2. Major changes in Roman religious life were mainly a result of ________.

A. foreign cultural invasion　　B. trade and commerce

C. territorial expansion of Rome　　D. interest in spiritual matters

3. Which of the following was NOT true about the early Christians?

A. They defied the Roman political authorities.

B. They accepted the idea that emperors were divine.

C. They banned paganism.

D. They suffered religious persecution.

4. Which of the following is NOT true about Emperor Constantine the Great?

A. He concentrated power in his own hands.

B. He made Christianity the state religion.

C. He abandoned Rome as the imperial capital.

D. He tolerated all religions in the Roman Empire.

5. Christianity originated from ________.

A. Turkey　　B. Palestine

C. North Africa D. the Western Europe

6. Jesus lived in the ________.

A. early 1st century B. late 1st century

C. early 2nd century D. late 2nd century

7. Constantine the Great declared ________.

A. Christianity as the only religion B. toleration for all religions

C. the end of Imperial Cult D. paganism illegal

8. Beginning in the 4th century, army units of German were ________.

A. suppressed by the Romans

B. eliminated by the Romans

C. welcomed into the Roman Empire to defend the Romans

D. driven by the Romans to settle in depopulated areas

9. The economic success of the early Roman Empire was mainly achieved by ________.

A. small farmers B. slaves

C. serfs D. Roman legions

10. The Roman Empire reached it largest territorial extent during the reign of ________.

A. Julius Caesar (46—44 BC) B. Octavian (27 BC—14 AD)

C. Trajan (98—117 AD) D. Constantine the Great (306—337 AD)

11. The gladiator show indicated Romans' love for ________.

A. adventure B. fun C. violence D. entertainment

12. Starting from the reign of which Roman emperor such jobs as bakery and military service became hereditray?

A. Octavian. B. Diocletian. C. Constantine. D. Theodocius.

13. All of the following statements about slavery in Roman society are true EXCEPT ________.

A. Wars provided the Romans with many new slaves

B. Slavery was a highly productive economic system

C. The offspring of slaves would automatically be slaves

D. Like in Sparta, slaves in Rome were public goods

14. In the year ________ Christianity became the official religion of the Roman Empire.

A. 311 B. 313 C. 324 D. 380

15. Constantine the Great named the new imperial capital ________.

A. Contantinople B. Byzantium C. New Rome D. Istanbul

16. Which people below were not of Germanic origin?

A. Anglos. B. Huns. C. Goths. D. Saxons.

17. Of all the Germanic kingdoms created in the late Roman time only the kingdom of ________ grew into a powerful one in the Middle Ages.

A. Franks B. Vandals C. Visigoth D. Burgundians

18. In the year of ________, Constantine the Great issued Edit of Milan which officially

made Christianity legal.

A. 311 B. 313 C. 324 D. 380

19. The ethnic origin of Jesus was ________.

A. Greek B. Roman C. Hebrew D. European

20. The second founding father of Christianity was ________.

A. St. Peter B. St. Paul C. St. Athanasius D. St. Augustine

21. Which one of the following statements about the condition of the Jews during the Roman time was NOT true?

A. In 64 BC Pompey conquered Judea and turned it into a Roman province.

B. The Jews had to pay heavy tax, but they enjoyed limited self-rule.

C. Faced with Roman persecution, the Jews had to worship the Roman emperors as gods.

D. The Jewish people hoped for salvation led by a prophet.

22. Three of the following statements are true with the early experience of Christianity. Which one is the exception?

A. Unlike the Jews, the early Christians of the Roman Empire suffered persecution.

B. Christianity was not the official religion of the Roman Empire until the 4th century.

C. Christianity spread in the cities of the empire, first in the east and later in the west.

D. It was Constantine's toleration for all religions that brought new life to Christianity.

23. Christians considered pagan gods ________.

A. as demons B. as humans C. incredible D. supernatural

Part Ⅱ The Medieval World

"The Middle Ages" (adjective: "medieval") is a term invented in the present day. It covers around a thousand years of European history, after the fall of the Western Roman Empire in 476, and followed by the Early Modern Era. History is commonly divided into three eras: Classic, Medieval, and Modern. To understand the Middle Ages better, we can subdivide them into: (1) Early Middle Ages (500—1000); (2) High Middle Age, also called by some Central Middle Age (1000—1300); and (3) Late Middle Age (1300—1500).

Some see the Middle Ages as an energetic and innovative time, one when classical culture was resurrected. Others see it as a cultural slump after the golden days of Greece and Rome. It is true that there are certain features common to the whole of this thousand-year period, but at the same time medieval Europe developed in a highly complex way involving many different ethnic groups of people and many gradual changes in social structures. We thus cannot generalize too much about the Middle Ages. Even their start and end are ill-defined: did the Middle Ages start in 476 at the final sack of Rome? What about the continuation of the Roman Empire in Constantinople until its conquest by the Ottomans in 1453? When did the "Renaissance" start? 1400? 1350? 1200? 1100?

It is wrong talk of a single "European" culture during this period. European history until the 14th or 15th century witnessed frequent disruptions of populations, migrations, and multiculturalism. New migrations were constantly and continually changing the cultural face of Europe, spreading new languages, social customs, and religions.

Perhaps the best way to define the Middle Ages is as the period during which Europe's tense and often disruptive multiculturalism standardized into a single, clearly definable cultural entity. At the start of the Middle Ages, there were European cultures. At their end, it was finally possible to use the term "European culture or European civilization" without adding a plural "s". The Middle Ages are the story of that transition.

Chapter 5
The Early Middle Ages (500—1000)

CHAPTER OUTLINE

1. Introduction
2. The **Byzantine** Empire
3. The Rise of **Islam**
4. The Western Christian World
5. Conclusion

Byzantium *n.* 拜占庭
Islam *n.* 伊斯兰教

FOCUS QUESTIONS

1. What factors accounted for Byzantium's stability and prosperity?
2. What were the main characteristics of the Byzantine civilization?
3. What role did Islam play in the Arabian expansion?
4. What was feudalism?
5. In what ways did the Byzantine and Islamic civilizations contribute to the civilization in Western Europe?

1. Introduction

The Early Middle Ages lasted from the 5th century until the High Middle Ages (1000—1300). In 476, Germanic invaders gave a final blow to the **crumbling** Roman Empire. Over the next two centuries it broke up into three quite different **spheres**. The eastern part of the old Roman Empire continued as the Byzantine Empire; in Western Europe, various Germanic tribes established their own kingdoms; meanwhile, the Muslim Arabs took control of parts of southern Europe as well as Persia, Palestine, and North Africa. While each of these three had its distinctive languages and ways of life, they saw continuing influence from the Roman intellectual and legal tradition. The Early Middle Ages is largely a story of the **rivalries** and interactions between these three civilizations.

crumbling *adj.* 摇摇欲坠的
sphere *n.* 范围
rivalry *n.* 竞争

The Byzantine civilization, a direct **descendant** of the Roman Empire, was Greek-speaking. Although its **successive** emperors in Constantinople no longer had any effective control over Western Europe,

descendant *n.* 后裔
successive *adj.* 相续的

strategically *adv.* 从战略而言
retain *v.* 保留
fuse *v.* 熔合
preserve *v.* 保全
Renaissance *n.* 文艺复兴
Arabic *n.* 阿拉伯语
assimilate *v.* 同化
cosmopolitan *adj.* 国际化
dynamic *adj.* 有活力
vernacular language 本国语
Carolingian Dynasty 卡洛林王朝
accomplishment *n.* 成就
lag behind *v. pr.* 落后于

they still claimed to be the rightful rulers of Rome and the West. The Byzantine Empire lasted till 1453. **Strategically**, it helped to stop Islamic expansion into Western Europe; Culturally, the Greco-Roman civilization was **retained** and **fused** with the Christian tradition. Byzantium helped **preserve** a large amount of classical texts and knowledge, as well as Roman bureaucratic and imperial practices, and thus paved the way for the **Renaissance** in Western Europe in the 14th century, as well as future legal and administrative traditions.

The Islamic civilization was **Arabic**-speaking. In the 7th century a new religion, Islam, unified the various Arab tribes into one people. These Muslim Arabs created an expansive empire and **assimilated** a multitude of other peoples. Drawing on the philosophy and scientific knowledge of the Hellenistic world and the literature and art of Persia, the Arabs enjoyed the most **cosmopolitan** and **dynamic** civilization of the early Middle Ages, many elements of which survive today.

Western Christian civilization was rooted in Latin, but it was also influenced by the Germanic and Romance (Latin-derived) **vernacular language** groups.① Although the Germanic kingdoms did not have imperial ambitions (except for the short **Carolingian Dynasty**), they borrowed Roman ideas of law and local government. Western Europe in the Early Middle Ages was politically violent and unstable with no central power; in terms of intellectual and literary **accomplishments**, it **lagged** far **behind** the Byzantine and Islamic worlds; and it was also the least economically developed of the three parts of the ex-Roman Empire. Despite great political and social struggles, the Church remained the most important player.

In what ways were the Byzantine and Islamic civilizations different to Western Europe? How did the interaction of these three transform European culture? In this chapter, we will examine each of these three civilizations in the Early Middle Ages.

2. The Byzantine Empire

Back in 285, the Emperor Diocletian had divided the Roman Empire into two. After the fall of the Western Roman Empire in 476, the eastern

① 今天欧洲各国本国语基本分属日耳曼语和罗曼语两大语系。日耳曼语系的欧洲语言包括英语、德语、荷兰语、丹麦语和瑞典语。自拉丁语衍生的罗曼语系包括法语、意大利语、葡萄牙语和西班牙语。英语虽划属日耳曼语系，但和其他日耳曼语相较而言，受到罗曼语传统的影响更为深广。

half developed its own distinctive **identity**, later known as the "Byzantine Empire" or "Byzantium". Its capital was **Constantinople**, founded on the site of the ancient city of Byzantium (today's **Istanbul**). The development of the Byzantine Empire was different to previous empires, as it was not created by invaders but was a continuation of the Roman Empire; indeed, at the time people did not speak of the "Byzantine Empire" but simply regarded themselves as Romans, **citizens** of the Eastern Roman Empire.

identity *n.* 认同感

Constantinople 君士坦丁堡

Istanbul 伊斯坦布尔

citizen *n.* 公民

In 610, Emperor **Heraclius** (rule 610—641) changed the official language from Latin to Greek, which was already the language used by most of the population. While this was a historic **milestone**, Byzantine history in fact started earlier. Although the Byzantine Empire was a successor to the Roman state, it had already gradually developed features different to the earlier Greco-Roman culture. These dated back at least to the earlier era of Emperor **Justinian.**

Heraclius 赫拉克利乌斯

milestone *n.* 里程碑

Justinian 查士丁尼一世

2.1 The Reign of Justinian (rule 527—565)

Justinian is generally considered the first great Byzantine emperor. During his reign, thinking and art began to look more distinctively "Byzantine" than "Roman". When he took power, Justinian was determined to restore the Empire to its past glory. He considered it his duty to re-conquer all the former Roman territories lost to the "barbarians". He never personally took part in military campaigns, which were in large part carried out by his capable general **Belisarius**. This goal finally appeared to be achieved in 552. Byzantium briefly regained control of much land in North Africa, Italy, and parts of Spain.

Belisarius 贝利撒留

Justinian (at the center) is sometimes called "The Last of the Romans". He was dynamic and ambitious. When he became emperor in 527, he set out to reclaim much of the western Empire, reform Roman law, and rebuild Constantinople.

Justinian's military campaigns were very costly; Just the recovery of Italy cost the empire more than 10 000 kilogram's of gold. A huge **burden** was thus placed on the Byzantine people, who deeply resented the heavy taxes which funded these campaigns. Although the reconquests of Italy and the southern Spanish coast greatly enlarged the empire, these proved short-lived. Only three years after Justinian's death (568), the greater part of Italy was lost to the invading **Lombards**, and within a century and a half Africa and Spain were forever lost. By then, it was clear that the new Byzantine emperors would have to concentrate on retaining the East. Western Europe would have to be abandoned.

burden *n.* 负担

Lombard *n.* 伦巴族人(属日耳曼民族)

Law had been a cornerstone of Roman rule, and one of Justinian's major accomplishments was the preservation and systematization of a large number of existing Roman laws. As supreme legislator and judge, Justinian ordered scholars to **codify** all Roman laws into one **coherent** body of law. The result was the famous ***Justinian Code*** (*Codex* in Latin), completed in 534. These laws included (1) the Twelve Tables, which were the original laws of the Roman Republic, (2) all imperial **edicts** from the time of the emperor Hadrian (rule 117—138) up to 533, (3) the writings of Roman **jurists** on previously-judged civil and criminal cases, and (4) 160 new laws, mainly relating to **contracts** and personal matters. The Codex emphasized the absolute legislative power of the emperor and helped strengthen Justinian's rule.

codify *v.* 编集成典

coherent *adj.* 前后一致的

Justinian Code《查士丁尼法典》

edit *n.* 诏令

jurist *n.* 法学家

contract *n.* 合同

Scholars also made a shortened version of the Codex, the "Institutes". Used as textbook, the Institutes helped develop the system of law and legal training for the rest of Byzantium's history. The Codex as well as the Institutes were also used in Western Europe, firstly by the Roman Catholic Church as a model for church law; later, from the 12th century onwards, the Codex became the strongest single influence on Western Europe's courts and law schools. Eventually it replaced most of the traditional laws on the Continent.

Justinian was also a **prolific** builder. A devout Christian, he ordered several splendid new churches to be built. He also strengthened the borders of the empire, from Africa to the East, through a system of **fortifications**. His engineers built an underground water storage system for Constantinople. He also restored cities damaged by earthquakes or wars and built a new city near his place of birth.

prolific *adj.* 高产的

fortifications *n.* 防御工事

An impressive building **enhances** a ruler's prestige, and serves as an important symbol of the empire. The best **visual** expression of

enhance *v.* 提升

visual *adj.* 视觉的

Justinian's imperial power is the Church of the Holy Wisdom, known as Hagia Sophia. In an effort to make the city of Constantinople impressive, Justinian ordered its rebuilding in 532, hiring the best architects, mathematicians and craftsmen from the whole empire.

Completed in 537, Hagia Sophia was the perfect representation of Byzantine civilization, a mixture of different cultural elements. Its balanced proportions reflected Greek influence; its engineering required the skills of Roman artisans; and its dramatic **dome** roof, a sphere set on a **rectangular** base, was inspired by Persian practices. Hagia Sophia is famous for its massive dome filled with **mosaics**, a unique feature of Byzantine art. For nearly one thousand years this remained the largest **cathedral** in the world. Hagia Sophia changed the history of architecture.

dome *n.* 穹顶
rectangular *n.* 长方形
mosaic *n.* 镶嵌画，马赛克
cathedral *n.* 教区总教堂

Built in 360, the original Hagia Sophia was burnt down in a riot in 532. Over the next 5 years Justinian rebuilt it into the largest cathedral in the world. Its huge dome is surrounded by smaller, smaller domes. The four slender towers are minarets (宣礼塔), added in 1453 when Constantinople fell to the Turks and Hagia Sophia was turned into a mosque (清真寺). In 1931, it stopped being used as a mosque and became a museum.

For centuries Hagia Sophia remained the centre of eastern Christianity. Faced with its **majesty**, worshipers felt as if time was suspended. Its huge, shallow dome still dominates the skyline of Istanbul. When Justinian went up to the **altar** to deliver his first speech, he declared, "Glory be to God, who has thought me worthy to finish this work. **Solomon**, I have **outdone thee**!" Majesty and splendor, softened by beauty, light and God's love—this was the message of the emperor. He saw himself as God's representative on earth, and declared Hagia Sophia to be better than the first Temple of

majesty *n.* 雄伟、壮丽
altar *n.* 祭坛
Solomon *n.* 所罗门王
outdo *v.* 超越
thee *n.* （古）你

the Jews in Jerusalem, built by the legendary king Solomon.

2.2 Economy and Society in Byzantium

During most of the Middle Ages, the Byzantine economy was the most advanced in Europe and the Mediterranean. Some say that before the rise of the Arabs in the 7th century, Byzantium had the most powerful economy in the world. Western Europe overtook it only in the late Middle Ages. Visiting foreign travelers were impressed by the wealth and luxury of the capital, Constantinople.

The Empire's economy relied primarily on agriculture. Agricultural development was slow but continuous, from the 5th to early 14th centuries. 90% of the Empire's population was **rural**. Among them, there was a clear distinction between tenants and free peasants. Free peasants usually owned small plots of land, and paid taxes to the state. Tenants lived on the **estates** of large landowners; they paid not taxes, but rent, paid to the landowner. From time to time the central government broke up large estates to make sure there were enough tax-paying free peasants. It worked continuously up to the 12th century to limit the amount of land an individual could own.

rural *adj.* 农村的
tenant *n.* 佃户
estate *n.* 私有土地

Another important part of the economy was trade. **Grain** and silk were major **commodities**. A popular luxury **fabric**, silk was in great demand. In the beginning, Byzantium relied on expensive imported silk. For more than a thousand years the Chinese government had kept a **monopoly** on silk production and **executed** anyone who tried to give away the secret of how it was made. Travelling to China to buy silk was long, dangerous, and expensive, especially as it involved passing through Persia which imposed heavy taxes. The turning-point, however, came during Justinian's reign when two Christian monks **smuggled** silkworm eggs out of China in their hollow bamboo canes. After they brought these back, a large local silk industry was able to develop in Byzantium, greatly reducing the price. This and other industries helped make Byzantium a major international trading centre.

grain *n.* 粮食
commodity *n.* 商品
fabric *n.* 织物
monopoly *n.* 垄断
execute *v.* 处决
smuggle *v.* 偷运

The city of Constantinople was a trade **crossroads**: trade routes ran northwards, southwards, eastwards and westwards, to Europe, West Asia, India and China. Constantinople's position as the most important trading centre in Europe was only slowly taken over by the Republic of Venice in the Central Middle Ages (1000—1400).

crossroads *n.* 十字路口

Most merchants in Constantinople were merely **middlemen**, and

middleman *n.* 经纪人，掮客

they used other people, including Jewish merchants, to transport their goods beyond the city. Many people were employed in manufacturing goods from imported raw materials. Byzantine artisans produced glassware, linen and wool cloth, gold and silver jewelry, **icons**, boxes and **badges inlaid** with precious stones for ceremonies. Most of the administrative and military **budgets** were paid for by a **customs duty** of 10%, which was imposed on all imports and exports.

The prestige and wealth of the capital **dazzled** visitors. Foreigners were left in **awe** of Byzantine power. An ambassador from **Kiev** once exclaimed, "For on earth there is not such splendor or such beauty, and we are at a loss how to describe it." During the first crusade (1095—1099), when Western Europeans saw the great city for the first time, one military leader explained:

> "... Those who have never seen Constantinople **marveled** greatly at it, for they could not **conceive** that the world held so mighty a city, when they saw the height of the walls, the great towers enclosing it all around, the splendid palaces, the lofty churches (the number of which was so great that none could believe it who had not seen it with his own eyes), and the length and breadth of the city that lorded it over all others. And know yet hat there was no man so bold that his flesh did not creep thereat, and this was no wonder."

Constantinople was also the political and intellectual center of the Middle Ages. Scholars came from far away to its libraries filled with Greek, Latin, Persian, and Hebrew documents. Byzantine scholars could read and write in classical Greek. Tutors taught classical Greek to wealthy merchants, aristocrats and candidates for jobs in the bureaucracy. Byzantine monks and scholars engaged in debates and tried to **reconcile** Jewish and Christian teachings with those of Plato, Aristotle, and other Greek philosophers. Many Greek and Roman traditions spread from Byzantium to the Muslim world, while ideas from the Muslim, Indian, and Chinese worlds travelled in the opposite direction. The classical knowledge and foreign ideas accumulated in Byzantium were an essential foundation for the later Renaissance.

Little information is available on how the average person in the Byzantine Empire lived. Historical materials show that merchants must have prospered. Peasants had a harder time because there was a high

icon *n.* 圣像
badge *n.* 徽章
inlaid *adj.* 镶嵌着……的
budget *n.* 预算
customs duty 关税
dazzle *v.* 令人目眩
awe *n.* 惊叹
Kiev 基辅(今乌克兰首都)
marvel *v.* 感到惊讶
conceive *v.* 构想出
reconcile *v.* 调和

tax on land. Collecting taxes was the bureaucrat's most important job. There were taxes on individuals, called a head tax, and on land, buildings, and services. One method for collecting taxes was to group people together and make each person responsible for the taxes of everyone else in the group.

mobility *n.* 流动性

Social **mobility** was possible, at least in theory. Individuals from any background could improve their status through success in the bureaucracy, army, trade, or the Church. The Imperial law said that as long as at least one son maintained the same family occupation, the others could seek different jobs. In practice, however, little mobility actually occurred. Byzantium was most prosperous when the empire had a large free **peasantry**, farming small plots of land. Some were able to build a surplus and move up the social scale, but most remained at the **subsistence** level and were often threatened by big landlords.

peasantry *n.* （集合名词）农民

subsistence *n.* 糊口

2.3 Byzantine Culture

Byzantine culture did not develop out of nowhere. Instead it developed slowly out of its "parent" civilizations, ancient Greece and Rome. Many have said that Byzantium was Greek in its culture, Roman in its government, and Christian in its religion.

2.3.1 Religion: Iconoclasm

Iconoclasm *n.* 反圣像崇拜运动

As the state religion, Christianity dominated Byzantine life. The greatest proof of its influence was probably the successful **conversion** of many **Slavic** peoples, especially those of Russia. Strong religious passions sometimes result in religious disputes; the Byzantines had religious disputes that could result in arguments, fighting and even death. This led to periods of conflict, the most violent one being the **Iconoclastic** movement in the 8th century.

conversion *n.* 皈依

Slavic *adj.* 斯拉夫的

iconoclastic *adj.* 反对圣像崇拜的

The iconoclastic controversy concerned the use of icons (drawings or paintings of Christ, the Virgin Mary, or saints) as aids to worship. Gazing at images and kissing them was an important part of worship in Byzantium, and church buildings contained many icons. Believers told of being miraculously **cured** by merely touching one. Shops hung them up to protect their goods, and soldiers carried them into battle. The use of icons in Byzantium was partly a Greek and Persian legacy. The early Christian Church had no problem with it.

cure *v.* 治愈

disapprove *v.* 反对

However, some church leaders began to **disapprove**. They were sensitive to the fact that Judaism and Islam were totally opposed to images. Emperor Leo Ⅲ (rule 671—741) decided that icons were a

form of idol worship and that they **violated** the Ten Commandment which **prohibited** "**graven** images". In 726 he launched the iconoclastic movement to destroy and forbid icons. In 754 the son of Leo, Emperor Constantine V passed a law to prohibit worship of icons.

idol *n.* 偶像
violate *v.* 违背
prohibit *v.* 禁止
graven *adj.* 雕刻的

Byzantine society became divided on the matter. Some church leaders maintained that the worship of religious objects was **legitimate**. The gaze from an icon caused "deep thoughts" and allowed the worshipper to communicate directly with the saint. Bishops argued that "simple folk" needed them, and that it would be hard for Byzantine Christians to give them up. Other church leaders said it was impossible to portray the divine nature of Christ by representing him in human form. They argued that worship without images was purer.

legitimate *adj.* 合理的，合法的

The Iconoclastic controversy was **resolved** in the second half of the ninth century by a return to the worship of images, but the conflict had some **profound** consequences. One was the destruction of a large amount of religious art. Today only a small amount of Byzantine art survives. A second consequence was a serious split between the eastern and western halves of the Christian Church. The pope in Rome, who had usually been a close ally of the Byzantines, strongly opposed the movement against icons during the 8th century. This led to worsening relations between East and West.

resolve *v.* 解决
profound *adj.* 深远的

Other matters also started to divide the Christian community. The Roman Church used Latin, while the Eastern Church used Greek. Then there was the dispute over the *filioque*. In the East people taught and believed that the Holy Spirit came "from the Father". In the West people said that the Holy Spirit came "from the Father *and from the Son*" (*filioque* in Latin). Furthermore, Greek monks shaved the front of their heads, whereas Western ones shaved a **circlet** on the top. The Greek Church used **leavened** bread in worship, whereas the Western church used unleavened bread. The biggest single issue was the power relationship between the pope of Rome and the **patriarch** of Constantinople.

circlet *n.* 小圈
leavened *adj.* 发酵的
patriarch *n.* 最高级主教

The Christian community gradually split into two groups. Neither wished to see a division in the Christian world, but physical separation and other differences produced two different traditions. The two groups formally separated in 1054 into the **Eastern Orthodox Church** and the **Roman Catholic Church**. This event was known as the Great **Schism** in the history of Christianity.

Eastern Orthodox Church 东正教教会
Roman Catholic Church 罗马天主教会
schism *n.* 分裂
classicism *n.* 古典主义
literate *adj.* 识字的

2.3.2 Byzantine Classicism

Besides their strong commitment to Christianity, the Byzantines also respected and preserved their ancient Greek heritage. **Literate** Byzantines read many works by the ancient Greek poets (Homer) and playwrights (Aeschylus, Sophocles, and Euripides). Byzantine scholars studied the philosophy of Plato and Aristotle, and writers imitated the prose of Thucydides. An educated Byzantine could quote Homer at will.

The influential University of Constantinople, founded in 425, trained not just clergy but also civil servants. It offered courses in law, medicine, philosophy, mathematics, astronomy, and rhetoric, and welcomed a wide variety of European and Muslim students. Major intellectual leaders of the time, such as **Cyril** (827—869) who developed the Cyrillic alphabet were among its graduates.① The university's courses were heavily reliant on classical Greek literature. Thanks to the Byzantines, a large body of Greek classics has been preserved and survives today.

Cyril 西里尔

Compared to the Muslim and Western European worlds, Byzantium offered exceptional opportunities for women. Although girls from aristocratic or rich families did not go to school, they received relatively good education at home from private tutors. **Eloquent** women were frequently praised when they engaged in philosophical debates. Byzantium had a number of female literary figures and physicians.

eloquent *adj.* 能言善辩的

By and large, Byzantine classicism emphasized tradition rather than innovation. This was essentially a good thing, but it did mean that some aspects of Byzantine culture were heavily **imitative**. Byzantine authors took the classical authors as near-perfect models, and often merely tried to imitate their style and even content, with only some small changes in detail. The Emperor Justinian even shut down the Athenian philosophical academy that had existed since Plato's day, declaring that everything worth knowing was already known. While emphasizing classical ideas and forms, the Byzantines neglected the Greek scientific and mathematical tradition. Byzantine culture was extraordinarily **sophisticated**, but can be seen as lacking in **originality** in this regard, especially when compared to the literature, science and technology that developed at the same time in Western Europe.

imitative *adj.* 模仿的

sophisticated *adj.* 高级的

originality *n.* 原创性

① 据认为9世纪时西里尔与其兄Methodius向斯拉夫人传教，共同创造西里尔字母，成为俄语、保加利亚语等斯拉夫语字母的本源。

2.4 What Made the Byzantine Empire Strong

Constantinople's **strategic** position, along with its trade and **manufacturing**, were important reasons for the empire's success. Other factors included the strength of the central government, its efficient military, and its relationship with the Church.

strategic *adj.* 战略的
manufacturing *n.* 制造业

While the Athenians experimented with direct democracy and Roman leaders attempted a republican form of government, the form of **governance** that emerged in Byzantium was centralized authority under an absolute monarch. Large territories ruled by emperors, not independent city-states, became its model. The prestige of the emperor was a major reason for Byzantium's strength. Unlike the Roman Empire, Byzantium had a **hereditary** monarchy. Though there were sometimes disputes over **succession**, most of the time the emperor remained the ultimate source of authority. He made the laws, judged the people, and led the army. The bureaucracy was responsible directly to him, as was the army. His civil service included capable ministers of internal and foreign affairs, public revenues, military funds, and imperial estates. Top bureaucrats, **recruited** from the leading families, answered directly to the emperor and he could fire them at will.

governance *n.* 治理
hereditary *adj.* 继承式的
succession *n.* 继位
recruit *v.* 征募

Perhaps the emperor's most important source of authority came from the Church. Besides his royal powers, the emperor served as a "friend" and "imitator" of Christ; he was the head of the Church, as well as the state. He thus appointed the **patriarch** of Constantinople and other important Church officials. The imperial government often made decisions on religious **doctrine**. The clergy gave sermons in support of the policies of the emperor, who was said to be carrying out the will of God. Anyone who opposed him was guilty of **blasphemy**, normally a religious offense. The only legitimate way to challenge the emperor was to **allege** that he had strayed from the godly path.

patriarch *n.* 大主教
doctrine *n.* 教条、教义
blasphemy *n.* 亵渎上帝的言行
allege *v.* 指称

Besides its strong central control and economy, the Byzantine Empire maintained a well-trained professional army of about 120 000 men, half of whom were **cavalry**. To ensure that there were enough soldiers, in the 7th century the government organized the provinces into themes (military districts) and appointed military generals to rule them. Generals had **jurisdiction** over both defense and civil administration. Free peasants were given land in return for military service. Legally every man in the empire had to serve in the military, but many rulers distrusted their subjects and preferred to accept money instead. They used the money to hire an army of well-paid

cavalry *n.* 骑兵
jurisdiction *n.* 权限

mercenary *n.* 雇佣军
navy *n.* 海军
lethally *adj.* 致命地
diplomatic *adj.* 外交的
maneuver *n.* 运作，手段
greed *n.* 贪婪
vanity *n.* 虚荣
bribe *v.* 贿赂
pit *v.* 使相斗
mistreat *v.* 亏待
cohesion *n.* 团结

mercenaries. Because soldiers received good salaries, it was relatively easy to hire them.

The Byzantine **navy** was also a formidable force. By the middle of the 7th century, ships were armed with firebombs that sailors hurled at enemy vessels. A weapon known as "Greek fire" even burned on water, and was **lethally** effective against the enemy's wooden ships. The Byzantine navy controlled the Mediterranean until the 9th century.

In diplomacy, the Byzantines were skillful. Byzantium faced almost constant pressure from nomadic groups on its borders, as well as the vigorous expansion of Muslim Arab forces. Because the borders were vast and using the army was expensive, Byzantine rulers attempted to resist these threats with **diplomatic maneuvers** and by handing out favors. They assumed every man had a price, and appealed to the **greed** or **vanity** of local rulers, often **bribing** them with riches or impressive titles. At other times they **pitted** feuding tribes against one another. Often diplomacy proved more effective and cheaper than fighting.

Byzantium worked hard to bond together the many different peoples in its empire. Many were Greek speakers and felt loyal to the Greek cultural tradition. The authorities encouraged everyone to speak Greek and practice common customs, but they never forced people to do so, nor did they **mistreat** those they conquered. Instead, they tried to win people over by welcoming their leaders into the bureaucracy if they learned to speak Greek, letting the upper classes intermarry with the Byzantine elite, and permitting them to take positions in the military. Commerce was another reason for Byzantium's tolerance; it required frequent interaction with outsiders. Influences from many areas came to the capital, and the Byzantines wanted to make foreigners feel at home.

Thus Byzantium had strong central control, flourishing trade, a well-trained and motivated army, a large tax base, and tolerance and **cohesion**. For more than a thousand years, Christian Constantinople was the richest, the most beautiful, and most cultivated city in Europe. Byzantium, along with the Islamic states, not only carried on Greek and Roman learning but also made important new contributions.

3. The Rise of Islam

By the 7th century, west Asia was divided between two major powers: the **Sassanids** (224—651), **heirs** to the earlier Persian Empire, and Byzantium. Both used religion to unite their ethnically and linguistically diverse **subjects**. Both were predominantly monotheistic: the Sassanids, following the Persian tradition, made **Zoroastrianism** the state religion; Byzantium was Christian. Monotheism strengthened and helped **integrate** their diverse populations. The two empires often fought, deploying thousands of soldiers and advanced military technologies. In 619 the Sassanids conquered Egypt and threatened Anatolia (the Asian part of today's Turkey), but in a series of battles from 623 to 627, Byzantine forces reclaimed those areas. As they exhausted each other in bloody battles, neither the Sassanids nor the Byzantines paid much attention to the Arabian Peninsula, an area they regarded as uncivilized.

Sassanid *n.* 桑萨王朝
heir *n.* 继承者
subject *n.* 臣民
Zoroastrianism *n.* 波斯拜火教
integrate *v.* 使成一体

Sometime around 610 in the town of **Mecca**, a merchant's son named **Muhammad** began to preach. He called upon the Arabs to **repent** and reform. Gradually he developed a new religion that he called Islam. The impact was explosive. Within a century after his death, his followers not only unified the Arabian Peninsula but also conquered other territories. The **adherents** of Islam, known as Muslims, created an Empire larger than the old Roman Empire and spread their religion across a much wider population.

Mecca *n.* 麦加
Muhammad 穆罕默德
repent *v.* 悔改
adherent *n.* 信徒

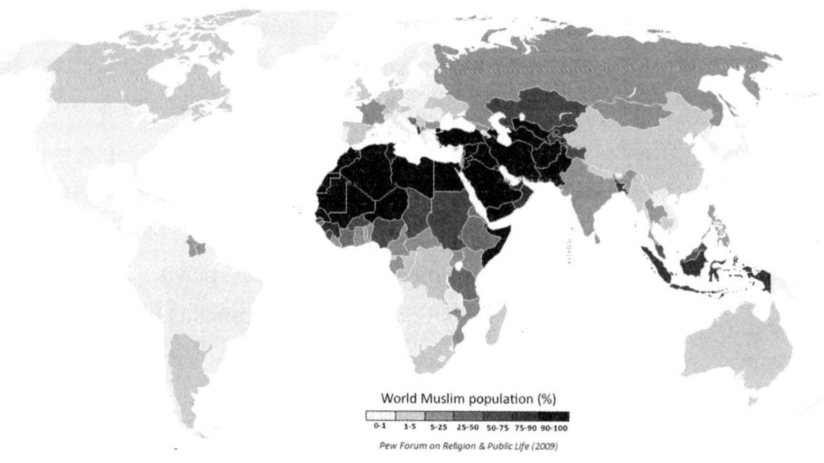

Map 19 World Muslim Population

Today Islam is the second-largest religion in the world (1.5 billion) and the fastest-growing. Islam is the main religion in the Middle East, North Africa, and large parts of Asia.

3.1 Arabia Before Muhammad

The Arabian Peninsula, the homeland of the Arabs, has some of the hottest and driest deserts of the world. As most of the land was too dry for agriculture, the Arabs raised sheep and camels and led a nomadic lifestyle, moving their animals from **oasis** to oasis in search of water. The harsh environment often led to rivalries over grassland and water. Although all nomads, Arabs lived in separate tribal groups and were fiercely loyal to their own blood relatives. Wars were fought over honor and social status. The Arabs were actively engaged in land and sea trade. They transported goods to and from the Indian Ocean via their Red Sea and Persian Gulf ports, overland through Palestine to Constantinople, and east to Central Asia and China. Important trade centers developed around oases.

oasis *n.* 绿洲
oases (*pl.*)

Before the rise of Islam, Arabia was backward and underdeveloped. The neighboring Byzantine and Sassanid empires had little interest in extending their rule over Arabian territories. Instead, they often hired the Arabs as **mercenaries**, **caravan** guides, and assistants for trade. In the second half of the 6th century, conflicts and wars between the Byzantine and Sassanid empires made Arabia a safe transit route for trade between Africa and Asia. Various towns grew out of these trading centers. The most prominent one was Mecca.

mercenary *n.* 雇佣军
caravan *n.* 旅行队，篷车

Mecca not only lay on a crossroads of major trade routes, but also had long been a local religious centre because it housed the Kaaba (Arabic meaning "cube"), a **sacred** black **meteorite**. Arabs called it "the black stone that fell from heaven in the days of Adam" and considered it the holiest **shrine** in Arabia. Every year, Arabs from near and far would come on a ***hajj*** (pilgrimage) to worship the Kaaba. They would offer sacrifices of sheep and camels, place images of their local gods and goddesses around the Kaaba, and then circle it seven times and kiss it, in the hope of heavenly blessing. Traders in and around Mecca guaranteed a month of peace in order to encourage pilgrims to visit the shine. This arrangement allowed Mecca to develop not only as a place of pilgrimage, but also as a trading centre.

sacred *adj.* 神圣的
meteorite *n.* 陨石
shrine *n.* 神龛
hajj *n.* 朝觐

Pre-Islamic Arabs were polytheists. Individual tribes had their own gods or goddesses. They also believed that divine spirits lived in trees, stones, springs, and wells. Besides these gods, the Arabs shared a common belief in a supreme deity called Allah, the creator and the giver of rain. Although Allah was believed to be present everywhere, he was not directly involved in everyday concerns. For more everyday matters, Arabs would pray to their tribal gods or goddesses. Allah thus had associates and companions, sons and daughters. This **conception**, however, was soon to be changed by the rise of Islam.

conception n. 观念

3.2 The Founding of Islam

The founder of Islam, Muhammad ("highly praised" in Arabic), was born in Mecca in 570. His parents died when he was very young, after which he was raised by a grand-uncle. After supporting himself with a variety of jobs, Muhammad was hired by Khadija, a rich widow, to manage her caravan business. The young Muhammad soon proved himself to be gifted at business. Khadija soon proposed to and married him, and for the rest of her life Khadija was Muhammad's only wife.

Other, monotheistic communities could also be found in Arabia: Christians, Jews, and ZoroastrianAs Muhammad travelled with Khadija's caravans to and from Syria and Mecca, he met many of these followers of centuries-old monotheistic faiths. He also accompanied caravans to **urban** areas where he probably asked people about their beliefs.

urban adj. 都市化的

When he was forty Muhammad had a life-changing experience. According to Muslim legend, while he was sleeping in a cave, the angel Gabriel appeared and told him that he had been selected to receive inspiration from God. There is only Allah, Gabriel told Muhammad, one all-powerful, all-knowing, and all-merciful God. In a way Allah resembled the same concept that Jews identify as Yahweh and Christians call God.

When Muhammad reported what he had heard, Khadija immediately took him seriously. She encouraged him to share the message with others. Over the next 22 years, Muhammad continued to receive messages from Allah via Gabriel and he continued sharing these **revelations** with others. Khadija supported Muhammad whenever others questioned his revelations. Muhammad founded a new monotheistic religion, Islam. Khadija was the first person to **convert** to Islam.

revelation n. 神示

convert v. 皈依，改信

As Muhammad accumulated supporters, he also found enemies. Some rich and powerful individuals felt **offended** by his **advocacy** of equality and sharing. His emphasis on monotheism also threatened the trade which had developed around the pilgrimage to the Kaaba in Mecca. Some Meccan aristocrats united against Muhammad and his followers. In 622 when a **delegation** from Yathrib invited Muhammad to make peace among the fighting tribes of that city, he and his followers slipped away from Mecca to Yathrib. This group of **migrants**, known as hegira, was the first Muslim community. This event is so important that Muslims

offend v. 反感

advocacy n. 提倡，主张

delegation n. 代表团

migrant n. 移民

Medina *n.* 麦地那
prophet *n.* 先知
integrity *n.* 正直
idol *n.* 偶像
pardon *v.* 宽恕
pledge *v.* 发誓
submission *n.* 服从
illiterate *adj.* 文盲的
Qur'an *n.*《古兰经》
recitation *n.* 背诵
rhymed *adj.* 押韵的
prose *n.* 散文

made 622 the first year of their calendar: A. H. 1 (anno hegira), and Yathrib was renamed **Medina**, "the city of the **prophet**".

Impressed with Muhammad's **integrity**, business skills, and ability to negotiate among tribal factions, the people of Medina looked to him for leadership. Muhammad became not only a prophet but also a political leader. He was also a skilled general and his army, which grew to over ten thousand men, brought many tribes under its control and united most of Arabia. In 630 Muhammad and his forces returned to Mecca, took control of the city, destroyed the polytheistic **idols** around the Kaaba, and **pardoned** his former enemies. The residents of Mecca became Muslims and accepted Muhammad's leadership. Before he died in 632, most of the tribes in the peninsula had either converted to Islam or **pledged** their loyalty to him.

3.3 The Religious Teachings of Islam

Islam in Arabic means "**submission**" and a person who submits to Allah is a Muslim. The faith of Islam calls for absolute submission to Allah, the Creator. Islam is thus a strict monotheistic religion, similar to Christianity and Judaism. Muslims believe that Muhammad was God's last and greatest prophet, but Muhammad never claimed any supernatural powers. He reminded people that he was an **illiterate** trader, a mouthpiece through whom Allah spoke to the people. Muhammad said that the great angel Gabriel told him that many prophets had been selected by God, including Abraham, Moses, and Jesus, and that now he was the last prophet chosen to spread God's word. Gabriel also asked Muhammad to help all people submit to Allah's will.

Muhammad preached that everyone was equal before Allah and the rich should share with the poor. Eventually everyone would face a final day of judgment. Those who had submitted to Allah would go to heaven, where they were promised gardens with flowing rivers as their eternal home. Those who had not submitted to Allah would be condemned to hell.

In the years after Muhammad's death, his followers tried to write down the messages Muhammad had received from God. These writings make up the **Qur'an**, the holy book of Islam. The word Qur'an means **recitation**. Muslims believe that the Qur'an contains the very words of God, and that Muhammad was God's mouthpiece. There are 114 chapters in the Qur'an, all written in Arabic in **rhymed prose**. The Qur'an is considered to be the most beautiful writing in the Arabic language. For Muslims the Qur'an is divine revelation, the closest any human being can come to Allah. It should not be translated because this would **distort** the original meaning; for a true understanding, it should be read in Arabic. The early spread of Islam through one single language gave believers a further common identity.

distort *v.* 扭曲

Islamic law **prescribes** five **principles** which all Muslims must follow. Muhammad spoke of Islam as a **brotherhood** of all believers, and the five principles help deepen this identity. The first principle requires Muslims to make the statement of faith by saying "There is no god but Allah, and Muhammad is his messenger." If a person makes this statement three times in **succession**, he or she becomes a Muslim. The second principle requires Muslims to pray at five precise times every day, facing Mecca. Muslims try to gather together to perform the noon prayers on Friday. The third principle requires Muslims to give zakat (money or gifts) to help the poor and the suffering. This is part of their concept of "brotherhood". The fourth principle requires Muslims to observe a month-long **fast** every year. From sunrise to sunset during the month of **Ramadan**, Muslims consume neither food nor drink. They break the fast each evening as the sun sets. The last principle of Islam is the hajj, a pilgrimage to the holy place of Mecca. No matter where they live, Muslims are expected to go on the hajj at least once during their lifetime if they can afford it.

prescribe *v.* 规定
principle *n.* 原则
brotherhood *n.* 手足情
succession *n.* 连续
fast *n.* 斋戒
Ramadan *n.* 斋月

Pilgrims walking around the Kaaba (2007) According to Islamic tradition, the Kaaba was built by the first man, Adam and is believed to be the first building ever built on earth. Inside the Kaaba, the Black Stone is located at the eastern corner. All Muslims face the Kaaba during their daily prayers, wherever they are in the world.

3.4 Conquest of Islam

Uniting the Arabic tribes was **critical** in the early years of Islam, but this **cohesion** did not come easily. Tribes, like other family-based groups, often challenge each other, and loyalty to one individual leader can suddenly end when the leader dies. In order to prevent the community from falling apart after his death, Muhammad tried to base

critical *adj.* 关键的
cohesion *n.* 团结

Muslims' loyalties upon their common religious faith instead of individual leaders or tribes. He told them that pledging their loyalty to Allah made them into one brotherhood.

procedure *n.* 程序

caliph *n.* 哈里发

When Muhammad died, the key problem was that he had never established a successor or a **procedure** for picking the next leader. Kings are succeeded by their children, but Muhammad had no son. When he died in 632, some followers supported Abu Bakr, the Prophet's father-in-law, as the next **caliph** (religious and political leader). Faced with widespread opposition, Abu Bakr organized an army to unite the Arabian Peninsula. After two years, the entire peninsula was brought under his control. The young Muslim state was now ready to expand.

offensive *n.* 进攻

The first major **offensive** to extend Muslim rule beyond Arabia was directed at Syria, another Arabic-speaking region. This was a challenge to the Byzantine Empire, which controlled much of the region. The Muslims heavily defeated the Byzantines in several battles, and by 648 Syria was firmly under their control. They also challenged the Sassanid Empire in Iraq. Despite some resistance, the Muslims quickly brought all of Iraq under their control by 642. They then turned to Byzantine-controlled Egypt; discouraged by defeat in Syria, the Byzantines quickly lost Egypt to the advancing Muslim armies.

scatter *v.* 分散
coordinate *v.* 协调
elite *n.* 精英
adversary *n.* 对手

The Muslims rapidly completed their control over the Middle East by the mid—600s. This was made easier as the Byzantine and Sassanid Empires had been weakened by internal conflicts and clashes with each other. Their large armies were **scattered** and poorly **coordinated**. In some areas, the Muslims benefited from the people's dissatisfaction with imperial rule. Most importantly, the Muslim ruling **elite** was well-organized and could build a powerful army, swifter and more skilled than those of its **adversaries**.

The Islamic expansion was interrupted by a civil war from 656 to 661, after which it continued but at a slower pace. Many new conquests took place far away from the Arabian heartland, including North Africa, Spain, Sicily, and western India. A powerful new empire was on the rise, and dominated much of the medieval world. It weakened the Byzantine Empire, created new international trading networks, and established a strong religion over a vast area. The new empire combined Islam with other cultural traditions. In many respects, this Islamic civilization was one of the most advanced and cultured in the world.

differentiate *v.* 区别
conversion *n.* 皈依

It is important to **differentiate** Muslim political control from

conversion to Islam. Just as many successful earlier empires tolerated diversity, Arab rulers, though devout Muslims, tolerated the cultures of people they had conquered, as long as the non-believers **observed** the rules, paid their taxes, and did not revolt. Muslims were especially tolerant of Jews and Christians, whom they called "People of the Book", and protected them as long as they paid a special tax. Muslim Arab leaders modeled their administration on the efficient Persian and Byzantine bureaucratic structures. Local non-Muslim administrators continued to govern faraway areas and collect taxes, so the conquests caused little disruption to everyday life. Most landowners kept their lands.

observe *v.* 遵守

Gradually, more and more non-Arabs converted to Islam. Many factors explain Islam's **appeal**. No doubt some people became Muslims for political or financial reasons; Muslims did not pay the protection tax, although they were expected to donate one-fortieth of their wealth to the community. Some others converted as a result of intermarriage. Some non-Muslim traders or administrators converted in order to help their business or enhance their political fortunes. The fact that Muslims were not allowed to **enslave** fellow Muslims encouraged some slaves to convert.

appeal *n.* 吸引力

enslave *v.* 奴役

Over time, Islam developed into a **universal** religion. It was strictly monotheistic, worshipping only Allah. It was open to all; Muhammad and the revelations in the Qur'an helped believers to gain salvation; the rules were few and easy to understand; and the faith addressed many of the issues people were facing. Islam spread most readily in cities rather than in rural settings, and it was shaped by intellectual elites who interpreted the original messages and developed various rules for living.

universal *adj.* 普世的

3.5 Economy of thc Islamic Empire

The economy of seventh-century Arabia was relatively **primitive**. But after Muhammad's followers continued their expansion, the Islamic world experienced a Golden Age from the mid-8th to the mid-13th centuries. During this period, the Islamic Empire was the world's leading economy, dominated by trade and commerce. Trade already had a long history in the Middle East's many settlements and towns; many of the territories conquered by Arab armies were wealthy and highly **urbanized**. Syria, Egypt, and Persia in particular were at the crossroads of the major trade routes between Africa, Europe, India, and China. **Baghdad** in the 800s and the 900s was the centre of this great empire. All kinds of products could be found in its markets:

primitive *adj.* 原始的，低下的

urbanized *adj.* 都市化的

Baghdad *n.* 巴格达

ruby *n.* 红宝石
ebony *n.* 乌木

rubies, **ebony**, and coconuts from India; donkeys, papyrus and fine cloth from Egypt; silk, paper and marble from China.

The Islamic Golden Age was an age of discovery and exploration. Arab traders and explorers travelled most of the Old World. On land, the Arab caravan traders reached southern Russian, India, and China; by sea, Arab sailors established new trade routes across the Indian Ocean, the Persian Gulf, and the **Caspian Sea**. Muslim traders established an early global economy across most of Asia and Africa and much of Europe. **Intellectual** and economic interaction between regions and civilizations became more frequent.

Caspian Sea 里海
intellectual *adj.* 知识的

One product deserves special mention: paper. Muslims learned papermaking from the Chinese, but quickly became masters of the art. Paper was cheaper to produce, easier to store, and far easier to write on than papyrus. By the early 11th century, paper had become the main medium even in Egypt, the heartland of papyrus production for almost 4 000 years. This shaped many of the characteristic features of Islamic civilization: bureaucratic record keeping, high levels of **literacy**, book production (especially copies of the Qur'an), and **calligraphy**. The Muslims then introduced paper-making to Western Europe in the 13th century, and this was a key driver of the Renaissance.

literacy *n.* 识字
calligraphy *n.* 书法

3.6 Islamic Culture

The culture of the Islamic empire was known both for its religious **sophistication**, and its absorption of multiple cultural heritages. The Islamic conquests brought the empire into intimate contact with older civilizations. Islamic culture successfully **blended** native Arabic elements with Christian, Jewish, Greek, North African, Iranian, Turkish, and even **Hindu ingredients**. Medieval Islamic cultural achievements greatly influenced the Western world.

sophistication *n.* 高度发达
blend *v.* 混合
Hindu *adj.* 印度(教)的
ingredient *n.* 成分

3.6.1 Philosophy and Science

The Arabs were particularly interested in the **intellectual** achievements of the Greeks. Scholars translated and studied Greek classics in astronomy, astrology, mathematics, medicine, **optics**, and philosophy. Muslim philosophers were greatly influenced by Aristotle and Plato, and extensively discussed the relationship between ancient Greek philosophy and Islamic theology. Many tried to **reconcile** the two, but their fundamental religious belief in God's will clashed with the Greek emphasis on the individual's free will. Although Muslim **theologians** strongly emphasized believers' responsibility to choose between good and evil, almost all Muslims agreed that nothing good

intellectual *adj.* 学识的
optics *n.* 光学
reconcile *v.* 调和
theologian *n.* 神学家

could happen unless God actively willed it. Such a **fatalistic** belief contradicted the Greek philosophical emphasis on human reason.

fatalistic *adj.* 宿命的

Islamic philosophers came to different conclusions on the relationship between religion and philosophy. For example, **Al-Farabi** (878—951), known as the Second Aristotle, used Aristotle's ideas to prove the existence of God. Like Plato, he believed it was the philosopher's duty to provide guidance to the state. But his effort to combine Greek philosophy with Islam led him into religious **mysticism**. By contrast, **Al-Ghazali** (1058—1111) bitterly **denounced** Aristotle, Socrates and other Greek writers as non-believers and labeled those who used their methods and ideas as **corrupters** of the Islamic faith.

Al-Farabi 法拉比

mysticism *n.* 神秘主义

Al-Ghazali 加扎利

denounce *v.* 痛斥

corrupter *n.* 腐化者

Another important Islamic philosopher, **Averroës** (1126—1198) found no conflict between religion and philosophy. For him, religion and philosophy were different ways of reaching the same truth. He held that the soul was divided into two parts, one individual and one divine; while the individual soul was not eternal, all humans also shared another common divine soul. Averroës **distinguished** two kinds of Knowledge of Truth. The first kind was based on religious faith and could not be tested, nor did it require training to understand. The second knowledge of truth was philosophy, which could be understood by intellectual development. For Averroës, **theological** truth was often given in a symbolic way and only philosophers could make rational interpretations of its symbolic meaning. Averroës wrote a series of commentaries on the work of Aristotle. Later his works were translated from Arabic into Latin and greatly influenced the way 13th century Christian scholars, including **Aquinas** and **Dante**, read and understood Greek philosophy.

Averroës 阿威罗伊

distinguish *v.* 区分

theological *adj.* 神学的

Aquinas 阿奎纳斯

Dante 但丁

Islamic philosophers were often excellent scientists. Although it might sound strange, Islamic religious teachings played an important role in science. For example, Islam advised Muslims to find ways of using the stars. The Qur'an says: "And it is He who **ordained** the stars for you that you may be guided thereby in the darkness of the land and the sea." The Qur'an also insists on observation, reason and **contemplation**. This led Muslims to develop an early scientific method based on **empirical** observation. They developed observational and **navigational** instruments which created a new astronomy based on observation, rather than philosophy. Muslim astronomers made such accurate observations that most navigational stars today have Arabic names. This observation of the stars also led some to question

ordain *v.* 授予

contemplation *n.* 冥想

empirical *adj.* 实证的

navigational *adj.* 航海的

stationary *adj.* 静止的

Aristotelian notions of a stationary Earth and begin to explore the concept of a moving Earth.

Another important contribution was the Arabic numeral system. This originated in India during the 500s or earlier, then spread to the Islamic world. In the late 1100s, it reached Western Europe via Muslim Spain, and Byzantium only a century later. Before the 1100s, European mathematics followed that of the ancient Romans, with calculations made on an **abacus**, and the results recorded using words, not **digits**. The Arabic system, on the other hand, allows the steps in a calculation to be easily recorded on paper. This was ideal for developing new and complex mathematical techniques, and mathematics and science soon progressed rapidly. It was the Muslims, inheritors of the rich mathematical knowledge of the Greeks, who passed it on to medieval Europe. Today the Arabic numeral system is used worldwide.

abacus *n.* 算盘
digit *n.* 数码

3.6.2 Literature and Art

At the beginning of the Middle Ages, Arabic was a fairly simple language. It was a language of desert nomads, who had little art except for oral poetry. Then it became the official language of the Islamic religion, and soon spread around the Mediterranean. As an international language it soon accumulated an extensive body of poetry and prose. Early poetry emphasized **virtues** such as courage and **generosity**. In the 700s and 800s as the Empire grew, literature flourished. Lyric poetry was especially popular. Muslim poets wrote brilliantly about love and life and showed great imagination in their use of Arabic. Religious poems and poems that praised powerful rulers in a **grandiose** style were also popular. A powerful and virtuous ruler might be described as "a sea of generosity" or "a lion in battle".

virtue *n.* 品德
generosity *n.* 慷慨
grandiose *adj.* 宏伟的

Arabic prose writing began with the Qur'an. Other medieval Muslim writers were interested in recording events and ideas, instead of **fiction**. History and philosophy were popular, as well as **biography** and autobiography. Scholarly discussions were often mixed with stories to **illustrate** an idea. The best-known fictional work from this period is *The Book of One Thousand and One Nights*, also known as the *Arabian Nights*. Mostly a compilation of earlier folk tales, it started in the 10th century and reached its final form by the 14th century. It has been influential in the West since it was translated in the 18th century.

fiction *n.* 小说
biography *n.* n. 传记
illustrate *v.* 说明

Calligraphy and architecture offer the best examples of Islamic art where art is the expression of abstract ideas instead of a simple imitation of nature.

Islamic art includes architecture, **calligraphy**, painting, and **ceramics**. Roman, Early Christian, Byzantine and Persian styles influenced early Islamic art and architecture, whereas there is a clear Chinese influence on Islamic painting, pottery, and textiles. Despite some specific regional peculiarities, certain elements are common to all art forms. These include highly decorated surfaces, patterns of **curving** and often **interlaced** lines, and the use of brilliant colors. Islamic art is a reflection of the social, political, cultural, and religious state of the Islamic world. It usually employed patterns and calligraphy rather than human figures; because many Muslims believe that the depiction of the human form is **idolatry**, a sin forbidden by the Qur'an. There are repetitive elements in Islamic art, such as the use of geometrical floral or vegetal designs, known as the **arabesque**. The arabesque is often used to symbolize the **transcendent**, indivisible and **infinite** nature of Allah.

calligraphy *n.* 书法
ceramics *n.* 陶瓷艺术
curving *adj.* 曲线的
interlaced *adj.* 交织的
idolatry *n.* 偶像崇拜
arabesque *n.* 阿拉伯式花饰
transcendent *adj.* 超验的
infinite *adj.* 无限的

4. The Western Christian World

After the fall of the Roman Empire in 476, Western Europe was very different to the Byzantine and Islamic worlds. For most of the Early Middle Ages, there was no strong central power, and Western Europe's economy **lagged behind** those of the Byzantine and Islamic empires. Politically and linguistically it was **fragmented**; its technology was primitive, and the **infrastructure** left by the Romans—roads, bridges, and schools—was collapsing. Violence and disorder were commonplace. No one at that time could have predicted that, of the three heirs to the Roman Empire, Western Europe would be the one to eventually dominate the world.

lag behind *v. pr.* 落后
fragmented *adj.* 支离破碎的
infrastructure *n.* 基础设施

Western Europe during this period was divided into several parts. In the south, the region now known as Spain was ruled first by the Visigoths, then after 715, the Muslims. The land which forms modern-day Italy was divided between the pope, the Byzantines, and the Lombards. The British Isles were home to many small **Anglo-Saxon** kingdoms. The only long-lasting Germanic kingdom was the Frankish kingdom in Gaul, but it was not until the 8th century that it strengthened and started to expand. The lack of centralized power in Western Europe, together with the emergence of **feudalism**, a new social system, led to a number of struggles. In all these struggles the church remained a major player.

Anglo-Saxon 盎格鲁—萨克森

feudalism *n.* 封建制度

4.1 The Rise of the Frankish Empire

Clovis (481—511) had established a strong Frankish kingdom in Gaul (see Chapter 4). After Clovis died, his successors in the Merovingian dynasty were known as "do-nothing kings", showing little political responsibility and relying mainly on violence to maintain power. Treating the kingdom as private property, they divided and re-divided the land among their heirs. Because of their **negligence**, the chief royal household officials, known as the mayors of the palace, gradually took over real power in government. One such mayor, Pepin of Heristal gained control over the entire kingdom in 687.

negligence *n.* 玩忽职守

When Pepin's son Charles Martel stopped the Muslim expansion into Europe at the battle of Tours in 732, the family gained much-needed support from the warrior **aristocracy** as well as the Christian church. In 751 an assembly of Frankish nobles declared that the last Merovingian king, the **feeble** Childeric III, was not truly a king and recognized Charles Martel's son **Pepin the Short** as the legitimate ruler. The pope also supported him and crowned him king of the Franks in 754. This implied that the Frankish king had a special tie to the **papacy** and thus to the Roman past. Through carefully-managed alliances with the aristocracy and church, continued battles against neighbors, and good administration, the Frankish kings expanded their territory beyond the Rhine River. In 768 the son of Pepin the Short, **Charlemagne** (also called Charles the Great) came to the **throne**.

aristocracy *n.* 贵族

feeble *adj.* 羸弱的

Pepin the Short 矮子丕平

papacy *n.* 罗马教廷

Charlemagne 查理曼大帝

throne *n.* 王位

Charlemagne (rule 768—814) was the greatest Frankish king. Over a 46-year reign, he undertook fifty-four military campaigns and established the vast Carolingian Empire, named after the Latin version of his name, "Carolus Magnus". War was the key to Charlemagne's success. Between 771 and 804, he conquered Lombardy, Saxony,

Bavaria, and parts of northern Spain. This made him **undisputed** ruler of almost all Western Europe—half of the Christian world. Only Britain, southern Italy, and Muslim Spain were outside his control.

undisputed *adj.* 无可争议的

An expansion of this size required a good army. Charlemagne's army was led by his faithful aristocrats and manned by free men, many the "**vassals**" of the aristocrats. The king had the right to call his subjects to arms and to command the army. He could also issue fines and punishments when his orders were not obeyed. Soldiers provided their own equipment; the rich went to war on horseback, the poor had to have at least a lance, shield, and bow. There was no standing army, and men had to be **mobilized** for each expedition. As long as the empire was expanding, such a system was very successful; aristocrats and free men were glad to go off to war when they could expect to return home rich with the **spoils** of war.

vassal *n.* 封臣

mobilize *v.* 动员

spoil *n.* 战利品

To rule this vast empire, Charlemagne divided it into **counties**, similar to the Roman provinces. He appointed Frankish aristocrats as **counts** (in Latin, *comites*, meaning "companion"). The count was the administrator, judge and military leader of the county. To make sure of his control over these counts, Charlemagne travelled widely around his empire. He also appointed special travelling inspectors to **scrutinize** local officials, hear complaints, and publish imperial **directives**. Charlemagne required all major administrative and religious figures to attend a general assembly almost every year. At this assembly they reported on their local areas, advised the emperor on important matters, and heard his directives. Charlemagne also **standardized** weights, measures, and money throughout his empire. His administrative system was far from perfect, but nonetheless produced the best government Europe had seen since the Romans. For the next three hundred years Western rulers used this system as a model.

county *n.* 郡

count *n.* 伯爵

scrutinize *v.* 详细检查

directive *n.* 指令

standardized *adj.* 统一标准的

A **devout** Christian, Charlemagne saw himself as the defender of a united Christian society. He saw it as the king's duty to carry out God's commands and build a society based on Christian ideals of order, justice, and morality. A wise statesman, Charlemagne also realized that the Catholic Church could provide valuable assistance. He undertook a number of religious reforms such as encouraging Christian missions, improving the moral and educational standards of **clergy**, strengthening the position of bishops, and funding the church through a 10% income tax (**tithe**) on all Christians.

devout *adj.* 虔诚的

clergy *n.* 神职人员

tithe *n.* 什一税

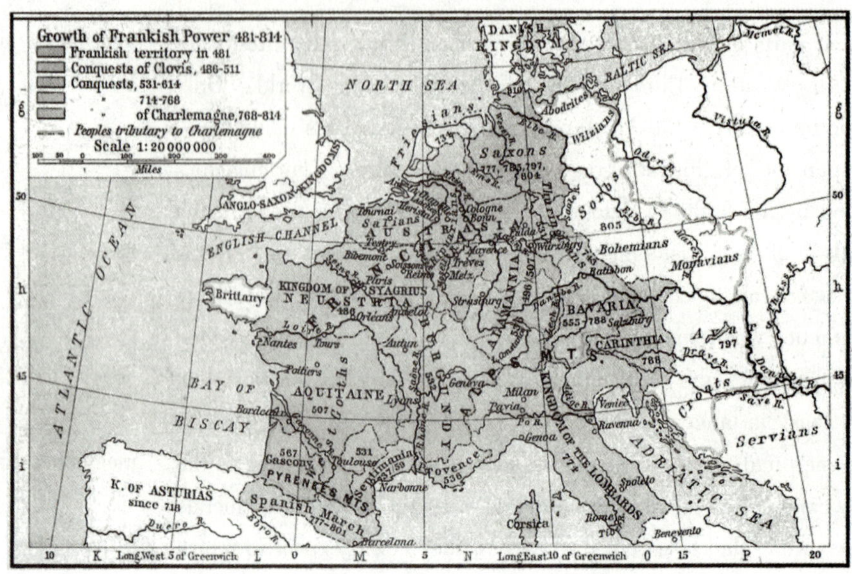

Map 20 Growth of Frankish power (481—814)

alliance *n.* 同盟

refuge *n.* 避难

crown *n.* 王冠

These reforms were supported by the pope. The Frankish kings had always had an **alliance** with the papacy, but Charlemagne took this further. He visited Rome four times. In 799, challenged by a rebellion, Pope Leo III escaped from Rome and took **refuge** at Charlemagne's court; Charlemagne later helped the Pope regain power. On Christmas Day, 800 AD, when Charlemagne visited Rome for the fourth time, Pope Leo placed a **crown** on his head and declared him emperor of the Romans.

The coronation of Charlemagne on Christmas Day, 800 AD marked the birth of a new civilization.

This **coronation** was the climax of Charlemagne's career and a historical moment for Western Europe. Until 800 only the Eastern Roman emperor in Constantinople could claim to be the direct **heir** of the Roman Empire. Although the Byzantines had lost most of their influence in the West, they continued to regard it as part of their empire. Charlemagne's coronation marked a major step for the developing Western European cultural identity. The coronation ceremony combined Greco-Roman, Christian, and Germanic elements; a Germanic king was crowned emperor of the Romans by the spiritual leader of Western Christendom. A new civilization was born.

coronation *n.* 加冕

heir *n.* 继承者

4.2 The Disintegration of the Carolingian Empire

disintegration *n.* 解体

Great empires in history have often faced similar problems. The Carolingian Empire was no exception, except that these were faster to come, due to its over-reliance on one man's skill and energy. Not long after Charlemagne's death, the Empire began to fall apart, and by the end of the ninth century it had disintegrated into small political entities.

Regional and ethnic diversity was one factor here. Many of the empire's major regions, such as Saxony, Bavaria, Brittany, and Lombardy had their own strong ruling elites, languages and cultures, which had a much longer history than the Empire. When **annexing** these regions, Charlemagne had tried to **compromise** between unity and diversity. On the one hand, he let the conquered peoples keep many of their own laws and customs. On the other hand, he made great efforts to create a sense of cohesion through the uniform administration and common Christian religion. Despite his good intentions, balancing this regional and ethnic diversity was never easy.

annex *v.* 吞并

compromise *v.* 妥协

Another key issue leading to the breakup of the Empire was succession—which had also been a problem for the Romans. The solution the Carolingians invented was to create subkingdoms for all their sons, while passing the main **imperial title** to the eldest son. Unfortunately, the younger sons often challenged their older brother.

imperial title 皇帝称号

In 814, Charlemagne was succeeded by his only surviving son Louis the Pious (rule 814—840). Louis the Pious was a weak personality, unable to maintain his father's system or control the aristocracy. He was unable to control his own sons, either, who fought continuously. In 843, three years after his death, his three sons signed the **Treaty of Verdun** to divide the empire into three parts: Charles the Bald (rule 843—877) received the western lands; Louis the German (rule 843—876) took the eastern lands; and Lothair (rule 840—

Treaty of Verdun《凡尔登条约》

855) kept the lands in the middle as well as the title of emperor.

The eastern and western kingdoms were relatively stable. They respectively evolved into (roughly) the later kingdoms of Germany and France. The middle kingdom lasted only a short time. When Lothair died in 855, the land was re-divided among his three sons. In 856, a civil war broke out between the East Franks and the West Franks for control over the middle kingdom and the imperial title. This ended with the **Treaty of Meerssen** (870), by which Lothair's kingdom disappeared. Lorraine, the northern part continued to be disputed between eastern and western kingdoms. The southern part was divided between a kingdom of Italy and the kingdoms of upper and lower Burgundy. The imperial title passed from one branch of the Carolingian family to another, but this now had little meaning. Historians traditionally see the year 888 as the end of the Carolingian Empire. The political future of Western Europe lay with the more stable eastern and western kingdoms of Germany and France.

Treaty of Meerssen 《莫尔森条约》

4.3 Early England

When the Roman **legions** returned to Italy in the fifth century, they left the Celtic natives in England with a new religion—Christianity—and a splendid system of roads, many of whose routes are still used today. The stability of Roman rule was soon broken by invaders: Angles, Saxons, and Jutes. The Anglo-Saxon invaders not only fought the **Celts**, but also fought among themselves. The conflicts among various Anglo-Saxon tribal kingdoms continued throughout the 5th and 6th centuries. As the kingdom of Kent took the upper hand, peace and order slowly returned.

legion *n.* 罗马军团

Celt *n.* 凯尔特人

In the 9th century, the kingdom of Wessex replaced the kingdom of Kent as dominant power. A new wave of invaders soon followed: the **Danes**. The Wessex king at the time, **Alfred the Great** (rule 871—899) defeated the Danes in battles, and then negotiated a treaty, allowing the Danes to settle in central England. Danes and Saxons soon intermarried and all differences between the two groups disappeared. One of England's finest monarchs, Alfred the Great also reformed the system of government. He reorganized the army, **issued** a set of laws, and **revitalized** intellectual life in England. His descendants were able rulers too, with the Anglo-Saxon monarchy reaching its height during the 10th century.

Dane *n.* 丹麦人

Alfred the Great 阿尔弗烈德大王

issue *v.* 颁布

revitalize *v.* 使得到复兴

The major structural weakness of the Anglo-Saxon monarchy was the king's inability to control his great nobles. This changed after the

Normans invaded in 1066. A more lasting legacy of the Anglo-Saxons was the representative local government structure they created. This led to a tradition of people participating in government.

Norman *n.* 诺曼人

4.4 Ninth-Century Invasions

A new wave of destructive attacks and invasions in the ninth century led to the final fragmentation of the Carolingian Empire. During the two centuries after Charlemagne's death, Western Europe was attacked by non-Christian invaders: **Magyars** from the East, Muslims from the South, and **Vikings** from the North. This period is often called the "dark ages".

Magyar *n.* 马扎尔人
Viking *n.* 维京人

The Magyars were also known as **Hungarians** because of a supposed relationship to the **Huns**. They were remarkable horsemen. They began fast, horse-borne raids on Western Europe in 889, attacking Italy, Germany, and even France. People's fear of them is shown by a common prayer of the time: "Lord save us from the arrows of Hungarians." It was not until the Magyars were defeated by the German king **Otto** Ⅰ in 955 that they settled down to form a stable kingdom, Hungary.

Hungarian *n.* 匈牙利人
Hun *n.* 匈奴人
Otto Ⅰ 奥托一世

In the ninth century, the Muslim Arabs based in North Africa started pushing across the Mediterranean. They occupied Sicily, Sardinia, and Corsica, and repeatedly attacked the coasts of Italy and southern France. They sacked the city of Rome in 846.

The largest-scale invasions came from the Vikings. Originally based on the **Scandinavian** Peninsula, the Vikings included Danes, **Norwegians**, and **Swedes.** These peoples had their own distinct language and culture. As the heavily forested Danish Peninsula and the rocky soils of Norway and Sweden did not favor agriculture, the Vikings developed their skills in **navigation**. In their long boats, the fierce Vikings ventured across the seas in search of riches.

Scandinavian *adj.* 斯堪的纳维亚
Norwegian *n.* 挪威人
Swede *n.* 瑞典人
navigation *n.* 航海

The extent of Viking expansion is astonishing. In the 8th century the Danes attacked the east coast of England, a land then divided into separate Saxon kingdoms. Their attacks continued through the 9th century and increased in size. Finally, the English King Alfred the Great (871—901) reached a compromise with the Danes, giving them the entire north-eastern half of England. Gradually the Danes were Christianized and adopted Saxon ways.

The Vikings also penetrated the European continent. Swedes crossed the Baltic Sea, and many sailed down the Dnieper River to the Black Sea and came into contact with Constantinople and the Byzantine

Empire. The Western European mainland also suffered from extensive Viking raids, including the French coast, Spain, the Mediterranean ports, and Italy. Vikings also sailed upstream in their long boats through the rivers of the Low Countries and France, attacking inland cities.

siege *n.* 围攻
tribute *n.* 贡金
chieftain *n.* 酋长

One of the greatest attacks was the **siege** of Paris in 885—886. Although the city was eventually saved after a ten-month defense, the French King, Charles the Fat was forced to pay a **tribute**. The next King, Charles the Simple made a compromise with the Norse **Chieftain** Rollo by signing a treaty in 911. The Norsemen were permitted to keep the part of the northern Frankish coastal region which was already under their control. This region later became known as **Normandy**, namely, "land of the Norse". In return, Rollo swore loyalty to the French king and became the Duke of Normandy, a **vassal** to the King. Gradually the Norse people converted to Christianity and became assimilated into French culture. In the eleventh century, the Normans brought their **hybrid** Norman-French culture to England which they conquered in 1066.

Normandy *n.* 诺曼底
vassal *n.* 封臣
hybrid *adj.* 混合的

The two centuries after Charlemagne's death were a dark period for Europe. Political disintegration was followed by widespread **chaos** and destruction. However, except for the Muslims, all the foreign invaders were eventually absorbed into European civilization. At the same time, people in Western Europe developed a new way of life.

chaos *n.* 混乱

4.5 Economy and Society in the Early Middle Ages

After Charlemagne's death, central governments in Western Europe were too weak to defend their subjects. Faced with the disintegration of the Empire and frequent invasions, the local nobility were generally the ones who ensured security. This led to the emergence of a new type of relationship between free individuals. This was known as **feudalism**, and was both a form of government and an economic system.

feudalism *n.* 封建制

4.5.1 Lords and Vassals

lord *n.* 领主
vassal *n.* 封臣
castle *n.* 城堡

Feudalism operated on two levels. At the local level, it involved the relationship between a lord of a **castle** and those who were in his service. On the state level, it defined the relationship between the king and the powerful lords under him.

On the local level, the lord of a castle was the military and administrative ruler of his district. Those who pledged their loyalty to him became his vassals. The lord gave his vassals land in return for their loyalty and service, such as fighting in his army or serving in his court.

Vassalage dates back to an early Germanic tribal custom, whereby warriors swore loyalty to their leader and fought for him; the leader in turn took care of their needs. When fighting the Muslims, the Carolingians discovered the need for a corps of well-equipped knights. A horse, **armor**, and weapons were however expensive to maintain. Consequently, in the post-Charlemagne era, powerful lords made changes to the old practice of vassalage. On top of the honorable relationship based on military service, the personal bond between a lord and his vassals was further strengthened by the holding of land. Lords had to grant each vassal a piece of land large enough to provide for the vassal and his family. In return for the land, the vassal provided his lord with one major service, his fighting skills. The Carolingians coined a new term, "**fief**" to refer to the property that a lord granted to his vassals in return for military service.① A vassal holding a fief could subdivide it into smaller fiefs. As a consequence, there were sub-vassals and fiefs within fiefs.

vassalage *n.* 采邑制，封臣制

armor *n.* 盔甲

fief *n.* 封地，采邑

Just as the vassals gave their service to the local lords, these lords in turn gave service to the king. On the state level, however, the **submission** of powerful lords to the king was largely symbolic. A feudal kingdom was in fact a kind of loose **federation** made up of all the different fiefs. In theory, the king was the supreme lord of all vassals, and his kingdom in turn was a fief held from God. Normally, however, a feudal king's actual power depended on the size of his own personal lands as compared to those of his vassals. Often powerful lords tended to be allies rather than **subordinates** of the king.

submission *n.* 服从

federation *n.* 联邦

subordinate *n.* 下级部属

The new feudal practice was a product of the Carolingian world, but also spread to England, Germany, central Europe, and in a changed form to Italy. Military service was the main reason for the feudal system to exist. Each vassal was expected to serve his lord personally as a knight. If the fief was large, it would have to provide several knights. A vassal was expected to perform military service for about forty days a year.

Apart from military ones, a vassal also had judicial and financial duties. He had to attend the lord's court at a certain time a year or whenever summoned. At the court he was expected to give his lord policy advice or to join other vassals in deciding legal cases. Whenever

① Fief 一词的拉丁文写法为 feodum，英文的 feudal（封建的）一词由此而来。

a decision was reached, he was required to help carry it out. Depending on the size of the fief, the vassal was required to provide his lord with financial assistance on certain **specified** occasions, such as the marriage of the lord's daughter or the knighting of the lord's eldest son.

specified *adj.* 特定的

A vassal also enjoyed certain rights. Within his personal fief he exercised political and legal authority. The obligations to provide military, political and legal assistance also gave the vassal certain powers and privileges. The lord was expected to protect his vassal, either by defending him militarily or by taking his side in a court of law if necessary. The lord and the vassal needed each other equally as much.

4.5.2 Serfs and Serfdom

Compared to the Byzantine or Muslim Empires, Western Europe in the Early Middle Ages was a **backward**, predominantly agricultural society. Towns were much less important administratively and culturally than in ancient Greece and Rome, and few of them were large. During the reign of Augustus, the population of Rome may have reached one million, but in 800 AD it was down to about thirty thousand. Paris had perhaps twenty thousand inhabitants at that time. And these were the largest cities in Western Europe!

backward *adj.* 落后的

The inland areas of Western Europe experienced economic **isolation**, as trade survived only along the coasts of the Mediterranean, North and Baltic Seas. Whether free peasants or serfs, up to 90% of the population farmed the land. The landholding class of nobles and knights made up military **elite**. When not busy with military service, they had free time, as the land was worked by a dependant peasant class, the serfs.

isolation *n.* 孤立

elite *n.* 精英

A fundamental change occurred among slaves. Faced with poor economic conditions, landlords started to settle slave families on small plots of land and turn them into serfs. During the **ploughing** and harvest seasons, the lord demanded services from his serfs, but at other times the serfs could work their own land. The serf and his family lived from the crops they themselves grew. In return for the land, the serf's family gave the lord an annual payment, usually in **grain** rather than in money.

plough *v.* 耕种

grain *n.* 粮食

Most European serfs were descended from slaves. Almost like slaves, they enjoyed little personal liberty, and were considered the property of their lords. Serfs were legally bound to the lord's land and could not leave without permission. Although free to marry, they could not marry anyone outside their manor without the lord's approval. Serfs had to pay rent and also pay for certain services, for example, the use of the lord's **mill**. They were also required to provide their labor services each week (often for three days). They were subject to the lord's political and legal authority. The lord's powers gave him almost complete control over his serfs. The lord's court was their only contact with any law, and their personal status was hereditary from generation to generation. Unlike slaves, however, they could not be sold away from their lands or families, and after paying their rent, they could keep the remaining harvest from their fields.

mill *n.* 磨坊

In the chaotic Early Middle Ages, free peasants often needed protection or food in times of bad harvest. Many gave up their freedom to powerful lords, and became serfs in return for protection and use of the lord's land. By the 9th century, serfs made up around 60% of the population of Western Europe. This number started to decline at the beginning of the 1200s with the movement to free serfs.

4.6 Culture in the Christian West

After the fall of the Western Roman Empire, **literacy** declined in Western Europe. **Deurbanization** reduced the extent of education. Cultural and educational standards dropped far below those of the Byzantine Empire or Muslim world. By the 6th century, learning took place in few venues apart from church and **monastic** schools. In Gaul, the centre of the Carolingian Empire, the old Roman schools had completely disappeared. Scholarship focused heavily on **biblical** texts. Most scholars were clergymen, for whom scientific study was only an **afterthought**. Their study of science was practical in nature; the need to care for the sick led to the study of medicine and of ancient texts on drugs, whereas the need to calculate the proper times to pray and the date of Easter called for a simple understanding of mathematics and the movements of the stars.

literacy *n.* 识字率，文化程度

deurbanization *n.* 去都市化进程

monastic *adj.* 修道院的

biblical *adj.* 圣经的

afterthought *n.* 可有可无

The highest cultural achievements took place in the Carolingian Empire between the late 8th and 9th centuries, when Pepin and Charlemagne promoted classical education and Christian wisdom. These rulers were concerned about the low **literacy rate**, which caused problems for religious and civil authorities as they needed people who could read and write. Another problem was the lack of a standard handwriting style and Latin grammar. Literate persons in one part of Europe had great difficulty recognizing or reading a text written in

literacy rate 识字率

another. This was because in the 6th and 7th centuries, with Western Europe divided into small kingdoms, different styles of writing had developed, and the Latin grammar used by scholars had taken on regional differences.

In response, Charlemagne ordered the founding of schools, and tried to attract many leading scholars to his court. A major reform was the creation of a standardized **curriculum** for use at these schools. **Alcuin** (732—804), the greatest of the English scholars of the time, played an important role here by writing textbooks, creating word lists, and establishing the **trivium** and **quadrivium** as the basis for education.① The trivium and quadrivium would form the undergraduate curriculum for the universities founded in the High Middle Ages (1000—1300).

Another great **milestone** was the reform of handwriting. Monks devised a new type of formal writing in around 800, known as the Carolingian **minuscule**. Previously, handwriting had used **capital letters** only and was difficult to read rapidly. The Carolingian minuscule used capital letters for the beginning of sentences and smaller (or lower-case) letters for the text. **Spaces** were inserted between words. It was easier to read a page written in this way; in addition, more letters could be written on a page, and thus more books were produced at lesser expense. All books in European languages today are based on this Carolingian innovation.

Another achievement was the standardization of Latin into what is now known as Medieval Latin. While retaining the rules of classical Latin, Medieval Latin was more **flexible** and open in its vocabulary. It allowed the invention of new words to express the new realities of the age. Medieval Latin was also different from the **vernacular languages** spoken by the people. Latin as a common scholarly language gave the vernacular languages freedom to develop on their own. Medieval Latin became the common language of scholarship, and allowed administrators and travelers to communicate easily across Europe.

This revival is sometimes called the "Carolingian renaissance". The period was crucial for the legacy of the Roman Empire; nearly 90% of the ancient Roman works that we still have today exist because they were copied by Carolingian monks. However, reforms were limited to the court and the clergy, unlike the wider social reforms of the later

curriculum *n.* 课程
Alcuin 阿尔昆
trivium *n.* 三学科
quadrivium *n.* 四学科
milestone *n.* 里程碑
minuscule *n.* 小书写体
capital letter 大写字母
space *n.* 空格
flexible *adj.* 灵活的
vernacular language 本国语言

① 三学科即语法、修辞、论理，四学科则为算术、几何、天文、音乐。

Italian Renaissance. As his Empire disintegrated, Charlemagne's educational system suffered considerable damage from barbarian invasions in the 9th and 10th centuries. But not all was lost; scholarly activity continued at church and monastery schools. In the High Middle Ages, some of these schools were transformed into universities, leading a new cultural revival.

5. Conclusion

In this chapter we have briefly surveyed three cultures—Byzantine, Islamic, and Western European. The Byzantine East and European West both developed from a single Greco-Roman-Christian civilization. Although they had much in common and never lost contact with each other, their political and religious separation **mirrored** a cultural **divergence** between the Greek east and the Latin west. To both of these, the brilliant Islamic civilization was largely **alien**.

mirror *v.* 反映
divergence *n.* 差异
alien *adj.* 异己的

Western European culture was the most backward during the Early Middle Ages, mainly due to numerous barbarian invasions. It would take time for the new **immigrants** to assimilate the culture of their new environment and start to make their own contributions.

immigrant *n.* 移民

Yet among the three, Western European culture ended up with the greatest **potential** and **vitality**. Byzantium would decline politically and culturally after the 10th century. Islam never again reached the same levels of power after the 11th century. Western Europe, on the other hand, continued to absorb the best of all the older cultures, combine diverse heritages in an innovative way, and achieve unity in diversity. Equally as important, Western European culture would be carried far afield by **missionaries**, colonists, **crusaders**, and explorers. One of the most significant modern historical trends is the **predominance** of European civilization. Its roots lie in the Middle Ages.

potential *n.* 潜力
vitality *n.* 活力
missionary *n.* 传教士
crusader *n.* 十字军
predominance *n.* 主导地位

Exercises

Ⅰ. Terminology: choose the suitable terms to fill in the blanks.

A. feudalism B. iconoclasm C. vassal D. Carolingian renaissance
E. Arabesque F. Justinian Code G. blasphemy H. coronation
I. tithe J. hajj

• __1__ is the body of Roman law codified under Justinian and the basis for many modern systems of civil law.

• The __2__ refers to the deliberate destruction of religious icons and other symbols or monuments, usually for religious or political motives.

• __3__ is something that is considered offensive to God or someone's religious beliefs.

• __4__ is the religious journey to Mecca which all Muslims try to make at least once in their life.

• A(n) __5__ is a type of decoration based on flowers, leaves and branches which are often twisted together, found especially in Islamic art.

• __6__ was the social system that existed in Europe in the Middle Ages, in which land belonged to powerful lords and the people they allowed to live on the land had to work and fight for them.

• A(n) __7__ is a man in the Middle Ages who promised to fight for and be loyal to a king or other powerful owner of land, in return for being given land to live on.

• __8__ is the ceremony of crowning a king, a queen or some other sovereign ruler.

• __9__ is a revival of classical art and architecture in parts of northern and western Europe begun under Charlemagne and lasting into the 10th century.

• __10__ is one tenth of the annual produce of a farm, formerly paid as a tax to support the clergy and the church.

Ⅱ. Decide whether the following statements are true (T) or false (F).

1. Among the Byzantine Empire, the Islamic Empire and the Frankish Empire, only the first one received continuing influence from the Roman intellectual and legal tradition. (   )

2. Hagia Sophia was the perfect representation of Byzantine civilization, apart from Byzantine artistic feature, it displays a mixture of Greek, Roman and Persian cultural elements. (   )

3. The economy of the Byzantine Empire relied primarily on agriculture. (   )

4. The official language of Byzantine Empire was Latin. (   )

5. Before the rise of Islam, Arabs did not believe in Allah. (   )

6. Muhammad was not only a prophet, but also a political and military leader. (   )

7. The Islamic Golden Age is a period of cultural and intellectual growth and activity that persisted throughout the Islamic world between the mid-8th and mid-13th centuries. (   )

8. Charlemagne was the greatest Frankish king, who founded the first empire in western

Europe after the fall of Rome. ( )

9. The Vikings originated from the Scandinavian peninsula and included Danes, Norwegians, Swedes and Magyars. ( )

10. Before the Carolingian renaissance, cultural and educational standards in western Europe had already surpassed those of the Byzantine Empire or Muslim world. ( )

Ⅲ. Multiple choices: choose the answer that best completes the statement or answers the question.

1. Which one is NOT the reason that Justinian is considered the first great Byzantine emperor?

A. He reconquered the lost territories of the former Western Roman Empire.

B. He ordered scholars to codify all Roman laws into one coherent body of law.

C. He declared himself to be God's representative on earth.

D. He commissioned the construction of Hagia Sophia.

2. Which is the correct description of life in the Byzantine Empire?

A. Peasants had a hard life due to the high tax on land.

B. Scholars were skeptical of Greek tradition.

C. Women were excluded from education.

D. Soldiers received poor salaries.

3. Which of the following descriptions of Constantinople is NOT true?

A. It was the most important trading centre in Europe in the Early Middle Ages.

B. It was the political and intellectual centre of the Middle Ages.

C. It dazzled visitors with its grand buildings and great wealth.

D. University of Constantinople did not have any Muslim students.

4. In the Early Middle Ages, the Roman Church and the Eastern Church were divided over the following issues EXCEPT for ________.

A. Iconoclasm B. official language

C. explanation of the Holy Spirit D. baptism

5. Which of the following statements about Byzantine classicism is true?

A. The Byzantines revered ancient Greek literature, philosophy and historiography.

B. The Byzantines emphasized Greek scientific and mathematical tradition.

C. The Byzantines were not only imitative, but also creative in their study of Greek tradition.

D. The Byzantine authors thought they could eventually surpass ancient Greek authors.

6. Which one is NOT the factor that contributed to the success of the Byzantine Empire?

A. Prestige of the emperor. B. Commitment to classicism.

C. Flourishing trade D. A well-trained army

7. Which of the following descriptions of pre-Islamic Arabia is not true?

A. Pre-Islamic Arabia was backward and underdeveloped.

B. Pre-Islamic Arabs showed no interest in sea trade.

C. Mecca was one of the most important trading centers.

D. Pre-Islamic Arabs would pray to their tribal gods or goddesses.

8. For some Muslims, Qur'an should not be translated because ________.

A. it is impious to translate the very words of Allah

B. it is too difficult to translate the rhymed prose of Qur'an

C. the original meaning of Qur'an would be distorted

D. the beauty of Arabic language would be violated

9. For those who want to convert to Islam, which of the following pillars of Islam is of the utmost importance?

A. Reciting the Muslim statement of faith with conviction.

B. Performing ritual prayers five times a day.

C. Giving money or gifts to the poor and the needy.

D. Observing a month-long fast every year and making a pilgrimage to Mecca.

10. Which factor did not facilitate the Islamic expansion?

A. The well-organized Muslim ruling elite and a powerful Muslim army.

B. People's dissatisfaction with imperial rule in some Middle East areas.

C. The tolerance of those cultures different from Islam.

D. The influence of the strict monotheism of Islam.

11. Which description of the Islamic philosophy is true?

A. Al-Farabi believed that philosophy and religion are not reconcilable.

B. Al-Ghazali regarded Greek philosophy as corrupters of Islamic faith.

C. Averroës believed that philosophical truth can not be tested.

D. Averroës thought that philosophers can not truly comprehend theological truth.

12. Which form of literature was unpopular in the medieval Islamic world?

A. Poetry. B. Prose. C. History. D. Drama.

13. What event marked the climax of Charlemagne's career and the formation of western European civilization?

A. Charlemagne became the Frankish king and ruled most of western Europe.

B. Charlemagne produced the best government Europe had seen since the Romans.

C. Charlemagne built a united Christian society and had an alliance with the papacy.

D. Charlemagne was crowned "Holy Roman Emperor" by the Pope.

14. Which one is not the factor that led to the disintegration of the Carolingian Empire after Charlemagne's death?

A. The regional and ethnic diversity.

B. The conflicts between different successors to the throne.

C. The destructive attacks of non-Christian invaders.

D. The emergence of feudalism.

15. What one is a correct description of the western European feudalism in the Early Middle Ages?

A. Feudalism was a product of the Carolingian world and it operated on two levels.

B. A feudal king's actual power depended on the number of his vassals.

C. A vassal holding a fief must not divide it into smaller fiefs.

D. Financial service was the main reason for the feudal system to exist.

16. What was the main difference between serfs and slaves in Western Europe?

A. The amount of personal liberty.

B. The hereditary personal status.

C. The military protection provided by the lord.

D. The obligation to work on the land.

17. Alcuin established ________ as the basis for education during the Carolingian renaissance.

A. the Carolingian minuscule B. trivium and quadrivium

C. medieval Latin D. biblical texts

18. In Early Middle Ages, Western European civilization differed from the Byzantine and Islamic Empires in the following aspects EXCEPT for ________.

A. the influence from the Germanic and Romance vernacular languages

B. the unstable political situation and a lack of central power

C. the influence of ancient Greco-Roman civilizations

D. the lower level of intellectual and literary accomplishment

19. Concerning the economy of the Byzantine Empire, Islamic Empire and western Europe during the Middle Ages, which statement is NOT true?

A. Byzantine had the most powerful economy in the world before the 7th century.

B. Islamic economy in the 7th century was already very prosperous.

C. Islamic Empire had the world's leading economy during the mid-8th and mid-13th century.

D. Western Europe overtook Byzantine in economy in the late Middle Ages.

20. Which city was NOT a prominent trading centre during the Early Middle Ages?

A. Constantinople. B. Mecca. C. Medina. D. Baghdad.

Chapter 6
The Central Middle Ages (1000—1300)

CHAPTER OUTLINE

1. Introduction
2. Economic Takeoff and Social Change
3. The Church Triumphant
4. The Emergence and Growth of National Monarchies
5. Intellectual Revival and Cultural Development
6. Conclusion

FOCUS QUESTIONS

1. What facts demonstrate the growth of church power in the Central Middle Ages?
2. What was the relationship between the Crusades and the social, cultural, economic changes in the Central Middle Ages?
3. How was the political development in England different from that in France and in Germany in the Central Middle Ages? Why?
4. What were the major intellectual and cultural achievements of European civilization in the Central Middle Ages?

1. Introduction

The Central Middle Ages, or the High Middle Ages, refer to the historical period that lasted from about 1000 to about 1300. Historians used to believe that most of the cultural, economic and political achievements of the Middle Ages occurred in this period, so they called it High Middle Ages. Only recently, as the accomplishments of the Early and Late Middle Ages have gained appreciation, has the term "High" fallen into **disuse**. Today, historians prefer to use the more **neutral** name, the Central Middle Ages, for this period.

disuse *n.* 不用
neutral *adj.* 中立的

No matter what term is chosen to label this period, the Central Middle Ages did mark a period of rapid change and growth in more than one way. The new European civilization that had emerged in the Early

Middle Ages began to flourish in the Central Middle Ages. From the 11th century through the 14th century, Europeans remade their world. They developed agriculture and commerce, revived old cities and built new ones, created universities, reformed the church, waged aggressive wars, made and unmade powerful kings and emperors. During this period, three key elements—the Greco—Roman tradition, Judeo-Christian tradition, and Germanic tradition—gradually integrated into one single civilization in Western Europe. At the same time, the balance among the three heirs of the Greco-Roman civilization—Byzantium, the Islamic world and Western Europe—began to shift and Western Europe grew into an important world power. The flowering of Western Europe took many forms. It was evidenced in a great **crusade** movement against Muslims in the Near East and the **Iberian Peninsula**, in colonial experiments outside Europe in Syria and Palestine, in pioneer contacts with faraway China.

crusade *n.* 十字军
Iberian Peninsula 伊比利亚半岛

In this chapter, we shall trace the emergence of a new Europe in the Central Middle Age. We will first examine the economic **takeoff** and social change, looking into the developments in agriculture, trade, and manufacturing, as well as changes in patterns of village and city life. In this period Christianity was central in both the daily life of ordinary Europeans and political life. This is why this period is often called an "Age of Faith." Given the centrality of Christianity, in the second section of this chapter we will examine the organization of the medieval church, the efforts to reform it. Then in the third section we will look at the development of feudal **monarchies** in three European areas—Germany, England, and France—and consider why the first failed and the latter two endured. In the last section we will discuss the cultural achievements in such fields as ideas, literature, and art in the Central Middle Age.

takeoff *n.* 腾飞
monarchy *n.* 君主国

2. Economic Takeoff and Social Change

During the period from 1000 to 1300, European society underwent a dramatic overall transformation. Social structure and economic activity in Europe became increasingly complex. Although most people remained directly involved in agricultural production, by the latter date many enjoyed their freedom. By 1300 a growing number of persons engaged in other occupations such as trade and manufacturing. They lived in towns rather than **manorial** villages. The growth of trade and rise of

manorial *adj.* 大农庄的

towns furthered economic and social changes, affecting life of the nobles and **clergy**, and changing conditions for the general working people. Behind this picture of more prosperous villages, more bustling towns, was an economic transformation that laid critical foundations for the religious, political, and cultural achievements of the Central Middle Ages.

clergy *n.* 神职人员

2.1 Agricultural Revolution and Rural Society

European society remained **overwhelmingly** agricultural throughout the Middle Ages, and agriculture constituted the lifeblood of the European economy. During the Central Middle Ages, significant new changes occurred in agriculture, which laid the foundations for the overall economic takeoff and social change.

overwhelmingly *adv.* 压倒性地

2.1.1 Agricultural Revolution: Causes and Impacts

New changes occurred in agriculture during the Central Middle Ages due to a couple of factors. The improvement in climate (a small rise in temperature) produced better growing conditions, as the summer growing season became longer. The social situation was more settled and peaceful, as the invasions of Europe by outside forces in the Early Middle Ages had stopped.

Another factor that contributed to increased agricultural production was a great expansion of the amount of land under cultivation. Growing numbers of Europeans not only resettled lands **depopulated** by the 9th and 10th centuries' invasions but also opened new lands for farming. Land-hungry peasants expanded arable land by **draining swamps**, clearing forests, cutting down trees, and building **dikes**. Many moved to frontier areas in central Europe or resettled in the Iberian Peninsula taken back from the Muslims. By such **endeavors**, Europeans doubled and possibly **tripled** the amounts of land they farmed and food they produced.

depopulated *adj.* 人口减少的
drain *v.* 抽水
swamp *n.* 沼泽地
dike *n.* 堤坝
endeavor *n.* 努力
triple *v.* 翻三倍

Technological developments also contributed to Europe's agricultural growth. One crucial improvement was the invention of the **heavy plow**. It made possible the cultivation of the thick, wet, and fertile north European soils. At first these plows were pulled by **oxen**. Later, with the invention of the horse **collar** and horseshoes in metal, peasants were able to make use of horses, which were more efficient than oxen. Another improvement was the expanding use of water **mills** and wind mills. The use of watermills and windmills to **grind flour** and press olives freed people for other tasks and increased **productivity**.

heavy plow 重型犁
ox *n.* 牛
oxen (*pl.*)
collar *n.* 项圈
mill *n.* 磨坊
grind *v.* 研磨
flour *n.* 面粉
productivity *n.* 生产力

Medieval farmers also improved their methods of cultivation. In farming, a new, three-field system of agricultural operation came into wide use. Previously, farmers divided their land into two fields, planted one in the autumn, and left the other **fallow**, or unused. Animals **grazed** the fallow fields and their **manure** fertilized the soil. Now in the three-field system, famers planted one field in the autumn for early summer harvesting, a second in the spring for autumn harvesting, and left the third fallow throughout the year. In the next year, the fields were rotated and the process repeated. The three-field system kept more land in production, increased food supplies by one-third, and reduced labor.

fallow *n.* 休耕
graze *v.* 啃食牧草
manure *n.* 粪肥

This agricultural revolution greatly benefited the Europeans. As much more food was produced than before, between 1000 and 1300 there were no widespread **famines**. As grain production increased, some farmers chose to grow vegetables and fruits, some chose to raise cattle and sheep. As farmers diversified their agricultural activities, many Europeans became able to enjoy more **protein-rich** and iron-rich diet than before: peas and beans, cheese and eggs, fish and meat, thick beer and wine. Over the course of the Central Middle Ages, Europeans became **enthusiastic** meat eaters.

famine *n.* 饥荒
protein-rich *adj.* 富含蛋白质的
enthusiastic *adj.* 热衷于

Largely as a result of the increased agricultural production, between 1000 and 1300 Europe's population grew rapidly. It rose from approximately 38 million to 74 million. This growing population was young; probably 40% of Europeans were under the age of fourteen and joined the labor force early in life. As their numbers increased, Europeans spread over the continent and brought new areas under cultivation. Moreover, they filled the countryside with villages and created many towns which provided markets for agricultural products. Increased food production promoted trade and freed people for non-agricultural occupations. As a result, the social structure of medieval Europe also underwent significant transformation.

2. 1. 2 *Villages and Manors*

manor *n.* 大农庄

As the technological improvements and the three-field system came into widespread use throughout Western Europe, a fundamental change occurred in the arrangement of the village, the basic unit of agricultural economy. Villages ranged in size from ten to several hundred peasant families, living in a **cluster** of cottages surrounded by their fields. Normally, each family worked several **strips** of land, and the members of a family produced food for the family's need. It was necessary for different families to cooperate in farming because plows and oxen were expensive, families often shared them. Peasants needed to pay **tithe** to the church and **rent** to their lords.

cluster *n.* 群
stripe *n.* 块
tithe *n.* 什一税
rent *n.* 租金

Most villages had woodland which provided burning wood and building materials. Many also had a stream or pond for water supply, fish and a water mill for grinding grain. Some rich villages could afford a common **oven** or **winepress**. All villages had a few artisans and traders who combined farm work with other labor. Some worked as the wheel makers, blacksmiths, and **carpenters**; others worked as butchers, bakers, and brewers. Many of these by-industries were men's work.

oven *n.* 烤炉
winepress *n.* 葡萄压榨机
carpenter *n.* 木匠
brewer *n.* 酿酒师

Peasants often had farmyards next to their cottages where they grew vegetables, planted fruit trees, and **raised** chicken and pigs. The also raised sheep and cattle on the village grassland, in addition to oxen and horses. Peasants in certain areas, particularly in Flanders and northern England raised sheep on such a large scale that they stopped growing grain. The lifestyle of the peasants was very simple. Villagers worked hard and enjoyed few comforts. While father and sons worked in the fields, mother and daughters did cooking and cleaning, made cheese and butter, milked cows, tended the vegetable garden, and made clothing.

raise *v.* 饲养

Most villages were included in manors, or great farms. Starting in the 9th century, the manor emerged as the key economic and social organization in the rural areas. Manorialism was the key economic organization in the medieval Europe. The term manorialism refers to the type of economic and social system which centered on the manor. The manorial system governed the methods of agriculture, the lives of the serfs and free peasants, and their relationship with each other and with the **lord** of the manor.

lord *n.* 领主

The manorial system was an institution which changed considerably, depending on the time and the location. The owner of a manor was a lord, who might be a king or queen, a great nobleman or noblewoman (**duke**, **count**, **baron**, **viscount**), a bishop or an **abbot**, or even a mere knight or lady. The lords formed an aristocracy or nobility that held real political, economic and social power. Some lords owned only one manor; others owned many. They lived in a manor house or a **castle**. Medieval Europe was dotted with castles.

duke *n.* 公爵
count *n.* 伯爵
baron *n.* 男爵
viscount *n.* 子爵
abbot *n.* 修道院院长
castle *n.* 城堡
dot *v.* 星罗棋布于

Peasants living in a manor were organized under the authority of the lord. The lord or his appointed officials **regulated** cultivation of the land as well as the labor services. The greatest advantage of the manorial system was the increased **productivity**. Large field could be farmed more efficiently than small fields. Investment costs were lower: working

regulate *v.* 管理
productivity *n.* 生产力

together, an entire village only needed a single plow and a dozen oxen or horses. Common fields also allowed the villagers to experiment with new crops and new **crop-rotation** systems. Common grassland could support larger numbers of animals.

crop-rotation 作物轮换

Despite the potential advantages the manorial system offered to peasants, lords played the dominant role in forcing its creation, and it was they who took the greatest benefits from this system. Lords benefited from the manorial system in several ways. Most lords kept the best land on the manor, called **demesne** for their private use. From demesne lords took all the produce for their own use. Then they rented some land to the tenants and received the rents in cash or goods (produce, eggs, hens, or other commodities). The lords also charged various fees for the use of **pastures**, woodlands, mills, winepresses, and ovens. The lords also enjoyed the jurisdictional rights associated with a manor. At manor courts, disputes were settled, misdeeds punished, and obligations enforced, but almost every such **transaction** resulted in a fee or fine paid to the lords.

demesne *n.* 领主私人土地

pasture *n.* 草场

transaction *n.* 处理

It is important to remember that, by and large, the manorial system was limited to England, northern France, and western Germany. Even in these areas, it was beginning to break down by the end of the 12th century. Many lords simply found it more **convenient** and less risky to accumulate their wealth in cash. They began to demand from their tenants cash payments instead of labor services and to live from rents rather than from the actual agricultural produce of their **estates**.

convenient *adj.* 便利

estate *n.* 私有地产

Most villages in Central Middle Ages had their own **parish** church. Together with castles and monasteries, parish churches were the largest buildings in the countryside. Some were built by **bishops**; others developed out of churches built by **monasteries**; many others were originally family churches, built by a local noble. The church was the center of village activity. Villagers celebrated baptisms and marriage there, and buried their dead in the churchyard. The churchyard was the site of village meetings and market. Celebrations of religious holidays, often including dancing and drinking, took place in the churchyard, too. Church bells provided the only timekeeping for most peasants and religious festivals marked major divisions of the agricultural year.

parish *n.* 牧区

bishop *n.* 主教

monastery *n.* 修道院

In all, the village, the manor, and the parish church made up the basic social structure of medieval rural communities. Each of them had different functions: for a peasant, the village regulated the routine agrarian work, the manor defined the economic, legal and social

consolation *n.* 慰藉
simultaneously *adv.* 同时
order *n.* 等级
Flanders *n.* 佛兰德地区
profit *n.* 利润
fleet *n.* 船队

relationship between the lords and peasants, and the parish was the source of spiritual **consolation** and religious obligation. Most peasants were **simultaneously** villagers, manorial tenants, and parishioners. Some manors or parishes covered two or more villages; in these cases, people from several villages shared a manorial court or parish church. But sometimes a manor or parish covered only part of a village, so that people in the same village owed rents to different manors or tithes to different parish churches. In the Central Middle Ages, the great majority of Europe's population belonged to one of the three **orders**—those who worked (peasants), those who fought (knights and lords), and those who preached (clergy). These three orders lived together in mutual dependence.

2.2 The Rise of Trade and Towns

Increased agricultural production made food available for town residents, who in turn had free time and energy to produce and market other products. As a result, European commercial activity expanded dramatically during the Central Middle Age. After 1000 commerce gradually became a powerful new force in European economic life. Towns grew along with trade, especially in north Italy and **Flanders**.① Throughout Europe, enterprising merchants responded to new opportunities by buying goods in one place, transporting them to another, and then selling them at a **profit**. English kings, French dukes, and German emperors alike encouraged trade: weekly markets were opened in villages, serving the local needs; annual fairs were organized in many regions, attracting international merchants and goods. By 1100 European ship were again sailing the Mediterranean; and for the next two centuries the traffic between Europe and the eastern end of the sea was lively. The growth of trade and the rise of towns laid the foundation for the eventual transformation of Europe from a rural society to an urban society.

2.2.1 Growing Trade

Italy undoubtedly played a leading role in the revival of European trade. To protect their merchant ships, Italian coastal cities such as Venice, Florence, Genoa, Naples, and Pisa, developed their own **fleets**. The city-state of Venice had joined the Byzantine Empire in the

① 佛兰德在欧洲中世纪是一个国家，今为欧洲西北部的一个地区，在北海沿岸，包括法国西北部部分地区、现比利时的东佛兰德省、西佛兰德省以及荷兰的西南部部分地区。中世纪兴起的佛兰德贸易重镇布鲁日（Bruges）、根特（Ghent）、安特卫普（Antwerp）今天都是比利时的主要城市。

Byzantine-Muslim War (1030—1035). This war decisively loosened the Islamic hold on the Mediterranean Sea from the 11th century onward. Italians became major military forces in the Mediterranean. Italian merchants dominated the Mediterranean and controlled the trade between Constantinople, Alexandria and the West, bringing goods from Islamic and Byzantine ports to Italian cities, and carrying them overland across the Alps into France and Germany. By the 13th century, Italian merchants had spread far beyond the Mediterranean. The merchant banking houses of Venice, Florence and Genoa had established offices around the Mediterranean and Black seas: south along the Atlantic coast of **Morocco**; east into Armenia and Persia; west to England (London) and Flanders (such as **Bruges** and **Ghent**); and north to Scandinavia. Some individual merchants, such as Marco Polo traded as far east as China and even entered the service of the Great **Khan**.

Morocco *n.* 摩洛哥
Bruges *n.* 布鲁日（今比利时城市）
Ghent *n.* 根特（今比利时城市）
Khan *n.* 可汗
Rhineland *n.* 莱茵河流域

By the year 1000, a triangular trade existed between England, Flanders and **Rhineland**, bringing raw wool from England to Flanders, and wool cloth from Flanders to the Rhineland. Flanders became a commercial center for the traders of northern Europe. English merchants were active in Constantinople and northern Spain, exchanging northern silver for Byzantine silks, Islamic **spices**, and African gold. Scandinavian merchants and warriors ranged even more widely, establishing cities in Ireland, **principalities** in Normandy and southern Italy, trading outposts along the Russian trade routes that ran from the Baltic to the Black Sea and to the Caspian Sea.

spice *n.* 香料

principality *n.* 公国

With the growth of trade, great **fairs** tying the southern and northern commercial worlds together came into being. In towns along the main European trade routes, smart lords set up fairs, which became meeting places for merchants from Italy and northern Europe. For two centuries these fairs were the most important European market places. The fair was different from the local market. Held once a week, the local market allowed the peasants to sell surplus food from the manor and to buy manufactured goods from the town; the fair was held only seasonally or annually in specified areas of each European country, it was a much more important and elaborate event. At the fair, not only goods but also ideas were exchanged. From all over Europe, men gathered and exchanged information about new methods in industry, agriculture, and transportation. The fairs pushed forward the development of a money economy. They helped break down the isolation of the towns.

fair *n.* 商品交易会

Champagne *n.* 香槟地区

The most famous fairs in all Europe were held in **Champagne** in northeastern France. Organized by the counts of Champagne, a series of six fairs were held annually in the chief towns of the region of Champagne. The fairs of Champagne attracted merchants from almost the entire Europe—Flanders, England, Scandinavia, Germany, Spain and Italy. Rich and poor people from the surrounding countryside also poured into the fairs, as merchants from north and south met to bargain and trade under the protection of the local counts. These trades connected the financial and marketing centers of the south with the manufacturing and trading communities of the north, tying the northern world to the south more effectively than any political system since the Roman Empire.

investing *adj.* 投资的
joint-stock *n.* 合股
liability *n.* 赔偿责任
accounting *adj.* 会计的
deposit *n.* 存储，定金
loan *n.* 贷款
credit transfer 银行转账

In Italy, new forms of business organization appeared to finance business enterprise. Partnerships were formed between **investing** partners who stayed at home and travelling partners who gained rewards for their risks (travelling partners could also be investors). A type of **joint-stock** arrangement also emerged in which several ship-owners would hold a number of shares in several ships to reduce their **liability** in the event of loss. As money became an accepted measure of value and means of exchange, European businessmen developed more efficient banking and **accounting** methods. **Deposits**, **loans**, and **credit transfers** became standard procedures. During this period, several cities, such as Vienna and Bruges, Siena and Florence, developed into prominent banking centers.

2.2.2 Towns: Growth and Development

extinct *adj.* 绝迹

Although towns continued to exist in Western Europe after the Germanic invasions, by 1000 population in most towns were greatly reduced, some even depopulated. Take Rome as an example, its population dropped from about a million to less than fifty thousand. The decline of the Roman Empire and the several waves of foreign invasions greatly disrupted the economy of town. Generally speaking, town life in Western Europe between 500 and 1000 was almost **extinct** and of little importance. But from 1000 to 1200 with the increase in trade, commercial activities revitalized older towns and brought new ones into existence. Trade and towns had an interacting effect on each other: the towns arose because of trade, but they also stimulated trade by providing greater markets and by producing goods for the merchants to sell.

In the revival of both commerce and cities, geography played an important role. It determined the location of certain strategic towns and conditioned the type of commercial activities in which the towns engaged. Rivers, which were important in the evolution of ancient civilizations, played an equally important role in the development of medieval towns. They were natural transportation routes for goods. Many towns' location, either near a mountain pass or on a good coastal harbor, was also advantageous. Italian costal towns were open to rich trade with the Near East and Africa.

Perhaps the most important social factor contributing to the rise of towns was the growth of population. As mentioned in the section on "agricultural revolution", the population in Europe by 1300 had almost doubled since the fall of Rome. The size of cities and towns grew fast. By the year 1300, Paris had about 200 000 people; Venice, Florence, Genoa, Milan had about 100 000 people each; London had about 80 000 people. Once cities and towns started to flourish, many of them began to specialize in certain enterprises. For example, Paris and Bologna became the homes of leading universities; Venice, Genoa, Cologne and London became centers of long-distance trade; Milan, Florence, Ghent and Bruges specialized in manufactures. The most important urban industries were those devoted to the production of wool cloth and cotton cloth. By the late 11th century, the production of wool cloth began to develop from a cottage occupation into Europe's first major industry.

The renewal of town life first appeared in three areas: northern Italy, Flanders, and southern France. Of the three areas northern Italy had the most flourishing cities. Controlling a large fleet of merchant ships by 1100, prosperous Venice was the envy of other towns in Europe. Milan, Genoa, Pisa, and Bologna had also become busy trade centers; and Florence, important for manufacturing, was soon to become internationally famous banking center. Towns in Flanders grew up mainly around the **textile industry**. Next in importance to the towns in northern Europe were those in southern France—Montpellier, Narbonne, and Marseilles. In central France, such river towns as Paris, Orleans, and Tours were slowly increasing in importance.

textile industry 纺织业

Throughout the course of the 11th and 12th centuries, the old Roman cities were again full of people from all walks of life. Residents included, besides merchants and artisans, free peasants seeking fortune, runaway serfs, ambitious young nobles, and also masters and students at a school or university. Meanwhile, many new cities or towns were also founded. Often these new towns developed near **forts** built in the ninth and tenth centuries. The strategic location of the forts offered

fort *n.* 堡垒，要塞

the merchants a good stopping place. As the German word for fort is burg, over time various forms of burg such as burgh, bourg, or borough, came to apply to the town, and town inhabitants became known as burghers or burgesses and later as a social class, the **bourgeoisie**. The growth of the bourgeoisie population brought a new order to the social structure of the medieval Europe.

bourgeoisie *n.* 中产阶级

2.2.3 *A New Urban Society*: *Guilds and Communes*

guild *n.* 基尔特，行会
commune *n.* 市镇(居民)

Most of the urban inhabitants were merchants involved in trade and artisans engaged in manufacturing. Generally, merchants and artisans had their own sections within a city. The merchant area included warehouse, inns and **taverns**. Artisan sections were usually divided along professional lines and each profession had its own street. When the merchants and artisans settled permanently in the towns, they organized themselves into guilds, i. e. associations of persons engaged in a common profession. These associations were useful not only from a business **standpoint** but also from a social and political viewpoint. The guild was set up to solve employer-worker problems, to regulate prices and wages, to govern production and distribution, to enforce rules of fair business practices, to protect the individual member, and to assure the social status of his family. There were two kinds of guilds: merchant and craft.

tavern *n.* 小酒店，小旅馆

standpoint *n.* 角度

The central purpose of the merchant guild was to **ensure monopoly** of trade within a certain town. Usually only merchants from a particular town could join the town's merchant guild. Within a monopoly of the town's import and export trade, the guild could enforce its standards. All merchants from other places were supervised closely and had to pay tolls. Disputes among merchants were settled at the guild court according to its own laws and rules. The guild regulated prices and standardized trading conditions such as weights, measures, and quality of goods to promote fair trade.

ensure *v.* 确保
monopoly *n.* 垄断

Learning from the merchants, artisans set up craft guilds to limit competition and to maintain a livelihood for all. The artisan guilds regulated wages, prices, conditions of labor, standards of quality, methods of manufacture, and amounts of production. They also controlled conditions for anyone who wished to enter into their professions. According to the general rules in most guilds, if a person wanted to enter a craft, he started as an **apprentice** to a master and had to work for perhaps seven years under the master's guidance, often living in the master's household. After this term, the apprentice

apprentice *n.* 学徒

became a **journeyman** and received wages for his work. When a journeyman earned enough money and developed sufficient skill, he might open his own shop and become a master. But his work (a masterpiece) had to first pass the examination by the guild.

journeyman *n.* 满师学徒工，熟练工

At the time there was not strong central government to protect merchants when they did business from one place to another, from one country to another. As a result merchants first organized guilds to protect their own interests. Later artisans followed their example. The guilds assumed some political functions that should have been played by governments. In a merchant was **imprisoned** in another town, the guild tried to secure his release at its own expense. If a merchant of a London guild refused to pay a debt owed to a merchant in Venice, the merchant guild in Venice would seize the goods of any London merchants coming to Venice.

imprison *v.* 监禁

In addition to its business and political functions, the guild also undertook **charitable** and social activities. If a guildsman fell into poverty, he would be helped by his guild. The guild also provided financial aid for the burial expenses of its members and looked after their families. These guilds also served important social **functions** as religious associations and drinking clubs.

charitable *adj.* 慈善的

function *n.* 功能

People living in towns did not fit into the "three orders" social framework (i. e. the peasants, the nobles, and the clergy). As new social elements in medieval society, town dwellers had to struggle to gain freedom to do their work and enjoy its rewards. The biggest problem town dwellers faced was the use of land. Initially, land on which a town sat was owned by its lord, who might be a noble, a bishop or the head of local monastery. To use the land, town dwellers needed a **charter** granted by the lord of the land. A lord might grant a charter for a money payment. But sometimes towns had to defeat lords in battle to get hold of such documents.

charter *n.* （成立自治市的）特许状

Charters enabled town dwellers to create **institutions** suitable to their new way of life. Charters gave the town dwellers some rights and powers of self-government, such as establishing their own courts and making their own laws to regulate their affairs. Through power of self-government, the charters **restricted** the lord's opportunities to raise money at will. Usually, a charter ruled that anyone living in a town for a year and a day would be freed from his **obligations** to serve his lord. Many **serfs** therefore escaped from the manors and moved to the towns. After living a year and a day in the town, a serf was considered a

institution *n.* 机构

restrict *v.* 限制

obligation *n.* 职责

serf *n.* 农奴

freeman. A former serf could completely change his old position and become a wealthy and influential craftsman or merchant in the town. Thus a common proverb stated, "City air makes one free." This specific regulation in the charter led to the growth of towns and the decline of **serfdom.**

serfdom *n.* 农奴制

Although there was a great diversity of people in the cities—**humble** street cleaners and powerful merchants, day laborers and master craftsmen, servants and financiers—all were united by a sense of common identity as city dwellers. City dwellers formed a revolutionary group who wanted no lords above them, who wanted freedom and self-government. Hence, a movement for urban self-government arose. By 1100, burghers were obtaining "charters of freedoms" or "urban charters" from their territorial lords. In effect, each urban charter created an independent or semi-independent political and legal entity called **commune**. Commune had its own local government, its own court, its own tax-collecting **agencies** and its own customs. Some communes gained their independence by paying lords to grant it to them, while others governed alongside their lord. Still others battled violently for rights of self-rule. Communes in Italy were particularly successful. They gained the right not only to govern themselves but also to rule the farmland and villages around them. By the 13th century, northern Italy was divided politically and economically into competing city-states, regions dominated by their chief city.

humble *adj.* 卑微的

commune *n.* 市镇

agency *n.* 中介

3. The Church Triumphant

Imagine a medieval traveler, when he approached a city he was guided by the tall towers of a church. Dominating the town and catching the eyes of the visitor, the physical importance of the church symbolized its importance in the lives of the people. As the traveler entered the city, he found monks, nuns, and **pilgrims** in the streets. Besides the churches, the traveler saw many other buildings which also belonged to the Church—colleges, hospitals, almshouses, as well as the elegant palace of the bishop. On leaving the city, he passed the massive buildings of a monastery. The road ahead would lead him to yet another church and another group of fellow Christians.

pilgrim *n.* 朝圣者

When St. Paul described the Church as "the body of Christ", he meant that the Church included all members of the Christian society.

Every child of Christian parents automatically began life within the Church: shortly after birth, they were **baptized**; when they died, they were buried in the Church yard; the Church was their moral guide and spiritual food; and it brought them comfort in this world and promised them **salvation** in the next life. Almost all Western Europeans, therefore, were subject to the Church's authority. **Obedience** to the Church was enforced by all political as well as religious rulers in western **Christendom.**

baptize *v.* 洗礼

salvation *n.* 救赎

obedience *n.* 服从

Christendom *n.* 基督教世界

The Central Middle Ages has often been called the Age of Faith. By the 13th century, Roman Catholic Christianity was the most obvious characteristic most Europeans shared. Nearly all accepted its beliefs and practices, as well as its ideals of living and its code of morals. Almost all Europeans were born, lived and died under the protection of the Church; this institution gave meaning and direction to their lives. The fundamental purpose of life was salvation of the soul, not the search for scientific fact and truth or the control of nature or other goals. To medieval Europeans, the biggest concern was to achieve salvation in the next life; in contrast, his achievement in the life on this earth was less important. Apart from its strong hold on individuals' minds and hearts, the Church also shaped the intellectual, artistic, and political life of Europe.

In our examination of medieval Christianity, we should remember that it contained three distinct aspects: (1) as a religion, it was personal faith in Jesus Christ and God; (2) as a Church, it was a highly organized institution; and (3) as a **theology**, it was a system of beliefs. But first let us consider briefly the organization and structure of the powerful Church during the Central Middle Ages. Like kings and princes who strove to create stable and effective governments, medieval religious leaders tried to centralize the organization and improve the quality of the medieval Church.

theology *n.* 神学

3.1 The Centralized Structure of the Medieval Church

Although by 1000, the rulers of most European kingdoms had adopted Christianity for themselves and their **subjects**, Christian society was confronted with many severe problems. The invasions of the 9th and 10th centuries by Vikings and Magyars not only destroyed many churches and monasteries but also greatly damaged the church institutions. As **lay** lords provided church officers protection against invaders, their economic and political authority over church officers increased. They absorbed church lands into their **estates** and used the resources of the

subject *n.* 臣民

lay *n.* 非神职的

estate *n.* 私有土地

church for their own benefits. Moreover, they controlled the appointment of church officers-priests, abbots, bishops, and during the 10th century even popes. Because the church was dominated by lay lords, church officers were often appointed for political rather than spiritual reasons. This gave rise to many serious religious **abuses**: some bought their way into the church office; some broke the church's rule of **celibacy**. At the same time, there were few schools to train clergy; many church officers were **shallow** and **incompetent.**

abuse *n.* 弊端
celibacy *n.* 独身生活
shallow *adj.* 肤浅
incompetent *adj.* 无能

By 1000, efforts to reform the church were under way. Reformers worked hard to create a centralized church organization under the pope's control. Based on the Bible and the writings of church fathers, the reformers viewed the church as a community of individual believers with a common faith **pursuing** the common goal of eternal salvation. Like political states, such a community needed its own head, law, and resources. The first step the reformers took to remove lay control over the church was to restrict the elections of popes to the **cardinals** (1059). Some reformers became popes and pushed the reform forward systematically. The popes of the 12th and 13th centuries were fully **committed** to establishing their authority over the church. They created a system of church courts in which the popes had final **jurisdiction**. They also greatly improved the collection of church taxes.

pursue *v.* 追求
cardinal *n.* 红衣主教
committee to *v. pr.* 致力于
jurisdiction *n.* 权限

By the early 13th century, after successive reforms, a highly centralized organization of the church was put in place. At the top of the pyramid-shaped power structure of the church was the pope. The pope was assisted by the **papal curia**. As the central governing body of the entire Roman Catholic Church, the curia was an extensive bureaucracy which contained specialized departments handling **correspondence** and records, finances, judicial cases, and the application of church law. The curia was directed by the College of Cardinals whose members were selected by the popes. Like kings, the popes issued laws, hired masters to collect **revenues** and judge cases, even declared wars. Such a system of government of the Church with the pope as its supreme head was called **papacy**.

Papal curia 罗马教廷
correspondence *n.* 信件往来
revenue *n.* 税收
papacy *n.* （罗马天主教）教皇制度

In addition to their own bureaucracy, the popes exercised authority over the **hierarchy** of archbishops, bishops, and priests below them. Archbishops and bishops administrated their territories, called **dioceses**. At the base of the institutional hierarchy, priests directed the religious life of the **laity** in their respective **parishes**. As they exercised more direct control of the increasingly centralized and hierarchically

hierarchy *n.* 等级制度
diocese *n.* 主教管辖的教区
laity *n.* 非神职人员
parish *n.* 牧区

organized church, the popes strove to free the church from the control of kings and lords.

In the reign of Pope **Innocent Ⅲ** (1198—1216), the papacy reached the height of its power. In order to place papal independence on a solid territorial foundation, Pope Innocent consolidated and expanded the papacy's territories in central Italy, and for this reason he is often regarded as the founder of the **Papal States**. On many occasions Pope Innocent acted as the judge of European affairs. For example, he forced King Philip of France to restore his wife to her rightful place as queen after Philip had tried to declare the marriage **invalid**. He intervened in the German affairs and established his own **candidate** as emperor (Frederick Ⅱ). He **compelled** King John of England to accept the papal choice of the archbishop of Canterbury. He supported the new religious **orders—Franciscan** and **Dominican**,① and called **crusaders** to **extinguish heresy**. More importantly, Pope Innocent summoned the **Fourth Lateran Council** in 1215.② The council's rulings covered many aspects of personal conduct. It defined fundamental doctrines (such as seven **sacraments**) and made the leadership of the papacy within the Christian world more apparent than ever.

Innocent Ⅲ 教皇英诺森三世

Papal States 教廷国

invalid *adj.* 无效
candidate *n.* 候选人
compel *v.* 迫使
order *n.* 修道会
Franciscan 方济各会
Dominican 多明我会
crusader *n.* 十字军
extinguish *v.* 消除
heresy *n.* 异端邪说
the Fourth Lateran Council 第四次拉特兰宗教大会
sacrament *n.* 圣礼仪式

Relation of Church and State

After the Gregorian Reform of the late 11th century, the power of kings and emperors over the Church began to decline. This painting shows how the Church viewed the relationship between Church and state. The pope is shown in the center of the picture, with other representatives of the Church to his left. To the right of the pope, and seated slightly lower, is the Holy Roman emperor, and to his right, other representatives of lay government.

① 方济各会由意大利天主教修士圣方济各（Saint Francis of Assisi，1182—1226）创立，规定修士恪守苦修，麻衣赤足，步行各地宣称“清贫福音”。多明我会由西班牙天主教修士圣道明古斯曼（Saint Dominic de Guzman，1170—1221）创立，会士均披黑色斗篷，因此称为“黑衣修士”。他们自称为主的看守犬，立志走遍欧洲去扑灭异端与无知。

② 大会在位于罗马的天主教最高位教堂拉特兰大教堂召开，因此得名。

enhance *v.* 增强

The popes of the 13th century continued to **enhance** their powers and centralize the government of the Church. But with the steady growth of royal power, toward the end of the 13th century, the papal monarchy met strong challenge from the national monarchies.

theological *adj.* 神学的
doctrine *n.* 教义，教条
chaotic *adj.* 混乱的
uniformity *n.* 一致性
interpretation *n.* 诠释

3.2 Unifying the Church's Theological Doctrine

To strengthen its power the Church in the Central Middle Ages was also active in unifying Christian belief. The **chaotic** conditions of the early Middle Ages had made it difficult for the Church to keep **uniformity** in doctrine and practices; Christians in different regions developed different **interpretation** of the Bible and adopted different practices. It was therefore necessary for the Church to develop a coherent and integrated system of belief and practice. Many scholars in the Central Middle Ages devoted much energy to solve the problems of theology. From the Bible, the writings of the church fathers, decision of councils, and papal statements, Catholic scholars tried to discover the nature of God and His relations to the universe and man.

essential n. 要素
Crucifixion *n.* 钉死于十字架
bliss *n.* 极乐
sacrament *n.* 圣礼
sacrifice *v.* 牺牲
atone *v.* 补偿
mediator *n.* 斡旋者
legitimize *v.* 使合法化

At the heart of the theological debate was the nature and process of salvation. The following points made up the **essentials** of the Catholic faith: (1) the creation and the fall of man, (2) the Birth and **Crucifixion** of Christ, (3) the Last Judgment, (4) the horrors of hell; (5) the eternal **bliss** of heaven, and (6) the usefulness of the **sacraments** in helping man win salvation. According to the theology of the Church, Adam had left the original sin to his descendants, so that the entire human race was sinner in the eyes of God. But God did not leave man without hope. Jesus, the Son of God, had **sacrificed** Himself on the cross to **atone** for mankind's sins, and through His sacrifice God gave man an opportunity to earn salvation. But how was salvation earned? Theologians taught that salvation was won only with God's grace given to man by means of sacraments through the Church and its officials. The Church and its officials, therefore, played the vital role of a **mediator** between common people and God. Such a doctrine naturally **legitimized** and strengthened the Church's position.

canon law 教会法规
decree *n.* 政令
heresy *n.* 异端邪说

To enforce its teachings and commands, the Church developed its own legal system of **canon law** and Church courts. Canon law was based on the Bible, writings of the Church Fathers, and **decrees** of Church councils and popes. In the twelfth century the Church issued its official body of canon law. Canon law guided the Church courts in judging various crimes against Christian teachings. **Heresy** was the most horrible of all crimes in medieval eyes. A murder was a crime against a fellow man, but the disbelief in the teachings of Christ or His Church was considered a crime against God himself. Punishment for **heretics** was severe. Although the medieval Church sometimes used physical punishment, the main weapons to support its authority were spiritual penalties. The most powerful of these was excommunication, which means exclusion from the Church. When a person was excommunicated, he was denied of the Church's protection and service and he would have little chance to save his soul after death.

heretic *n.* 异教徒，持异端者

Seven Sacraments 七大圣礼

"Seven Sacraments" refer to seven particular rites or rituals performed in and by the Church., including: ①Baptism 受洗; ②Confirmation (or Chrismation) 坚振; ③Eucharist (or Holy Communion) 圣体; ④Reconciliation (or Penance, or Penance and Reconciliation) 告解（忏悔）; ⑤Anointing of the Sick (formerly known as Last Rites or Extreme Unction) 终傅; ⑥Marriage (or Holy Matrimony) 婚配; ⑦Holy Orders (or Ordination) 圣秩（神品）.

3.3 Christian Conquests and the Crusades

The most dramatic expression of European's religious **ardor** was the Crusades. The word crusade itself is derived from "taking the cross," after the example of Christ. The Crusades were a series of Holy Wars launched by Latin Christian Europe against Muslims in the Middle East to restore Christian control of the Holy Land. On the way to the Holy Land, a crusader wore the red cross on his outfit. The devout Christian believed that if he took the cross and fulfilled his duty, he would enjoy forgiveness of his sins.

ardor *n.* 激情

Fought over a period of nearly 200 years between 1095 and 1291, the Crusades arose from complex causes, underwent dramatic process, and produced far-reaching effects. The rise and fall of the crusading movement was closely related to the **fortunes** of the papal authority in the Central Middle Ages. The First Crusade was started by the papacy, and its success was a great early victory for the papal monarchy. The papacy hoped that the religious enthusiasm in the crusades would strengthen its own position. But the later decline of the crusading movement helped **undermine** the pope's authority.

fortune *n.* 运气

undermine *v.* 逐渐削弱

3.3.1 The Causes of the Crusades

Generally speaking, the causes of the Crusades lie in the **deteriorating** situation of the Byzantine Empire in the east caused by a

deteriorating *adj.* 不断恶化的

new wave of Turkish Muslim attacks as well as the economic-political-military-social-religious developments in Western Europe. After the Macedonian dynasty was **extinguished** in 1056, the Byzantine Empire got into internal struggles for power between military leaders and aristocratic families. The growing division and official split between the Catholic Church of the west and the **Eastern Orthodox Church** of the Byzantine Empire also weakened the Byzantine state. Moreover, the Byzantine Empire faced external threats to its security as well. The greatest challenge came from the Islamic **Seljuk Turks** in the Middle East.

extinguish *v.* 消亡

Eastern Orthodox Church 东正教教会

Seljuk Turk 塞尔柱突厥人（土耳其人）

Abbasid caliphate 阿巴斯哈里发

By the 11th century, the Islamic empire led by the **Abbasid** caliphate in Baghdad was also in a process of disintegration. The Seljuk Turks, originally from Central Asia and converting to Islam, captured Baghdad in 1055 and took Jerusalem in 1065, killing 3 000 Christians. Later in 1071, the Seljuk Turks defeated the Byzantine army at the Battle of Manzikert and occupied Asia Minor (Anatolia), the heartland, breadbasket and population center of the Byzantine Empire.

The Seljuk Turkish invasion not only threatened the Byzantine Empire, but also disrupted the Western Christian **pilgrim** traffic to the Holy Land. Pilgrimage to the Holy Land, where Jesus Christ was born, **crucified** and **resurrected**, was of great spiritual importance to European Christians, because it was a demonstration of their religious devotion and a way of saving their sins. Unlike the Arabs who had been fairly tolerant of Christian pilgrimage to the Holy Land, the Islamic Turks created considerable hardships for Western pilgrims, attacking the Christian pilgrims, killing many of them and selling many others as slaves.

pilgrim *n.* 朝圣

crucify *v.* 钉上十字架

resurrect *v.* 复活

In 1095, the Byzantine emperor **Alexius Ⅰ** (1081—1118) asked **Pope Urban Ⅱ** (1088—1099) for military help against the Seljuk Turks. Pope Urban II responded to emperor's appeal and called for a Crusade to rescue the Byzantines from Islamic Seljuk Turks' threat and liberate the Holy Land from the Muslim. Thus came the Crusades. This religious-military **motivation** to stop the Muslim invasion and re-conquer the Land of Christ was the **immediate** and **primary** reason for the Crusades.

Alexius Ⅰ 阿里克西乌斯一世

Pope Urban Ⅱ 教皇乌尔班二世

motivation *n.* 动机

immediate *adj.* 直接的

primary *adj.* 首要的

For many Christians, the crusading movement was a holy war. But some crusaders were motivated by material considerations. When a crusader put the red cross on his **outfit**, he became a privileged person. Through the influence of the Church, he was freed from taxes, and his debts were temporarily cancelled; the Church took care of his property

outfit *n.* 外衣

and his families while he was away from home. Among the crusaders, there were **criminals** trying to escape justice, debtors running away from their creditors, nobles seeking to gain new lands, and merchants looking for new business opportunities and more profits. Like many historical movements, the crusades were influenced by both **idealism** and **materialism.**

criminal *n.* 犯罪分子

idealism *n.* 理想主义

materialism *n.* 物质主义

Besides religious and material motivations, there were other more complex reasons for the Crusades. One reason behind the Crusades was to offer an **outlet** for the constantly warring feudal lords and knights in Western Europe. In the medieval Europe, almost all nobles were trained as knights in the spirit of **chivalry**. These noble warriors had defended Christian civilization against successive waves of barbarian **assaults**, but by the 11th century the barbarians (including Vikings, Magyars and others) were either **tamed** or destroyed, except the Muslims. In areas far from the Muslim frontier, these noble warriors turned their energy to fight each other over land, possessions, romance, right of succession, or even attack the local common people. The Crusades redirected the goals of warfare from attacks against other Christians to the defense of Christian society against Muslims.

outlet *n.* 出口

chivalry *n.* 骑士

assault *n.* 袭击

tame *v.* 驯服

Another reason involved Roman-Byzantine **rivalry** and the **rift** between the Western Roman Catholic Church and the Eastern Orthodox Church following the **Great Schism** of 1054. Pope Urban Ⅱ saw Byzantine emperor Alexius' request as an opportunity to **heal** the Schism of East and West once and for all, especially when Alexius promised he would take measures toward recognizing Rome once Byzantine was safe from the Turks. If the West proved capable of defeating the Muslim threat which had for so long troubled the East, then the West was possible to bring the Orthodox Church back into communication with the papacy and reunify the Eastern and Western churches. Thus the Christian interest in the Crusades was not only to end the Muslim threat, but also to end the Christian schism.

rivalry *n.* 敌对

rift *n.* 不和

Great Schism 东西方宗教大分裂

heal *v.* 愈合

Furthermore, the Crusades had something to do with the issue of the **Investiture Controversy** where popes and German emperors struggled over the control of the appointment of church officers. Both sides of the Investiture Controversy participated in the Crusades, hoping to guide public opinion in their favor. People became personally engaged in a dramatic religious controversy. The public interest in religious affairs was further strengthened by religious **propaganda**, which **advocated** Just War to retake the Holy Land from the Muslims.

Investiture Controversy 叙任权斗争

propaganda *n.* 宣传

advocate *v.* 主张

Pope hoped that an expedition to the East, carried out under papal leadership and comprised of noblemen from across Western Europe, would **enhance** his position in the ongoing Investiture Controversy with the Holy Roman Empire.

enhance *v.* 提高

Socio-economic factors contributed to the formation of the Crusades as well. In the Central Middle Ages, agricultural advances increased the food supply, permitted population increase, and led to more wealth and commerce, making manpower and **facility** for military expeditions available. On the other hand, more population also created pressure on existing resources, which led the West to begin looking for external adventures to get new land and vast wealth in the East. In addition, the Italian merchant states, already powerful and influential, wished to expand their trade in the Mediterranean. This was being blocked by Turk Muslim control of many strategic seaports, so if Muslim domination of the eastern Mediterranean could be ended or at least significantly weakened, then cities like Venice, Genoa, and Pisa had a chance to enrich themselves further. Of course, richer Italian states also meant a richer **Vatican.**

facility *n.* 设备

Vatican *n.* 梵蒂冈

3.3.2 The Process of the Crusades

The Crusades went on about 200 years. Generally speaking, there were altogether nine main Crusades, as well as various small expeditions. We should bear in mind that the process of the Crusades was a complex one, and it was difficult to make any **categorization** or division of the Crusades. Where did one Crusade end and the next begin? It was quite **controversial**. We should also remember that because of internal conflicts among Christian kingdoms and political powers, some of the crusade expeditions were **diverted** from their original aim. For example, the Sixth Crusade was the first crusade to set sail without the official blessing of the Pope. And the Fourth Crusade led to the sack of Christian Constantinople and the **partition** of the Byzantine Empire between Venice and the Crusaders.

categorization *n.* 分类

controversial *adj.* 有争议的

divert *v.* 偏离

partition *n.* 分割

The Crusades (1096—1291)		
Crusade	Period	Results
1st Crusade	1096—1099	Crusaders captured Holy City of Jerusalem and established four Crusader states which were also called Latin States.
2nd Crusade	1147—1149	Failure of the crusade, including the loss of one of the four Latin States.
3rd Crusade	1189—1191	A strong start, but a weak end. German emperor Frederick drowned on the way; French king Philip quarreled with English king Richard and went home; only Richard stayed longer, but failed to take Jerusalem.
4th Crusade	1202—1204	The Crusaders sacked Constantinople, and established the so-called Latin Empire and a series of other Crusader states throughout the territories of the Byzantine Empire.
5th Crusade	1217—1221	Defeat of the crusade by the ruler of Egypt, Ayubid Sultan Al-Kamil
6th Crusade	1228—1229	Treaty with Al-Kamil
7th Crusade	1248—1258	Defeat of the crusade by the Egyptians.
8th Crusade	1270—1270	Failure of the crusade.
9th Crusade	1271—1272	Defeat of the crusade.

The early crusading armies enjoyed astonishing success. Allying with the Byzantine emperor Alexius, they defeated Seljuk armies in Anatolia. They then conquered cities in Syria and finally entered Jerusalem in 1099. To control their newly won territories, the crusaders established a feudal monarchy and made one of their members the king of Jerusalem.

Despite the marked success, the crusaders faced several persistent problems. For one thing, the crusaders' interest in seeking land and glory for themselves conflicted with Alexius' desire to restore his empire. Although by their success the crusaders restored the unity of Christendom, their colonial ambition **crippled** the Byzantine Empire. The crusaders' **greed** further **embittered** the Eastern Orthodox Christians. As a result, the gap between the Eastern Orthodox and the Roman Catholics became wider and deeper. It was not until the 20th century before the division was ended by pope and patriarch permanent.

cripple *v.* 削弱
greed *n.* 贪婪
embitter *v.* 使怨恨

The crusaders also had difficulties in receiving enough additional warriors from Europe to **consolidate** their position. Over time, they were forced to trade and make treaties with their Muslim neighbors. This

consolidate *v.* 巩固

facilitate *v.* 有利于
acquire *v.* 获取
Acre *n.* 阿克城（今以色列境内）

in turn **facilitated** later Turkish expansion into southern-eastern Europe. Christian territories **acquired** during the First Crusade were gradually lost over the next 200 years. Jerusalem was recaptured by Muslim forces in 1187. Muslim capture of **Acre** in 1291 marked the end of the Crusades.

3.3.3 *Impact of the Crusades*

disturbance *n.* 混乱
Christendom *n.* 基督教国度
estimate *n.* 估算

The Crusades kept all Europe in a **disturbance** for two centuries, directly and indirectly costing **Christendom** several millions of lives (from 2 millions to 6 millions according to different **estimates**), in addition to incalculable expenditures in treasure and suffering. On the other hand, the Crusades directly and indirectly brought about so comprehensive and significant effects that they formed a most important factor in the history of the progress of civilization. Some of the effects were short-lived, while others have lasted into contemporary times.

foster *v.* 助长
accustom *v.* 使……习惯于……

Without doubt, the Crusades increased the power of the Papacy. The important role which the Popes played in the Crusades naturally **fostered** their authority and influence, by placing in their hands the armies and resources of Christendom, and **accustoming** the people to look up to them as guides and leaders. The Church therefore benefited a lot from the Crusades in terms of wealth.

undermine *v.* 逐渐削弱
revert *v.* 回复
private warfare 私战
turbulent *adj.* 骚乱的

The Crusades also strengthened the power of national monarchies and **undermined** feudalism. Thousands of barons and knights sold their lands in order to raise money for a crusading expedition. Thousands more died and their estates **reverted** to the crown. Moreover, **private warfare** also tended to die out with the departure for the Holy Land of so many **turbulent** feudal lords. The decline in both numbers and influence of feudal lords was helpful to the growth of the royal authority and the development of centralized bureaucracies (the foundation of the modern nation-state).

henceforth *adv.* 自此以后

The Crusades fatally weakened the Byzantine Empire. Both the failure to recover Anatolia from the Turks and the sack of Constantinople destroyed the Byzantine Empire as a first rate power. **Henceforth**, the Byzantine Empire was but a shell of its former self. Encouraged by the decline of the Byzantine Empire, the Turks later invaded the Balkans. In 1453, the Turks finally took Constantinople. Although the Byzantine Empire finally collapsed in 1453, yet its turning point occurred during the Crusades, especially the 4th Crusade.

ignite *v.* 激起

The Crusades **ignited** a long tradition of organized violence against

Jews in European culture. The first widespread attacks on the Jews occurred during the Crusades. Some Christians argued that to undertake the holy wars against the Muslims in the Holy Land while the "murderers of Christ" (i. e. the Jews) ran free at home was unthinkable. During the first Crusade, especially the Popular Crusade, on their way across Europe, the crusaders killed thousands of Jews in the Rhineland (now western Germany). This was in fact the first organized **anti-Semitic** persecution in European history. It established a terrible precedent and the **massacre** of Jews became a regular feature of medieval European history.

anti-Semetic *adj.* 反犹太人的
massacre *n.* 大屠杀

The Crusades created deeper distrust between Islam and Christianity. The Crusades helped to **crystallize** both Christian and Islamic doctrines of holy war against each other. The conflict between them deepened the **mutual hostility** that already separated the Islamic world and Christian Europe. The image of barbaric Christian Crusaders has been continuing to **haunt** Arab Muslim's **perspections** of Europe and Christianity, especially when combined with the more recent history of European colonialism in the Middle East. Even in the 21st century, sentiments in the Western world as well as in the Muslim world came to a level of tension which not only resembled the crusader times, but was also inspired by the same ideas as the crusades.

crystallize *v.* 变得明朗而具体
mutual *adj.* 相互的
hostility *n.* 敌意，敌对态度
haunt *v.* 缠绕
persepection *n.* 看法

In addition, the Crusades opened the first chapter in the history of Western colonialism. The process of Christian military conquest and territorial expansion brought parts of the Muslim, Byzantine and Slavic worlds into the boundary of Western Christendom. In consequence, Western Christendom roughly doubled in area during the Central Middle Ages. This process also in part gave birth to the intellectual, cultural, economic, political, religious revival.

The Crusades produced important effect on trade and commerce. They created a constant demand for the transportation of troops and supplies, encouraged ship-building and extended the market for Eastern products in Europe. The products of the East (silks, **tapestries**, perfumes, spices, pearls, jade, diamonds, ivory, glass-manufacturing techniques, early forms of gun powder, and many other products) were carried across the Mediterranean to the Italian seaports and coastal cities, whence they found their way into all European lands. The Italian cities (especially the Maritime Republics of Venice, Genoa and Pisa) prospered and replaced Byzantines and Muslims as merchant-

tapestry *n.* 挂毯

traders in the Mediterranean. This commercial power became the economic base of the Italian Renaissance. It also **provoked** such **Atlantic** powers as Spain and Portugal to seek trade routes to India and China. Their efforts helped to open most of the world to European trade dominance and colonization and to shift the center of commercial activity from the Mediterranean to the Atlantic.

provoke *v.* 激起
Atlantic *adj.* 大西洋的

The Crusades had important effect on the intellectual and cultural development of Europe. Above all, the Crusades **liberalized** the minds of the crusaders, opened up a new world, and brought about a vast increase in cultural **horizons** for many Europeans. Romantic and imaginative literature also **blossomed** during the Crusades. Furthermore, although Europe had been exposed to Islamic culture for centuries through contacts in Iberian Peninsula and Sicily, much knowledge in areas such as science, medicine and architecture was transferred from the Islamic to the western world during the Crusade era. Most of all, the knowledge gained by the Crusaders through their expeditions, greatly stimulated the Latin intellect, and helped to awaken in Western Europe the mental activity which resulted finally in the great intellectual outburst known as the Revival of Learning and the period of the Renaissance.

liberalize *v.* 使自由化
horizon *n.* 眼界
blossom *v.* 繁荣发展

4. The Emergence and Growth of National Monarchies

In 900, the Carolingian Empire was collapsing. Three major areas in the former Empire—Germany, Italy, and France—followed different paths in their political and institutional development. By 1300 France had emerged as a large, stable kingdom, and Italy had turned into several relatively **coherent entities**. We might have expected these outcomes based on the pre-Carolingian experiences in these two areas. The most surprising political development within the old Carolingian lands was Germany. In the 10th century it rose to a **premier** position in Europe and then it entered into a long period of slow decline. Strong feudal monarchy flourished first in the Carolingian lands of Germany, but it eventually failed there; as a result, national unity in Germany was long **postponed**. Outside of the European continent, the English kings began the process of creating more centralizing authority. Eventually England became one of the most successful monarchies in Europe.

coherent *adj.* 一致的
entity *n.* 实体
premier *adj.* 最重要的
postpone *v.* 延迟

4.1 England

In 1066, William (**Duke of Normandy**) defeated English King Harold at the Battle of Hastings and was crowned king of England as William Ⅰ (rule 1066—1087). Norman Conquest started the process of creating a new England by combining Anglo-Saxon and Norman institutions. Right from the start, all of William's policies were pointed toward a single goal—the organization of a centralized government. To enhance his power, William introduced Norman political **principles** and feudal **practices** to England. But the feudal relationships he introduced were different from the traditional ones. In traditional feudal relationship, it was more important for lesser lords and knights to be loyal to the lord directly above them. Loyalty to the king was of **secondary** importance. Claiming all England as his by right of conquest, William demanded all landholders to swear loyalty directly to him. Such a measure greatly strengthened the royal power.

Duke of Normandy 诺曼底公爵

principle *n.* 原则

practice *n.* 实践

secondary *adj.* 次要性的

Besides keeping one-fifth of the conquered territory as royal lands, William also ordered a thorough survey of the entire land in England and its wealth. The survey provided a basis for calculating tax and making other financial **assessments**. He kept the power of coining money and collecting land taxes and also acted as judge in major criminal cases, such as **homicide** and robbery or cases involving barons. To consolidate his control of the English church, he also replaced Anglo-Saxons in leadership positions with Norman reformers and worked with them to **promote** religious reform in England.

assessment *n.* 评估

homicide *n.* 谋杀

promote *v.* 促进

By the 11th century, Anglo-Saxon England had combined strong local government, effective royal authorities, and **rigorous** nobles in a well-balanced political system. England's royal administration became highly centralized and efficient. Its kings received the direct **allegiance** of all subjects, commanded the army, and obtained advice from an informal council of nobles, clergy, and officials. Members of the royal household performed such administrative duties as regulating the royal finances and sending royal commands to local officials. England was divided into regions called **shires**; each shire had a royal administrative officer (called "**sheriff**") and district courts controlled by local lords. Sheriffs collected land taxes and recruited soldiers for the royal army.

rigorous *adj.* 缜密的

allegiance *n.* 忠诚

shire *n.* 郡

sheriff *n.* 郡长

Kings of England

William Ⅰ (the Conqueror)(1066—1089)
William Ⅱ (1089—1100)
Henry Ⅰ (1100—1135)
Stephen Ⅰ (1135—1154)
Henry Ⅱ (1154—1189)
Richard Ⅰ (Richard the Lionheart)(1189—1199)
John (1199—1216)
Henry Ⅲ (1216—1272)
Edward Ⅰ (1272—1307)

In the 12th century, the power of the English monarchy was greatly enlarged during the reign of Henry Ⅱ (rule 1154—1189). The new king strengthened the monarchy's control over England by establishing a new centralized system of justice and enhancing the power of the royal courts. By standardizing laws throughout his kingdom and by putting the law in the hands of royal officials instead of local **barons**, Henry II began to establish a common law in England—a law common to all people, courts, and cases. This system of justice united England under one set of laws and under one system of justice, giving the king not only power and prestige but also money (He collected **fines** from criminals and fees from civil cases.)

The nobles, however, were not happy about the expansion of royal authority. They were especially angry about the king's **arbitrary** decision to raise heavy taxes or to start a war. Various attempts were made to limit the king's power. In 1215 a large group of **disgruntled** barons forced King John (rule 1199—1216) to sign the **Magna Carta**, or "Great Charter" (so called because it was written on an unusually large sheet of **parchment**). As required by this document, the king must respect and consult the barons on important issues; he should administer justice according to established **procedures** rather than in an arbitrary manner; and he should also recognize and respect certain rights enjoyed by all free men in England. Magna Carta was a major step in the development of **constitutional** government in England. Its great significance lies in its acknowledgment that the king was not above the law.

The attempts to limit the royal power also led to the establishment of the English **Parliament.** The barons wanted to have some say in naming the king's closest advisers and in controlling the king's **agents**, especially judges. In 1259, King Edward held several meetings of the

baron *n.* 男爵
fine *n.* 罚金
arbitary *adj.* 随心所欲的
disgruntled *adj.* 不满的
Magna Carta《大宪章》
parchment *n.* 羊皮纸
procedure *n.* 程序
constitutional *adj.* 宪政的
parliament *n.* 议会
agent *n.* 代理人

royal court. The meetings included two knights from every county, two **burghers** from every town, and the king's Great Council (barons, bishops, judges, advisors). These meetings were called ***parliaments***, a French word meaning "talking together." In the early days, these meetings had no fixed rights or procedures, no set group of attendees, and no defined role. The kings viewed them as clever political devices to win support for royal policies. The barons viewed them as opportunities to play a real role in the government. Although at the time the parliament was not yet a major **check** on royal authority, the groundwork was being laid for England's transformation from an absolute monarchy into a constitutional monarchy. Eventually, barons and church lords formed the House of Lords; knights and burgesses, the House of Commons.

burgher *n.* (自治市的)市民

check *n.* 限制

4.2 Capetian France (987—1314)

Capetian 卡佩王朝

When the Treaty of Verdun created the West Frankish kingdom in 843, no one knew what the future of France would be. During the late 9th century and much of the 10th century, the area suffered cruelly from constant waves of Viking attacks. The Carolingian family also failed repeatedly to produce adult **heirs** to the throne. When the last Carolingian king died without an heir in 987, the barons chose the duke of Paris, Huge Capetian to be the king. In theory, the king was the overlords of the great lords of France, such as the dukes of Normandy, Brittany, Burgundy and Aquitaine. But in reality, the Capetians directly ruled only their small **domain**, the Ile de France whose central town was Paris. Earlier Capetian kings were thus weak kings. But over time the Capetians increased royal power bit by bit and ruled France for more than three hundred years—impressive achievements in comparison with the repeated failure of German dynasties.

heir *n.* 继承人

domain *n.* 领地

Unable to establish strong royal power by conquest, as William had done in England, the Capetian kings built their royal power slowly but steadily. They struggled hard to increase their power. As the growth of agriculture and trade in the royal domain supplied the French kings with **adequate** tax income, they worked to extend the royal power and to systemize the royal administration. The Capetians at the same time kept the support of the popes by defending the Christian faith and by going on crusades. While using church officials as administrators, the French kings carefully defined the powers of their officials and closely supervised them. Moreover, they developed Paris as both a trading center and a royal capital.

adequate *adj.* 充裕的

The Capetian Kings of France

Huge Capet (987—996)
Robert Ⅱ (996—1031)
Henry Ⅰ (1031—1060)
Philip Ⅰ (1060—1108)
Louis Ⅵ (1108—1137)
Louis Ⅶ (1137—1180)
Philip Ⅱ (1180—1223)
Louis Ⅷ (1223—1226)
Louis Ⅸ (1226—1270)
Philip Ⅲ (1270—1285)
Philip Ⅳ (1285—1314)

quadruple *v.* 成四倍

purchase *v.* 购买

surpass *v.* 超越

thorough *adj.* 彻底的

The reign of King Phillip Ⅱ (1180—1223) was an important turning point. He used military force to gain control of northern French territories that had been held by the English king. Through military conquest, Phillip more than doubled his territory and **quadrupled** the income of the French monarchy and greatly enlarged its power. Other kings after Phillip II continued to add lands to the royal domain both by **purchase** and marriage. On these solid foundations, a series of 13th century Capetian rulers developed strong monarchical government. By the end the 13th century, France **surpassed** England to be the largest, wealthiest, and best-governed monarchical state in Europe.

In contrast to the rapid growth of feudal monarchy in England, feudal monarchy in France developed slowly. England's size was small, internally it was not divided, and William I's conquest offered opportunity for **thorough** reform. All these made its experience unique. France, by contrast, was a large land of many provinces with widely different institutions; its conditions were more similar to those in other European lands. As France eventually developed into a powerful monarchy, it became a model for other European lands.

4.3 The Land of the Holy Roman Empire: Germany and Italy

Germany as well as Italy in the Central Middle Ages followed a very different pattern from the unified and centralized France and England. Unlike France and England, neither Germany nor Italy created a unified national monarchy in the Central Middle Ages. The Treaty of Verdun created something new in 843: an East Frankish Kingdom. But before 843 no united kingdom had ever existed in the territories east to the Rhine River. The lands had no tradition of common or unified rule. There were no single "German" people; Saxon thought of themselves as Saxon, for example, not as German. The **penetration** of Roman culture into German lands was weak, and Christian culture was recent and **fragile.** "Germany" had no natural frontiers. And finally, Germany was the most under-developed area of the Carolingian world.

penetration *n.* 渗透

fragile *adj.* 脆弱

The political situation in Germany had much to do with its tradition. Under the Carolingians, tribal areas in Germany had formed **duchies**. Each duchy was governed by a duke with his own governmental assembly and an army of tribal freemen. When the last Carolingian ruler in Germany died in 911, the dukes in Germany elected one of themselves, Henry of Saxony to be king. The German monarchy thus started off as a loose political union of five duchies—Bavaria, Franconia, Saxony, Swabia, and Lorraine. The German monarchy thereafter remained elective, despite the efforts of many rulers to make it **hereditary**.

duchy *n.* 大公国

hereditary *adj.* 世袭的

Throughout the 10th century, successive dukes of Saxony ruled as kings of Germany, forming the Saxon dynasty (919—1024). Able and ambitious, the Saxon kings **initially** succeeded in creating the first strong monarchy in Western Europe. During the 10th and 11th centuries, Germany became the first European land to recover from the disorder caused by the collapse of the Carolingian empire and foreign invasions.

initially *adv.* 开始

When in 1024 the last of Saxon king, Henry II died without an heir, the German dukes elected a member of the Salian family to be king. The Salians died out in the middle of the 12th century and was replaced by the Hohenstaufen, who ruled until 1250. This record of frequent dynastic change in Germany was in sharp contrast to the situation in France, where the Capetian family ruled from 987 to 1328. The repeated change of ruling family in a country with powerful dukes inevitably made political development **fragmented** and unstable.

fragmented *adj.* 支离破碎的

Rulers of Medieval Germany

Saxons	Salians	Hohenstaufen
Henry Ⅰ (919—936)	Conrad Ⅱ (1024—1039)	Conrade Ⅲ (1138—1152)
Otto Ⅰ (936—973)	Henry Ⅲ (1039—1056)	Frederick Barbarrosa (1152—1190)
Otto Ⅱ (973—983)	Henry Ⅳ (1056—1106)	Henry Ⅵ (1190—1197)
Otto Ⅲ (983—1002)	Henry Ⅴ (1106—1125)	Frederick Ⅱ (1212—1250)
Henry Ⅱ (1002—1024)		

Although the German kings enjoyed prestige and support, the strength of the dukes seriously limited royal power. The kings themselves were dukes, and therefore they could only control directly their own duchies. The Saxons were based in the north, the Salians in the center, and the Hohenstaufen in the south. As few nobles below the dukes held lands directly from the kings, the kings had little authority over these lesser lords. Lesser lords as well as common people living in a duchy remained more loyal to their duke than to the king. In fact, the loyalty of Germans to their regional governments (duchies at the time) rather than to a central government had colored the history of Germany from the days of Charlemagne to those of **Hilter** (1889—1945).

Hitler 希特勒

To overcome their mighty dukes, the German kings relied on the use of military force to increase their authority. The most powerful of the Saxon kings, the true restorer of the German Emperor, was **Otto Ⅰ** (936—973). Otto was primarily a warrior, and conquest was a main foundation of his power. In his early career he successfully **crushed** rebellions led by several dukes who felt threatened by his ambition. After he put down these rebellions, Otto I **appointed** new dukes from his relatives and favorites. He also controlled the appointment of lesser lords in these duchies.

Otto Ⅰ 奥托一世

crush *v.* 镇压

appoint *v.* 任命

lay investiture 世俗叙任

To reduce dependence on the dukes for assistance in governing, Otto and his successors increasingly relied on churchmen as royal officials. Since the time of Charlemagne, the Holy Roman Emperor had the right to appoint bishops and all other high-ranking churchmen and used them as government officials. This practice was called **lay investiture**. This practice had several apparent advantages. First, church officials had the educational and administrative **expertise** the rulers needed. And then the churchmen could not get married and had no **offspring**, they could be trusted to support royal policies rather than

expertise *n.* 专门知识技能

offspring *n.* 子女

pursuing family interests. Representing the king, churchmen exercised governmental authority in different duchies and provided army from those lands on the king's request. To some extent, the use of church officials helped reduce the dukes' control of government. All in all, by bringing the church into their political system, German kings tried to reduce the influence of the dukes.

For a century this cooperation worked quite well; the German kings provided the popes protection and helped promoting Christianity in the newly conquered lands. From Otto Ⅰ onwards successive German kings were crowned emperors by the popes. German kings appointed the great bishops and even controlled the elections of the popes. But beneath the **surface** of smooth **alliance**, a deep and inevitable rivalry between pope and emperor gradually built up. In the 12th century when the Church started to push for reform and to centralize its organization, the German emperors and the popes started to engage in a series of bitter conflicts over the appointment of church officials, also known as the **Investiture Struggle**. The Investiture Struggle would eventually bring out the final collapse of central authority in the Holy Roman Empire.

surface *n.* 表面
alliance *n.* 联盟
Investiture Struggle 叙任权斗争

Also, despite the great efforts made by Otto Ⅰ and later German kings to limit the powerful dukes and control the appointment of new officials, they never sought to establish a **uniformed** administration system and legal system. This was partly due to the strong tradition of **tribal autonomy** in the German society. But when there was no uniformed administration system, the kings could not enjoy the benefit of an independent tax income. As the people continued to be ruled by local officials, their loyalty to the king remained limited.

uniformed *adj.* 统一的
tribal autonomy 部落自治

Otto Ⅰ further increased his reputation and power by military victories and conquests outside of Germany. He defeated the Magyar invaders and drove them to **Hungary**; he continued German expansion eastward against the Slavs and actively promoted German colonization beyond **the Elbe River**; he marched into Italy and proclaimed himself ruler of the kingdom of Italy. In 962, Otto Ⅰ was crowned emperor by the pope. Like so many men of the Middle Ages, Otto I tended to look back over his shoulder into the past. Regarding the Roman and Carolingian empires as the golden ages of man, he firmly believed in the imperial tradition. As an American history put it: "His **objective** was Empire, and his model was Charlemagne."

Hungary *n.* 匈牙利
the Elbe River 易北河
objective *n.* 目标

This pursuit of an empire continued to drive Otto's successors to expand German influence in all directions throughout the 11th century.

intervene *v.* 干预
depose *v.* 废黜

In 1046, the Holy Roman Emperor Henry Ⅲ (1039—1056) used his imperial authority to **intervene** in the politics of papal Rome. He marched into the Italian peninsula and **deposed** Pope Benedict Ⅸ and his two rivals. He then appointed the first of a series of German-born reform popes and ruled both Germany and Italy.

preoccupation *n.* 对……的全神贯注
confusion *n.* 混乱
preeminence *n.* 卓越,超群

Later in the 12th and 13th centuries, the two most famous members of the Hohenstaufen dynasty, Frederick Barbarossa ("Red Beard") (1152—1190) and Frederick Ⅱ (1212—1250), tried to build the Holy Roman Empire with Italy as the center. Their attempts to conquer northern Italy met severe resistance from the alliance of the papacy and Italian cities. Both Frederick Barbarossa and Frederick II failed in their attempts. Their **preoccupation** with the creation of an empire in Italy left Germany and Italy in considerable political **confusion** and chaos. In the long run the German kings' imperial policies eventually led to the loss of Germany's position of **preeminence** among the nations of Europe.

insignificant *adj.* 不重要的
exert *v.* 施加控制
fragmentation *n.* 割裂状态
principality *n.* 侯国

In 1273, the major German princes, serving as electors, chose an **insignificant** German noble Rudolf of Habsburg as the new German king. In choosing Rudolf king, the princes wanted to make sure that the German monarchy would remain weak and incapable of re-establishing a centralized state. Rudolf and his successors made no attempt to **exert** imperial rule over either Germany or Italy, although they held the title of emperor of the Holy Roman Empire. Germany in the 13th century was weak and disunited. Meanwhile, Italy remained in political **fragmentation**. In the north were self-governing city-states under the weak German imperial rule, in the center was the papal state, and in the south were various **principalities** and kingdoms.

Henry Ⅳ at Canossa

Holy Roman Emperor Henry Ⅳ, together with his wife and young son, spent three days barefoot in the snow at Canossa, in northern Italy. Pope Gregory Ⅶ had excommunicated (开除教籍) Henry following a clash over secular control of the empire, and Henry was seeking from the pope readmission to the Church.

5. Intellectual Revival and Cultural Development

The Central Middle Ages was a time of **tremendous** intellectual and artistic **vitality**. This period witnessed the growth of educational institutions, a rebirth of interest in classical philosophy, advancement in **theological** thought, the development of a **vernacular** literature, and a burst of activity in architecture. While monks continued to play an important role in intellectual activity, kings, princes, or high church officials, began to exert a newfound influence. The towns and cities were especially significant in the creation of new cultural expressions.

tremendous *adj.* 巨大的
vitality *n.* 活力
theological *adj.* 神学的
vernacular *adj.* 本国语的

5.1 Education and the Rise of Universities

One important feature of medieval intellectual life was expanding interest in education. Such an interest gradually led to the creation of a distinctive new institution, the university. Before 1000, most education in Europe took place in schools set up in **monasteries**. During the 11th and 12th centuries, expanding royal bureaucracy, and increasingly complex church organization, and reviving commercial activity created a growing demand for educated persons. In response to that demand, schools grew larger and evolved into universities.

monastery *n.* 修道院

In the 12th and 13th century, many of these schools were organized into universities, the direct **ancestors** of modern European and American universities. The word university is derived from the Latin word universitas, meaning a **corporation** or guild, and referring to either a guild of students or a guild of teachers. Italy and France led the way in developing universities and became the centers of the new educational movements. The first European university appeared in 1088 in Bologna, Italy. The University of Paris established in 1200 became the first recognized university in northern Europe. Bologna University was governed by a corporation of students, a pattern followed by other southern universities, while the University of Paris was dominated by a corporation of teachers, a pattern followed by other northern universities. Bologna specialized in the study of law, while Paris became the leader in the study of **liberal arts** and **theology**. The University of Oxford in England, organized on the Paris model, was founded in 1208. A **migration** of scholars form Oxford led to the establishment of Cambridge University the following year. By the end of the Middle Ages, there were nearly 80 universities throughout Europe, most of them located in Italy, France, England, Germany and Spain.

ancestor *n.* 祖先
corporation *n.* 社团，企业
guild *n.* 基尔特，行会
liberal arts 文科
theology *n.* 神学
migration *n.* 迁徙

curriculum *n.* 课程设置
curricula (*pl.*)
logic *n.* 逻辑学
rhetoric *n.* 修辞学
reasoning *n.* 推理
arithmetic *n.* 算术
enforce *v.* 实施
lecture *n.* 讲座
committee *n.* 委员会
Bachelor of Arts 文科学士
Master of Arts 文学硕士
decade *n.* 十年
doctoral degree 博士学位
civil servant 公务员
clash *v.* 与……发生冲突
charter *n.* 特许状
immunity *n.* 豁免权

To meet the demands for educated persons, universities revised their **curricula** to include the study of seven liberal arts from classical civilization. Particularly important were the three disciplines of grammar, **logic**, and **rhetoric**. Grammar taught people to read and write effectively, rhetoric contributed to both capable writing and competent speaking, and logic promoted clear thinking and careful **reasoning**. The other four liberal arts, **arithmetic**, geometry, astronomy, and music, although less central, also helped enlarge interest.

Largely self-governing, universities **enforced** their own rules about dress, classroom activities, and the materials taught. All classes were taught in Latin and mostly by a **lecture** method. The word lecture is derived from the Latin verb meaning "to read". The master, i. e. the teacher, read a text aloud and commented on its important or difficult passages, while the students followed along, often with a copy of the text. There were other classes organized as discussions in which both masters and students asked and answered questions one another.

After a four or six year period of study, a comprehensive oral examination was given to students by a **committee** of teachers. The first degree a student could earn was **Bachelor of Arts**; later he might receive a **Master of Arts**. After completing the liberal arts curriculum, a student could go on to study law, medicine or theology (philosophy) for about a **decade** or more. A student passed final oral examinations was granted a **doctoral degree**. Besides teaching, many of the students who had successfully completed their studies went on to careers in the church. Others became lawyers and doctors, often serving wealthy merchants and their families. Still others became **civil servants** and worked for kings or princes.

Medieval universities shared in the violent atmosphere of the age. Conflicts between teachers, between students, between teachers and students were quite common. Moreover, students and teachers often **clashed** with city authorities and townspeople, because universities were granted **charters** by kings, enjoying legal **immunity** from city laws. Universities served only a limited sector of the medieval population, only for men and the wealthy; women and the poor were kept out of education.

Classes in medieval universities

5.2 Philosophy and Theology

During the Early Middle Ages, a large body of the classical works had been destroyed in Western Europe. Then in the Central Middle Ages, the crusaders re-conquered former Islamic lands and brought back to Europe many works of Jewish, Islamic, and Greek philosophy (especially Aristotle). Many scholars engaged in translating classical works from Greek and Arabic into Latin. The rediscovery of Greek and Roman scientific and philosophical works, particularly the works of Aristotle had an overwhelming impact on Western Europe. Aristotle became the leading authority on logic, but his thought presented problems for Christian thinkers. The biggest challenge was the relationship between **reason** and faith. For example, Aristotle taught that nature was good and **purposeful** and that the earth is **eternal**. Such ideas **contradicted** Christian views.

During the 13th century numerous scholars (who were called "**scholastics**" because they worked in the medieval schools) responded to the challenge. Some scholars tried **in vain** to **forbid** the study and teaching of Aristotle's thought; some argued that reason alone could lead to truth; still some argued that **ultimate** truth could not be discovered by reason, but was revealed to human by God in His mystical ways.

The most **fruitful** response to the challenge was the attempt to harmonize faith and reason. The leading scholar in this attempt was **Thomas Aquinas** (1225—1274), a professor of theology and the most brilliant intellect of the Central Middle Ages. To start with, Aquinas

reason *n.* 理性
purposeful *adj.* 有意义的
eternal *adj.* 永恒的
contradict *v.* 与……相违背
scholastics *n.* 经院哲学派
in vain 徒劳
forbid *v.* 禁止
ultimate *adj.* 终极的
fruitful *adj.* 富有成效的
Thomas Aquinas 托马斯·阿奎纳斯

took it for granted that God is the source of truth, and that the world is created by God. He then argued that **revelation** and reason were two ways of knowing the truth, in other words, there were truths **derived** by reason and truths derived by faith. For him, the two truths could not be in conflict because human reason, a gift from God, could not contradict **divine** revelation. If there were any conflict, it must come from the limits of human reason. In his ***Summa against the Gentiles*** and his incomplete ***Summa of Theology*** sought to **reconcile** systematically Christian doctrine and Greek philosophy. Aquinas's views would influence Christian intellectuals for centuries.

revelation *n.* 神示
derive *v.* 获得
divine *adj.* 神的
Summa against the Gentiles《反异教大全》
Summa of Theology《神学大全》
reconcile *v.* 调和

Saint Thomas Aquinas

Education in the 13th century was shaped profoundly by the work of Italian philosopher and theologian Saint Thomas Aquinas. The writings of Aquinas attempted to reconcile the philosophy of Aristotle with the ideas of Christian theology. Aquinas employed both reason and faith in the study of metaphysics, moral philosophy, and religion.

5.3 Science

Science was also **prominent** in medieval intellectual activity. The Latin Christian tradition preserved some scientific knowledge in early medieval **encyclopedias.** Translators of Greek and Arabic scientific works during the 11th and 12th centuries enlarged Europe's store of scientific knowledge and gave new **impetus** to the study of science. During the 13th century, a new combination of mathematical studies and direct observation of natural phenomena helped lay the foundation of modern science.

The medieval people saw the **universe** as quite small. The church adopted the model suggested by Aristotle, who had placed the earth in the center of the solar system. This was adopted because it supported the idea that the universe had been created by God just for humans, and that He had placed humans at the center of the universe. On the Earth, there were changes, things lived and died, but in Heaven there was no

prominent *adj.* 重要
encyclopedia *n.* 百科全书
impetus *n.* 推动力
universe *n.* 宇宙

change.

Arabic numbers were introduced in 1202 by Italian mathematician Leonardo de Pisa (most commonly known as **Fibonacci**, 1170—1250), including a new concept, the Indian **zero**. Fibonacci is considered by some "the most talented western mathematician of the Middle Ages," best known to the modern world both for the spreading of the Arabic numeral system (also called **Hindu-Arabic numeral system**) in Europe, primarily through the publication in the early 13th century of his *Book of Calculation* (the *Liber Abaci*) and for a **number sequence** named after him known as the Fibonacci numbers. The merchants in Italy preferred the use of Arabic numeral system to the Roman one because the former was easier to use. The new numeral system had much influence on science, the organization of texts, and the **notion** of time. The chapters of the Bible were numbered by Archbishop of Canterbury, Stephen Langton (1155—1228) and a library **categorization** system was devised. The hours became fixed and of the same length. **Perspective** in art also began its development in the 13th century, when artists began to study mathematics and **optics**.

Robert Grosseteste (1168—1253), **Roger Bacon** (1214—1294) and others made Oxford University the center of scientific studies during the 13th century. Grosseteste's emphasis on methodical and **inductive** use of observation and mathematics **dominated** English scientific thought for another two centuries. Bacon carried Grosseteste's work farther. Bacon wrote three important books, *Great Work*, *Small Work and Third Work*. In them he **urged** scientists to adopt an inductive investigation method involving observation and experimentation with appropriate instruments and methods, rather than mere reasoning. Applying these techniques, he described the **nerve system** of the eye, made **magnifying glasses**, and proposed high-technology warfare using gigantic mirrors to **focus** the sun's rays and **incinerate** opponents. All these contributed to the advance of science.

5.4 Literature

In addition to numerous scholarly writings, medieval writers **composed** a great quantity and variety of imaginative literature, both in Latin and in the vernacular languages of everyday speech.

Besides functioning as the international scholarly language for the church and university, Latin was used for **lyric poetry**. Religious writers used Latin for devotional works, particularly **hymns** expressing the intense religious feeling of love for God. **Secular** writers used Latin

Arabic number 阿拉伯数字
Fibonacci 斐波那契
zero *n.* 零
Hindu-Arabic numeral system 印度—阿拉伯数字体系
number sequence 数列
notion *n.* 观念
categorization *n.* 分类
perspective *n.* 透视法
optics *n.* 光学
Robert Grosseteste 罗伯特·格罗赛特斯特
Roger Bacon 培根
inductive *adj.* 归纳的
dominate *v.* 主导
urge *v.* 力劝
nerve system 神经系统
magnifying glass 放大镜
focus *v.* 聚焦
incinerate *v.* 将……烧成灰
compose *v.* 创作
lyric poetry 抒情诗歌
hymn *n.* 赞美诗
secular *adj.* 与教会无关的

Goliardic poet 游荡诗人
satirize *v.* 嘲讽
folly *n.* 愚蠢
foible *n.* 怪癖
parody *v.* 滑稽地模仿

to treat non-religious themes and produced poetry about all aspects of life. A group of students and churchmen called the **Goliardic poets** wrote poems for all occasions, including begging songs, drinking songs, and love songs. They **satirized** the **follies** and **foibles** of churchmen and **parodied** religious beliefs and institutions. They used accent and rhyme to express their deep feelings freshly and vigorously, making Latin sing.

appeal *v.* 吸引
nobility *n.* 贵族
romance *n.* 罗曼史

In both quantity and artistic quality, poetry in vernacular languages became more important than Latin poetry. The most popular vernacular literature was a variety of poetry that **appealed** to the **nobility**, such as epic poetry, lyric poetry and **romance** poetry.

contest *n.* 竞争
combat *n.* 战斗
genre *n.* 体裁

Vernacular epic poetry was enormously popular first among the northern French aristocracy and was later spread to other countries. There it was known as "*chansons de geste*", meaning "heroic epic" or "songs of great deeds". Heroic epics were written for a male-dominated society. The chief events described in these poems were battles and political **contests**. The world described was one of **combat** in which knights fought courageously for their kings and lords. Women played little or no role in this literary **genre**. Among the leading heroic epics were the French *Song of Roland*, the Norse Eddas and Sages, the German *Song of the Nibelungs*, and the Spanish *Poem of the Cid*. The most famous heroic epic of all was the The *Song of Roland* written in Old French, which told of a bloody battle between a Muslim army and some troops of Charlemagne.

Count Roland never loved a coward,
Nor arrogant men nor those of evil character,
Nor any knight, unless he were a good vassal.
He called to Archbishop Turpin:
"Lord, you are on foot and I am on horseback;
For love of you I shall make a stand here.
Together we shall endure both good and ill;
I shall not abandon you because of any man."
(from *The Song of Roland*)

The vernacular lyric poetry first appeared in southern France and soon spread to northern France, England, Italy and Germany. Similar to heroic epic, this genre of poetry was chiefly the product of nobles and knights. It focused, however, on love between men and women, especially the love of a knight for a lady, generally a married noble lady. This **unrequited love** that lyric poets wrote about was called **courtly love**. In courtly love, it was generally men who loved, **agonized** and undertook heroic deeds to attract the attention of the women they loved. Women were more **passive**, mere mirrors of male desire. But there were some lyric poetresses, whose poems reversed the pattern, even twisting it a bit.

unrequited love 单相思
courtly love 典雅爱情
agonize *v.* 痛苦
passive *adj.* 被动的

<table>
<tr><td colspan="2">Below are two extracts of lyric poems. The one on the left was written by well-known poet Jaufre Rudel (1125—1148), and the one on the right was composed by celebrated poetresse Beatrice of Dia (1140—1175).</td></tr>
<tr><td>Most sad, most joyous shall I go away,
Let me have seen her for a single day,
My love afar,
I shall not see her, for her land and mine
Are sundered, and the ways are hard to find,
So many ways, and I shall lose my way,
So wills it God.
(Jaufre Rudel)</td><td>I would truly love to hold
my knight, naked, in my arms one night,
and that he would consider himself in ecstasy
if only I would serve him as a pillow;
for I am more in love with him
than was Floris with Blanchefleur:
I give him my heart and my love,
my mind, my eyes and my life.
(Beatrice of Dia)</td></tr>
</table>

A new poetic form known as romance emerged out of the **convergence** of vernacular epic and vernacular lyric. Like the northern epic, the romance was a long **narrative**; like the southern lyric, it was **sentimental** and concerned with love. It was commonly based on stories from the remote past, such as the Trojan War, Alexander the Great, and King Arthur. In those stories, love destroyed the lovers in the end, yet their destruction was romantic, even glorious. Along the theme of love in the romances, was the theme of Christian purity and **dedication**. The romance first flourished in France and among the French-speaking nobility of England. It later spread into the Italian and Iberian Peninsulas, and became a crucial factor in the **evolution** of vernacular literature in Germany. An important work of vernacular romance literature was the *Romance of the Rose*. It was in fact not a romance in the ordinary sense but an **allegory** of the whole courtly love tradition in which the feelings of the lover and his lady are **personified** in **characters** such as Love, Reason, and Jealousy.

convergence *n.* 汇合
narrative *n.* 叙述
sentimental *adj.* 伤感的
dedication *n.* 奉献精神
evolution *n.* 演变
allegory *n.* 寓言
personify *v.* 拟人化
character *n.* 人物

In addition to epics, lyrics, and romances for noble audiences, medieval writers produced **fabliaux**, **fables** and dramas for town dwellers. Fabliaux were short satirical poems filled with crude humor, depicting ordinary people in events of everyday life while ridiculing conventional morality. In them, all priests and monks were described as **gluttons** and **lechers**; all women were depicted as easily **seduced** and **lustful**; young men were characterized as clever upstarts. Because fabliaux were usually short and emphasized plot and climax, they are regarded as **forerunners** of the modern short story.

fabliau *n.* 闹剧，趣剧
fable *n.* 寓言故事
glutton *n.* 贪食者
lecher *n.* 好色之徒
seduced *adj.* 受引诱
lustful *adj.* 淫荡
forerunner *n.* 前身

Fables were brief stories that taught moral truths. They were in the ancient Greek tradition of *Aesop's Fables* and many of them came from France. In such fables, the characters were **disguised** as animals. The most popular fable was the ***Romance of Renard***, in which the clever Renard the Fox persistently **outwitted** King Lion and his loyal but stupid vassals.

disguise *v.* 伪装
Romance of Renard《狐狸列那的故事》
outwit *v.* 智胜

Medieval drama developed from brief Latin language performances in church during religious ceremonies, to illustrate events associated with the important holy days of Christmas and Easter. As these performances became more dramatic and attracted larger crowds, they were presented outside the church and used **lay** actors and vernacular dialogue. In time, some **guilds** assumed responsibility for presenting these dramas during religious festivals. By the 13th century, three distinct types of plays existed: miracles plays recounting events of saints' lives, mystery plays enacting **biblical** stories, and morality plays teaching correct behavior by personifying virtues and vices. These plays combined **coarse** humor with Christian piety, both entertaining audiences and teaching them Christian history. The use of spoken dialogues, songs and dances, or **puppets** and **pantomimes** also contributed to the entertainment of townspeople and the development of European drama.

lay *adj.* 非神职的
guild *n.* 基尔特，行会
biblical *adj.* 圣经的
coarse *adj.* 粗俗的
puppet *n.* 木偶剧
pantomime *n.* 童话剧

5.5 Art

The artists and artisans of medieval era created impressive works of architecture, sculpture, and painting. As religion had the most powerful influence on people's lives and the Church was the main **promoter** of activity, churches were the primary focus of artistic creation.

promoter *n.* 主办者

Architecture was the foremost art form of the medieval period. It **integrated** all other forms of visual arts to present Christianity's rich symbolic and spiritual values. Other forms of arts—painting, sculpture,

integrate *v.* 融入

woodcarving, metalwork, and **stained glass**—were mostly used to decorate churches. So many churches were built that a writer shortly after 1000 remarked that the Earth was being covered with a white robe of churches.

The architectural style that emerged shortly after 1000 and flourished during the 11th and 12th centuries is called **Romanesque** style, because builders used Roman-type building materials and architectural features in their work. Special needs at the time also contributed to the popularity of the Romanesque style. The destruction caused by invaders and the frequency of fires in wood-roofed churches made Europeans realize the **desirability** of having churches made entirely of stone. Christian rituals in this period also stimulated a need for spacious buildings that could hold both large **congregations** and numerous **pilgrims**.

Combining features of ancient Roman and Byzantine buildings, Romanesque architecture was known by its **massive** quality. The most characteristic feature was the **round arches** which were used for the church's doors and windows as well as for the church's **vaults**. Because the round arches gave the vaults a **tunnel-like** appearance, they were often called tunnel vaults. Romanesque churches were very large and were built with thick stone walls and **pillars** to hold the weight of the heavy arched vaults and roofs. The massive walls and pillars gave Romanesque churches a sense of **solidity** and a look of **fortress**. Little space was left for windows, making the churches quite dark inside. Inside the church, the walls were decorated with paintings of important religious scenes or events in the lives of the **saints**. Massive **columns** leading from floor to vault were decorated with sculptures depicting scenes from the Bible or from other religious texts.

woodcarving *n.* 木刻
stained glass 彩色玻璃
romanesque *adj.* 古罗马式
desirability *n.* 可取性
congregation *n.* （教堂里的）会众
pilgrim *n.* 朝拜者
massive *adj.* 厚重的
round arch 圆拱
vault *n.* 穹顶
tunnel-like *adj.* 像隧道似的
pillar *n.* 房柱
solidity *n.* 坚固
fortress *n.* 堡垒
saint *n.* 圣徒
column *n.* 圆柱

Cathedral Group at Pisa

This group of buildings, built from 1053 to 1272 at Pisa, in Italy, includes a bell tower, better known as the Leaning Tower (rear right), a cathedral (center), and a baptistery (left). The series of columns throughout the group are characteristic of the Romanesque style of architecture, which preceded the Gothic style in Western Europe.

Cathedral of Notre-Dame in Paris

Locates on the island Il de Cité in the middle of the Siene River. The construction began in 1163, but was not completed until the beginning of the 14th century.

Left: Kohl Cathedral, Germany. Construction of the Cathedral began in 1248 and took, with interruptions, until 1880 to complete. **Right**: Interior of a Gothic church.

Gothic *adj.* 哥特式的
pointed arch 尖顶的拱形
ribbed vault 有棱线的穹顶
flying buttress 飞檐扶壁
stained-glass 彩绘玻璃
compact *adj.* 紧实

During the 12th and 13th centuries, Romanesque style was gradually replaced by a new style, the **Gothic** style. As the first Gothic-styled church was built in France, this style was also known as "the French Style." In sharp contrast to the Romanesque style, the characteristic features of the Gothic style included **pointed arches**, **ribbed** vaults, **flying buttresses**, thinner walls, large and **stained-glass** windows. Churches built in the Gothic style appeared higher, lighter and more **compact** than Romanesque churches.

feature *v.* 以……为特色
soaring *adj.* 高耸入云
upward *adv.* 向上
distribute *v.* 分配
install *v.* 安装

The Gothic style was influenced by religious writers' emphasis of the effect of light and space on prayer and meditation; consequently, Gothic architecture **featured** space, light, and height. The use of pointed arches and ribbed vaults created an impression of weightless **soaring upward** movement that implied the energy of God. The flying buttresses built onto the outside of the church walls evenly **distributed** the vault's weight outward and downward, reducing the weight on the walls. The thinner walls were **installed** with magnificent stained-glass windows which opened up to give more colorful light, a symbol of the divine light of God.

The Gothic style became popular for city churches, especially large cathedrals. It was first adopted by the cities in the region around Paris, and later cities in the rest of France, England, the Netherlands, Spain, Italy, Germany, and eventually all the rest of Europe. The Gothic cathedral, with its towers soaring toward heaven, gave witness to an age dedicated to spiritual ideal. **Cathedral of Notre-Dame in Paris** was among the most brilliant Gothic cathedrals.

Cathedral of Notre-Dame in Paris 巴黎圣母院

6. Conclusion

As mentioned in the Introduction, the Central Middle Ages were also called the High Middle Ages, because Europe, especially Western Europe in this period developed to a new **height** in almost every aspect. In the year 1000, Europe was the least powerful, the least prosperous, and the least intellectually advanced of all three Western civilizations that had emerged out of the Roman world. It remained politically **fractured** and weak, militarily threatened by Viking, Hungarian and Muslim attacks, economically dependent on Byzantine and Islamic traders, culturally lagged far behind Byzantine and Islam who had inherited cultural and intellectual riches from the classical world.

height *n.* 高度

fractured *adj.* 割裂的

By the year 1300, however, the position of Europe **vis-à-vis** both the Byzantine and the Islamic world had been transformed. Europe had become the dominant power among the three successor civilizations to ancient Greece and Rome. This transformation rested on a series of profound changes occurred in economic, social, cultural, political, religious and military fields.

vis-à-vis *prep.* 同……相比

However, by the end of 13th century, certain tensions and crises began to **creep** into European society. These tensions and crises led to the end of the Central Middle Ages and the beginning of the Late Middle Ages.

creep *v.* 渐渐侵入

Exercises

Ⅰ. Terminology: choose the suitable terms to fill in the blanks.

A. manor	B. guild	C. papacy	D. Magna Carta
E. The Crusades	F. Sacraments	G. Investiture Controversy	H. clergy
I. diocese	J. fallow	K. manorialism	L. Great Schism

- __1__ refers to the power struggle between kings and popes over the appointment of high cleric officers during the Middle Ages.
- __2__ was the first document forced onto an English King by a group of his subjects, the feudal barons, in an attempt to limit his powers by law and protect their privileges.
- A __3__ was a self-sufficient stationary estate, or fief that was under the control of a lord who enjoyed a variety of rights over it and the peasants attached to it by means of serfdom.
- __4__ is the term used to describe the formal religious leadership within a given religion, such as deacons, priests, bishops, and ministers in Christianity.
- The land ploughed and left unseeded for a season or more is called __5__.
- __6__ is the district overseen under the supervision of a bishop. It is divided into parishes.
- An association of craftsmen in a particular trade in the Middle Ages is called __7__.
- __8__ refers to the key religious ceremonies and rituals determined by the Catholic Church for Christians.
- __9__ refers to the system of government of the Roman Catholic Church of which the pope is the supreme head. It might also refer to the office of pope, a succession or line of popes, or the reign of a pope.
- __10__ were a series of holy wars waged by much of Roman Catholic Europe against the Muslims in the Middle Ages.
- __11__ refers to the division of the once united Christian Church into the Roman Catholic Church and Eastern Orthodox Church in 1054 because of religious disputes and power struggle.
- __12__ is a feudal system of self-sufficient "house economy" in the Middle Ages. Under this system, the land of a large area belonged to a lord. The lord kept some of the land for his own use, and rented the rest to farmers. The farmers had to pay by giving services and part of the crops they grew.

Ⅱ. Decide whether the following statements are true (T) or false (F).

1. During the 12th and 13th centuries, Romanesque style gradually took the place of Gothic style in architecture. (　　)

2. Romanesque architecture was known by its massive quality, round arches, barrel vaults, thick walls, sturdy pillars, small windows, large towers and decorative arcading. (　　)

3. The characteristic features of the Gothic style included pointed arches, ribbed vaults, flying buttresses, thinner walls, large and stained-glass windows. (　　)

4. All classes in universities were taught in Latin and mostly by a lecture method. (   )

5. Seven Sacraments are recognized by Catholic Church, Orthodox Churches and Protestant Churches. (   )

6. Universities served only a limited sector of the medieval population, only for men and the wealthy; women and the poor were kept out of education. (   )

7. An important product of vernacular romance literature was the Romance of the Rose. (   )

8. Romance combined features of both vernacular epic and vernacular lyric. (   )

9. In his incomplete Summa of Theology, Thomas Aquinas sought to reconcile systematically Christian doctrine and Greek philosophy. (   )

10. Medieval fables are regarded as forerunners of the modern short story. (   )

Ⅲ. Multiple choices: choose the answer that best completes the statement or answers the question.

1. Which one of the following statements was NOT a factor that brought about the agricultural growth during the Central Middle Ages?

A. The climate improved and the temperature was higher.

B. More lands were under cultivated.

C. Farming technology improved greatly.

D. The food price dropped drastically.

2. Which one of the following statements about the medieval universities is NOT true?

A. The first university appeared in Italy.

B. Bologna University was governed by a corporation of students, a pattern followed by other southern universities.

C. University of Paris was dominated by a corporation of teachers, a pattern followed by other northern universities.

D. A migration of scholars from Cambridge led to the establishment of the University of Oxford in England.

3. 1066 marked the ________.

A. defeat of the Vikings

B. Norman Conquest of England

C. death of William I

D. death of Alfred the Great

4. Magna Carta in 1215 in England was significant in that it ________.

A. really weakened the power of the church

B. spoke for the common people

C. really weakened the power of the king

D. spoke for the nobles

5. Which one of the following statements about the English Parliament in 1259 is NOT true?

A. It included two knights from every county.

B. It included two burgesses from every town.

C. It included the king's Great Council (barons, bishops, judges, advisors).

D. It was a major check on royal authority.

6. Which factor directly resulted in the first great split in Christianity in 1054?

A. The rulers of most European peoples adopted Christianity for themselves and their subjects.

B. The invasions from Vikings and Magyars not only destroyed many churches and monasteries but also greatly damaged the church institutions.

C. There were few schools to train clergy, and many church officers were shallow and incompetent.

D. Pope Leo IX asserted the supreme authority of the papacy and clashed with the Patriarch of Constantinople Michael Cerularius.

7. Which of the following statements is NOT true?

A. The pope was assisted by the papal curia.

B. The curia was an extensive bureaucracy which contained specialized departments.

C. The curia was directed by the College of Cardinals whose members were selected by kings.

D. Like kings, the popes issued laws, hired masters to collect revenues and judge cases, even declared wars.

8. Which of the following statements about villages in the Middle Ages is NOT true?

A. Villages ranged in size from ten to several hundred peasant families, living in a cluster of cottages surrounded by their fields.

B. Most villages had woodland which provided burning wood and building materials.

C. Many villages had a stream or pond for water supply, fish and a water mill for grinding grain.

D. Few villages had a few artisans and traders who combined farm work with other labor.

9. Which of the following statements about the Crusades is NOT true?

A. On the way to the Holy Land, a crusader wore the white cross on his outfit.

B. The Crusades increased the power of the Papacy and the wealth of the Church.

C. The Crusades strengthened the power of national monarchies and undermined feudalism.

D. The Crusades set the first example of European expansionism.

10. All the following statements about the medieval commune are true EXCEPT ________.

A. Commune had its own local government, its own court, its own tax-collecting agencies and its own customs

B. Some communes gained their independence by paying lords to grant it to them, while others governed alongside their lord

C. No communes battled violently for rights of self-governance

D. Communes in Italy gained the right not only to govern themselves but also to rule the farmland and villages around them

11. All the following statements featured the Capetian kings of France, EXCEPT ________.

A. The Capetian kings established strong royal power by conquest, as William had done in England

B. They kept the support of the popes by defending the Christian faith and by going on crusades

C. They carefully defined the powers of their officials and closely supervised them, while using church officials as administrators

D. They developed Paris as both a trading center and a royal capital

12. All the following statements about the Scholasticism are true, EXCEPT ________.

A. Some scholars tried in vain to forbid the study and teaching of Aristotle's thought

B. Some argued that reason alone could lead to truth

C. Some argued that ultimate truth could not be discovered by reason, but was revealed to human by God in His mystical ways

D. The most fruitful achievement was the attempt to harmonize faith and reason by the leading scholar St. Augustine

13. What is the Central Middle Ages also called?

A. "Age of Art". B. "Age of History".

C. "Age of Faith". D. " Age of Science".

14. All the following made up the basic social structure of medieval rural communities EXCEPT ________.

A. The village B. The manor

C. The parish church D. The guild

15. What were the three classes of people in the Central Middle Ages?

A. Pope, peasants and nobles.

B. Kings, lords and monks.

C. Clergy, lords and peasants.

D. Warriors, peasants and priest.

16. Which of the following statements about the third Crusade is NOT true?

A. It had a strong start, but a weak end.

B. Frederick drowned on the way.

C. Philip quarreled with Richard and went home.

D. Richard stayed longer, and took Jerusalem.

17. Which of the following statements about the development of science in the Central Middle Ages is NOT true?

A. Translation of Greek and Arabic scientific works gave new impetus to the study of science.

B. Arabic numbers were introduced by Italian mathematician Leonardo de Pisa.

C. Robert Grosseteste, Roger Bacon and others made Cambridge University the center of scientific studies during the thirteenth century.

D. Bacon wrote three important books, *Great Work*, *Small Work and Third Work.*

18. What were the three forms of vernacular Literature for nobles?

A. Epic poetry, romance poetry and dramas.

B. Fabliaux, fables and romance poetry.

C. Lyric poetry, epic poetry and romance poetry.

D. Fabliaux, fables and dramas.

19. What were the three forms of vernacular literature for town dwellers?

A. Epic poetry, romance poetry and dramas.

B. Fabliaux, fables and romance poetry.

C. Lyric poetry, epic poetry and romance poetry.

D. Fabliaux, fables and dramas.

20. Which of the following statements about art in the Central Middle Ages is NOT true?

A. Architecture was the foremost art form.

B. Schools were the primary focus of architectural endeavors.

C. Architecture integrated all the visual arts in presentations of Christianity's rich symbolic and spiritual values.

D. Other arts were used to decorate churches with sculpture and painting, woodcarving and metalwork, and stained glass.

Crisis in Late Medieval Western Europe (1300—1500)

CHAPTER OUTLINE

1. Introduction
2. Economic Crisis and Recovery
3. Social Crisis and Popular Unrest
4. Political Crisis and Recovery
5. The Crisis of the Western Christian Church
6. Conclusion

FOCUS QUESTIONS

1. What major problems did European states face in the Late Middle Ages?
2. What were the causes of the popular rebellions in the Late Middle Ages?
3. What were the main causes and impacts of the Hundred Years' War?
4. How and why did the authority and prestige of the Church decline in the Late Middle Ages?

1. Introduction

The late Middle Ages (1300—1500) are often described as a period of crisis and decline. In this period of time, the vigorous expansion that marked European history in the previous centuries came to an end. From the 1300s onward, Europe experienced many natural and manmade disasters. **Plague** and **famine** caused millions of deaths in Europe. Along with **depopulation** came social unrest and conflicts. Peasant uprisings and urban revolts broke out in many countries. Rivalry between feudal governments led to wars, the most violent being the Hundred Years' War (1337—1453) fought between France and England. More lives were lost in these **recurrent** conflicts and wars.

plague *n.* 瘟疫
famine *n.* 饥荒
depopulation *n.* 人口剧减
recurrent *adj.* 反复出现的

secular *adj.* 世俗的，非宗教的
heresy *n.* 异端邪说

To add to the many problems of the period, the authority of the Christian Church also came under attack. Challenged by both **secular** governments and **heresies**, the Church was forced to redefine its place in both the religious life and the political life of Europe.

renewal *n.* 更新

Yet out of the crises came a number of significant changes. In truth, the late Middle Ages was not merely an age of total breakdown. It was also an age of **renewal**. Toward the early 15th century crisis gave way to a dramatic economic, social, and political recovery. In 1500 Europeans were fewer in number than in 1300, but they had developed a more productive economy and a more powerful technology. The European population was again on the increase. England and France emerged strengthened by military and political conflicts. Experiences of disasters and conflicts led to new thinking which paved the way for the cultural and intellectual **revival** in the later periods of **Renaissance** and **Reformation.**

revival *n.* 复苏
Renaissance *n.* 文艺复兴
Reformation *n.* 宗教改革

So, exactly what kinds of crises did Europe suffer in the late Middle Ages? What were the causes of these crises? How did Europeans react to the crises and eventually succeed in turning the challenges to their advantages? This chapter will focus on the crisis-driven transformation of late Medieval Europe. We will look into the transformation in Europe's social and economic structures, political **arena**, and religious institution. Europe's cultural and intellectual rebirth will be dealt with in the next two chapters ("The Renaissance" and "The Reformation").

arena *n.* 领域

2. Economic Crisis and Recovery

As discussed in the preceding chapter, Europe in the Central Middle Ages experienced agricultural revolution and booming trade. Economic growth was coupled with a dramatic increase in the size of the population. In the span of three hundred years, the total population size in Europe doubled. Then, in the 14th century Europe was struck by a series of famines and plagues. Initially, these disasters led to the death of millions and widespread hardship. European prosperity came to a halt. But between 1350 and 1450 Europeans learnt how to turn crises into opportunities. As they reorganized their economic activities to greatly changed **demographic** conditions, they were able to significantly increase the **efficiency** of economic production. Economic recovery altered the socials structures in many parts of Europe. In the late 15th century,

demographic *adj.* 人口的
efficiency *n.* 效率

Europe emerged with a healthier economy than it had known earlier.

2.1 Agricultural Failure and Great Famine

By 1300, Europe was **overpopulated**. The explosive population growth of the previous centuries began to **take its toll** on the society. People in many parts of Europe were living on the edge of disaster. European agriculture had expanded to the limits allowed by such earlier **technological innovations** as the **heavy plow**, the **three-field system**, and **windmills**. There was no more new land to clear, and the cultivated soil itself had become **exhausted** after years of continuous over-cultivation. The existing land, no matter how well it was cultivated, could no longer support the growing number of people who lived on it. Farm size shrank throughout Europe as parents tended to divide their land among their children. Rents for farmland increased as landlords found that they could play one land-hungry farmer against another. In towns and cities, competition for jobs kept wages low. When taxes were added to high rents and low wages, poor townspeople and peasants found it difficult to raise families. Many tended to marry late and have smaller families. Simply put, the number of people in Europe **exceeded** the productive **capacities** of its lands.

overpopulated *adj.* 人口过密
take its toll 对……产生不良影响
technological innovation 技术革新
heavy plow 重型犁
three-field system 三块地轮耕体系
windmill *n.* 风力磨坊
clear *v.* 开垦
exhausted *adj.* 被用尽的
exceed *v.* 超出
capacity *n.* 能力

To make matters worse, around 1300, there was a noticeable change in the climate pattern in Europe as the Medieval Warm Period gave way to the Little Ice Age. Whereas Western Europe had been favored with a drying and warming trend in the 11th and 12th centuries, in the 14th century the weather became colder and wetter. Cold climate significantly shortened growing seasons, especially in northern Europe. Increased rainfall caused terrible floods, ruining crops.

Overpopulation and worsened farming conditions led to a **prolonged**, deadly famine known as the **Great Famine**—the worst famine in European history. It lasted for seven hard years, from 1315 to 1322. In cities and rural areas alike, there was shortage of food supplies. Wheat, **oats**, **hay** and consequently **livestock**, were all in short supply. Starvation even drove some people to eat cats, dogs, and rats. By the time it ended, the Great Famine had wiped out 10% to 15% of the entire European population. Those who survived the Great Famine often suffered from **chronic malnutrition**. As a result, their **immune systems** were greatly weakened, leaving them highly **vulnerable** to **infections** and diseases.

prolonged *adj.* 长期的
Great Famine 大饥荒
oat *n.* 燕麦
hay *n.* 作饲料的干草
livestock *n.* 牲口
chronic malnutrition 长期营养不良
immune system 免疫系统
vulnerable *adj.* 易受攻击的
infection *n.* 感染

If Europe's problem had merely been one of famine brought on by overpopulation and harsh farming conditions, rapid recovery should have

the Black Death 黑死病
epidemic *n.* 流行病

been possible. But the difficulties were worsened by plague. In 1347, Europe was struck by a great plague known as **the Black Death**. The disease spread quickly throughout the Mediterranean region and Western Europe. The **epidemic** was so horrifying that it seemed to many it was the end of the world.

2.2 The Black Death

Gobi Desert 戈壁滩沙漠
infect *v.* 感染
Ukraine *n.* 乌克兰

Although today we still cannot determine the exact cause of the Black Death, we do know from where the Europeans got this disease. Originated in the **Gobi Desert** of Mongolia, in the mid-14th century plague spread along caravan routes of central Asia and arrived at Black Sea ports. Europe's active trade in luxury items from the East gave the plague a route to Europe. In 1347, sailors and traders from Genoa (in Italy) became **infected** with the plague in Caffa, a city in today's **Ukraine** on the Black Sea coast. Infected sailors carried the disease south into Egypt and west into Italy. From there it spread throughout Western Europe along the trade routes, first striking the seaports, then moving inland. Although a few people recovered from the plague, and some did not catch it, the majority of those who caught the disease died from it within a week. Some scholars think the weather, which had become colder and wetter, created a favorable environment for the spread of the plague.

devastating *adj.* 毁灭性的
demography *n.* 人口总况
Florence *n.* 佛罗伦萨
mortality rate 死亡率
cease *v.* 停止

As the Black Death was the first major epidemic to strike Europe since the 7th century, it had a **devastating** effect on Europe's **demography**. It is estimated to have killed 30% ~ 60% of Europe's population. Death rates varied from one region to another. The death rate in some larger cities in Italy may have been as high as 60 percent. In **Florence**, for example, the population probably declined from about 90 000 to about 50 000 or even less. In northern France, villages suffered **mortality rates** of 30%, and cities experienced losses as high as 40%. In England and Germany, some villages disappeared entirely. The shock and disruption were immense. Governments in some towns **ceased** to function at the height of the epidemic. Chroniclers reported that no one could be found to care for the sick or bury the dead.

They died by the hundreds, both day and night, and all were thrown in... ditches and covered with earth. And as soon as those ditches were filled, more were dug. And I, Agnolo di Tura... buried my five children with my own hands... And so many died that all believed it was the end of the world.

—*The Plague in Siena: An Italian Chronicle*

In the first stage of the plague between 1347 and 1351, 25% ~35% of the European population may have died. Just as some areas were recovering from the **initial** outbreak of the plague, it returned between 1360 and 1363, and then for three centuries thereafter almost no generation could avoid it. For example, in central Italy, the plague returned **on average** every eleven years between 1350 and 1400. It was not until the 19th century that the plague disappeared from Western Europe.

initial *adj.* 最初的

on average 平均

Not knowing the true cause of the disease, many Christians considered the Black Death a signal of the Last Judgment. Their logical reaction was to **urge** various moral reforms to create a purer, truly Christian society. Some blamed outsiders, especially **Jews**, who were suspected of spreading the plague in an attempt to bring down Latin Christendom. Despite official rejection of popular rumors and fears, from the mid-14th century, life became more difficult for the Jews of Christian Europe.

urge *v.* 催促

Jews *n.* 犹太人

Illustration of the Black Death from the Toggenburg Bible (1411)

At first, the Black Death caused great hardships for most of the **survivors**. After burying the dead, the survivors often gave up working

survivor *n.* 幸存者

in the fields or looking after their shops. What was the point in working for the future when it was so uncertain? Harvests were left rotting; manufacturing was disrupted, and trade collapsed. The survivors needed time to overcome the shock, but eventually in the long run they adapted to the new conditions. **Paradoxically**, death caused by the Black Death improved the situation of surviving peasants and laborers since the most common **victims** were the very young, the elderly, and the poor-those least likely to pay taxes, own shops, or produce children. By 1400, the new demographic realities began to change the basic patterns of the European economy.

paradoxically *adv.* 十分矛盾的是
victim *n.* 受害者

2.3 A New Economic Equilibrium Out of the Depression

equilibrium *n.* 均衡

In the **aftermath** of the plague, the economy of Europe changed in a number of profound ways. As depopulation left vast areas of farmland **untended**, more fertile lands were made available for the survivors. Farmers quickly realized that with labor in short supply they could demand higher wages for their labor, and that they could even break the bonds of their serfdom and move around the countryside or to towns to follow higher wages. However, the landowners attempted to protect their own interests by **re-imposing** serfdom. One **tactic** was to pass laws to limit peasants' freedom from the labor demands of serfdom. For example, the English Parliament passed **the Statute of Laborers** in 1351, which fixed prices and wages at the pre-plague levels. The Statute also forbad peasants to move away from their own manor. Similar laws were passed in other parts of Europe. Like any move against **market mechanism**, such laws were dead letters. So long as the demand for labor force was larger than the supply, landowners were unable to stop the peasants from moving from one manor to another in search of higher wages. As a result, the systems of manorialism and serfdom were greatly weakened. By the 15th century serfdom had almost disappeared in England, France, Italy, and western Germany.

aftermath *n.* 余波
untended *adj.* 无人料理
re-impose *v.* 再次强加
tactic *n.* 策略
the Statute of Laborers 《劳工法令》
market machanism 市场机制

The sudden shortage of cheap labor forced landowners to find other ways to increase **profits**. Landowners began to **invest** in a more profitable industry. Noticeably, landlords in England **converted** their lands to grassland for sheep raising as the prices for wool, sheep skins, mutton and cheese were high. They fenced large fields and drove the peasants away from these lands. This process, called **enclosure**, continued for centuries and played an important role in English economic and social history. Other countries also began to develop more profitable

profit *n.* 利润
invest *v.* 投资
convert *v.* 转变
enclosure *n.* 圈地运动

agricultural **specialization.** **Netherlands** promoted **diary** production, Spain specialized in merino wool, and parts of Italy invested in canals, irrigation, and new crops.

Following the new process of agricultural specialization, in some parts of Western Europe woolen **textile** production shifted from **urban** workshops to the countryside, leading to the growing process of urbanization. Over time, **rural** production became the most **dynamic** part of the textile industry. The advantages of such a rural production were obvious. Processed cloth promised a higher return in profit than **raw** wool. In the countryside, wool could be **processed** into cloth more cheaply because it could be done as occasional or part-time labor by farmers, or by their wives or children. Cloth produced in rural areas was free of the control of guild over the product's quality or price. Merchants were free to move the cloth to wherever it could be sold most easily and profitably.

The economic transformation of England was closely tied to the development of rural cloth production. Long recognized as a producer of raw wool, England reduced the exports of its high-quality raw wool and began instead to export its own finished cloth during the 15th century. The growth of cloth exports contributed enormously to the expansion of London as a major trade center. Soon after 1500, over 80% of the cloth for export passed through the hands of the Londoners. This development, coupled with the rise of London as a center of **administration** and **consumption**, laid the foundation for the economic and demographic growth that would make London the largest and most prosperous city in Western Europe by the 18th century.

Hard times and labor shortages also inspired more technical advances to provide workers with better tools. Technical improvements in turn laid the basis for economic recovery. A series of inventions after 1460 lowered the cost of metals and extended their use. Better techniques allowed miners to **exploit** the deep, rich mineral resources of central Europe. Between 1460 and 1530, the output from the mines of **Hungary**, **Bohemia**, and **Saxony** grew as much as five times. During this period, miners in Saxony discovered a method for getting pure silver from **lead ores**. By the late 15th century, European mines were providing a large amount of silver for **coinage**. Money became plentiful, which stimulated the economy. Exploitation also began in the rich coal **deposits** of northern Europe. Expanding iron production meant more and stronger machine parts, tools, and iron wares. Skill in

specialization *n.* 专门化
Netherlands *n.* 尼德兰地区
diary *adj.* 乳业
textile *n.* 纺织
urban *adj.* 城市的
rural *adj.* 农村的
dynamic *adj.* 有活力的
raw *adj.* 未经加工的
process *v.* 加工
administration *n.* 行政
consumption *n.* 消费
exploit *n.* 勘探
Hungary *n.* 匈牙利
Bohemia *n.* 波西米亚（约等于捷克）
Saxony *n.* 萨克森（今德国一州）
lead ore 铅矿石
coinage *n.* 硬币
deposit *n.* 矿藏

metalworking contributed to two other inventions: firearms and **movable metal type**.

movable mental type 活字印刷术

By 1500, the overall economic prospects of Western Europe improved. The **revitalized** economy meant a higher standard of living. As production gradually returned to normal and there were fewer mouths to feed, the food prices began to decline. With sufficient grain supply, more meat was available on the market; the consumption of meat and dairy products went up. Adults in part of Europe could enjoy bread, meat, and wine each day. Housing was also improving for most people in the Late Middle Ages. With the increasing use of brick and **tile**, buildings were more solid and more spacious. A higher standard in living brought a new emphasis on polite behavior, particularly at the table. Consumption pattern for artistic works also changed. In the past the main buyers of the arts had been churches and nobility, and the major artistic **themes** had been religious. Now with the rise of a larger middle class, the demand for fine decorative objects **soared**. In particular, oil paintings, including portraits, were the favored items on the shopping lists of the rising middle class.

revitalized *adj.* 重新复苏的

tile *n.* 瓦片

theme *n.* 主题

soar *v.* 激增

3. Social Crisis and Popular Unrest

European society had been remarkably stable and peaceful in the Central Middle Ages. Social uprisings and warfare were rare. In fact, it had been remarkably stable and mostly peaceful from the Early Middle Ages until around 1300, and there is little evidence of uprisings. The 14th and 15th centuries, however, witnessed numerous revolts in both rural and urban areas. To provide an example of how common and widespread these popular revolts became, in Germany between 1336 and 1525 there were no fewer than sixty instances of **militant** peasant unrest. It was once thought that these were all caused by extreme economic hardship, but as we will see, often that was not the case.

militant *adj.* 激进的

3.1 Revolts in the Rural Areas

The one large-scale rural uprising that was most clearly caused by economic hardship was **Jacquerie**, a French peasant revolt in northern France in 1358. The rebellion took its name from "Jacques" or "Jacques Bonhomme", a **contemptuous nickname** used by the French nobles for any peasant. Life was already hard enough for peasants after the first wave of the Black Death (1347—1351). To make matters

Jacquerie 扎克雷农民起义

contemptuous *adj.* 轻蔑的

nickname *n.* 绰号

worse, France at the time was engaged in the Hundred Years' War against England, a war mainly fought on the French soil. As usual in many other wars, peasants suffered most from the **looting** and burning carried out by the soldiers. Then in 1356, in the Battle of Poitiers France was defeated by England. Many French aristocrats were captured by the English, including the king of France, John II. The English demanded a **ransom** for the **captives**. The French nobles shifted the burden onto the peasants by forcing them to pay more taxes.

loot *v.* （在战争中）抢劫

ransom *n.* 赎金

captive *n.* 俘虏

Angry peasants had had enough. In 1358 they rose up against the nobles. The outburst of their anger led to **savage confrontations** and large-scale violence. Rebellious peasants burned down castles, murdered their lords, and raped their lords' wives. Economic hardship was undoubtedly the major cause for the uprising. The peasants involved in the rebellion did not seem to have any political program. Nor did they have any clear organization. Within a month the rebellion was **suppressed** by French nobles, tens of thousands of peasants savagely **massacred.**

savage *adj.* 野蛮的

confrontation *n.* 对立

suppress *v.* 镇压

massacre *v.* 屠杀

By contrast, the English Peasants' Revolt of 1381 had very different causes from the Jacquerie. Instead of a product of **desperation**, the Peasants' Revolt in England arose out of **frustrated** rising economic expectations. As mentioned earlier, after the Black Death, the condition of the English peasants had improved: they enjoyed more freedom from the labor burden of serfdom; with the shortage of labor force, peasants could **bargain** for higher wages, lower rents, and fewer hours of work. Some historians have called the period a golden age for peasantry.

desperation *n.* 绝望

frustrated *adj.* 受挫的

bargain *v.* 讨价还价

However, aristocratic landlords had fought back with **legislation** to protect their interest, an example being the Statute of Laborers passed by the English Parliament in 1351. Although the law was later proven unworkable, it caused much popular **discontent**. What really **triggered off** the great revolt of 1381 was an attempt to collect a new type of national tax to pay for the failing war with France. Peasants in eastern England, the wealthiest part of the country, refused to pay the tax and **expelled** the tax collectors from their villages.

legislation *n.* 立法

discontent *n.* 不满

trigger off 激起

expel *v.* 驱逐

This action produced a widespread rebellion led by a well-to-do peasant called Wat Tyler and a preachernamed John Ball. The rebels burned local records, **torched** the manor houses of aristocrats; then they marched into London and **executed** several important officials,

torch *v.* 付之一炬

execute *v.* 处决

Lord Chancellor 大法官
Lord Treasurer 财政大臣
Archbishop of Cantebury 坎特伯雷大主教
confine *v.* 局限于
magistrate *n.* 治安法官

including the **Lord Chancellor**, **Lord Treasure**, and **archbishop of Canterbury**. Though called the Peasants' Revolt by today's historians, participation in the Revolt was not **confined** to serfs or even to the lower classes. The peasants received help from members of the noble classes—one example being William Tonge, a **magistrate** of London, who opened the London city gate for the masses.

Realizing the gravity of the situation, the fourteen-year-old king, Richard Ⅱ (rule 1377—1399) went out to meet the peasants and promised to accept their demands if they returned home. Mistakenly thinking they had achieved their aims, the peasants quickly went home. But once the boy king was no longer in danger of his life he broke his promise. The peasants involved in the rebellion were hunted down and the trouble-makers were executed. The revolt therefore did not **accomplish** its **objectives**.

accomplish *v.* 实现
objective *n.* 目标

Although the Revolt itself was a failure, it did succeed in showing the nobles what peasants were capable of when dissatisfied. In the long run, it increased **awareness** in the upper classes of the need for the reform of feudalism in England. The revolt later came to be seen as a mark of the beginning of the end of serfdom in medieval England.

awareness *n.* 意识

3.2 Revolts in the Cities

erupt *v.* 爆发

Revolts also **erupted** in the cities. Like the Jacquerie and the Peasants' Revolt, most urban rebellions arose from a complex combination of political, economic, and social forces. Most famous was the revolt of Florence's wool workers, the ***ciompi***, in 1378. Woolen industry had long been a key economic engine of Florence's prosperity in the Middle Ages. The masters of the woolen industry thus had great political power and could pass laws in their own favor. The industry employed a large number of wool combers, known as the ciompi. In the 14th century, the ciompi made up approximately 25% of the Florentine population. They worked 14—16 hours a day; they were poorly paid and labored in a depressed working condition. The woolen industry owners had the right to fire *ciompi* from their jobs without warning. Furthermore, the *ciompi* were not **guild** members and therefore had no political rights.

ciompi *n.* 梳毛工人
guild *n.* 基尔特，行会

In the 1370s, the woolen industry was **depressed** as trade declined after the Black Death. Some woolen workers lost their jobs, while others were cheated or underpaid by their masters. But the economic depression did not automatically lead to social unrest. As later events revealed, it was a political crisis that stirred up the revolt. In 1378

depressed *adj.* 衰退

Florence had become **exhausted** by three years of war with the **papal states**. The ruling class of Florence **split**, some demanding to change the war policy. One fraction of the ruling class called upon the lower classes, in particular, the *ciompi* to take part in the revolt.

exhausted *adj.* 耗尽
papal states *n.* 教廷国
split *v.* 分裂

On July 22, the *ciompi* **forcibly** took over the government and pushed through their own radical reform program. The most important reforms of the *ciompi* were an increase in wages, the granting of political **representation** in the government, the formation of a ciompi guild (which would have granted the ciompi full citizenship), the formation of a people's **militia**, and the establishment of equality of all inhabitants of the city. For the first time a European government represented all the classes of society. But their newly won rights were short-lived. A **counter-revolution** by government authorities brought an end to *ciompi* revolt by 1382. The *ciompi* lost their hold on power, and their reform programs were **abolished.**

forcibly *adv.* 强行地
representation *n.* 代表权
militia *n.* 民兵
counter-revolution *n.* 反革命
abolish *v.* 废除

If we try to draw any general conclusions about these various uprisings, we can certainly say that most occurred because of an economic crisis. But political **considerations** always had some influence, and the rebels in some uprisings were more prosperous than in others. Although the lower-class uprisings, both in the rural and the urban areas, sometimes resulted in short-term gains for the participants, all failed quickly. This was certainly because the upper classes were **accustomed** to ruling, and they also had the money and troops to suppress the revolts. In addition, the lower classes put much emphasis on economic problems at the moment. Without an **overall** economic and political plan, unity of the lower classes was easily disrupted after the first victory. Nevertheless, the rural and urban revolts of the 14th century ushered in an age of social conflict that characterized much of later European history.

consideration *n.* 考量
be accustomed to 习惯于
overall *adj.* 全面的

4. Political Crisis and Recovery

Famine, plague, economic **turmoil**, and social **upheaval** were not the only problems of the Late Middle Ages; medieval Europe was also **disrupted** by constant military warfare and political instability.

turmoil *n.* 动乱
upheaval *n.* 剧变
disrupt *v.* 打断

4.1 The Hundred Years' War

Of all the warfare of the Late Middle Ages, the most violent and the most significant was the Hundred Years' War. The Hundred Years'

War was a series of wars between England and France, lasting for 116 years from 1336 to 1453, with periods of savage warfare **alternating** with long periods of **truce.**

alternate *v.* 交替
truce *n.* 休战

4.1.1 Causes of the War

The war arose from a number of causes. First, there were conflicts of interests between the two countries, both **territorial** and political. As mentioned earlier, in 1066, William, the French Duke of Normandy conquered England and made himself the king of England. According to the feudal arrangement, William and his **descendents** remained the **vassals** of the French king and they continued to hold lands in France. After the Norman conquest, the power of the kings of England increased. France in turn considered England as a **potential** threat. French kings had tried constantly to extend their influence in the French territories controlled by the English kings, and the two sides had fought several wars over these lands. By 1327, when Edward Ⅲ (1327—1377) became the king of England, England only controlled two areas of France—**Gascony** in the south and **Ponthieu** in the north. Many English aristocrats considered the lost territories in France their **ancestral** homeland, and wanted to regain possession of these territories. The French king, Philip was determined to take over Gascony and Ponthieu, the last two English possessions in France.

territorial *adj.* 领土的
descendent *n.* 后代
vassal *n.* 封臣
potential *adj.* 潜在的
Gascony *n.* 加斯科尼
Ponthieu *n.* 皮卡第区
ancestral *adj.* 祖先的

Apart from the territorial disputes in France, England and France had clash of economic interest in **Flanders**. The County of Flanders was formally a part of France. Since the 12th century, it had grown increasingly wealthy in the **triangular** trade between Flanders, France and England. **Raw** wool exported from England was **processed** into cloth in Flanders, which then was sold on the French market. Because of differences in economic interest, the land-holding aristocracy in Flanders remained loyal to the French king while the wealthy merchants and cloth manufacturers were dependent on the English. In 1302 the Flemish **burghers** rebelled against their count and **proclaimed** the independence of Flanders from France.① In the Flemish civil war, the English supported the manufacturing middle class in the cities while the French supported the land-owning nobles. King Edward also began to tax wool leaving England and encouraged the Flemish **weavers** to come to England to set up workshops under his special protection. Incidentally, this move was the beginning of the woolen cloth industry in

Flanders 弗兰德地区
triangular *adj.* 三角的
raw *adj.* 未经加工的
process *v.* 加工
burgher *n.* 城镇居民
proclaim *v.* 宣布
weaver *n.* 纺织工

① 到1328年以前佛兰德地区一直维持其独立地位。

England.

The relationship between the two kingdoms was further worsened by a dispute over the French royal **succession**. While most noble families had direct father-to-son succession for only a few generations, the Capetian dynasty in France had produced male **heirs** for three hundred years (see Chapter 6). In 1328, the last Capetian king, Charles Ⅳ, died. The nearest surviving male relative was King Edward Ⅲ of England, whose mother, Isabella was Charles Ⅳ's sister. Because of this family relationship, Edward believed that he should succeed Charles Ⅳ to be the next king of France. However, the Parliament of Paris proclaimed that a cousin of Charles, Philip, should be crowned king. They based their decision on an old Frankish law which forbade females from **inheriting** or **transmitting** the claim to the crown. Despite his obvious **discontentment** Edward did not dispute the Parliament's decision as he did not have **sound** legal argument. But when King Philip Ⅵ of France seized Gascony in 1337, King Edward Ⅲ of England declared war on Philip and claimed himself "King of France" in 1340. Most nobles on both sides welcomed war, seeing it as a chance for excitement, honor, **plunder**, **revenge**, and even fun.

succession *n.* 继位
heir *n.* 继承人
inherit *v.* 继承
transmit *v.* 传递
discontentment *n.* 不满
sound *adj.* 合理的
plunder *n.* 抢劫
revenge *n.* 复仇

4.1.2 The Course of the War

The Hundred Years' War was actually a series of conflicts that lasted for even more than one hundred years-from 1337 to 1453. At the start, France should have had no difficulty in defeating England: it was the richest country in Europe and it had a much larger population than England, at least three times larger. However, until the 1420s the English had won most of the battles. Perhaps, the biggest victory for the English was the Battle of Poitiers (1356) when they captured the King of France. The French paid a large sum for the king's **ransom** and signed a treaty **ceding** two-fifths of their country to England.

Several factors **contributed** to English victory. From their recent experiences in fighting with the **Welsh** and **Scots**, the English had learned better military **tactics** and learnt to use new weapons such as the **longbow** and **cannon**. Then there was the fact that the war was fought mainly on French soil. Except for the southern coastal ports, England did not suffer much destruction of war. The English soldiers were eager to fight in France because they looked forward to rich **plunder**. Despite its size, France lacked internal unity. Many provincial leaders took advantage of the confusion to **assert** their autonomy and seek their own advantage. Some even became English **allies**. The most dramatic

ransom *n.* 赎金
cede *v.* 割让
contribute to 导致
Welsh *n.* 威尔士人
Scot *n.* 苏格兰人
tactic *n.* 策略
longbow *n.* 长弓
cannon *n.* 大炮
plunder *n.* 赃物
assert *v.* 坚持
ally *n.* 盟友

instance was the breaking away of Burgundy. From 1419 to 1435 the dukes of Burgundy allied with the English, directly threatening the very existence of an independent French crown.

In 1428 military and political power seemed firmly in the hands of the English. But a **stunning** series of events were able to reverse the situation. In 1429, the arrival of a peasant girl, **Joan of Arc** turned French fortunes and led to victory. Born in 1412 in a well-to-do peasant family in Champagne, Joan of Arc grew up with a strong religious belief. During **adolescence** she began to hear voices, which she later said belonged to Saints. In 1428 these voices urged her to help the **Dauphin**, Charles be crowned king and to help the French army expel the English from France. Joan went to the French court, and persuaded the Dauphin to let her take command of his troops. Hoping that Joan would provide a miracle to save the country, Charles allowed her to accompany the army. Joan **inspired** the French soldiers with **confidence**, and they defeated the English decisively in **Orleans** in May 1429. Aided by the victory, Charles gained popular support and was crowned king.

In 1430 England's allies, the Burgundians, **captured** Joan and sold her to the English. The English accused Joan of **witchcraft** and contact with the **devil**, and sent her to be tried by church authorities. In 1431 the court **condemned** her as a **heretic** and burned her at the stake in the marketplace in Rouen. Joan had become a national symbol. Joan's intervention marked the turning point in the war. A series of French success followed Joan's death, and by 1453, only **Calais** was left in English hands. No formal treaty ended the war, but both sides accepted the outcome: England was no longer a continental power.

4.1.3 The Effects of the War

Like all the disasters of the era, the Hundred Years' War **accelerated** change. The most immediate change occurred in military affairs. The war **stimulated** the development of new weapons. The most famous weapons were the **longbow** and **cannon** used by the English. Arrows from the longbow had more penetrating power than a **bolt** from a **crossbow**, and the longbow could be fired much more rapidly. Moreover, firearms also played a significant role in the battles. **Gunpowder** probably arrived in the West from China in the late 13th century. By 1300 Europeans relied more and more on cannons for defensive wars. With the introduction of new weapons, **infantry** became a more important army force in battle than horse-riding knights.

stunning *adj.* 令人惊奇的
Joan of Arc 圣女贞德
adolescence *n.* 青少年期
dauphin *n.* 王太子
inspire *v.* 激发
confidence *n.* 信心
Orleans *n.* 奥尔良
capture *v.* 抓捕
witchcraft *n.* 施行女巫巫术
devil *n.* 魔鬼
condemn *v.* 指责
heretic *n.* 异教徒
Calais 加来港
accelerate *v.* 加速
stimulate *v.* 刺激
longbow *n.* 长弓
cannon *n.* 大炮
bolt *n.* 弩箭
crossbow *n.* 十字弓
gunpowder *n.* 火药
infantry *n.* 步兵

Another positive development was the steady growth of effective governmental institutions. During the reign of Edward Ⅲ (1327—1377), English political institutions developed fast. The most significant development was the English Parliament, which changed from an **occasional** assembly into a **permanent** institution. Due to his constant need for money to fight the Hundred Years' War, Edward came to rely on Parliament to **levy** new taxes. In return for regular grants, Edward made several **concessions**, including a commitment to levy no direct tax without Parliament's **consent** and to allow committees of Parliament to examine the government **accounts** to ensure that the money was being spent properly. The Parliament evolved into two houses, the **House of Lords** (high-born nobility and high-ranking clergy) and the **House of Commons** (representatives from shires and boroughs, such as knights and burghers). Although the House of Commons did little beyond approving measures proposed by the Lords, it did begin to gain control over taxation and any new legislation. By the end of Edward's reign, Parliament had become an important **component** of the English governmental system.

occasional *adj.* 不经常的
permanent *adj.* 常设的
levy *v.* 征税
concession *n.* 让步
consent *n.* 同意
account *n.* 账户
House of Lords 贵族院
House of Commons 平民院
component *n.* 组成部分

The war harmed France more than England. As a whole, France was **devastated**: lives were lost, farmlands ruined, commerce disrupted. Despite the damage, once the war over French economy quickly recovered as the land was so rich. The expulsion of the English from French lands greatly **boosted** the prestige and power of the French monarch. More importantly, the **emergency** situations in the war period allowed the French kings to gather new powers, above all, the rights to collect national taxes and maintain a **standing army**. The standing army represented an entirely new form of power for kings. Not only could they defend their kingdoms from invaders, but standing armies could also protect the king from internal threats and also keep the population in check. The war **accelerated** the process of transforming France into a highly centralized state.

devastated *adj.* 被毁坏
boost *v.* 提高
emergency *n.* 紧急情况
standing army 常备军
accelerate *v.* 加速

In both countries, the war **promoted** the growth of modern **nationalism** and awakened the national **consciousness** in the mind of their people. Before the war there had been very little national feeling. People identified with their local regions or towns instead. Local lords rivaled with the kings, and some even sought independence, for instance, the breaking away of Burgundy in France. The governments of both sides **rallied** public opinion to support the war. England held that the war was waged for one reason: to get back for King Edward the

promote *v.* 促进
nationalism *n.* 民族主义
consciousness *n.* 意识
rally *v.* 召集

evilness *n.* 邪恶
fortune *n.* 财富

French crown that he had been denied. While condemning the **evilness** of the French, the English government also stressed the great **fortunes** to be made from the war. Perceiving the English as invaders, the French developed a deep hatred of the English. The anti-English sentiment in the course of the Hundred Years' War resulted in a **surge** in national self-consciousness. The idea of France as a nation was born. Joan of Arc further helped inspire this idea. Perhaps no one expressed this national consciousness better than Joan of Arc, when she urged that the enemy should be "driven out of *France*."

surge *n.* 飙升

In the long run, the war had a major effect on the political development in England and France. England emerged from the war an island country. Separated from the European continent by the **English Channel**, England had more **diplomatic flexibility** in dealing continental European countries. With the loss of lands in France, the English monarch could avoid war with the French. Such a freedom enabled England to invest its energies in overseas expansion in America and elsewhere in the 16th century. As the English **aristocrats** lost their **possessions** in France, the strong French influence on English society and culture **diminished**. A clear indication was the status of the English language. From the Norman Conquest until the 14th century, French was the preferred language of the English crown and aristocracy, but after 1400 English gradually replaced French as the language of law courts and administration.

English Channel 英吉利海峡
diplomatic flexibility 外交灵活性
aristocrats *n.* 贵族
possession *n.* 财产
diminish *v.* 减弱

4.2 Political Crisis and Recovery

From 1300 to 1450, despite the unique history of the internal politics of each state, all were marked by aristocratic **factionalism**; European states were also troubled by internal political instability. All across Europe, the great families of the noble class competed with the **monarchs** for control of the state, often resulting in civil wars. Apart from the challenges of great nobles, monarchs in many European countries were not the direct descendants of those ruling in 1300. The founders of these new **dynasties** had to struggle for position. At the end of 14th century and beginning of the 15th century, there were two **claimants** to the throne of France; two aristocratic factions fought for control of England; three princes struggled to be recognized as emperor of Germany.

factionalism *n.* 派系斗争
monarch *n.* 君主
dynasty *n.* 王朝
claimant *n.* 继承人

Beginning in the 15th century, western European rulers began the work of reducing violence, limiting the power of nobles, and establishing domestic order. With the exception of Italy and Germany, national monarchies in France, England, and Spain became stronger than they had been two centuries before. Some scholars called **Louis Ⅸ** of France (rule1461—1483), **Henry Ⅶ** of England (rule1485—1509), and **Ferdinand** and **Isabella** of Spain (rule 1474—1516) "new monarchs." The new monarchs of late 15th century England, France and Spain laid the foundation for three of the great nation-states of modern Europe. These monarchs stressed the royal **majesty** and royal **sovereignty** and insisted that all must respect and be loyal to them. They also started to pursue **aggressive** expansionist policies overseas. The result of this transformation would be felt around the globe. For now, let us examine the political transformation in England, France, and Spain. We will leave the discussion of the political situation in Italy and Germany for the next two chapters, "Renaissance" and "Reformation."

Louis Ⅸ 路易十一
Henry Ⅶ 亨利七世
Ferdinand 费尔迪南
Isabella 伊萨贝拉女王

majesty *n.* 崇高地位
sovereignty *n.* 主权
aggressive *adj.* 挑衅性的

4.2.1 England

After the Hundred Years' War, England began to experience the internal **instability** of **aristocratic factionalism**. In 1422, the death of **King Henry** Ⅴ (rule 1413—1422) left the throne to his nine-month-old son, **Henry** Ⅵ (rule 1422—1461). As young Henry Ⅵ turned out to be **immature** and mentally unstable, his rule was challenged by his cousin, Edward, the **Duke of York**. Rivalry between Henry's family of **Lancaster** and the house of York led to a series of devastating civil wars from 1455 to 1485. These wars were commonly called the **Wars of the Roses** because the symbol of the house of Lancaster was a red rose and that of the house of York a white rose.

instability *n.* 不稳定
aristocratic factionalism 贵族派系斗争
Henry Ⅴ 亨利五世
immature *adj.* 不成熟
Duke of York 约克郡公爵
Lancaster 兰卡斯特郡
Wars of the Roses 玫瑰战争

In 1461, after a six-year struggle, Edward finally succeeded in **ousting** Henry Ⅵ and ruled until 1483. But when Edward died, his brother Richard murdered Edward's two sons and made himself king, becoming **Richard** Ⅲ. Political stability in England **collapsed** once again. In 1485, Richard Ⅲ was defeated and killed by the last surviving Lancastrian heir, Henry Tudor. Henry then resolved the rivalry between the two houses by marrying Elizabeth of York. With the two royal houses reunited, the Wars of Roses came to an end. The rival symbols of the red and white roses were merged into the new **emblem** of the red and white Tudor Rose. King Henry Ⅶ (1485—1509) founded the **Dynasty of Tudor**, which subsequently ruled England and Wales for 117 years.

oust *v.* 把……撵走
Richard Ⅲ 查理三世
collapse *v.* 崩溃

emblem *n.* 徽章

Dynasty of Tudor 都铎王朝

Gradually and **cautiously**, Henry Ⅶ rebuilt the monarchy. He encouraged the cloth industry and built up the English **merchant fleet**.

cautiously *adj.* 谨慎地
merchant fleet 商务舰队

Both English exports of wool and the royal export tax on that wool steadily increased. The king also earned support of the English merchants. By destroying castles and **confiscating** the lands and wealth of over-powerful lords, Henry Ⅶ further consolidated the royal authority. He also **crushed** an invasion from Ireland and secured peace with Scotland through the marriage of his daughter Margaret to the Scottish king. When Henry Ⅶ died, his son **Henry Ⅷ** (rule 1508—1547) inherited from his father a full **treasury** and a stable government. By the time Henry Ⅷ's daughter, **Elizabeth Ⅰ** (1558—1603) came to power, England had become one of Europe's most powerful nation-states and an **emerging** empire on the global stage.

confiscate *v.* 没收
crush *v.* 击溃
Henry Ⅷ 亨利八世
treasury *n.* 国库
Elizabeth Ⅰ 伊丽莎白一世
emerging *adj.* 崛起中的

4.2.2 France

In France, too, the power of the monarchy was threatened by rival factions of nobles. Between 1407 and 1435 when France was **ravaged** by the Hundred Years' War against the English, a civil war broke out between the **Armagnac** and the **Burgundian** factions. The war's causes are rooted in a confrontation between two different economic, social and religious systems. On one hand was France, very strong in agriculture, with a strong feudal and religious system, and on the other was England, a country whose rainy climate favored **pasture** and sheep-farming and where **artisans**, middle classes and cities were important. The Burgundians were in favor of the English model (the more so since Flanders belonged to the **duchy** of Burgundy) and thus **allied** with England. Defending the French model, the Armagnacs wanted to fight off the English. The Burgundians also had territorial ambitions. The dukes had tried to establish a Burgundian "middle kingdom" between France and the Holy Roman Empire. Such a state would have greatly **undermined** the position of the French king. The civil war created chaos for the French government and the French people.

ravage *v.* 严重破坏
Armagnac *adj.* 阿曼涅克的
Burgundian *adj.* 勃艮第人的
pasture *n.* 草场
artisan *n.* 手工匠人
duchy *n.* 大公国
ally *v.* 结为盟友
undermine *v.* 削弱

When both the Hundred Years' War and civil war ended in 1453, France did not immediately achieve territorial consolidation. But the **expulsion** of the English from the French lands and the **disintegration** of the Duchy of Burgundy left the French king without a major rival. The monarch emerged from the war with high prestige. Charles Ⅶ began France's long recovery.

expulsion *n.* 驱逐出境
disintegration *n.* 分崩离析

Charles Ⅶ worked to **reconcile** the Burgundians and Armagnacs. He reorganized the royal council, giving increased influence to the middle-class men. Through taxes on salt and land, he strengthened royal finances. Charles also reformed the justice system and created the

reconcile *v.* 调节关系

first permanent royal army. In 1438 he published **the Pragmatic Sanction of Bourges**, **affirming** the special rights of the French king over the French church. The Sanction gave the French king control over the **appointment** of bishops in France and **deprived** the pope of French **ecclesiastical revenues**. Greater control over the church, the army, and the legal system helped to consolidate the authority of the French crown.

the Pragmatic Sanction of Bourges《布尔日国事诏书》
affirm *v.* 确立
appointment *n.* 任命
deprive *v.* 剥夺
ecclesiastical revenue 教会税

The process of developing a strong French monarchy was greatly advanced by King Louis Ⅺ (rule 1461—1483), the son of Charles Ⅶ. Called the "Spider King" by his subjects because of his cruel character and **devious** ways, Louis Ⅺ **repressed** the French nobility and brought the provinces of Anjou, Maine, Bar, and Provence under royal control. Building on the system begun by his father, Louis Ⅺ worked tirelessly to remodel the government. Like Henry Ⅶ of England, Louis Ⅺ was a new monarch, using old **measures** to produce a more stable and prosperous **realm.**

devious *adj.* 狡诈的
repress *v.* 打压
measure *n.* 手段
realm *n.* 王国

4.3.3 Spain

Political development in the **Iberian Peninsula** followed a pattern different from that of France and England. Iberia throughout the Middle Ages was marked by **disunity** and **plurality**. The land had often been often invaded by foreign peoples such as the Romans, Germanic tribes, and Muslims. Different languages, laws, and religious communities made for a rich diversity. For centuries, three strong Christian kingdoms—**Castile**, **Aragon** and **Portugal**—had tried to drive the Muslims off Iberia. But at the same time, they also competed against each other to gain control of the entire peninsula.

Iberian Peninsula 伊比利亚半岛
disunity *n.* 分裂
plurality *n.* 多元
Castile *n.* 卡斯提拉
Aragon *n.* 阿拉贡
Portugal *n.* 葡萄牙

In 1469, Isabella of Castile (1474—1504) married Ferdinand of Aragon (1479—1516). The wedding was a major step in the **unification** and **Christianization** of Spain. This marriage, however, created a union of two royal houses, not a political union of two peoples. Although Ferdinand and Isabella **pursued** a **common** foreign policy, Spain under their rule remained a **loose confederation** of separate states. Each kingdom continued to keep its own parliament, laws, courts, bureaucracies, and systems of coinage and taxation.

unification *n.* 统一
Christianization *n.* 基督化
pursue *v.* 遵循
common *adj.* 共同点
loose *adj.* 松散的
confederation *n.* 邦联
counterpart *n.* 地位相当的人物

Like their **counterparts** Henry Ⅶ in England and Louis Ⅺ in France, Isabella and Ferdinand were new monarchs, and they were determined to strengthen royal authority. In order to limit aristocratic power, they gave local communities the right to organize police forces and punish criminals. Isabella and Ferdinand also restructured the

royal council by appointing only people of middle-class background. This measure intended to reduce the influence of the nobility on state policy. With the council as the center of the governmental system, the king and queen controlled full **executive**, **judicial**, and **legislative** power. Thereafter, an efficient central administration governed the two realms and eventually transformed them into the kingdom of Spain.

In the expansion of royal authority in Spain, the control of the church was the key. The church possessed vast power and wealth, and churchmen did not have to pay tax. Most of the higher **clergy** were descended from great aristocratic families. They controlled armies and **strategic fortresses**. The major issue confronting Isabella and Ferdinand was the appointment of bishops. If they could select the higher clergy, then they could influence the church policy. Isabella and Ferdinand formed a **diplomatic alliance** with the **papacy** to fight off the Muslims in Spain. As part of the agreement, the papacy granted Isabella and Ferdinand the title of "Catholic Kings of Spain."

The Spanish monarchs thereafter enjoyed the right to appoint bishops in Spain and in the Spanish **colonies** in America. In effect, the Spanish rulers now had the power to establish a national church. Using their power to reform the church, they put some of the church wealth to the use of national purposes. With taxation from church land, Ferdinand and Isabella were able to raise an army to continue their struggle against the Arabs in southern Spain. In the early 16th century, the Arabs had been defeated and their last force driven out of Spain, finally placing all the Iberian Peninsula under Christian control.

The reign of Isabella and Ferdinand marked a **profound** change in politics and society not only in Iberia but also in Europe in general. Ferdinand and Isabella married their daughter Joanna to Philip of Habsburg in 1496 to draw the Holy Roman Empire into the Italian wars brought on by the French invasion. The marriage of their daughter Catherine of Aragon to Prince Arthur of England in 1501 was designed to get another ally against the French. Those two marriages would have **momentous consequences** for European history in the 16th century.

royal council 皇家委员会
executive *adj.* 行政
judicial *adj.* 司法
legislative *adj.* 立法
clergy *n.* 神职人员
strategic fortress 战略性要塞
diplomatic alliance 外交结盟
papacy *n.* 教廷
colony *n.* 殖民地
profound *adj.* 深刻的
momentous *adj.* 重大的
consequence *n.* 后果

5. The Crisis of the Western Christian Church

When Europe was hit by the Black Death, terrified Christians looked to the Church for both physical and spiritual help. The Church

interpreted the plague as a sign of God's will, but it could not explain why God willed this awful punishment on His followers. No one, the Church included, was able to **cure** the plague **victims**. Many clergy even abandoned their Christian duties and fled. As the Church could not keep its promises of **salvation**, people grew increasingly **disillusioned** and **cynical** toward church officials. By the time the most severe blow of the Black Death was over, there was a **severe shortage** of clergy. A large number of new clergy members were trained in a hurry and had little experience. The lack of educated personnel among the clergy gravely reduced the intellectual strength of the Church. The lack of moral **discipline** of the clergy further resulted in **abuses** and **corruption**. In fact, the leaders of the church added to the sorrow and misery of the times.

interpret *v.* 解释
cure *v.* 治愈
victim *n.* 受害者
salvation *n.* 救赎
disillusioned *adj.* 幻灭
cynical *adj.* 冷嘲热讽
severe *adj.* 严重的
shortage *n.* 缺乏
discipline *n.* 纪律
abuse *n.* 滥用职权
corruption *n.* 腐败

The Black Death thus struck a serious blow to the Catholic Church. After the plague, angry and frustrated villagers started to revolt against the Church. The church's power was weakened, and in some cases, the social roles it had played were taken over by **secular** groups. At the same time, the Church also faced the challenge of internal and external threats.

secular *adj.* 非宗教的

5.1 The Babylonian Captivity

Babylonian Captivity 巴比伦沦陷

In 1305, French King, Philip Ⅵ secured the election of a Frenchman as **Pope Clement** Ⅴ (1305—1314). In order to control the church and its policies, Philip Ⅳ pressured Pope Clement Ⅴ to settle in the city of **Avignon** in south-eastern France. Clement, seriously ill with cancer, lacked the will to resist Philip. From 1305 until 1378, seven popes lived in Avignon. The leadership of the Church was thus cut off from its historical roots and the source of its ancient authority, the city of Rome. In the absence of the **papacy**, the Papal States in Italy lacked stability and good government. The economy of Rome had long been based on the **presence** of the papal court and the rich tourist trade the papacy attracted. The 73-year-long papacy at Avignon left Rome **poverty-stricken.**

Pope Clement Ⅴ 教皇克雷芒五世
Avignon 阿维尼翁
papacy *n.* 教廷
presence *n.* 存在
poverty-stricken *adj.* 极度贫困

During the 73 years of the Papacy at Avignon, several popes were Frenchmen, and 113 out of the 134 new **cardinals** created by the popes were French. Many people believed that the popes at Avignon were **puppets** and **captives** of the French monarchy. This period in church history is often called the Babylonian Captivity, recalling the biblical story of the Jews who were taken from Israel to work as slaves for the Babylonians. The Babylonian Captivity badly damaged papal prestige.

cardinal *n.* 红衣大主教
puppet *n.* 傀儡
captive *n.* 俘虏

As long as the French kings dominated papal policy, papal influence in England and in Germany declined.

The Avignon papacy reformed its financial administration and centralized its government. But the seven popes at Avignon concentrated on bureaucratic matters. Such reform measures turned the papacy into a more political than spiritual institution. Furthermore, some of the Avignon popes, especially Clement Ⅵ (1342—1352), were **corrupt** and **immoral**. The cardinals led equally **luxurious** lives. Avignon had become a powerful symbol of abuses within the Church.

corrupt *adj.* 腐败的
immoral *adj.* 不道德的
luxurious *adj.* 奢华的

Many devout Christians urged the popes to return to Rome. One of the most prominent calls came from Catherine of Siena (1347—1380). She was sent by the city of Florence on a special **mission** to Avignon to **plead** with the pope to return. In 1337 **Pope Gregory** Ⅺ (1370—1378) brought the papal court back to Rome. Unfortunately he died shortly after the return. At Gregory's death, Roman citizens demanded the College of Cardinals to elect an Italian pope as he would remain in Rome. Determined to pressure the cardinals, a Roman **mob** surrounded St. Peter's **Basilica**, blocked the roads leading out of the city, and seized all boats on the Tiber River. Sixteen cardinals—eleven Frenchmen, four Italians, and one Spaniard—held the election meeting on April 7, 1378 and voted an Italian pope, **Urban** Ⅵ (1378—1389).

mission *n.* 使命
plead *v.* 恳请
Pope Gregory Ⅺ 教皇格里高利十一世
mob *n.* 暴民
basilica *n.* 大教堂
Urban Ⅵ 教皇乌尔班六世

Pope Urban Ⅵ started immediately to reform the church. He wanted to abolish simony (the sales of the position of clergy), pluralism (one clergyman holding several church offices at the same time), **absenteeism**, and clerical **luxury** and **ostentation**. These were the very abuses being increasingly criticized by Christian peoples across Europe. Despite his good intention, Urban was **tactless** in carrying out the reform. He **denounced** individual cardinals by name and even threatened to **excommunicate** certain cardinals. Before he could consolidate his position in the church hierarchy, his reform measures met strong opposition from many high-ranking church officials.

absenteeism *n.* 玩忽职守
luxury *n.* 奢华无度
ostentation *n.* 炫耀
tactless *adj.* 缺乏策略
denounce *v.* 谴责
excommunicate *v.* 开除教籍

A number of French cardinals fled Rome and declared Urban's election **invalid** because it came about under threats from the Roman mob. They then announced the decision to excommunicate Urban and elected the cousin of King Charles V of France to be **Pope Clement** Ⅶ (1378—1394). There were thus two popes in 1378—Urban at Rome and the **antipope** Clement at Avignon. This led to the so-called **Western Schism** which divided Christians in Western Europe until

invalid *adj.* 无效的
Pope Clement Ⅶ 教皇克雷芒七世
antipope *n.* 对立主教
Western Schism 西方教会大分裂

1417.

5.2 The Western Schism (1378—1417)

For nearly four decades, Christian society in Western Europe was **split**. The religious divide was further **reinforced** by political rivalry among European rulers. Religious division fell along strictly political lines. France naturally **recognized** the French antipope, Clement. England, France's historic enemy, recognized Pope Urban. Scotland, whose attacks on England were supported by France, followed the French. Aragon, Castile, and Portugal **hesitated** before deciding for Clement. The emperor of the Holy Roman Empire in Germany, who had ancient **hostility** to France, recognized Urban. At first the Italian city-states recognized Urban; when his reform damaged their interests, they opted for Clement. Whenever a pope died his supporters quickly elected a successor, thus **prolonging** the Western Schism.

split *v.* 分裂
reinforce *v.* 强化
recognize *v.* 承认
hesitate *v.* 犹豫
hostility *n.* 敌意
prolong *v.* 延长

The Western Schism badly damaged the faith of Christian believers and introduced uncertainty into the daily lives of ordinary Christians. Both lines of popes **denounced** the other as the **Antichrist**, and such a situation could not help but **undermine** the very foundation of the Church. The Western Schism also led large numbers of serious churchmen to seek a revolutionary approach to solving the Church's institutional problems.

denounce *v.* 谴责
Antichrist *n.* 反基督分子
undermine *v.* 削弱

In response to continued Europe-wide calls for a **council**, the two colleges of cardinals from both sides **summoned** a council at **Pisa** in 1409. This Council of Pisa **deposed** both popes and **named** a new pope. But the two deposed popes refused to step down. As a result, there were now three popes, turning the two-way schism into a three-way schism. The church seemed more hopelessly divided than ever.

council *n.* 会议
summon *v.* 召集
Pisa (意) 比萨
depose *v.* 废除
name *v.* 任命

Finally, due to the pressure of the German emperor Sigismund, a great council met at the imperial city of Constance in 1414. The **Council of Constance** (1414—1417) was the largest religious gathering of the Middle Ages. It had three major **objectives**: to end the schism, to **eradicate** heresy, and to reform the church from top to bottom. After three years of lengthy debates, the council ended the Western Schism. This council succeeded mainly because of the strong support from several European princes, including the German emperor and the king of England. The council deposed all three popes and elected **Martin** Ⅴ (1417—1431) as new pope, who made Rome his headquarters. To prevent any future division, the Council of Constance had declared that **supreme authority** within the church rested not with

Council of Constance 康士坦会议
objective *n.* 目标
eradicate *v.* 清除
Pope Martin Ⅴ 教皇马丁五世
supreme *adj.* 至高无上的
authority *n.* 权威

the pope, but with itself and all future such "general councils". It also ordered that general councils should meet regularly thereafter to **oversee** the **governance** and reform of the church. This started the **conciliar movement**, a movement to make Church councils, not popes, the supreme authority within the Church. Although the council managed to end the schism, it was much less successful in dealing with the problems of heresy and the church reform.

oversee *v.* 监督
governance *n.* 治理
conciliar movement 会议运动

5.3 Religious Protest

In times of crisis or disaster, people often seek the **consolation** of religion. In the late medieval period, however, the official Christian Church failed to provide people with confidence and hope. Distrusting the formal institutions of the Church, many turned to private **devotions** and to **mysticism** to achieve union with God. Most of these stayed within the Church, but a few broke sharply with it. Strong dissatisfaction with the Church led to the rise of religious protest, or **heresies**. To a large extent, religious development in this period paved the way for the sixteenth-century Reformation movement.

consolation *n.* 慰藉
devotion *n.* 虔诚
mysticism *n.* 神秘主义
heresy *n.* 异端邪说

One form of heresy was mysticism. Even as Europeans were losing respect for the Church, people everywhere were seeking closer relationships with God. In the 14th and 15th centuries, a great many pious lay men and women chose to live together to strive for spiritual perfection. Throughout Europe, particularly in Germany and England, male and female **lay** Christians sought union with God by means of contemplation or spiritual exercises. An influential and eloquent mystical theorist was **Master Eckhart** (1260—1327), a German cleric. For Eckhart, there was a "**spark**" deep within every human soul that was really the **dwelling** place of God; it was through inward meditation instead of outward rituals that one could find this spark and achieve union with God. In the early 15th century, an unknown author in northern Germany wrote the ***Imitation of Christ***.① It taught individual Christian how to become the "partner" of Jesus Christ by receiving **communion**, engaging in biblical meditation, and leading a simple, moral life. This book of spiritual direction remains today the most widely read religious text after the Bible. Such teachings greatly reduced the importance of the **institutional** Church and were **condemned** by the papacy.

lay *adj.* 非神职的
Master Eckhart 爱克哈特大师
spark *n.* 火花
dwelling *adj.* 居住地
Imitation of Christ《效仿基督》
communion *n.* 圣餐
institutional *adj.* 机构的
condemn *v.* 谴责

① 也有学者认为作者是 Thomas à Kempis。

An opposite route to mysticism was **flagellantism**. In an imitation of Christ's life and sufferings, flagellants ritually beat (flagellated) themselves between the shoulders with **metal-tipped whip**. Through their sufferings, these Christians hoped to win the forgiveness of God and to bring about a moral and religious transformation of society. **Originated** in Hungary, the movement spread quickly into Germany, and across France and the Low Countries. In Germany, flagellants believed that severe punishment of each other with whips would reduce their sin. Church authorities considered the flagellants dangerous and announced them heretical.

flagellantism *n.* 鞭笞派

metal-tipped whip 鞭头包金属的鞭子

originate *v.* 发端于

The other form of heresy was **outright** religious protest. In England and **Bohemia**, heretical movements became serious threats to the Church. The **initiator** of heresy of late medieval England was **John Wycliffe** (1330—1384), a professor at the University of Oxford. Wycliffe argued that popes and clerics did not make up the Church. Instead, the Church was the community of all believers. For Wycliffe, the Bible alone declared the will of God; neither the pope nor the Scholastic theologians could tell Christians what they should believe; truth came through study of the Bible, not through the rituals of priests and bishops. By such arguments, Wycliffe questioned one of the central **dogmas** of the Church that emphasized the special power of the priest: **transubstantiation**.① Wycliffe claimed that the true Church included only those elected by God. Popes and bishops who were not elected by God had no right to rule. According to him, the **prince**, not the pope, should control church reform, and the pope could exercise only as much authority as the prince allowed. He also denied the authority of the clerics to hold property.

outright *adj.* 无掩饰的

Bohemia *n.* 波西米亚

initiator *n.* 发起者

John Wycliffe 约翰·威克里夫

dogma *n.* 教条

transubstantiation *n.* 圣餐变体论

prince *n.* 君主

Although many of Wycliffe's views were labeled heretical, they were extremely popular in England. Some of the peasants in the 1381 Peasants' Revolt were influenced by him. He had support among the nobles as well who protected him unharmed until he died. His ideas were even adopted by many priests. His followers, mostly ordinary people known as **Lollards** pushed for religious reform. Although they were constantly persecuted by Church authorities, they managed to survive as an underground movement in the countryside until the Protestant Reformation exploded more than a century later. To make the Bible **accessible** to common people, Wycliffe translated the official Latin

Lollard *n.* 罗拉德派

accessible *adj.* 易于使用的

① 天主教的神学理论，认为面饼和葡萄酒在弥撒中经神父的祝圣后变成耶稣的身体和血。

version of Bible into vernacular English, now known as the *Wycliffe Bible*. Wycliffe's writings later inspired leaders of the Protestant Reformation such as Martin Luther and John Calvin. For this reason, he is often considered a **precursor** to the Protestant Reformation, sometimes called "The Morning Star of the Reformation".

precursor *n.* 先驱

Wycliffe's ideas spread faraway to **Czechs** in Bohemia, where they were taken up by the Czech religious reformer **Jan Hus** (also spelt as John Huss) (1373—1415). A **distinguished** churchman and scholar, he served as president of the Charles University in **Prague**, one of Europe's best-known universities. Like Wycliffe, Hus argued that the Church was made up of all the faithful; that priests were not a holy and privileged group, set apart from laypersons. Hus demanded changes in the Church, focusing on the ritual of communion at Mass, which involved the eating of bread (a symbol of Christ's body) and the drinking of wine (a symbol of Christ's blood). He rejected the division that allowed the ordinary believers at Mass to receive only bread but not the wine, which only the priests could drink. This was more than an argument over ritual—it was a demand for equality. **Defying** the leadership of the Church, he shared the cup of wine with all worshipers.

Czech *n.* 捷克人
Jan Hus 扬·胡斯
distinguished *adj.* 出类拔萃的
Prague *n.* 布拉格
defy *v.* 公然蔑视

In 1415, Hus was condemned as a heretic and was burned at the stake. His followers, called **Hussites** were also persecuted. All levels of Czech society saw the attack on Hus as an attack on Czech independence and national interest by a Church and an empire controlled by Germans. Unlike the Lollards who stayed out of sight in England, the Hussites refused to retreat in the face of persecution. Under the leadership of the king of Bohemia, John of the Chalice, the Hussites organized an army and a civil war broke out in Bohemia. At this moment, the Hussites movement took a new and powerful turn. The Hussites were not only fighting for religious reform but also for Bohemia's independence from the Holy Roman Empire. The resistance lasted twenty years before the Hussites' final defeat in 1436. But eventually the Hussites were allowed to establish a special church in which both bread and wine were shared by all worshippers at Mass. The people of Bohemia emerged from the ordeal with a solid sense of national identity. Like Wycliffe, Hus was also a key **predecessor** to the Protestant movement of the 16th century, and his teachings had a strong influence on the states of Europe.

Hussite *n.* 胡斯派
predecessor *n.* 前辈

As a result of these religious protests, the Church lost prestige, spiritual authority and leadership over the people. However, the decline of the Church authority did not mean a **decrease** in Europeans' religious **enthusiasm**. The turmoil of the Late Middle Ages actually **intensified** religious enthusiasm. But it took on new forms of expression as evidenced by the rise of national churches in the sixteenth-century Reformation.

decrease *n.* 减少
enthusiasm *n.* 热情
intensify *v.* 强化

6. Conclusion

The Late Middle Ages saw decline, disruption, and **disintegration** in most of Europe. It has been described in such terms as "the decline of the Middle Ages", or "the **waning** of the Middle Ages". Certain developments support these descriptions. European expansion temporarily ended. Population decreased significantly, due in great part to poor harvests, disease, and war. Economic conditions varied greatly, contributing to the considerable social unrest of the period. Extended political conflicts led to an unusually intense period of wars. The Roman Catholic Church faced a series of conflicts including internal divisions and heresy. In short, these developments paint a picture in marked contrast to our image of the Central Middle Ages.

disintegration *n.* 分崩离析
wane *v.* 日渐衰败

However, periods of decline and disintegration are often fertile grounds for change and new developments. Periods of crisis usually give rise to new ideas and new practices. **Dislocation** itself promotes innovation. The confidence the Europeans had developed in the Central Middle Ages was not destroyed by the **travails** of the Late Middle Ages. Europeans seized the opportunities their new world presented to them. Europeans stood on the **threshold** of a new age of cultural rebirth, stood on the verge of a new age of expansion and conquest that would take European armies, merchants and settlers together with European civilization around the globe. In short, out of the dissolution of medieval civilization came a new era of Renaissance, Reformation, and Discovery.

dislocation *n.* 扰乱
travail *n.* 阵痛
threshold *n.* 门槛

Exercises

Ⅰ. Terminology: choose the suitable terms to fill in the blanks.

A. Statute of Laborers B. enclosure C. The Hundred Years' War

D. Wars of the Roses E. conciliar movement F. heresy

G. flagellantism H. The Black Death I. The Parliament

J. ciompi.

• __1__ was a series of wars between England and France, lasting from 1336 to 1453.

• __2__ was a movement to make Church councils, not popes, the supreme authority within the Church.

• __3__ were wool combers.

• __4__ was a law enacted by the English parliament under King Edward III in 1351 in response to a labor shortage, designed to stabilize the labor force by prohibiting increases in wages and prohibiting the movement of workers from their home areas in search of improved conditions.

• The process of conversion of land use from arable to pasture—usually sheep farming is called __5__.

• __6__ is a controversial or novel change to a system of beliefs, especially a religion, which conflicts with established dogma.

• __7__ was a practice of imitating Christ's life and sufferings through beating each other with whips, in hope of winning the forgiveness of God and bringing about a moral and religious transformation of society.

• __8__ was one of the most devastating pandemics in human history, peaking in Europe between 1348 and 1350.

• __9__ was an important component of the English governmental system, consisting of two houses, the House of Lords and the House of Commons.

• __10__ was a series of civil wars from 1455 to 1485.

Ⅱ. Decide whether the following statements are true (T) or false (F).

1. The Late Middle Ages are often described as a period of crisis and decline. ( )

2. Knowing the true cause of the disease, many Christians considered the Black Death a signal of the Last Judgment. ( )

3. Economic hardship was undoubtedly the major cause for the Jacquerie uprising. ( )

4. What really triggered off the English Peasants' Revolt of 1381 was an attempt to collect a new type of national tax to pay for the failing war with France. ( )

5. Joan's intervention marked the turning point in the Hundred Years' War. ( )

6. The new monarchs of late 15th century Germany, Italy and Spain laid the foundation for three of the great nation-states of modern Europe. ( )

7. Throughout the Middle Ages the Iberia Peninsula was marked by unity and plurality. (　　)

8. From the Norman Conquest until the 14th century, French was the preferred language of the English crown and aristocracy, but after 1400 English gradually replaced French as the language of law courts and administration. (　　)

9. The anti-English sentiment in the course of the Hundred Years' War resulted in a strong feeling of hatred in France. (　　)

10. The confidence the Europeans had developed in the Central Middle Ages was destroyed by the travails of the Late Middle Ages. (　　)

Ⅲ. Multiple choices: choose the answer that best completes the statement or answers the question.

1. The Late Middle Ages were marked by the following features, EXCEPT ________.

A. Plague and famine caused millions of death in Europe

B. Along with depopulation came social unrest and conflicts

C. Rivalry between feudal governments led to wars, the most violent being the Hundred Years' War fought between Germany and Italy

D. Peasant uprisings and urban revolts broke out in many countries

2. Which one of the following statements about the Great Famine is NOT true?

A. It was the worst famine in European history.

B. It lasted for seven hard years.

C. In cities alone, there was shortage of food supplies.

D. By the time it ended, the Great Famine had wiped out 10 percent to 15 percent of the entire European population.

3. Which one of the following statements about the Black Death is NOT true?

A. It is estimated to have killed 30% ~60% of Europe's population.

B. The death rate in some larger cities in Italy may have been as high as 60 percent.

C. In northern France, villages suffered mortality rates of 30 percent, and cities experienced losses as high as 40 percent.

D. Death caused by the Black Death worsened the situation of surviving peasants and laborers.

4. Which one of the following statements about "Jacques rebellion" is NOT true?

A. The peasants involved in the rebellion had a clear political program and organization.

B. The rebellion took its name from a contemptuous nickname used by the French nobles for any peasant.

C. Rebellious peasants burned down castles, murdered their lords, and raped their lords' wives.

D. Within a month the rebellion was suppressed by French nobles.

5. The following statements about the English Peasants' Revolt of 1381 are true EXCEPT

________.

A. it accomplished its objectives

B. it received help from members of the noble classes

C. it succeeded in showing the nobles what peasants were capable of when dissatisfied

D. it marked the beginning of the end of serfdom in medieval England

6. The Hundred Years' War arose from the following causes, EXCEPT ________.

A. The territorial disputes between England and France

B. The clash of economic interest in Flanders

C. Famine, plague, economic turmoil, social upheaval

D. The dispute over the French royal succession

7. Which of the following statements is NOT true?

A. The Hundred Years' War harmed England more than France.

B. The war stimulated the development of new weapons.

C. The war speeded up the development of the English Parliament.

D. The war promoted the growth of modern nationalism and awakened the national consciousness in the mind of their people.

8. The Wars of Roses ended up in ________.

A. the emergence of the new emblem of the red and white Tudor Rose

B. the split of the two royal houses

C. the establishment of the Dynasty of Tudor by King Henry Ⅷ

D. the subsequent ruling of England and Scotland for 117 years

9. Which of the following statements about Papacy at Avignon is NOT true?

A. The reform measures of Avignon papacy turned the papacy into a more spiritual than political institution.

B. Several popes were Frenchmen, and 113 out of the 134 new cardinals created by the popes were French.

C. Papal influence in England and in Germany declined.

D. This period in church history is called the Babylonian Captivity.

10. The Council of Constance marked ________.

A. the largest religious gathering of the Late Middle Ages

B. the end of the Western Schism

C. the success in dealing with the problems of heresy

D. the success in dealing with the problems of the church reform

11. All the following constitute the main forms of heresy, EXCEPT ________.

A. mysticism　　B. flagellantism

C. Lollards and Hussites　　D. worshipers

12. The following kings were called "new monarchs", EXCEPT ________.

A. Louis Ⅺ of France　　B. Friedrich I of Germany

C. Henry Ⅶ of England　　D. Ferdinand and Isabella of Spain

13. Pope Urban VI started to reform the church and wanted to abolish the following abuses, EXCEPT ________.

A. Simony B. Pluralism

C. Absenteeism D. homosexual

14. Which of the following statements about Joan of Arc is NOT true?

A. She was born in a well-to-do peasant family.

B. She grew up with a strong religious belief.

C. Charles refused her to accompany the army.

D. She was burned at stake.

15. Which of the following statements about ciompi is NOT true?

A. They formed a ciompi guild.

B. They formed a people's militia.

C. They granted political representation in the government.

D. They had not lost their hold on power.

16. During the Great Famine, starvation even drove some people to eat the following living creatures, EXCEPT ________.

A. cats B. rats C. snakes D. dogs

17. During the Wat Tyler Rebellion, the rebels marched into London and executed the following important officials, EXCEPT ________.

A. Lord Chancellor B. Lord Treasurer

C. magistrate of London, William Tonge D. Archbishop of Canterbury

18. Which of the following statements about The Hundred Years' War is NOT true?

A. The most famous weapons were the longbow and cannon used by the English.

B. Firearms played a significant role in the battles.

C. Horse-riding knights became more important army force than infantry.

D. Europeans relied more and more on cannon for defensive wars.

19. The Black Death struck a serious blow to the Catholic Church in the following ways, EXCEPT ________.

A. the Church failed to explain why God willed this awful punishment on His followers

B. many clergy stuck to their Christian duties and died

C. there was a severe shortage of clergy

D. church was unable to cure the plague victims

20. Which of the following statements about Western Schism is NOT true?

A. France recognized the French antipope Clement.

B. England recognized Pope Urban.

C. Scotland followed the French.

D. The emperor of Holy Roman Empire in Germany recognized Clement.

Part Ⅲ Transition from Middle Ages to Early Modern Era

The Early Modern Era (Age, Period, Time) is the term used by historians to refer to a period in the history of European civilization (especially Western Europe and Central Europe) which spanned the centuries between the end of the Middle Ages and the beginning of the Industrial Revolution, roughly the 14th century to the 18th century, although the chronological limits of the period are open to debate.

The Early Modern Era was characterized by a shift away from medieval age and a series of profound changes in many realms of human endeavor. Regardless of the precise dates used to define its beginning and end points, the Early Modern Era is generally agreed to have comprised several important historical events—the Renaissance, the Reformation, the Discovery and Colonization, the Scientific and Industrial Revolution, the Enlightenment, etc. As such, the Early Modern Era is often associated with the decline and eventual disappearance (at least in Western Europe) of an old age featured by feudalism, and the beginning of a new age featured by capitalism and globalization.

Among these historical events, the Renaissance and the Reformation played a vital role in the formation of the new age. It is first due to the Renaissance and then to the Reformation that the Europeans were liberated from the feudalistic autocracy and the theological yoke and the culmination in her historical development began. The Renaissance and the Reformation together were a turning point in the development of Western culture and civilization by providing a new perception and a new belief for the West. Western civilization was thus able to take on a new look and opened a new page in her historical process towards modernity by stepping up her efforts at an unprecedented pace.

Chapter 8
Renaissance (1350—1600)

CHAPTER OUTLINE

1. Introduction
2. The States of Northern Italy
3. Italian Renaissance Culture
4. Northern Renaissance
5. Scientific Accomplishments
6. Conclusion

FOCUS QUESTIONS

1. Why did the Renaissance originate in Italy?
2. What were the principal characteristics of Italian Renaissance art?
3. What were the similarities and differences between the Italian Renaissance and Northern Renaissance?
4. How did the Renaissance change the European society?

1. Introduction

In the latter half of the 14th century, a number of Italian scholars and artists began to take a strong interest in the Greek-based culture of ancient Rome. According to them, one thousand years of darkness had separated them from the **glorious** Roman era (an era known as the classical period). The **humanists** believed that classical art, science, philosophy, and literature had been lost during the "dark ages" that followed the fall of the West Roman Empire. They considered it their **responsibility** to rediscover, rescue, and revive the classical culture. Their efforts **ushered** in a period of remarkable **intellectual**, **literary**, and artistic activity. Today we use the French word for "rebirth", *renaissance*, to describe this period of intense creativity and change.

glorious *adj.* 辉煌的
humanist *n.* 人文主义学者
responsibility *n.* 责任
usher *v.* 引入
intellectual *adj.* 智识的
literary *adj.* 文学的

The Renaissance started in northern Italy around 1350. By the 1500s scholars and traders were spreading the Italian Renaissance to the rest of Europe, where it was called the Northern Renaissance. Today we tend to view these separate movements as a single Europe-wide cultural and intellectual movement. In terms of time span, the Renaissance (1350—1600) **overlapped** with most of the Late Middle Ages (1300—1500) and the **Reformation** (1500—1600). In spite of this, historians today all agree that the Renaissance represents a break with the earlier medieval periods. It is thus treated as a separate period of history with **unique** qualities in focus and emphasis. Historians have not determined an exact date for the end of the Renaissance, though most agree that it reached a peak at the end of the 15th century. In some parts of Europe, achievements associated with the Renaissance continued into the first half of the 1600s.

overlap *v.* 重叠
Reformation *n.* 宗教改革运动
unique *adj.* 独特的

The Renaissance began as a literary movement, but by the time it reached a peak in the 15th and 16th centuries, a **transformation** was taking place in all areas of public and private life—philosophy, science, the arts, architecture, music, politics, social customs, and popular culture. The Renaissance also contributed to the rise of the Reformation, a widespread religious reform movement that began in the 16th century. The Renaissance and Reformation period is regarded as the beginning of the modern age—the time in Western (non-Asian) history when people **rejected** familiar traditions and found new ways to express their experience of the world.

transformation *n.* 转型
reject *v.* 摒弃

In this chapter, we will trace the growth and development of the Renaissance. The next section will begin with an overview of the Italian Renaissance, examining the **specific** historical context of Italy at the time to explain the rise of the Italian Renaissance. Then after a general discussion of the **characteristics** of the Italian Renaissance, we will present the **representative figures** in the Italian Renaissance, introducing their ideas or works in the fields of arts, literature, and philosophy. Moving out of Italy, the focus will be shifted to the spread of the Renaissance in Europe as well as the features of the Northern Renaissance. The final section will examine the development in science and technology in the Renaissance period.

specific *adj.* 特定的
characteristics *n.* 特点
representative *adj.* 代表性的
figure *n.* 人物

2. The States of Northern Italy

Although the Renaissance eventually became a Europe-wide intellectual and artistic movement, it developed first and foremost distinctively in 14th century northern Italy, then moving northward to other parts of Europe in the early 15th century. Its early rise had much to do with the economic, social, and political context of northern Italy at the time.

The history of Italy during the Renaissance is extremely ***complex***. Italy at the time was not unified under a single ruler. In fact, the united nation of Italy was not created until 1861. In 1350 the Italian Peninsula was mainly made up of a **dozen** of city-states. They differed in size, shape, and form. Some were large seaports; others were small inland villages. Among these dozen of city-states, five had emerged to **dominate** the politics of the peninsula. In the south was the kingdom of **Naples**, the only city-state ruled by a **hereditary monarchy**. In the central Italy was the **Papal States** under the control of the pope, whose capital was Rome. Northern Italy was dominated by three city-states—Florence, Milan, and Venice.

complex *adj.* 错综复杂

dozen *n.* 十几个

dominate *v.* 主导

Naples *n.* 那不勒斯

hereditary *adj.* 世袭的

monarchy *n.* 君主制

Papal States 教皇国

With the exception of Venice, northern Italy was part of the **Holy Roman Empire**. But since the 11th century, the influence of most German emperors in Italy had been weak. Furthermore, the struggle between the popes and rulers of the Holy Roman Empire created favorable opportunities for the northern city-states to **enlarge** their own power and independence. During the 14th century, these cities slowly increased their power and expanded their scope of control.

Holy Roman Empire 神圣罗马帝国

enlarge *v.* 扩大

2.1 Milan

Located in the far northern region of Italy, along the border of percent-day **Switzerland**, Milan had been one of Italy's largest and wealthiest cities since the late Roman Empire. The city occupied a strategic position at the **crossroads** of major routes between the Italian Peninsula and northern Europe. Although Milan was surrounded by a fertile agricultural area, the economy was based mainly on commercial trade. Merchants in the area conducted active trading relationships with most of the European states and with kingdoms along the eastern coast of the Mediterranean Sea.

Switzerland *n.* 瑞士

crossroads *n.* 十字路口

At the time of the Italian Renaissance, Milan was a **duchy** that consisted of the capital city of Milan and other, less influential cities.

duchy *n.* 大公国

Like most Italian city-states, Milan was also dominated by a few powerful families. The foremost families were the Viscontis and the Sforzas. Moving in and out of power in Milan for 136 years, the Viscontis controlled Milan at the beginning of the Renaissance. The Sforzas came into power in 1450, and their eighty-five-year **reign** covered the remainder of the Renaissance period.

reign *n.* 统治时期

Both the Viscontis and the Sforzas were **patrons** of the arts. For instance, Galeazzo Ⅱ Visconti (1321—1378) built a **castle**, founded the University of Pavia, and also financed **Petrarch** (1304—1374), the "father of humanism." Galeazzo Ⅱ's son, Gian Galeazzo Visconti (1351—1402; ruled 1378—85) ordered construction to begin on the **cathedral** of Milan, a gigantic building that still stands today. Another magnificent building **commissioned** by Gian Galeazzo was the Certosa di Pavia, a richly decorated **monastery** church in Pavia, which is considered one of the architectural **masterpieces** of the Renaissance. Likewise, the Sforzas also actively supported the art and beautified Milan. Ludovico Sforza (1451—1508; ruled 1494—1499) was one of the wealthiest and most powerful rulers of the Italian Renaissance. With his wife, he **hosted** grand **spectacles** and financed works of many Renaissance artists, poets and musicians. Numerous artists were invited to his splendid court, including the painter **Leonardo da Vinci** and the architect **Donato Bramante.**

patron *n.* 赞助人
castle *n.* 城堡
Petrarch 彼得拉克
cathedral *n.* 大教堂
commission *v.* 委托制作
monastery *adj.* 修道院的
masterpiece *n.* 杰作
host *v.* 主办
spectacle *n.* 活动
Leonardo da Vinci 列奥纳多·达·芬奇
Donato Bramante 多纳托·伯拉孟特

2.2 Venice

Situated on 118 islands in a **shallow** body of water at the extreme northern end of the **Adriatic Sea**, Venice was one of the most important cities of Renaissance Italy and perhaps the most beautiful. It was the only Italian city-state to remain independent while others were being invaded and occupied. During the Renaissance, Venice reached the height of its power. Compared to the other Italian city-states, Venice was relatively free from internal political struggle. The main reason was its **distinctive** form of government. The head of the republic was a duke elected for life. But the real power was located in the Great Council. Comprised of all Venice's noblemen from about 180 families, the Great Council was in charge of electing officials and making laws. Thus Venice, a republic in name, was in reality governed by a small group of wealthy **merchants**. Stability in the Venetian republic **guaranteed** a relatively peaceful life in the republic during the Renaissance.

shallow *adj.* 浅的
Adriatic Sea 亚得里亚海
distinctive *adj.* 与众不同的
merchant *n.* 商人
guarantee *v.* 确保

By the 13th century Venice was the main trade link between Europe and Asia. From the East the six fleets of the republic brought back such

luxury items as teas, **spices**, and silk, and made huge profits in the European market. The republic was also a major ship-building center. Its ship-building and arms manufacturing facility, **the Arsenal** was the largest industrial enterprise in Europe. The Arsenal could build a fully equipped warship in just one day. It attracted the finest artisans from all over Europe and gave Venice the reputation of the **artisans' haven.**

luxury item 奢侈品
spice *n.* 香料
arsenal *n.* 军工厂
artisans' haven 工匠收容所

2.3 Florence

Unlike the port city of Venice, Florence was an inland city without easy **access** to water transportation. Banking instead of sea trade was an important source of the city's income. Florence became the banking center of Italy in the early 14th century and an international financial center in the 15th century. Florentine bankers had offices in all most all important cities in Europe, Paris, London, Bruges, Barcelona, Marseilles, Geneva, and of course, Naples and Rome. The **florin**, the city's gold coin, was one of the most **reliable currencies** at the time. Huge profits from **loans**, **investments**, and money **exchanges** poured back to Florence.

access *n.* 入口
florin *n.* 弗罗林（硬币）
reliable *adj.* 可靠的
currency *n.* 货币
loan *n.* 贷款
investment *n.* 投资
exchange *n.* 兑换
capital *n.* 资本
fetch *v.* 获得

Such profits provided the city with sufficient **capital** to develop its industries. The Florentine wool industry, in particular, pushed further the city's financial expansion and population increase. At its height, the Florentine textile industry employed 30 000 people. Florentine woolen cloth **fetched** the highest prices in the fairs and markets of Europe, Asia, and Africa. Besides its woolen clothes, Florence also produced other luxury goods such as silk, fine leather, and silver and gold objects. The training offered by its guilds in design and craftsmanship was a major reason for the high skills of its artists.

In theory, Florence was a self-governing **democracy**, but during the Renaissance, real political power was in the hands of wealthy businessmen. Powerful and influential families were all **striving** to gain control of the city. At the same time, Florence was involved in conflicts with neighboring city-states over rights to trade routes. As a result, political life in Florence was potentially unstable.

democracy *n.* 民主政体
strive to 极力

In the mid-14th century, situation became worse with the arrival of the Black Death. Nearly 40% of the entire population was lost in the single year 1348. Loss of workers and market seriously disrupted manufacturing. By 1380, cloth production had fallen by more than 70%. Florence was further **devastated** by the wars with Milan and Naples. The combined impact of the Black Death and warfare drove many leading Florentine families into **bankruptcy**. Florence turned for

devastate *v.* 破坏
bankruptcy *n.* 破产
the Medicis 美地奇家族

aid to the wealthiest banking family in Europe, **the Medicis**. The male head of the Medici family, Cosimo de Medici (1380—1464) became the ruler of the city in 1434. Combining their enormous amount of wealth with political skills, the Medici family secured more than one century long dynastic rule in Florence.

The Medicis were active supporters of artists and intellectuals. In his life time, Cosimo collected a large number of books and paintings, built the Medici library, and founded the **Platonic Academy**. The son of Cosimo, Piero (1416—1469; ruled 1464—1469) continued to support artists and architects. The wife of Piero, Lucretia, was a respected Florentine poet. She helped Piero spread the family's wealth to talented artists. Cosimo's grandson, Lorenzo (1449—1492; ruled 1478—1492), known as "**Magnificent Lorenzo**", continued the support of the arts. He expanded the Medici library, invited leading artists and intellectuals to his table and garden, periodically held poetry readings and stage performances.

the Platonic Academy 柏拉图学园

Magnificent Lorenzo 伟大的洛伦佐

In short, without the economic success in Italy, the Italian Renaissance would not have occurred. Economic success had made Italy the most advanced **urban** society in Europe. As Italian towns grew larger and wealthier, urban populations became a mixture of social classes different in background and power. In such new societies based on merchants and commerce, there was a widespread secular (non-religious) spirit among the increasingly wealthy townspeople. They demanded new opportunities for the enjoyment of worldly things. This encouraged writers and artists to seek **inspiration** from the classical art and literature. Although the wealthy Italian noblemen and merchants often supported artists in order to **glorify** their own success, they played a major role in **promoting** the Renaissance, both in Italy and elsewhere in Europe.

urban *adj.* 都市化的

inspiration *n.* 灵感

glorify *v.* 颂扬

promote *v.* 推动

3. Italian Renaissance Culture

The Italian Renaissance produced many artists, thinkers, writers, and scientists. The main ideas of the Renaissance movement in Italy were first introduced by a number of scholars through their writings. Then the works of great artists provided **visual** evidence that these ideas were taking roots. By capturing the spirit of the time in word or song or image, they set the stage for the modern era. In the Renaissance

visual *adj.* 视觉的

period, Europe was growing less medieval and increasingly modern. A fundamental transformation of the European society was set in motion by the Renaissance. Through such a process of transformation, the European society moved toward **secularism**, **individualism**, **skepticism**, and **materialism**. This does not mean that all scholars or artists of the Renaissance simply abandoned medieval qualities and embraced modern values overnight. It does mean that most could be found moving away from the older standards, somewhere on the path toward the newer ones.

3.1 Italian Renaissance: Humanism at a Glance

The **learned** men in the Italian Renaissance called themselves humanists. Based on the study of the classical literary works of Greece and Rome the Renaissance humanists **launched** an intellectual movement. Medieval scholars had also studied the classics (see the section of "philosophy and thought" in Central Middle Ages), but the Renaissance humanists took the studies of the classics up to a new level. They rediscovered many classical texts forgotten or lost for a long time, for instance, the works of **Homer**, Plato, **Cicero**, and **Tacitus**. They also made many copies of the existing classical texts and spread the knowledge beyond the small **circle** of scholars.

The rise of humanism was a reaction to the **domination** of Christian beliefs in people's thinking. Though searching and studying the classical works, humanists hoped to find some **guidance** for a better life. They were more concerned with man's world and life on earth rather than God's kingdom and life after death. But it would be wrong to **assume** that the humanists were anti-religious. Nor were they **hostile** to the Church. What they tried to do was to pay more attention to this life on earth so as to make it meaningful. In fact, many famous humanists were employed by the **papal court** at some time in their careers. Their interest in human achievement and human potential must be set beside their religious belief. As Petrarch, the father of humanism, once said, "Christ is my God; Cicero is the prince of the language I use."

In order to better understand classical texts, humanists not only read the original texts written in ancient Latin and Greek, but also read these texts **critically** within their historical contexts. The results were strong **criticism** of medieval **commentators** and new **interpretations** of classical works. One of the most remarkable contributions made by the humanists was in the field of Greek studies. Despite the long contacts between Western Europe and the Byzantium, almost nobody in the West

secularism *n.* 世俗主义
individualism *n.* 个人主义
skepticism *n.* 怀疑主义
materialism *n.* 物质主义
embrace *v.* 拥抱
humanism *n.* 人文主义
learned *adj.* 有学问的
launch *v.* 发起
Homer 荷马
Cicero 西塞罗
Tacitus 塔西佗
circle *n.* 圈子
domination *n.* 控制
guidance *n.* 指导
assume *v.* 认为
hostile *adj.* 有敌意的
papal court 教廷
critically *adv.* 批判性地
criticism *n.* 批判
commentator *n.* 评论家
interpretation *n.* 诠释

exile *n.* 流亡者
free-lance writer 自由撰稿人
reshape *v.* 重新型塑
individuality *n.* 个性
universal man 全面发展的人
excel *v.* 擅长于
rhetoric *n.* 修辞
diploma *n.* 学历证书
enhance *v.* 强化
elite *n.* 精英
inhibit *v.* 阻碍
Tuscany 托斯卡纳
Dante 但丁
Divine Comedy《神曲》

before the late 14th century knew Greek or cared about Greek literature. Greek studies before the Renaissance in Western Europe mainly focused on the works of Aristotle which were often translated from Arabic versions. With the help of Greek **exiles** and visitors, the humanists began to teach Greek in the universities and to translate works by ancient Greek authors into Latin.

Only a few humanists were what we would call "**free-lance writers**; most were teachers in schools or universities. Their thinking greatly **reshaped** educational theory and practice. The goal of education, they believed, was to produce persons whose actions expressed their **individuality** and who would lead good and useful lives later in their careers. According to humanist teaching, one ruled one's own life, and success and failure depended on one's own abilities and accomplishments. The humanist ideal was the "**universal man**," one who **excels** in many different fields. To achieve this goal, classical training was made a central part of elementary and secondary education. Besides grammar and **rhetoric**, the program of study included classical literature, mathematics, music, science, athletics, and outdoor activity. Those studies would encourage harmonious development of students' body and mind, stimulate imagination, and guide their moral conducts. Many humanist schools were founded in the Italian cities. A **diploma** of humanist studies soon became necessary for a position in the Church or the government. Education **enhanced** the impact of the humanist ideas on the ruling class as well as the future generations of **elite**.

3.2 Italian Intellectual Renaissance: Literature and Thought

One of the earliest manifestations of the Renaissance humanism in Italy was the development of literature written in Italian. Throughout the Middle Ages the strong position of the Latin language and the political disunity of Italy had long **inhibited** the growth of Italian language. Population in the peninsula used regional dialects rather than a national language. During the 14th century eloquent writers from **Tuscany** (the area around Florence) made their dialect the basis of the modern Italian language.

The first Italian to compose in his native language was the poet **Dante** (1265—1321). Born into a noble family in Florence, Dante held several positions in the city government. His best-known poem is the epic, the ***Divine Comedy*** (composed 1308—1321), which is considered one of the masterpieces of Western literature. The epic consists of one hundred sections, written in a complex verse form called **terza rima**.① Divided into three parts, the *Divine Comedy* tells the story of the poet's imaginary journey toward the City of God through three parts of the next world—Hell, **Purgatory**, and Paradise. In the journey, the poet was first guided by the Roman poet **Virgil** and then Beatrice, a young lady whom Dante fell in love in real life. Virgil represented **reason** while Beatrice symbolized love. The message is clear: only reason and love can lead one to the City of God. In Paradise, St. Bernard—representing **mystic contemplation**—led Dante to the Virgin Mary. Through her **mediation** Dante at last had a glimpse of God and discovered the secret of the universe.

terza rima 隔行韵脚

purgatory *n.* 炼狱

Virgil（古罗马诗人）维吉尔

reason *n.* 理性

mystic contemplation 神思冥想

mediation *n.* 求情

In many ways Dante was still very much a medieval man: he lived at the end of the Middle Ages, and his writing reflects the concerns of a devout medieval Christian. And yet the **theme** in his work marks the early **sparkles** of the Renaissance spirit. The *Divine Comedy* portrays contemporary and historical figures and comments on religious and non-religious affairs. Dante greatly influenced the next generation of Renaissance poets through his sharp philosophical and religious criticism, creative literary imagination. His use of the Tuscan dialect formed the basis of modern Italian language. For all these, later generations regard Dante both as the last poet of the Middle Ages and the first poet of the modern time.

theme *n.* 主题

sparkle *n.* 火花

After Dante, **Petrarch** (1304—1374) was the next Italian poet to make a major contribution to Western literature. Known as the "father of humanism", Petrarch strongly rejected the medieval tradition of focusing on religion and spiritual matters. Instead, he analyzed his own thoughts and emotions. He perfected the **sonnet** form of poetry and is considered by many to be the first modern poet. In ***Canzoniere*** (Song Book), a collection of 366 sonnets and other poetic forms written in Italian, Petrarch celebrated his unreturned love for Laura, a woman he had seen in a Florence church. *Canzoniere* was first printed in 1470, after Petrarch's death, and by 1600 there were 170 editions. Petrarchan sonnets were imitated by numerous Italian poets, and by the first half of the sixteenth century the sonnet had arrived in other parts of Europe. It was especially popular in England, where writers developed the English

Petrarch 彼得拉克

sonnet *n.* 十四行诗，商籁体

Canzoniere《歌集》

① 《神曲》的韵律形式是民间诗歌中流行的一种格律三韵句，即第三行为一音节，隔行押韵，连锁循环，贯穿全诗始终。

sonnet, the form that is best known today.

Although Petrarch promoted writing in the Italian language, he regarded his Canzoniere and other Italian poems as less important than his works written in classical Latin. Admiring and imitating the Roman rhetorian **Cicero**, Petrarch produced his great epic, *Africa* in classical Latin. By describing the virtues of the Roman Republic in *Africa*, Petrarch criticized the Middle Ages and called for the revival of the Roman glory. In fact, it was him who first used "dark age" to name the period between the death of Constantine the Great and his own time. Petrarch's sense of himself as an individual and his desire for individual achievements had a huge impact on his fellow humanists. His art and ideas influence latter days' European literature.

Cicero（古罗马）西塞罗

As Petrarch perfected the sonnet, his friend **Giovanni Boccaccio** (1313—1375) developed the short story form. His ***Decameron*** is a collection of 100 stories taken from other sources. In the book, the stories were told by a group of ten young people who were passing the time in a rural castle while Florence was hit by the Black Death. The stories **depict** commonplace events and a variety of people from all social classes, reflecting the everyday life of the time. The *Decameron* shows love for humans and tolerance for their failures and weaknesses. Written in a satirical and humorous language, it continues to delight today's readers. In contrast to Dante's *Divine Comedy*, it is sometimes called the "Human Comedy".

Giovanni Boccaccio 乔万尼·薄伽丘
Decameron《十日谈》
depict *v.* 描绘

In Florence, the humanist movement took a new direction at the beginning of the 15th century. Some Florentine scholars and thinkers, such as Leonardo Bruni (1370—1444) and Leon Battista Alberti (1404—1472) developed a different version of humanism called "**civic humanism.**" For Petrarch, an ideal life was a quiet one devoted to serious thinking and understanding; **contemplation** in solitude was the path to true **virtue**. For the civic humanists after Petrarch, however, an individual could only obtain true virtue by participating in public life, by making use of their wisdom for the benefit of one's society and state as well as oneself. In their view it was not wrong for people to pursue material pleasures and to strive for a more comfortable life; ambition and the desire for glory should be encouraged.

civic humanism 公民式人文主义
contemplation *n.* 冥想
virtue *n.* 德行

But in the late 15th century the Renaissance movement gradually turned away from the practical concerns of the civic humanists. Scholars became again interested in such philosophical ideas as "truth" and "perfection". This shift in focus was a result of the growing interest in

Greek classical works—especially the works of Plato. A group of Florentine philosophers led the way. They were known as "**Neo-Platonists**," or, "new" followers of Plato.

Neo-Platonist 新柏拉图主义者

The most gifted of these Neo-Platonist was the philosopher **Marsilio Ficino** (1433—1499). The Medici family played a vital role in the development of Ficino's career. When he was still a boy, his talents were discovered by Cosimo de Medici who gave him lifelong support. Ficino was the first to translate from Greek into Latin Plato's complete works and the writings of Plato's chief followers. From his study of the idealism of Plato, Ficino argued that Plato's ideas proved the **dignity** and **immortality** of the human soul. Ficino and other Neo-Platonist made an ambitious effort to reconcile Platonic philosophy and the Christian religion. They believed that Platonic philosophy and Christianity were two faces of a single truth. We humans were driven by nature to seek perfection in either direction. With the gift of free will from God, humans were free to become all things, but a good life should be an effort to achieve personal perfection. Because of the Neo-Platonists' **reconciliation** Platonic philosophy and Christian belief, and also because of their passionate **idealism**, Neo-Platonist philosophy exerted a major influence on artists and thinkers for the next two centuries.

Marsilio Ficino 马尔西利奥·费奇诺

dignity *n.* 尊严

immortality *n.* 永生不死

reconciliation *n.* 调和

idealism *n.* 理想主义

3.3 Italian Renaissance Art

The Renaissance art movement began in the early 15th century when humanist ideas were put into practice by painters, sculptors, and architects. This great movement lasted for nearly two hundred years. It is divided into three periods: Early Renaissance (1420—1495), High Renaissance (1495—1520), and the Late Renaissance (also called **mannerism**, 1520—1600). In all the arts, the city of Florence led the way. But Florence was not the only artistic center. In the High Renaissance period, Rome took the lead.

mannerism *n.* 风格主义

Numerous works of art produced by Italian Renaissance masters show three great achievements: the discovery of **linear perspective**, the knowledge of **anatomy**, and the knowledge of the classical forms. By using linear perspective, painters represented on paper images as they were seen by the eye. The knowledge of anatomy perfected the creation of the beautiful and idealized human body. The classical forms, especially in architecture, were considered in the period to stand for everything that was **dignified** and beautiful.

linear perspective 直线透视法

anatomy *n.* 解剖学

dignified *adj.* 不失尊严的

3.3.1 The Early Renaissance Art (1420—1495)

experimentation *n.* 实验
subject matter 主题对象
imitate *v.* 模仿

The Early Renaissance was a time of **experimentation**, which started among artists in Florence and then spread to other Italian city-states. Artists began to experiment with new **subject matters**, styles, and techniques in painting, sculpture, and architecture. Through their artistic activities, they were determined to apply humanists' ideas to art. They **imitated** the classic art in both style and subject matters, and at the same time put humans and nature at the center of their works.

Revolutionary change in the art was started by three friends. They wanted to break with the medieval styles and create paintings, statues, and buildings that would bring the glories of the ancient past back to life. All three went to Rome in the 1420s. They observed directly and studied ancient masterpieces to improve the qualities of their own works. The lessons they learned enabled them to transform the styles and purposes of art.

Masaccio 马萨乔
inspiration *n.* 灵感
Brunelleschi 布鲁内莱斯基
interplay *n.* 相互作用
dimension *n.* 维度

Among these three friends, the painter **Masaccio** (1401—1428) is considered by many to be the father of Renaissance painting. Using the **inspiration** of the ancients he put a new emphasis on nature and on individual human bodies. He depicted figures that seemed to come to life. A major contribution made by Masaccio to western painting was the use of linear perspective. He may have learned the technique from his friend, the architect **Brunelleschi** (see below). Masaccio used perspective to achieve the effect of light coming from one direction and making it shine on figures. Through the **interplay** of light and shadow, these figures seem to have three **dimensions** and exist in actual space. This technique also gives the viewer a sense of looking at a scene along with the painter. With humans and human emotions as the themes of his works Masaccio transformed the very purpose of art: arts in the Middle Ages mainly served the purpose of praising God the creator; now Masaccio's stressed the value of humans, God's finest creation. Although he died at age twenty-seven, he had a profound impact on the art world.

Donatello 多纳泰罗

Masaccio's friend **Donatello** (1386—1466) is regarded as the first true Renaissance sculptor. He was the most influential Florentine sculptor before Michelangelo. Like Masaccio, Donatello imitated the Romans by creating nude bodies. One of his most famous works, the bronze status of David (created around 1440s) is the first free-standing nude male sculpture made since antiquity. Once again the focus was on the beauty of the body itself, a notable and distinctive feature of the classical art. The nudes created by Donatello, whether in bronze, marble, or wood, all represented the ideal human form.

The most impressive of these three pioneers was the architect **Brunelleschi** [1337 (?)—1446]. Considered the first Renaissance architect, Brunelleshi developed the concept of linear perspective, which influenced the depiction of space in painting and sculpture till the modern time. Imitating the classical style, he used both the Greek style Corinthian columns and Roman style rounded arch and dome in his designs. Through the symmetry and simplicity of his buildings, Brunelleschi tried to realize harmony and balance in the classical standards of beauty. Brunelleschi's interests also extended to mathematics and engineering. He invented **hydraulic machinery** and complicated **clockwork.**

Brunelleschi 布鲁内莱斯基

hydraulic machinery 水利机械

clockwork *n.* 发条装置

During the remaining years of the 1400s, other artists, not just in Florence but in other parts of Italy as well, progressed on the achievements of the three pioneers. They experimented with perspectives and made close observations of nature. Imitation of the Greek and Roman styles was visible in different artistic productions. Subject matters also changed: artists produced more **portraits** and status of rich Italians of the day and depicted stories and figures out of Greco-Roman myths. By the end of the 1400s, the leading Florentine painter at the time, **Botticelli** (1444—1510), was presenting ancient subjects like the Birth of Venus in exactly the Roman fashion.

portrait *n.* 肖像画

Botticelli 波提切利

3. 3. 2 The High Renaissance Art (1495—1520)

The artists working in the early years of the 1500s are often referred to as the generation of the High Renaissance. In this period of time, Renaissance art reached its peak. Three masters, in particular—Leonardo da Vinci, Raphael, and Michelangelo—brought the artistic creation up to a new level. While the traditions of the Florentinc school still had a strong influcncc, Rome became the major artistic center of the Italian peninsula.

Leonardo da Vinci (1452—1519) was the oldest of the three great masters. If there is anyone who can embody the Renaissance ideal of man completely and totally, it is da Vinci. In fact, he has often been described as the representative of the Renaissance Man. A self-educated genius, da Vinci was interested in almost all knowledge known to man at the time. And he was an expert in different subjects: he was painter, sculptor, architect, musician, scientist, mathematician, engineer, inventor, **anatomist**, **geologist**, **cartographer**, **botanist** and writer. He was always experimenting; as a result few of the

Leonardo da Vinci 达·芬奇

anatomist *n.* 解剖学家

geologist *n.* 地质学家

cartographer *n.* 制图家

botanist *n.* 植物学家

projects he started were finished. Though he left only a small number of paintings, they all show his achievements as an artist. His portrait of the *Mona Lisa*, for example, is famous not only for her mysterious smile but for the amazing rocky **landscape** in the background. Always seeking new ways of doing things, da Vinci made contributions to every artistic form. These few paintings together with his notebooks, which contain drawings, scientific **diagrams**, and his thoughts on the nature of painting, had an enormous influence on artists of his own day and later times.

The Italian painter **Raphael** (1483—1520) is considered the **supreme** representative of the High Renaissance. He was very productive, running an unusually large workshop, and despite his death at 37, a large body of his work remains. In his early career, he was especially attracted to Leonardo's work. In a series of **Madonna** that he painted he used Leonardo's techniques. He also adopted Leonardo's design in the *Mona Lisa* in his own portraits. His admiration for Leonardo can be seen from his masterpiece, *The Athens School*; the portrait of Plato in the painting has Leonardo's face. In fact, many of the philosophers in this painting are portraits of the artists of the day. If the philosophers were the representatives of the glory of ancient Athens, Raphael seems to be suggesting that the artists were the central players of his age. Over time, Raphael developed his own style by combining new techniques and ancient styles. Through a distinctive use of color and an emphasis on **gesture** and movement, his paintings show perfect harmony, beauty, and **serenity**. They leave the viewers an impression of complete relaxation, balance, and peace.

Michelangelo (1475—1564) considered himself first and foremost a sculptor, but he also excelled at painting, poetry, architecture, and engineer. During his long life, Michelangelo produced extremely large number of powerful works. Two of his best-known sculptures, the ***Pietà*** and *David*, were sculpted before he turned thirty. Although he did not think highly of painting, Michelangelo also created one of the most influential fresco in the history of Western art: the scenes from **Genesis** on the **ceiling** of the **Sistine Chapel** in Rome. At the age of 74, Michelangelo was appointed the architect of **St. Peter's Basilica**. Revising the previous plan of construction, Michelangelo designed the western end of the Basilica with a magnificent Roman style **dome.**

landscape *n.* 风景
diagram *n.* 图表
Raphael 拉斐尔
supreme *adj.* 最高的
Madonna *n.* 圣母
gesture *n.* 姿势
serenity *n.* 安详
Michelangelo 米开朗琪罗
Pieta 圣殇像（圣母哀悼耶稣之死）
Genesis *n.* 创世纪
ceiling *n.* 天花板
Sistine Chapel 西斯廷教廷
St. Peter's Basilica 圣彼得大教堂
dome *n.* 穹顶

The **individualism** and **idealism** of the High Renaissance have no greater representative than Michelangelo. Indeed, there is something almost **superhuman** about him and his art. His superhuman energy enabled him to complete the entire work of painting the ceiling of the Sistine Chapel in four years, and his art **embodies** a superhuman ideal of man. Embracing Neo-Platonism as a philosophy, Michelangelo was more concerned with expressing enduring, abstract truths. At the center of all of his paintings is the **idealized** human figure, which is always extremely large, powerful, magnificent. Michelangelo's depiction of the human, particularly the male figures offers the best visual representation of the humanistic concern of Italian Renaissance culture.

indvidualism *n.* 个人主义
idealism *n.* 理想主义
superhuman *adj.* 超人的
embody *v.* 体现
idealized *adj.* 理想化的

3. 3. 3 The Late Renaissance Art (1520—1600)

The impressive achievements of the High Renaissance masters left little room for improvement. In both painting and sculpture, there was a gradual shift from classicism to anti-classicism; harmonious modeling was replaced by dramatic **distortion**. In a way, the change in the artistic trend reflected the change in the spirit of the time: Italy after 1520 was destroyed by wars and conflicts; religious reforms pushed people to pay greater attention to human suffering. Between 1510 and 1520, some artists in Florence and Rome began to experiment with new styles to express this new spirit of the 16th century. Many artists were no longer interested in representing the classical ideals of balance and harmony; instead, they sought to express their **intuition** and imagination.

distortion *n.* 扭曲
intuition *n.* 直觉

Michelangelo's later works demonstrate these changes. Abandoning the balance, **proportion**, and beauty in his earlier works, his later sculptures are **exaggerated**; the human figures are distorted, often made longer. Through this style, Michelangelo hoped to increase the works' emotional and religious qualities. In 1534, he was commissioned by the Pope to paint *The Last Judgment* on the Sistine Chapel's end wall. There are remarkable differences between *the Last Judgment* (finished in 1541) and the ceiling painting of the stories of Genesis (finished in 1512); in contrast to the proportion, harmony, and **restraint** of classical style in the ceiling painting, *The Last Judgment* is full of violence, tragedy, and horror.

Artists in Italy and elsewhere worked "in the manner" of Michelangelo and became known as **mannerist**. They twisted the figures in their paintings at will and **juxtaposed** elements in **unconventional** ways. The most well-known mannerist was **El Greco**

proportion *n.* 比例适当
exaggerated *adj.* 夸张的
restraint *n.* 克制
mannerist *n.* 风格主义，又译为矫饰主义
juxtapose *v.* 把（通常不放在一起的东西）并置一起
unconventional *adj.* 非常规的
El Greco 埃尔·格列柯

[1548 (?)—1614].① He used strong colors and elongated features to express Spanish religious **zeal** in his powerful and emotional paintings. For El Greco as well as other mannerist artists, paintings served the purpose of representing ideas or teaching a moral lesson.

zeal *n.* 狂热

The artistic Renaissance in Italy gave birth to the idea of the artist as creative **genius**. In the Middle Ages, people believed that only God created; artistic products by individual artists had no independent value except for glorifying God. In the Renaissance, however, human beings became the central focus of artistic expression in painting, sculpture, and architecture. A piece of excellent work of art was valued as the creation of a unique individual. Now a genius artist shared in the power of creation of God. Art became a source of individual and collective pride, produced by creative artists, but enjoyed by all.

genius *n.* 天才

Between 1426 and 1427, Masaccios painted ***The Expulsion of Adam and Eve from Eden*** on the wall of the Church of Santa Maria del Camine in Florence. In showing Adam and Eve, he not only depicted the first nudes (裸体) since antiquity but showed them coming through a rounded arch (圆拱) which was a mark of Roman architecture. The painting vividly portrays their profound remorse (悔恨) and anguish (痛苦) through their body language and facial expressions. Masaccio achieved this sense of human drama in all of his works.

① 画家本名为 Domenico Theotocopuli，出生在当时为威尼斯共和国治理的克里特岛，1577 年后一直在西班牙生活、创作。El Greco 在西班牙语中意为“希腊人”，是根据画家的血统而取的别名。其独特的艺术风格受西欧中世纪传统画派、拜占庭艺术和意大利文艺复兴风格的熏染。其画作以弯曲瘦长的身形为特色，用色怪诞而变化无常。

Donatello's Saint Mark (1411—1413) is a marble statue that stands approximately 236 cm high outside of the Orsanmichele church, Florence. This sculpture is notable for its detailed realism, evidence of the artist's skills. Even the veins of St.Mark's left hand are visible as he holds a text upon his hip.

Donatello's bronze statue of David (1440, h.158 cm)is famous as the first unsupported standing work of bronze cast during the Renaissance, and the first nude male sculpture made since antiquity.

Brunelleschi's famous dome of Florence cathedral(built 1420—1436) The first dome built in Italy since the fall of the Roman Empire, it embodies the revival of classical forms in architecture. The dome was also an achievement of engineering. Brunelleschi himself invented the machines that made the construction possible.

Bottichelli:
Birth of Venus(维纳斯的诞生)(1485).

Botticelli:
Allegory of Spring (春之寓言)(1482).

Leonardo da Vinci's Mona Lisa(produced 1503—1505) is considered by many to be the greatest painting of all time. By skillful techniques, such as shadow at the corner of eyes and mouth, and the use of two different perspectives in the background, da Vinci makes the woman seem alive.

Raphael's paintings. Left: ***The Madonna of the Meadow*** (1506),Raphael used Leonardo's pyramidal composition for subjects of the Holy Family. Right: ***The Athens School*** (1509)

4. Northern Renaissance

During the 1400s commerce and trade recovered slowly in Western Europe. Trade routes linked different European regions with Italy. Italian humanist scholars often travelled with traders outside of Italy. They took with them the ideas of the Italian Renaissance. Italian artists and artisans also went to work for monarchs and noblemen in other European countries. At the same time, large number of students from the Low Countries, France, Germany, and England travelled to Italy to study the "new learning" and then carried it back to their countries. Scholars and artists from outside of Italy interpreted Italian ideas about classical antiquity, individualism, and humanism in terms of their own traditions. Soon they began making their own cultural contributions, which became known as the Northern Renaissance.

The Northern Renaissance is the term used to describe the Renaissance in Europe outside Italy. Before 1450 Italian Renaissance humanism had little influence outside Italy. From the late 15th century the ideas spread around Europe. During the northern Renaissance, advances took place in literature, painting, sculpture, architecture, and music. Many northern European artists gained international **reputations.**

reputation *n.* 声誉

The Northern Renaissance should not be seen as a mere copycat of the Italian Renaissance. In some areas the Northern Renaissance was **distinct** from the Italian Renaissance. While Italy was dominated by independent city-states, parts of central and Western Europe began emerging as nation-states. Centralization of political power gave the Renaissance movements in these areas a strong national flavor. Compared to Italy, areas outside of Italy also had a lower level of economic development. In their more traditional economic and social networks, the Church's influence remained strong. As a result, the Northern Renaissance was also more religious in nature.

distinct *adj.* 独特

4.1 Northern Christian Humanism

Like the Italian humanists, Northern Renaissance thinkers drew their inspiration from the languages and literature of ancient times, and they also believed in the human **potential** for self-improvement. The Italian humanist scholars and artists were certainly Christian, but they were more interested in secular (non-religious) subjects. By contrast, the Northern Renaissance was more concerned with religious matters.

potential *n.* 潜力

Because of this strong religious concern, humanism in the Northern Renaissance differed from that of the Italian: it was more than a philosophy; it was a social and spiritual movement. By combining the best elements of classical and Christian cultures, northern humanists tried to push forward social reforms and to make better Christians through better education. Although Christian humanism as a movement **faded** rapidly after about 1520, the northern Renaissance continued to flourish throughout the 16th century in primarily literary and artistic forms.

fade *v.* 消退

Desiderius Erasmus 伊拉斯谟

biblical study 圣经研究

The Dutch scholar **Desiderius Erasmus** (1466—1536) was the most important and respected humanist in northern Europe. Known as the "scholar of Europe," Erasmus was regarded by many the leader of the Northern Renaissance humanist movement. An unusually learned scholar and a highly productive writer, Erasmus published innumerable works on a wide range of subjects, including **biblical studies**, education, and religious reform. He also wrote more than three thousand letters to kings, popes, scholars, financiers, humanists, and reformers. He was probably the best writer in Latin prose style since the days of Cicero.

Gospel *n.* 福音书

contemporary *n.* 同时代人

guidance *n.* 指导

At the heart of Erasmus' thought is, in his own words, "the philosophy of Christ." For Erasmus, the entire society of his day was caught up in corruption and immorality because people had lost sight of the simple teachings of the **Gospels**. Erasmus thus offered to his **contemporaries** three different categories of publication: clever satire to show people the error of their ways, serious moral books to offer people **guidance** toward proper Christian behavior, and scholarly editions of basic Christian texts.

The Praise of Folly《愚人颂》

scholastic *adj.* 学者的

pedantry *n.* 迂腐

dogmatism *n.* 教条主义

ignorance *n.* 无知

credulity *n.* 轻信

mass *n.* 大众

Handbook of the Christian Knights《基督徒士兵须知》

formalism *n.* 形式主义

compile *v.* 编撰

manuscript *n.* 手稿

The Praise of Folly (1509) is the best sample of Erasmus's first category of writings. In this essay still widely read today, Erasmus criticized the **scholastic pedantry** and **dogmatism** as well as the **ignorance** and **credulity** of the **mass**. In the second type of writing, such as ***Handbook of the Christian Knights*** (1503), Erasmus condemned the **formalism** of the Church and urged a return to the simple teachings of Jesus. For Erasmus, Christians should follow Christ-his life and what he said and did as recorded in the Bible, not what theologians had written about Him. It was because of this belief that Erasmus devoted much time and energy to the third type of writings, i. e. scholarly edition of the Bible and the writings by such early Church Fathers as Augustine, Jerome, and Ambrose. He spent ten years studying and **compiling** all the best early Greek biblical **manuscripts** he could find in order to establish an **authoritative** text. His New Testament in Greek finally came out in 1516, together with explanatory notes and his own new Latin translation. It became the basis of various translations into the vernacular languages. To this day, it remains one of the most important works of biblical study of all time. Erusmus's version was the basis of many later vernacular translations of Bible during the Reformation.

authoritative *adj.* 权威性的

The development of humanism in England was greatly strengthened after 1500, partly by Erasmus' first visit. The most well-known English humanist was the statesman **Sir Thomas More** (1478—1535), one of Erasmus' closest friends. Unlike most humanists, More never studied in Italy and was neither a scholar nor a teacher. Instead, he followed a successful career as a lawyer and as speaker of the House of Commons and in 1529 he was appointed **Lord Chancellor** of England. He was an active leader of educational reform activities among English churchmen. His active promotion of bible study made London a favored meeting place for scholars from all over Europe. Many English scholars studied Greek intensively and eagerly analyzed the New Testament and the writings of the early Church Fathers.

Sir Thomas More 托马斯·莫尔爵士

Lord Chancellor 大法官

More was best remembered for the ***Utopia*** (1516). Written in Latin, the novel describes an ideal society located on the island of Utopia (meaning "nowhere"). This powerful work is written in two parts. The first part is a debate over the moral value of public service between Morus, a well-intentioned but practical politician, and Hythloday, a widely traveled idealist. Through the debate, More strongly criticizes the unjust and immoral governments. Then in the second part Hytholoday describes the **commonwealth** of Utopia where he lived once. The members of Utopia hold all their goods in common; they work only six hours a day so that they may have free time for intellectual pursuits. As wisdom, moderation, and justice are highly valued, the community is free of **greed** and violence. Through the description of such an idealized community, More strengthens his criticism of the evil and corruption of his time.

Utopia《乌托邦》

Commonwealth *n.* 联合体

greed *n.* 贪婪

Despite the achievements made by Christian humanists in different countries, the movement was weakened by the rise of Protestant Reformation in the 1520s. The **irony** here is obvious: the Christian humanists emphasis on the Bible as the true authority and their criticisms of the corruption in the Church and **excessive** religious **ceremonies** and rituals certainly helped pave the way for the Protestant

irony *n.* 讽刺

excessive *adj.* 过度的

ceremony *n.* 仪式

Martin Luther 马丁·路德
Catholic camp 天主教阵营
persecution *n.* 迫害
shame *n.* 羞辱
Inquisition 异端裁判所
imprison *v.* 监禁
martyr *n.* 烈士
figure *n.* 人物
Geoffrey Chaucer 乔叟
Milton 弥尔顿
Dickens 狄更斯

Reformation started by **Martin Luther** in 1517. And yet despite their criticisms, most Christian humanists tried to remain within the **Catholic camp**. But as time went on, these Christian humanists faced pressure and even **persecution** from both the Catholic Church and the Protestant groups. Erasmus died early enough to escape public **shame**, but several of his less fortunate followers became victims of the Spanish **Inquisition**.① Refusing to acknowledge Henry as head of the Church of England, More was **imprisoned** and later died as a Catholic **martyr.**

4.2 Northern Renaissance Literature

The influence of humanist ideas on literature throughout Europe was obvious: literary works emphasized the revival of ancient and traditional literary forms, the exploration of human creativity, and the use of native languages. Writers in most European countries produced large amount of works in every imaginable literary form. It is therefore impossible to give a complete overview of the Northern Renaissance literature. This section will then only focus on a few **figures** in England, France, and Spain, countries where the major literary contributions were made in the period.

In England, the days when Norman nobles spoke French and peasants spoke Saxon had passed. A common national language, made up of Germanic and Romance elements, had emerged as "middle English" and was being used in the 14th century for literary purposes. The outstanding figure in this formative period of English literature was a poet, **Geoffrey Chaucer** (1340—1400). He was the first major writer of an English that can still be read today with relatively little effort. Similar to Dante, Chaucer the poet and his works show both medieval and early Renaissance features. Both Dante and Chaucer helped lay the foundation of their national languages. Most critics rank him just behind Shakespeare and in the same class with **Milton** and **Dickens**.②

Chaucer wrote several highly impressive works, but his masterpiece

① 西班牙宗教裁判所于1478年由西班牙伊莎贝拉女王（Isabella）要求教宗思道四世准许成立，用以维护天主教的正统性，以残酷手段惩罚异端，经教宗思道四世指责，直至19世纪初始取消西班牙宗教裁判所，但从1483年至1820年期间共有38万人被裁定成异端，被火刑处死的达10万人。

② 约翰·弥尔顿（John Milton，1608—1674）英国诗人、政论家，民主斗士。弥尔顿是清教徒文学的代表，代表作《失乐园》是和《荷马史诗》、《神曲》并称为西方三大诗歌。查尔斯·狄更斯（Charles Dickens）(1812—1870)，英国小说家，19世纪英国现实主义文学的主要代表，代表作品有《匹克威克外传》、《雾都孤儿》、《双城记》、《远大前程》等。

is unquestionably the ***Canterbury Tales*** (1386—1400). Like Boccaccio's Decameron, this is a collection of stories held together by a frame. In Chaucer's case, the stories were told by a group of thirty men and women on their pilgrimage from London to Canterbury for entertainment on the road. From these stories we learn not only what Chaucer's **contemporaries** were like but also what they said and thought. In depicting these typical characters, Chaucer presents a rich "human comedy" of the English society in the 14th century.

Canterbury Tales《坎特伯雷故事集》

contemporary *n.* 同时代人

The high standard set for English literature by Chaucer in the 14th century was not kept in the 15th. Then literary development reached a high level when the **Tudors** gained control of the throne in 1485. Then by the time Queen Elizabeth Ⅰ (ruled 1558—1603) came to power, the English Renaissance was firmly established. In this period, the poet **Edmund Spenser** (1552—1599) invented new poetic forms that influenced the work of later poets.① His masterpiece, the unfinished huge epic poem, ***The Faerie Queene*** (1590—1609), is an **allegorical** celebration of the Tudor dynasty. This golden age of English literature produced some of the most brilliant dramas in Western literature. **Christopher Marlowe** (1564—1593) wrote half a dozen plays in a language full of poetic beauty.② Mixing scholarship and wit, **Ben Johnson** (1572—1637) explored human nature in his satiric comedies. Above all, the **immortal** dramas of Shakespeare mark the peak of the English Renaissance.

the Tudors 都铎王朝

Edmund Spenser 埃德蒙·斯宾塞

The Faerie Queene《仙后》

allegorical *adj.* 寓言式的

Christopher Marlowe 克里斯多夫·马洛

Ben Johnson 本·琼生

immortal *adj.* 不朽的

The **playwright**, poet, and actor William Shakespeare (1546—1616) is generally acknowledged to be the greatest of English writers and one of the most extraordinary creators in human history. The son of a successful glove maker in a small town in Warwickshire, Shakespeare chose a career on the London stage. Devoting his entire life to the public theater, he gained recognition as an actor and playwright. His surviving works consist of about 37 plays, 154 sonnets, two long narrative poems, and several other poems. Traditionally, Shakespeare's 37 plays are divided into the genres of tragedy, history, and comedy. They have been translated into every major languages and

playwright *n.* 剧作家

① 斯宾塞在长诗《仙后》中探索出一种新的十四行诗格律形式：每节9行，前8行都是每行10个音节，第9行为12个音节，按ababbcbcc押韵，被称作"斯宾塞诗节（the Spenserian stanza）"。

② 马洛共写了7部剧本，均属悲剧或带有悲剧意味的历史剧：《帖木儿》、《浮士德博士的悲剧》、《马耳他的犹太人》、《爱德华二世》、《迦太基女王狄多》和《巴黎的大屠杀》。马洛革新了中世纪的戏剧，在舞台上创造了反映时代精神的巨人性格，为莎士比亚的创作铺平了道路。

are still read and performed throughout the world today.

genius *n.* 天才
originality *n.* 原创性
psychology *n.* 心理

Shakespeare's **genius** lies in the **originality** of his characterizations, the diversity of his plots, his understanding of human **psychology**, and his amazing gift for language. Shakespeare was a Renaissance man in his deep appreciation for classical culture, individualism, and humanism. Such plays as *Julius Caesar*, *Pericles*, and *Anthony and Cleopatra* deal with classical subjects and figures. Several of his comedies have Italian Renaissance settings. The nine history plays, including *Richard* Ⅱ, *Richard* Ⅲ, *and Henry* Ⅳ, **recount** England's struggles leading up to the glory of the Tudor dynasty. Written during the decade after the defeat of the Spanish Armada, the history plays express English national consciousness. Shakespeare's later plays, above all the tragedies *Hamlet*, *Othello*, *King Lear*, and *Macbeth*, explore an enormous range of human problems.

recount *v.* 叙述

The Renaissance in France is often thought to begin with the reign of King Francis Ⅰ (rule 1515—1547). Though strongly influence by the Italian Renaissance, by the mid-16th century the French had developed their own version of the Renaissance, particularly in literature. The writer **Francois Rabelais** (1494—1553) was perhaps the most popular writer in the French Renaissance. Recognized as a comic genius, Rabelai is best known for **Gargantua and Pantagruel** (1532—1545). Set against the medieval background around the time of the legendary English **King Arthur**, the novel consists of a series of fanciful tales of the adventures of Gragantua and his son Pantagruel, both of whom are giants. Written in an extremely down-to-earth French, Rebelais satirized religious ceremonialism, **ridiculed Scholasticism**, and laughed at **superstition**. While rejecting Christian doctrine and morality, he glorified the human and the natural. Rabelais saw people as essentially good and able to achieve self-fulfillment by reason; for him, the only rule in life was "do what you will." Despite the condemnation by Paris theologians, *Gargantua and Pantagruel* was an immediate popular success. Scholars note that it most certainly influenced *Don Quixote* by Spanish author Miguel de Cervantes (see below).

Francois Rabelais 弗朗索瓦·拉伯雷
Gargantua and Pantagruel《巨人传》
King Arthur 亚瑟王
ridicule *v.* 嘲讽
Scholasticism *n.* 经院哲学
superstition *n.* 迷信

Another important French author was **Michel de Montaigne** (1533—1592). A humanist, Montaigne loved the Greek and Roman writers and was always eager to learn from them. Like the Greeks, he believed that the object of life was to "know thyself" for self-knowledge teaches men and women how to live happily. In his masterpiece ***Essays***

Michel de Montaigne 米歇尔·德·蒙田
Essays《蒙田随笔全集》

(written between 1570 and 1580) Montaigne tried to express his thoughts and ideas. He was not a **systematic** thinking, however, and he did not keep a single point of view. In writing Essays, Montaigne developed a new literary **genre** (form), the essay-from the French verb *essayer*, meaning "to test or try."

systematic *adj.* 有系统的

genre *n.* 体裁

Spanish literature's golden age came somewhat later than that of France. Among the Spanish Renaissance literary works, ***Don Quixote*** by **Miguel de Cervantes** (1547—1616) is often called the first modern novel, sometimes regarded as the greatest novel ever written. Don Quixote is a retired country gentleman around 50 living in La Mancha. Obsessed with books of **chivalry**, Don Quixote sets out on his old horse to seek adventure, bringing with him his practical **squire**, Sancho Panza. During their travels, Don Quixote's overexcited imagination blinds him to reality: he thinks windmills to be giants, flocks of sheep to be armies, and slaves to be oppressed gentlemen. From one failure to another his faithful squire keeps him company. Finally the hero returns to La Mancha, and only at his deathbed Don Quixote **confesses** the **folly** of his past adventures. Through the vivid depiction of the two central figures, Cervantes laughs at both the pretensions of nobles and the literature of his days, which featured chivalric romances and sentimental novels.

Don Quixote《堂吉珂德》

Miguel de Cervantes 塞万提斯

chivalry *n.* 骑士精神

squire *n.* 随从

confess *v.* 忏悔

folly *n.* 愚蠢

4.3 Northern Renaissance Art

The great achievements and inventions of the Italian masters of the Renaissance made a deep impression on the people north of the Alps. After 1500, Italian influences upon northern European art became more direct. Northern artists went to Italy to study the Italian theories and techniques of art. When it comes to the purpose of art, northern art was influenced by the strong religious nature of the Northern Renaissance. Unlike Italian Renaissance artists whose central concern was the representation of idealized human beauty, the goal of northern artists was to **stimulate** religious feeling in their viewers. So artists in each country adopted and assimilated only those Italian concepts and techniques that suited their purpose.

stimulate *v.* 激发

Innovations in painting appeared primarily in Germany and the Low Countries and then spread to other parts of northern Europe. An early pioneer was the Dutch painter **Jan van Eyck** (1390—1441). Rediscovering the ancient art of oil painting, van Eyck developed a new method of mixing colors in oil. This way he could paint several layers of thin **oil glaze**, which created lights and depth of color. He also used

Jan van Eyck 让·范爱克

oil glaze 油质釉彩

varnish *n.* 清漆

Albrecht Dürer 阿尔布雷特·丢勒

graphic artist 版画家

treatise *n.* 专著

ideal proportion 理想比例

varnish, giving a shiny surface to all of his paintings. Even today colors in his paintings remain bright and clear. Because of his mastery of the new technique, he was traditionally known as the "father of oil painting."

The German artist **Albrecht Dürer** (1471—1528) has been regarded greater than any other northern artist of his time. Dürer made two trips to Italy especially to study ideas and techniques of the Italian artists. He was the first to introduce the achievements of the Italian Renaissance into northern European art. Better known as a **graphic artist** than a painter, Dürer's influence was most widely felt through his woodcuts and engravings. The rapid reproduction of his graphic works by printing made Dürer hugely successful as an artist at the time. Combining intensive religious feelings and humanistic concerns, his works are a mixture of Gothic and Italian Renaissance styles. Apart from artistic works, Dürer also wrote detailed **treatises** on the principles of mathematics, perspectives, and **ideal proportion**, which influenced northern artists then and later.

Two paintings by van Eyke. **Left:** Annunciation(oil, 1434—1436) **Right:** the Alnolfi Portrait (oil, 1434)

Two works by Dürer. **Left:** Self-portrait(oil, 1500) **Right:** Saint Christopher(engraving, 1521)

5. Scientific Accomplishments

Some extraordinarily important accomplishments were made in the history of science during the Renaissance. Scientists developed new theories that eventually made science a separate field from philosophy. It is important to note that development in science was not achieved by Renaissance humanism. The educational program of the humanists placed a low value on science because it seemed irrelevant to their aim of making people more moral. None of the great scientists of the Renaissance Age belonged to the humanist movement.

Nonetheless, the revival of the classical learning did prepare the way for great new scientific advances. The works of the Greek philosopher Aristotle were especially popular among 15th and 16th centuries scientists. Aristotle was a pioneer in the **systematic classification** of all fields of knowledge. He considered the ideal form of knowledge to be science, which he defined as universal and necessary knowledge. For Aristotle this knowledge was gained through analyzing the causes of things. Influenced by Aristotle, scientists in the Renaissance period paid more attention to answer how things happened

systematic classification 系统分类

in nature. This marked a significant shift in thinking as the medieval Europeans were mainly concerned with why things happened. The ancient Greeks introduced the concept of using a particular method to study nature or solve an abstract problem. For instance, both Plato and Aristotle wrote about methods of investigation and logic. Interest in method was revived during the Renaissance. Scientists in this period developed the idea of the "scientific method." Notably, the Italian astronomer **Galileo** (1564—1642) and the English philosopher **Francis Bacon** (1561—1626) introduced new scientific methods.

Galileo 伽利略
Francis Bacon 培根

The actual scientific accomplishments of the Renaissance period were international and multi-disciplinary in scope. The most outstanding achievement was in astronomy. Since ancient times astronomy was linked with **cosmology** and **astrology**. During the Renaissance, astronomy began to develop into a separate scientific field, which would have a profound impact on the scientific revolution in the 17th century. Central to the development of astronomy was the formulation and proof of the **heliocentric theory** that the earth revolves around the sun. Until the 16th century Western Europeans held the **geocentric conception**, believing that the earth stands still at the center of the universe.

cosmology *n.* 宇宙起源
astrology *n.* 占星术
heliocentric theory 日心说
geocentric conception 地心说

The Polish theologian **Nicolas Copernicus** (1473—1543) was the first to suggest the heliocentric system. Based on observations, Copernicus thoroughly reinterpreted the old astronomical evidence. In his *On the Revolutions of Heavenly Spheres*, he argued that the universe was made up of eight **spheres** with the sun standing still at the center. Six fixed stars, including the earth move around the Sun in **concentric circles**. The moon, however, **revolves** around the earth. Moreover, according to Copernicus, it is because the earth daily **self-rotation** and its annual journey around the sun that the sun and the fixed stars seemed to move around the earth. Copernicus's system itself was still highly imperfect; moreover, it **contradicted** some passages in the Bible and people's common-sense assumptions. As a result, most people at the time were not ready to accept his thinking.

Nicolas Copernicus 哥白尼
spheres *n.* 球体
concentric circles 同心圆
revolve *v.* 旋转
self-rotation *n.* 自转
contradict *v.* 与之相矛盾

The next step in destroying the geocentric conception and supporting the Copernican system was taken by the German scientist **Johannes Kepler** (1571—1630). A brilliant mathematician, Kepler firmly believed that God had created the universe according to mathematical laws. Relying on new and accurate astronomical observations, Kepler revised Copernicus's assumptions and developed

Johannes Kepler 开普勒

three laws of **planetary motion**.① Kepler then raised the question of what kind of force was holding the planets in their paths. He concluded that it was the **magnetic attractions** between the sun and the planets. By identifying a **physical** force in the universe, Kepler laid the foundation for a relationship between physics and astronomy.

planetary motion 行星运动
magnetic attraction 磁性吸引力
physical *adj.* 物理的

As Kepler perfected Copernicus's heliocentric system from the point of view of mathematical theory, so Galileo (1564—1642) promoted the new theory by gathering more evidence. With a **telescope** he made himself, he discovered the moons of **Jupiter** and spots on the sun. He also identified a large number of stars and determined that the solar system is only a part of the Milky Way. Though criticized by many, the Church in particular, Galileo's discoveries gradually convinced the majority of scientists that the main conclusion of Copernicus was true. By the time of Galileo's death, the Copernican view of the universe was being accepted as scientific truth. The final victory of this idea is commonly called the Copernican Revolution. It was one of the most significant events in the intellectual history of the world, for it **overturned** the medieval worldview and paved the way for modern conceptions of **mechanism**, **skepticism**, and the **infinity** of time and space.

telescope *n.* 望远镜
Jupiter *n.* 木星
overturn *v.* 颠覆
mechanism *n.* 机械主义
skepticism *n.* 怀疑主义
infinity *n.* 无限性

6. Conclusion

In the Middle Ages, man had thought of himself primarily as part of a universal order of things created by God and represented on earth by the Church. But gradually, he began to attach importance to himself as an individual and to the physical world around him. This change in attitude was **manifested** in art, literature, and learning we call the Renaissance.

manifest *v.* 表现

The change took place earliest in Italy and first expressed itself in the great intellectual movement known as humanism. In its early stages humanism was a revival of classical learning. Scholars searched for

① 开普勒第一定律，也称椭圆定律。每一个行星都沿各自的椭圆轨道环绕太阳，而太阳则处在椭圆的一个焦点中。开普勒第二定律，也称面积定律。在相等时间内，太阳和运动中的行星的连线所扫过的面积都是相等的。开普勒第三定律，也称调和定律。各个行星绕太阳公转周期的平方和它们的椭圆轨道的半长轴的立方成正比。由这一定律不难导出：行星与太阳之间的引力与半径的平方成反比。这是牛顿的万有引力定律的一个重要基础。

ancient manuscripts and early introduced the literature of Greece and Rome into schools and universities. The **comprehensive** knowledge of classical literature and thought made it possible for humanists to develop new concepts and theories. They reintroduced into western culture an emphasis on the dignity of man as an individual and stimulated a concern for the problems and challenges of the contemporary world.

comprehensive *adj.* 全面的

The Renaissance period produced numerous remarkable intellectual, literary, and artistic works. The vernacular writings of Petrarch and Boccaccio developed Italian poetry and prose. Humanists produced quality work in history, philosophy, and philology. Italian Renaissance artists employed various knowledge and techniques to represent creatively **three-dimensional** realistic and idealized world. Outside of Italy, vernacular literature flourished in England, France, and Spain. Humanism in these lands developed with a distinct Christian concern. Both Italian and northern humanists shared an **optimistic** view of human nature and believed in the power of education. In advocating a return to the classical texts, the humanists raised fundamental issues about the Church and its teaching. In the 16th century, the cultural movement of the Renaissance gave away to a religious revolution, that is, the Reformation.

three-dimensional *adj.* 三维的

optimistic *adj.* 积极乐观的

Exercises

Ⅰ. Terminology: choose the suitable terms to fill in the blanks.

A. Renaissance B. humanism C. Medici D. sonnet
E. Mannerism F. patron G. geocentric theory H. heliocentric theory
I. secularism J. Neo-Platonism

• A __1__ is a type of poem containing 14 lines, each of 10 syllables, and with a formal pattern of rhymes.

• __2__ is a system of thought that centers on human beings and their values, capacities, and worth.

• A __3__ is someone who supports the work of writers, artists, musicians, etc. especially by giving them money.

• The __4__ is a theory that places the Sun as the centre of the universe, and the planets orbiting around it.

• The __5__ is the belief that the Earth is the centre of the universe and that all other objects orbit around it.

• The __6__ was a rich and powerful Italian family of bankers who ruled Florence from the 15th to the 18th centuries, and spent much of their money on art and on providing financial support to artists.

• __7__ is the belief that religion should not be involved with the ordinary social and political activities of a country.

• __8__ is a philosophical system developed at Alexandria in the 3rd century AD by Plotinus, which is composed of elements of Platonism and Aristotelianism and oriental mysticism.

• The __9__ was the period in Europe, especially Italy, in the 14th, 15th, and 16th centuries, when there was a humanistic revival of classical art, architecture, literature, and learning.

• __10__ is a style of 16th century art, common in Italy, France and Spain, which did not show things in a natural way but made them look strange or out of their usual shape.

Ⅱ. Decide whether the following statements are true (T) or false (F).

1. All city-states of northern Italy belonged to the Holy Roman Empire during the Renaissance. ( )

2. During the Renaissance, all scholars and artists abandoned medieval qualities and embraced modern values overnight. ( )

3. Florence was the major centre of the High Renaissance Art at the early 16th century. ( )

4. The Italian Renaissance was largely credited to the economic success in Italy at that time. ( )

5. The Northern Renaissance is the term used to describe the Renaissance in northern Europe, or more broadly in Europe outside Italy. (　　)

6. "Middle English" was the national language of the England during the Early Middle Ages. (　　)

7. During the Renaissance, many Italian scholars began to learn Greek because they wanted to translate Latin works into Greek. (　　)

8. Dante was the first Italian writer to compose in his native language rather than in Latin. (　　)

9. Marsilio Ficino, the first man to translate Plato's complete works from Greek into Latin, was known as a Neo-Platonist. (　　)

10. Christian Humanism helped paved the way for the Protestant Reformation. (　　)

Ⅲ. Multiple choices: choose the answer that best completes the statement or answers the question.

1. Which description of the Age of Renaissance is correct?

A. The Renaissance happened right after the Late Middle Ages in time.

B. The Renaissance reached a peak at the end of the sixteenth century.

C. The Renaissance began as a literary movement.

D. The Renaissance was opposed to humanism.

2. The Italian Renaissance scholars did all the following things except for ________.

A. reviving many classical texts forgotten or lost for a long time

B. spreading the knowledge beyond the small circle of scholars

C. refusing to accept religious teaching or read religious works

D. paying more attention to man's world and life on earth

3. Which is not one of the things that the Viscontis, the Sforzas and the Medicis had in common?

A. They were wealthy and powerful families in Italy.

B. They were rulers of Milan during the Renaissance.

C. They ordered the construction of great architectures.

D. They were generous patrons of artists and intellectuals.

4. Which statement about the humanist education during the Renaissance is wrong?

A. The goal of education was to produce independent, virtuous and capable men who excelled in many different fields.

B. The program of study relied heavily on classical training, but it also contained many other subjects.

C. The Renaissance education enhanced the impact of the humanist ideas on the ruling class and the elite.

D. The educational program of the humanists placed a high value on science.

5. Which of the following Renaissance writers was not known for his sonnets?

A. Dante.
B. Petrarch.
C. Edmund Spencer.
D. William Shakespeare.

6. Which description of Petrarch is wrong?

A. He was known as the "father of humanism".
B. He was the first to coin the term "Dark Ages".
C. He valued his Italian writings more than his Latin writings.
D. He was financed by Galeazzo II Visconti.

7. Which statement about the "civic humanism" is wrong?

A. It was developed by some Florentine scholars during the fifteenth century.
B. It believed that virtue could only be obtained by participating in public life.
C. It encouraged people to pursue material pleasures and fulfill their desires.
D. It was the same with the "Christian Humanism" of Northern Renaissance.

8. Which one is not a period of Italian Renaissance Art?

A. Early Renaissance.
B. Middle Renaissance.
C. High Renaissance.
D. Late Renaissance.

9. Which is not one of the three great achievements of Italian Renaissance art?

A. the revival of classical texts.
B. the discovery of linear perspective.
C. the knowledge of anatomy.
D. the knowledge of the classical forms.

10. Who did not belong to the Florentine School of the Early Renaissance art?

A. Brunelleschi.
B. Donatello.
C. Masaccio.
D. Raphael.

11. Who was not one of the three masters of the High Renaissance art?

A. Leonardo da Vinci.
B. Raphael.
C. El Greco.
D. Michelangelo.

12. Which is the key feature of the Mannerism of the Late Renaissance art?

A. the invention of new artistic techniques.
B. the imitation of Greek and Roman styles.
C. the representation of idealized human figures.
D. the use of intense colors, strange themes and twisted figures.

13. Compared with Italian Renaissance, Northern Renaissance had the following distinctive features except for ________.

A. strong national flavor
B. great religious concern
C. influence of classicism
D. belief in Christian humanism

14. Which categories of publication does Erasmus's The Praise of Folly belong to?

A. clever satires to expose people's errors.
B. serious moral books to offer people Christian guidance.
C. scholarly editions of basic Christian texts.

D. collection of stories to amuse people.

15. Which is not the similarity shared by Chaucer's Canterbury Tales and Boccaccio's Decameron?

A. a collection of stories.

B. satirical and humorous language.

C. vivid characterization.

D. religious themes.

16. Which one is not the main characteristic of Shakespeare as a Renaissance man?

A. His interest in classical culture.

B. His belief in humanism.

C. His support of individualism.

D. His consciousness of national identity.

17. Who was not a representative writer of Northern Renaissance?

A. Giovanni Boccaccio. B. William Shakespeare.

C. Fran? ois Rabelais. D. Miguel de Cervantes.

18. Who was regarded as the "father of oil painting"?

A. Masaccio. B. Botticelli.

C. Albrecht Dürer. D. Jan van Eyck.

19. In terms of science, what was the significant shift in thinking during the Renaissance Age?

A. the inclusion of science in the educational program.

B. the emphasis on how things happened in nature.

C. the development of new scientific methods.

D. the acceptance of heliocentric theory.

20. Who was not a believer in the heliocentric theory?

A. Nicolas Copernicus. B. Johannes Kepler.

C. Galileo. D. Francis Bacon.

Chapter 9
Reformation (1500—1600)

CHAPTER OUTLINE

1. Introduction
2. Religious and Social Background of the Reformation
3. Luther and the German Reforamtion
4. The Spread of the Protestant Reformation
5. The Catholic Counter-Reformation
6. General Effects of the Reformation
7. Conclusion

FOCUS QUESTIONS

1. What were the main causes of the Protestant Reformation in Germany?
2. What are the similarities and differences between Lutheranism and Calvinism?
3. What measures did the Roman Catholic Church take to reform itself and to combat Protestant Reformation?
4. What impact did the Protestant Reformation have on 16th-century European society?

1. Introduction

After two centuries of economic, political and social **turmoil**, Europe in the year 1500 was well on the way to recovery. The population and economy were rebounding, cities and towns flourishing anew, and the kingdoms of France, England, Spain, Scotland, and Poland exercising firm control over their subjects' lives. Europeans were also busy with overseas commercial and colonial expansion. Despite the split with the **Orthodox Church** and continuous threat of **heresies** the Church of Rome seemed all-powerful and unchallenged. Overall, the future of Europe looked brighter than it had done for several centuries.

turmoil *n.* 动乱

Orthodox Church 东正教教会

heresy *n.* 异端邪说

No one in 1500 could have predicted that within fifty years Europe's

monopoly *n.* 垄断
rupture *v.* 撕裂

religious **monopoly** would be **ruptured** by a new reform movement. None could have foreseen that the call for reform would lead to a series of destructive wars and shake the foundations of European political and religious life.

newly-coined *adj.* 新造的
launch *v.* 发起
protestant *n.* 新教徒
branch *n.* 分支，派别

Historians label the 16th century the Age of Reformation. This **newly-coined** word primarily meant religious reform. People were increasingly unhappy with some of the Church of Rome's practices and beliefs. They **launched** a protest against the Church and called for reform. This is the origin of the word "**protestant**". Although they originally had no intention of forming a new church, Protestants came into violent conflict with the Church of Rome. The once-united Christian community split into Roman Catholic and Protestant camps. In the second half of the 16th century, differences among the reformers further resulted in the creation of new Protestant **branches**. Thus it is appropriate to speak of "Reformation movements" rather than a unified Protestant Reformation.

chronology *n.* 年代学
eve *n.* 前夜

In this chapter we will examine the causes, the **chronology**, and the effects of the Reformation. Its causes are rooted in the general historical background of Western Europe and in particular Germany on the **eve** of the Reformation. We will then compare the development of major Reformation movements in Germany, Switzerland, and England. Moving on from their historical progression, we will explore the effects of the Reformation on European society and culture as a whole.

2. Religious and Social Background of the Reformation

spontaneous *adj.* 自发的
culmination *n.* 顶点
erupt *v.* 爆发

The Reformation was not **spontaneous**; it was the **culmination** of a series of changes starting in the 14th century. The huge creative energy and destructive conflicts of the 16th century owed their existence to forces that had been building up since the late Middle Ages and the Renaissance. To examine the roots of the revolution, we will first look at the Christian Church in Western Europe just before it **erupted**.

2.1 The Church of Rome Around 1500

sophisticated *adj.* 成熟的

At the dawn of the 16th century the Roman Catholic Church had a very special position throughout western and central Europe. Its role was vastly bigger than it is today. The Church dominated Medieval Europeans' life. Village peasants or more **sophisticated** townspeople, all believed that God, Heaven and Hell existed. From the earliest of ages, people were told of the horrors awaiting them in Hell; they were warned that they could go to Heaven if the Church allowed them to. Every child of Christian parents was born a member of the Church. The Church was official and public, not private and voluntary. States all supported the Church and a person who attacked or disrespected it would be punished by the authorities.

The Church imposed heavy taxes and **dues** on ordinary people. All Christians had to pay 10% of what they earned in a year to the Church (this tax was called **tithe**). Tithe could be paid in either money or **in kind**; as peasants had little money, they almost always had to opt for the latter and pay in seeds, harvested grain, or livestock animals. This caused considerable hardship as seeds, for example, were needed for the next year's crop and thus the family's **subsistence**. Failure to pay their tithe, so the peasants were told by the Church, would lead to their souls going to Hell after death. Fear kept people paying their tithes, despite the difficulties it caused. There were other taxes as well, such as **Peter 's Pence**, a tax on the use of the **hearth** charged to every household. Peasants also had to work for free on Church land. This was difficult too, as time spent working on Church land could have been better used by the peasants to work their own plots of land and produce food for their families. Besides these taxes and dues, people also had to pay for church **rites** such as **baptism**, marriage and burial.

Over the fifteen centuries that had **elapsed** since Jesus Christ, the Christian Church had developed into a **sophisticated** organization. At the head of this structure was the bishop of Rome, the pope, who was the successor of St. Peter. The pope was elected for life by certain clergymen called **cardinals**. The pope was the **supreme** lawgiver of the Church, its supreme judge, and the supreme administrator of all its finances and business activities. Besides his religious functions he was also ruler of the city of Rome and the surrounding papal state. He collected fees, dues, and taxes from all Christian lands. By the 15th century the popes were immensely powerful figures—both within the Church and in terms of their political influence across Europe. Emperors and kings were often made to follow papal policy. The pope also had the right to **depose** an emperor or king and to **nullify** a civil law of which he **disapproved**.

Subordinate to the pope, the bishop took charge of all church affairs in a **diocese**, usually a city or town with a certain amount of

dues *n.* 会（员）费
tithe *n.* 什一税
in kind 以实物（支付）
subsistence *n.* 维持生活
Peter's Pence 彼得捐
hearth *n.* 灶
rite *n.* 仪式
baptism *n.* 洗礼
elapse *v.* 流逝，过去
sophisticated *adj.* 缜密严谨的
cardinal *n.* 红衣主教
supreme *adj.* 至高无上的
depose *v.* 废黜
nullify *v.* 宣布无效
disapprove *v.* 反对
subordinate *adj.* 下级的
diocese *n.* 主教辖区

surrounding land. Several dioceses together would constitute a province, with an **archbishop** at its head. As bishops were amongst the most powerful landowners in any kingdom, the appointment of bishops was a very sensitive issue between the Popes and emperors. The diocese, in turn, was divided into **parishes**, which might be a village or small town, or a section of a larger town or city. Each parish had its church and its parish priest. This **pyramidal** structure, which ran from the parish priest up to the cardinals and the pope, was called the **secular clergy** because they worked among the people, "in the world".

The other kind of clergy was called "**regular**" because they lived under a special rule (regula in Latin). The regular clergy consisted of monks and nuns. Some regular clergy lived in **monasteries**. They worked the soil, **transcribed manuscripts**, wrote books, and ran schools. Some organized crusades, took up arms or tended to holy places. Yet others moved about among common people, engaging in preaching and teaching, but were not bound to a locality like the secular clergy. The regular clergy were the chief **missionaries** of the Church, and established many **charitable institutions** such as schools, poorhouses, and hospitals. The regular clergy system was answerable only to the Pope. The larger monastic houses were ruled over by **abbots** who might control large **estates** and be as powerful and as independent as any bishop or lord.

Ordinary people outside of the Church organization had no say in running the Church, but they did form their own religious clubs called **confraternities**. In some cities these numbered several dozens. Majority Europeans from the 13th century onwards were members of one or more confraternities.

2.2 Corruption and Malpractices within the Church

Like most great and growing organizations the Church was also **plagued** by threats, for example, the constant challenges of heretics, and the **Great Schism** between the Church of Rome and the Orthodox Church in 1054. Before the Reformation, the greatest challenge came, however, from within: malpractice within the Church was serious enough to trouble many faithful Christians.

As Lord Acton famously said, "Power tends to corrupt, and absolute power corrupts absolutely". With no other authority to hold it to account, the medieval Church **abused** its power. The Church engaged in the practice of **simony**, that is, the raising of cash through

archbishop *n.* 大主教
parish *n.* 教区，牧区
pyramidal *adj.* 金字塔形的
secular clergy 在俗教士
regular *adj.* 受教规约束的
monastery *n.* 修道院
transcribe *v.* 誊写
manuscript *n.* 手稿
missionary *n.* 传教士
charitable institution 慈善机构
abbot *n.* 修道院院长
estate *n.* 地产
confraternity *n.* 宗教社团
corruption *n.* 腐败
malpractice *n.* 玩忽职守
plague *v.* 不断困扰
Great Schism 宗教大分裂
abuse *v.* 滥用
simony *n.* 买卖圣职

the sale of **posts** in the Church. By the 15th century this was very common: Pope Leo X (1475—1521) raised large sums by selling 2 000 Church offices each year, often to rich families seeking positions for their **offspring**. As a result, the highest ranks in the Church were increasingly filled by powerful and rich families. A case in point was the Medici family in Florence. In the 16th century this family alone produced two popes. Worse still, to increase their income, some high church officials would hold several church offices **concurrently**.

Simony meant clergymen often had low religious and personal standards. Those who had bought their way into the Church often had little knowledge of the Bible or Latin. Many **neglected** their duties and **violated** Church discipline. Marriage of clergy was forbidden, but many married or kept **mistresses** and had **illegitimate children.**

Then there was the sale of **indulgences**, the holy trade developed by the Church around the late 13th century. These **purported** to allow a person to buy God's forgiveness and ransom his way out of hell. Church officials argued that clergy were doing more good works than they needed to; they had more **merits** in their spiritual "**accounts**" than needed in order to pay for their own sins. Why not sell off the **excess**? Reselling its own good works was precisely what the Church started to do. With the approval of the pope, individual bishops could sell good works carried out by clergy to individual believers. Proof of the sale was in the indulgence itself, a piece of paper, like a piece of money or a check, which certified that the meritorious works of the clergy had paid off the "good works debt" of the individual believer.

Indulgences were invented by the Church for one and only one reason: to collect money. The only reason this worked is because everybody accepted the value of indulgences in the same way that everybody accepts the currency of paper money as a **substitution** for things that have value. With the invention of the printing press, printed indulgences became big business for the Church.

post *n.* 职位
offspring *n.* 子女
concurrently *adv.* 同时
neglect *v.* 无视
violate *v.* 违反
mistress *n.* 情妇
illegitimate child 私生子
indulgence *n.* 赎罪券
purport *v.* 据称是
merit *n.* 优秀品质
account *n.* 账户
excess *adj.* 多余的，过量的
substitution *n.* 替代品

An indulgence granted by the Pope in 1517 and sold by John (Johannes) Tetzel (Tietzel). The text written in Latin reads: "By the authority of all the saints, and in mercy towards you, I absolve you from all sins and misdeeds and remit all punishments for ten days."

rampant *adj.* 猖獗的
trigger off 引发
Wittenberg (德) 魏登堡
nail *v.* 钉
poster *n.* 海报
theses *n.* 论纲
summon *v.* 传召
renounce *v.* 正式宣布放弃
excommunicate *v.* 开除教籍
papal Bull 教皇诏令
chain reaction 连锁反应

The **rampant** sale of indulgences was the central issue that **triggered off** the Reformation. In 1517 a preacher named John Tetzel came to **Wittenberg** in Saxony to raise money by selling indulgences for the building of St. Peter's Basilica in Rome. On October 31, a monk named Martin Luther **nailed** a **poster** to the church door in Wittenberg. On the poster he had written 95 **theses**—or points for discussion-criticizing the selling of indulgences. Four years later, in April 1521, Luther was **summoned** by the Holy Roman Emperor Charles V to present himself before the Diet (parliament) in Worms. All the princes and great men of the empire were there. The emperor ordered Luther to **renounce** or change his arguments. When Luther refused, he was declared an outlaw in the Empire and **excommunicated** from the Church. Pope Leo X also issued a **papal Bull** condemning Luther's beliefs and ordering the public to burn his books. In response, Luther burnt a copy of the Bull and a book of canon (Church) law. Quite remarkably, Luther's action set off a **chain reaction** that quickly resulted in a major social, economic, and intellectual revolution in Europe.

Who was this Martin Luther? Why and how did he want to reform the Church? What were his teachings about? Besides the public acceptance of his teachings, what other factors helped turn this one-man revolt into a Europe-wide revolution? Why did the Reformation start off first in Germany? Why and how did it spread to other parts of Europe?

To explain the rise of the Lutheran revolt in Germany, we will look at Martin Luther the person, his ideas, and the relationship between his personal spiritual journey and German society at large.

3. Luther and the German Reformation

3.1 Martin Luther (1483—1546)

Luther was born into a **miner**'s family in Saxony in central Germany. His father, the most powerful figure in the family, provided him a good education and wanted him to become a lawyer. Young Luther proved to be a good student. At the age of nineteen, he entered the University of Erfurt and received his master's degree four years later. Following his father's wishes, he **enrolled** in law school at the same university. But shortly after starting his legal study, Luther had a life-changing experience. According to his **biography**, one day he was **trapped** in a thunderstorm and was overcome by fear of death and hell. He promised Saint Anne he would become a monk if he survived the thunderstorm. When he did, he entered the Augustinian monastery at Erfurt. In 1507, he became a priest of the Augustinian order.

miner *n.* 矿工
enroll *v.* 注册
biography *n.* 传记
trap *v.* 受困

Luther's life as a monk was one of constant struggle. He felt he had to get rid of his sin to satisfy the mighty God. He tried everything the Church offered to achieve that-constant prayers, devotion to church services and especially the Mass, and generally punishing himself to the extent that he damaged his health by not eating or sleeping enough. But none of these did any good; he was overwhelmed by his sense of guilt and sin. The constant emotional struggle made him a most unusual monk: he arrived at a point where he even felt hatred for God. He became increasingly doubtful that the Church could actually offer him **salvation** at all. A trip to Rome only intensified his doubt as he discovered the capital of Christianity to be **swamped** in **corruption.**

In spite of his emotional and religious **torment**, Luther continued to prove a remarkable **intellectual**. A master of both **theology** and the liberal arts of the day, in 1508, at the age of twenty-five, Luther was appointed a teaching position at the newly established University of Wittenberg. Shortly after he received his doctoral degree in theology, he was **promoted** to a professorship at the same university.

salvation *n.* 救赎
swamp *v.* 陷入，面临
corruption *n.* 腐败
torment *n.* 煎熬，折磨
intellectual *n.* 学者
theology *n.* 神学
promote *v.* 提升

During the following ten years in Wittenberg, Luther found his ideas growing clearer from his reading of the Bible and from his theological teaching. To prepare his lectures, he often turned to the letters of St. Paul to the early Christian community advising them on Christian belief and practice. This return to the sources of Christian thought offered Luther insight that he could not find in the large body of church doctrine and theological debates. From this reading of the Bible, he discovered that it was not the Church, but his own individual faith that would **guarantee** his salvation. Departing from Church teaching of the time, Luther's new understanding of salvation was to become the central argument of the Ninety-Five Theses in 1517 and most of his later works.

guarantee *v.* 保障

3.2 Luther's Teachings

To most historians, the publication of Luther's *Ninety-Five Theses* marks the beginning of the Reformation. To Luther, it was simply an effort to draw attention to the corrupt practices of the Church. What angered Luther most was that the Church would **mislead** people into thinking that sins could be forgiven with money, that God's free, forgiving love and mercy could be bought. This anger led Luther to prepare his *Ninety-Five Theses* on issues relating to the sale of indulgences. Luther argued that forgiveness came only through **repentance**. The pope had no power to forgive sins. He could only **confirm** what God already had done. The pope could free Christians from the self-punishment placed on them by the Church but could not free dead Christians from **purgatory**. Even if the pope had the power to free human souls from purgatory, he should do so out of love, not for money. In short, the selling of indulgences went against the true spirit of Christianity.

mislead *v.* 误导

repentance *n.* 悔改，忏悔

confirm *v.* 确认

purgatory *n.* 炼狱

There was nothing explicitly revolutionary about what Luther did. Many pieces of evidence suggest that Luther's only intention was to push for church reform. For one thing, when he finished writing his theses, he did not immediately publish them. He first sent copies to the Archbishop in Saxony and to his local bishop. Only when he got no reaction did he put up copies on the church door. This, again, was nothing unusual: in those days the church door often served as the town **bulletin board** for announcements and topics for debate. Besides, Luther's theses were written in Latin, and were thus clearly not meant for the general public but for the small world of **academia.**

bulletin board 布告栏

academia *n.* 学术界

In 1520, responding to some attacks on his *Ninety-Five Theses*, Luther published three more **pamphlets** to outline his fundamental position. In *Address to the Nobility of the German Nation* written in

pamphlet *n.* 宣称手册

German, Luther called on the German princes to reject the foreign pope's authority and establish a reformed German church. In The *Babylonian Captivity of the Church*, Luther attacked the belief that the **sacramental system** was the only means to salvation and called for the reform of monasticism. He insisted that **justification** was by faith alone. In *The Liberty of the Christian Man*, Luther further explained his **doctrine** of faith and justification. He insisted that a Christian could be justified, freed, and attain salvation only by his faith. Being saved and freed by his faith in Jesus, however, does not free the Christian from the duty to perform good works; rather, he performs good works out of **gratitude** to God: "Good works do not make a good man, but a good man does good work." By then he had gone so far as to challenge the authority of the pope itself. An eventual **break** with the Church of Rome was **inevitable.**

sacramental system 圣礼仪式
justification *n.* 赦免
doctrine *n.* 信条，教义
gratitude *n.* 感恩
break *n.* 破裂
inevitable *adj.* 不可避免

Justification by faith and the Bible as the sole authority in religious affairs are the two fundamental **assertions** of Luther's teachings. They later became the central doctrines of the Protestant Reformation. Nothing but faith matters, said Luther. All else is **superfluous**. All an individual needs to do to be saved is his own unshakable belief and faith in God. No one can obtain God's grace, mercy, and love on behalf of someone else. A priest of the Church is no more than a teacher and helper. Every believer is his own priest. A believer must not be content to accept the teachings of the Church. He must look to the Bible for God's purpose and seek it out for himself. For, in Luther's opinion, the truth was only to be found in the Bible.

Justification by faith
assertion *n.* 主张
superfluous *adj.* 多余的

Selection from Luther's *Ninety-Five Theses*

5. The Pope has neither the will nor the power to remit any penalties beyond those he has imposed either by his own authority or by canon law. 教皇没有免除任何罪孽的意志和权力，他只能赦免凭自己的权力或教会法加于人们的惩罚。
21. Therefore those preachers of indulgences are in error, who say that by the pope's indulgences a man is freed from every penalty, and saved. 所以那些宣讲赎罪票者，说教皇的赎罪票能使人免除各种惩罚，而且得救，乃是犯了错误。
27. It is mere human talk to preach that the soul flies out [of purgatory] so soon as the penny jingles into the money-box. 他们鼓吹的仅仅是人的主张，说什么当钱柜中的银币叮当作响，炼狱中的灵魂即会应声飞入天堂。

28. It is certainly possible that when the penny jingles into the collection box greed and avarice can increase; but the intercession of the Church depends on the will of God alone. 显然，当钱币在钱柜中叮当作响，增加的只是贪婪和利己之心。至于教会代祷的功效，仅由神主宰。

82. For example: "Why does not the Pope empty purgatory for the sake of most holy love and the supreme need of souls? This would be the most righteous of reasons, if he can redeem innumerable souls for sordid money with which to build a basilica, the most trivial of reasons." 譬如有人问："既然教皇为了筹集修建圣彼得教堂的那笔可怜的款项而解救炼狱中的无数灵魂，那他为何不因圣爱的缘故和炼狱中灵魂的迫切需要，将他们统统释放呢？而前者的理由微不足道，后者则正大光明。"

90. To suppress these most conscientious questionings of the laity by authority only, instead of refuting them by reason, is to expose the Church and the Pope to the ridicule of their enemies, and to make Christian people unhappy. 不用理性来消除信徒的疑虑和争端，而仅凭武力压制，那就只能使教会和教皇成为敌人的笑柄，而使广大基督徒感到痛心。

94. Christians should be exhorted to seek earnestly to follow Christ, their Head, through penalties, deaths, and hells. 应当告诫基督徒通过苦行、死亡和地狱，忠心追随其主基督。

95. And let them thus be more confident of entering heaven through many tribulations rather than through a false assurance of peace. 唯有经历各种苦难，而不是虚假的平安担保（徒14：22），才能有把握进入天国。

Jan Hus 扬·胡斯
heretic *n.* 异端分子
duke *n.* 公爵
kidnap *v.* 绑架
castle *n.* 城堡
false *adj.* 假的
stir *n.* 骚动

Luther was not the first to have such thoughts. A hundred years earlier a priest called **Jan Hus** (1369—1415) had taught the much the same in Prague. He was burned as a **heretic**. Luther himself could not have survived if he did not have the protection of Frederick Ⅲ (1463—1525), **Duke** of Saxony, where Luther lived. When Luther was announced an outlaw in 1521, Frederick had Luther **kidnapped** and taken in secret to his **castle** in Wartburg. There Luther lived under a **false** name and started to translate the Bible into German so that every German could read it and receive God's message. However, this was not easy as in those days there was no language that all Germans could read: Bavarians wrote in Bavarian, Saxons in Saxon. So Luther had to invent a language that everyone could understand. And in his translation of the Bible he actually succeeded in creating one that was to become the basis of a unified German language.

Luther did not foresee the **stir** his critical views would cause. His pamphlets written in Latin were soon translated into German. Printers used the power of the new printing press to spread his messages throughout Europe. Most people could not read or write in 1517 but it was common for a person who could read to do so aloud in a public place (such as a market square) if he believed that he had something of interest that others might want to hear. Luther's views soon became public knowledge. When Luther found out what had happened he was **disturbed**. But there was nothing he could do. The response of the public to his works was outside of his control.

disturb *v.* 困扰

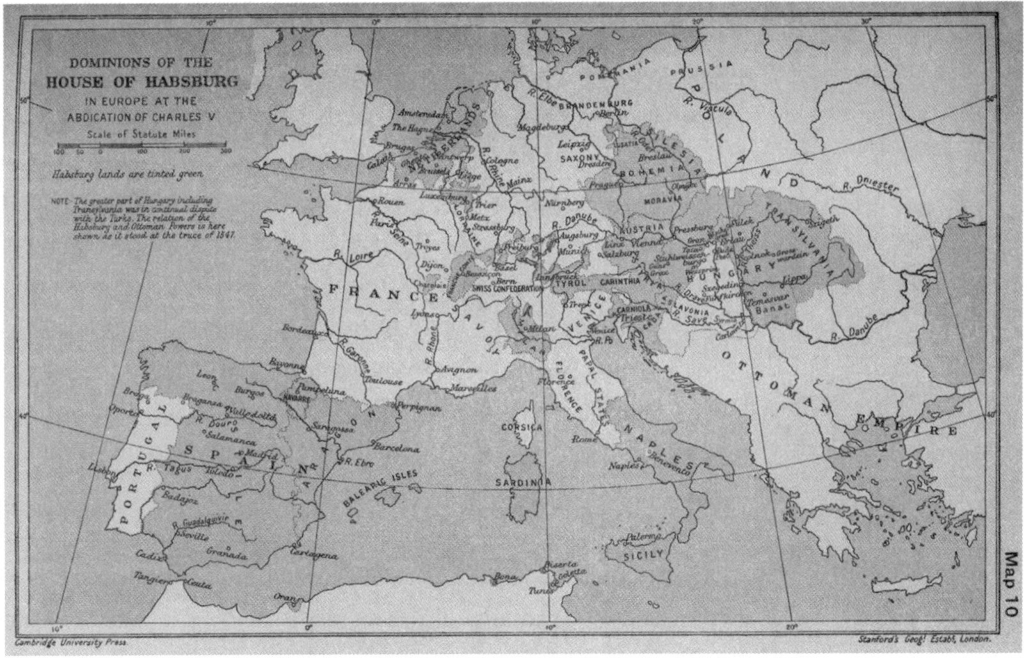

Map 21 Holy Roman Empire under Charles V

The vast Empire consisted of Spain (together with the Spanish overseas territories, not shown on this map), the Habsburg kingdom (including parts of today's Germany, Austria, Hungary and Slovenia), Bohemia (today's Czech and Slovak republics), the Low Countries (Belgium, the Netherlands, Luxembourg), some eastern regions of today's France, and northern Italy. Charles V also ruled over extensive Spanish colonies in North, Central, and South America, the Caribbean, Asia, and the Philippines. Despite the name "Holy Roman Empire", Rome was never part of the Empire.

3.3 The Reformation in Germany

From its very beginning, the fate of Luther's movement was closely tied to political interests. The politics of Germany at the time had an important influence on the destiny of the movement. Certain characteristics made Germany particularly **ripe** for religious revolt. To begin with, "Germany" in the early 16th century was not a unified

ripe *adj.* 条件成熟

kingdom on its own but belonged to the Holy Roman Empire. At the time the Reformation broke out, the emperor of the Holy Roman Empire was **Charles V** (rule 1519—1566). King of Spain, Charles was elected emperor at the age of nineteen. **Inheriting** the vast empire from his family, Charles had only limited power in Germany. In theory, the emperor was superior to the kings, dukes, counts, princes, cities, archbishops, bishops, and abbots within the Empire. In practice, the power of the emperor depended on his relations with the towns and princes of Germany. Germany itself was made up of more than three hundred separate states. Rulers of these states often warred with one another or in league against the emperors.

Charles V 查理五世
inherit *v.* 继承

Throughout Europe in the Late Middle Ages, state and Church were **pitted** in increasing competition against each other, in both religious and secular matters. Powerful rulers—primarily the kings of France and Spain—were able to **trade** their support for the Church for considerable autonomy. In the Holy Roman Empire, however, due to the lack of political unity there were no agreements between pope and emperor limiting papal authority in Germany. In addition, almost one third of land in Germany was owned by the Church. The high papal taxes on Germans also led to public discontent. Despite paying such large sums of money to Rome, Germans had almost no influence over papal policy. Frenchmen, Spaniards, and Italians dominated the ranks of cardinals and the papal bureaucracy, and the popes themselves were always Italian. **Graduates** of the rapidly expanding German universities almost never found employment in Rome. In a word, people in Germany felt particular **resentment** towards the power of the pope.

pit *v.* 绞尽脑汁与（某人）较量
trade *v.* 交换
graduate *n.* 毕业生
resentment *n.* 不满

Against this historical backdrop, Luther's ideas hit at the heart of the political and social **tension** between authorities and the Church. Between 1521 and 1525, his teachings spread like wildfire through northern and central Germany. The initial spread of Luther's ideas produced **chaos**. In Wittenberg, some **radical** supporters of Luther started to destroy images of Christ on the cross and statues of saints in churches. Although Luther spoke out strongly against the vices and corrupt practices of the Catholic Church, he did not believe in violence as a solution. He was forced to return to Wittenberg in March 1522, where he moved to stop the unrest together with Frederick's support. He took over leadership of the Reformation in Wittenberg; and as a response to his message having been well received but badly interpreted, Luther decided to start his own church.

tension *n.* 张力
chaos *n.* 动乱
radical *adj.* 激进的

What Luther started, a number of German princes soon took into their hands. Several German princes formally **converted** to Lutheranism, making it the official religion in their territories too. Many churches and towns had turned "**evangelical**" (a term used to refer to Christians in the Lutheran tradition in Europe). Of course, these princes had a number of **motives** for rallying behind Luther. Religious concerns surely played a role, but political factors were generally more important. By "establishing" Lutheranism (making it their territories' official religion), Protestant princes could **consolidate** their authority by appointing church officials, stopping the payments to Rome, **confiscating** church property, especially monastic property, and limiting the power of church courts. They also used Luther's teachings as a new weapon in their struggle against the emperor, himself a devout Catholic.

convert *v.* 皈依

evangelical *adj.* 福音派

motive *n.* 动机

consolidate *v.* 巩固

confiscate *v.* 没收

Similar considerations also pushed other social classes to adopt Lutheranism. Below the level of the princes, in 1522 a number of German knights revolted against the Catholic Church and the Holy Roman Empire. Although the revolt was short-lived—it was put down in lees than a year-their refusal to pay church tithes during the Revolt soon spread to the peasant classes. Refusal to pay the tithe was one of the factors leading up to the German Peasants' War.

The Peasants' War of 1524 and 1525 posed Luther his greatest challenge. Luther had taught that all Christians were equal. Each had the right to interpret the Bible for himself, guided by reason. The peasants took the ideas of Luther to mean that all people were equal. Inspired by this and the text of the Bible, they demanded freedom from **serfdom**, and a number of other rights. In June 1524, they rose in revolt against their lords and looked to Luther for support. But Luther had no intention to **extend** his doctrine of religious equality to the broader social **domain**. Luther wanted order to be maintained, within both society and the Church. He intended his church to be respectful of established political authority. In the early days of the Peasants' Revolt, he tried to reason with the peasants, asking them to suffer quietly. When they refused he urged the princes to hunt the rebels down like dogs, as "nothing can be more poisonous than a man in rebellion." Protestant and Catholic princes united and suppressed the revolt. More than one hundred thousand peasants died in the revolt. After the bloody punishment of the peasant rebels there was never again to be a mass lower-class uprising in Germany.

serfdom *n.* 农奴制

extend *v.* 扩展

domain *n.* 领域

By the later 1520s, Lutheranism was spreading in more peaceful ways, usually when a prince or a city formally adopted Luther's ideas and **disestablished** the Catholic Church within their territory. The new faith had won the devotion of a large part of the German people, particularly in the north and the east, farthest away from the center of imperial power. Some of the great cities in the south, such as **Nuremberg** had also come over to the Lutheran side. By the 1550s Lutheranism had **captured** about half of the population of the Empire.

disestablish *v.* 废除
Nuremberg 纽伦堡
capture *v.* 获得

The unstable political situation in the Holy Roman Empire contributed to the success of the Reformation. Right from the start, Charles was determined to keep a **check** on the spread of Lutheranism as it posed an open challenge to the authority of the Emperor and the Catholic Church. However, politics in the Empire, both internally and externally, were not in his favor. Upon coming to the throne, Charles had to deal with a series of border disputes with the king of France, Francis Ⅰ (1515—1547). For more than two decades (1521—1544) the Holy Roman Empire and France fought **intermittently** in southern France, the Netherlands, the Rhineland, northern Spain, and Italy. At the same time, Charles was faced with an invasion by the **Ottoman Turks** in the eastern part of the empire. The Turks **overran** most of Hungary, moved into Austria, and advanced as far as the gates of **Vienna**. Fearful of Charles V's new power, many Catholic princes refused to cooperate in his attempt to impose his authority throughout the empire. Charles was forced to rely on the military support of the Lutheran princes, in exchange for his **tolerance** of the **initial** spread of Lutheranism in the Empire.

check *n.* 阻止
intermittently *adv.* 断断续续地
Ottoman Turks 奥斯曼土耳其人
overrun *v.* 蔓延
Vienna 维也纳
tolerance *n.* 容忍
initial *adj.* 开始的

In 1531, Charles V decided that he would put a stop to the spread of Lutheranism. This decision led the Lutheran princes to form a defensive alliance of their own, known as the **League of Schmalkald**. The outbreak of war was only prevented because the Empire faced a new wave of threats from the French and Turks. Charles V was forced again to seek the help of the Lutherans to defend against invaders. Luther then died in 1546. His death and other events weakened the Schmalkald League. In April 1547 the forces of the league, betrayed by one of their leaders, were defeated by imperial armies. Charles' victory was so decisive that it looked as if the Protestants might be crushed. Greatly alarmed by the **prospect** of a united Germany, the French decided to enter the war. In 1552 a French army invaded Germany. By 1554, the Protestants had regained much of their lost ground.

League of Schmalkald 施马加登同盟
prospect *n.* 前景

In 1555 Protestants and Catholics finally agree to the **Peace of**

Augsburg. According to the terms of the agreement, each prince could **dictate** the religion of his subjects; the Protestants could keep all the church property they had seized up to 1552; Lutherans and Catholics living in areas where their religion was not recognized could **emigrate**. However, the agreement was reached between Catholics and Lutherans only. The peace did not extend to members of other branches of the Reformation. No form of Protestantism other than Lutheranism was to be tolerated. The Peace of Augsburg was merely a **truce**; it did not settle the religious conflict in Germany for once and for all. Both sides were exhausted and at an **impasse**, so everyone accepted matters as they stood. Thus religious conflict in Germany did not break out into general war for another sixty years. When it did, though, the consequences were devastating.

Peace of Augsburg《奥格斯堡和约》
dictate *v.* 决定
emigrate *v.* （向外）移民
truce *n.* 休战
impasse *n.* 僵局

Between 1520 and 1555 Lutheranism won an established position and found general acceptance throughout the northern half of Germany. Its **triumphs** were not limited to Germany. To the north, Sweden broke away from Denmark in 1523 in a general uprising. A new king, Frederick Ⅰ (1523—1533) came to the throne of Denmark and Norway, while the Swedes chose Gustavus Vasa (1523—1560) as their ruler. Both the new rulers saw the possibility of increasing their political control and their power by adopting Lutheranism. Both met with considerable opposition, but through **propaganda** and **legislation**, and especially by armed force, they gradually converted their countries to the new faith. Catholicism died slowly in the Scandinavian lands. Before the end of the 16th century Scandinavia was firmly Lutheran.

triumph *n.* 胜利
propaganda *n.* 宣称
legislation *n.* 立法

The Peace of Augsburg was an important turning point in the history of the Reformation. The division of Christianity was formally acknowledged, with Lutheranism granted equal legal standing with Catholicism. When the peace settlement accepted the right of each German ruler to determine the religion of his subjects, Charles' hopes for a united empire were completely **dashed**, and the medieval ideal of Christian unity was lost. The future of Lutheranism was secure. At the same time, different branches of Protestantism had developed in Germany and other places in Europe.

dash *v.* 破灭

4. The Spread of the Protestant Reformation

Luther asserted that the Bible was the sole source of religious constitute *v.* 构成

sow *v.* 播种

authority. For Protestant reformers, this raised the question of what **constituted** a correct interpretation of the Bible. Disagreement on this issue could boil over into bloody warfare. As Lutheranism took root in northern Germany and Scandinavia, competing forms of Protestantism soon emerged from the seeds that Luther had **sown**. Protestantism had become a truly international movement, but one split into a number of competing traditions. While Luther and his followers pursued a more conservative religious and social outlook, in several cities of Switzerland Protestantism took on more radical forms.

4.1 The Reformation in Switzerland

confederation n. 邦联
canton *n.* 郡
Zurich 苏黎世
Bern 伯尔尼
Basel 巴塞尔
autonomous *adj.* 自治的

In the early 16th century Switzerland was neither ruled by kings nor dominated by powerful princes. Instead the Swiss **Confederation** was a loose association of thirteen prosperous cities called cantons. The six forest cantons were democratic republics, while the seven urban cantons, including **Zurich**, **Bern**, and **Basel**, were governed primarily by city councils. Theoretically part of the Holy Roman Empire, they became virtually **autonomous** in 1499. So when the leading citizens of a Swiss canton decided to adopt Protestant reforms, no one could stop them. Although religious arrangements varied from city to city, the Reformation in Switzerland generally followed the so-called Reformed tradition. The best known of its early leaders was **Ulrich Zwingli**. After Zwingli's death, leadership of the movement was taken on by **John Calvin**. Because of Calvin's powerful influence and sharp theological mind, the Reformed tradition is also known as **Calvinism**. In this section we will briefly review the beginnings of the Reformed tradition in the hands of Zwingli, and its theological development under Calvin.

Ulrich Zwingli 胡尔德莱斯·茨温利
John Calvin 约翰·加尔文
Calvinism *n.* 加尔文教派

4.1.1 Ulrich Zwingli and the Swiss Reformation

Ulrich Zwingli (woodcut by Hans Asper ***1531***)

Only a year after Luther nailed his theses to the door at Wittenberg, a Swiss priest named Ulrich Zwingli (1484—1531) launched a quieter reform in Zurich. A year younger than Luther, Zwingli was aristocratic and well-educated. His studies were influenced by humanists. Between 1516 and 1518 Zwingli was pastor at Einsiedeln. He spoke against both pilgrimages and selling indulgences. He also preached against the practice of hiring out Swiss soldiers to foreign rulers, a business in which the church played a part. Increasingly doubtful about many church practices, he reached conclusions similar to Luther's.

By 1519 when Zwingli was assigned as preacher in the cathedral of

Zurich, his **sermons** were drawing huge crowds. Like Luther, Zwingli insisted that the Bible, not the Church, was the true guide to faith and morals. By so doing, he began to speak against the supremacy of the pope. Like Luther, Zwingli taught of salvation by faith alone. He thought the appeal of saints and use of candles, **incense**, and images were "**superstitions.**" He began a trend of church buildings being almost undecorated halls. Like Luther, Zwingli **objected** to the idea that priests had miraculous powers. He denied the position of the priest as mediator between God and human. Good priests could and should play a role in **enlightening** the people, but before God they were equal to the general public. Like Luther, Zwingli argued against various forms of self-punishment within the church such as **fasting** and the practice of **celibacy**. His own marriage was publicly celebrated in 1524. Luther did not marry until the next year.

sermon *n.* 讲道，布道
incense *n.* 熏香
superstition *n.* 迷信
undecorated *adj.* 无装潢的
object *v.* 反对
enlighten *v.* 启蒙
fasting *n.* 禁食
celibacy *n.* 独身，禁欲

In 1522 Zwingli undertook a major set of reforms in Zurich. He persuaded the town council to forbid any religious custom that was not in agreement with the Bible. He advocated democracy in religious terms, as well as in state politics. The government of Zurich and most of its citizens followed Zwingli's teachings. Many of the other German-speaking towns of Switzerland became Protestant.

As his movement began to spread, Zwingli tried to form an alliance with Luther and the German reformers. Although both German and Swiss reformers realized the need for a **united front** against Catholic opposition, they were unable to agree on the interpretation of the Last Supper. In the Catholic tradition, the bread and wine at the Mass is the body and blood of Christ. Although Luther denied the miracle of the Mass, he held that the body and blood of Christ are somehow *present* in the bread and wine. Zwingli believed that the bread and wine only *symbolize* the body and blood. Zwingli's belief has become the usual Protestant doctrine.

united front 统一阵线

The Swiss reform led by Zwingli was mainly an **urban** movement. Despite its rapid success, five forest cantons with few large towns or cities remained Catholic. In 1531 Zwingli and his followers attempted to convert the forest cantons by force of arms. Zwingli was killed at Kappel. His enemies cut up his body, burned the pieces, and **scattered** the ashes. In November 1531 the Catholics and the Reformers signed the **Peace of Kappel**. The peace treaty allowed each canton free choice in matter of religion. To this day Switzerland is part Catholic and part Protestant.

urban *adj.* 城市的
scatter *v.* 分散
Peace of Kappel《卡普尔和约》

4.1.2 John Calvin and the Development of Calvinism

After Zwingli's death a number of leaders continued to spread Protestant ideas in Switzerland, Germany, and France. However, it was not until several years later that the Swiss movement would find its greatest leader in John Calvin (1509—1564). Calvin was perhaps the most influential of all religious leaders of the Protestant Reformation in 16th-century Europe. He built up a systematic body of theological doctrine and developed a strong church.

priesthood *n.* 圣职

French-born and educated in Paris, Calvin was trained first for the Catholic **priesthood** and then as a lawyer. Influenced by of the writings of Erasmus and Luther, Calvin converted from Catholicism to Protestantism. In 1534 he fled from Paris to Basel in Switzerland as pressures against reformers in France increased. Two years later, Calvin arrived in **Geneva**, where he would remain, except for a short exile, until the end of his life.

Geneva 日内瓦

Institutes of the Christian Religion 《基督教原理》

theology *n.* 神学

Upon his arrival in Geneva Calvin published his first edition of the ***Institutes of the Christian Religion***. After several revisions and expansions (the four-volume complete edition appeared in 1559), this work became the most authoritative and systematic summary of Protestant **theology**. The Institutes are still regarded as a masterwork of French literature because of their cool, clear, concise language. They contain all the beliefs and practices of Calvinism.

personality *n.* 性格

volatile *adj.* 易激动的

On most important doctrines, Calvin stood very close to Luther. Both preached the doctrines of justification by faith alone; both regarded the Bible as the only spiritual authority. But Luther and Calvin differed greatly in their **personality** and spiritual journey. Whereas Luther was always highly **volatile**, Calvin remained a cool-headed legalist from start to finish. Luther and Calvin adopted different theological paths: for Luther the starting point of his understanding of God and God's activity was his personal experiences of sin, guilt, and fear of God's punishment; whereas for Calvin, right from the beginning his theology was built around the "power, grace, and glory of God" and worked on a top-down basis. Although Calvin always acknowledged Luther's influence on him, in the *Institutes* he developed several doctrines that set Calvinism apart from Lutheranism.

abandonment *n.* 抛弃

sacraments *n.* 圣礼

discipline *n.* 纪律

Unlike Luther, Calvin called for the **abandonment** of all the **sacraments** except baptism and the Last Supper. In church organization, Calvin believed that the order and **discipline** of the early church should be restored. Thus he introduced many changes.

Calvinist churches kept only their own priest, and did away with bishops, archbishops, and regular clergy. For the Calvinists, the church was a place for men to come close to God through reading the Bible. Public worship did not require complicated ceremonies, a richly decorated church building, or music. Calvin was also much stricter than Luther in his standards of a good or "godly" Christian life. He not only insisted that Christians should go to the church regularly, but also urged them to lead an **austere** and pure life. Dancing, games, and other amusements were forbidden. Hard work and self-control were encouraged. This way of life is known as "**puritanical**", a word inherited from the later English Calvinists.

austere *adj.* 简朴的

puritanical *adj.* 清教徒

Most striking, perhaps, were Calvin's new teachings of salvation. He developed a strong **doctrine of predestination**, which means man, from birth, is predestined by God for salvation or damnation. The chosen ones, or the elect, will go to heaven; the others will go to hell **regardless** of their deeds or their manner of life. Christ died for man, but only for the elect, not for all people. According to Calvin, God's choices cannot be understood by humans as a huge **gulf** separates God and humans. People's actions cannot change their fate.

doctrine of predestination 先定论

regardless of 无论

gulf *n.* 鸿沟

Theory alone did not satisfy Calvin. He set out to put his teachings into practice. In Geneva Calvin helped to unite the followers of Zwingli and other reformers and to throw off the rule of the Catholic Duke of Savoy. Soon, Calvin was made both the religious and political leader of the city, and he held this position till his death in 1546. Constantly preaching and writing, Calvin involved himself in all aspects of Genevan affairs including education, trade, and diplomacy. Strict moral order was enforced by the Calvinists. Dancing, card-playing, theatre performances, and work or play on the **Sabbath** were all outlawed. Any sort of wrongdoing would result in severe **penalties**. During the first four years after Calvin gained control in Geneva, there were no fewer than fifty-eight executions out of a total population of only 16 000.

Sabbath *n.* 安息日

penalty *n.* 处罚

Calvin was not interested in Geneva alone but also in spreading the Reform movement abroad, especially in his native country, France. In 1559 Calvin founded the Genevan Academy (now the University of Geneva) to train **clergy**. Because of its advantageous location in Geneva and the power of Calvin's theology, it quickly came to rival the University of Wittenberg as the center of Protestant thought. Many earnest students and preachers came to Geneva from France, Scotland, England, and the Low Countries. They absorbed Calvin's teachings and carried them

clergy *n.* 神职人员

back home. Calvin gave advice and guidance to his followers from all over Europe. He wrote enough letters to fill thirty huge volumes. Calvin earned himself the name of the "Protestant Pope."

Calvinism achieved remarkable success in many parts of Europe. By the end of the 16th century, Calvinists were a majority in Switzerland, Scotland (where they were known as **Presbyterians**), Holland (where they founded the Dutch Reform Church), and England (where the Church of England adopted reformed theology but not reformed worship; other Calvinists who pushed for further reforms were known as **Puritans**). There were also substantial Calvinist minorities in France (where they were called **Huguenots**), Germany, Hungary, **Lithuania**, and Poland. God's kingdom on earth had not yet been fully realized, but an extraordinary revolution had taken place in European religious life.

Presbyterian *n.* 苏格兰长老教会
Puritan *n.* 清教徒
Huguenot *n.* 胡格诺教派
Lithuania *n.* 立陶宛

4.2 The Reformation in England

As late as 1500, the Catholic Church was as firmly rooted in England as on the continent of Europe. A century later, the church in England had broken off from Rome. A separate English national church came into being, called **Anglican Church** or the Church of England, with the king at its head. In many ways the Reformation in England was a political movement with religious **implications**. It was partly the result of growing English **nationalism**. The change started from events that took place in the reign of **Henry Ⅷ**.

Anglican Church 英国国教，又称为英格兰圣公会教会
implication *n.* 意义
nationalism *n.* 民族主义
Henry Ⅷ 亨利八世

4.2.1 Henry Ⅷ and the Early Reformation

Lutheran teachings had come into England by 1521 and aroused discussion in Oxford, Cambridge, and London. Initially, Henry Ⅷ was not impressed with the reformers' ideas. For many years, he seemed to be a most devoted son of the Catholic Church. He also wrote an essay against Luther's teachings, and dedicated it to the Pope. The Pope responded by awarding him the title "Defender of the Faith." In international terms, Henry Ⅷ also allied with Pope Leo X on several occasions to defend Catholicism.

Indeed, England would never have broken with Rome had it not been for its king's **marital** troubles. Henry's father had initially married his eldest son Arthur to Catherine (aunt of the Holy Roman Emperor Charles V) to form an alliance between Spain and England. Arthur died four months after the wedding. The English and Spanish states then agreed to have Catherine marry her husband's younger brother, Henry. Now it is against Catholic rules for a man to marry his brother's **widow**,

marital *adj.* 婚姻的
widow *n.* 寡妇

and so it took a special **authorization** from Pope Julius Ⅱ (rule 1503—1513) for Henry and Catherine to **tie the knot**. However, the marriage was not a happy one, and in addition five of their six children died, leaving only a girl, Princess Mary. It seemed unlikely to Henry that Catherine would give him a son. Furthermore, Henry was having a secret **affair** with Anne Boleyn, a lady-in-waiting to Queen Catherine.

authorization *n.* 许可
tie the knot 结婚
affair *n.* 婚外恋

Whatever his reasons, Henry Ⅷ requested Pope Clement Ⅶ (rule 1523—1534) to **annul** his marriage with Catherine.① He argued that church law forbade a man to marry his brother's widow and questioned whether it had been right for Pope Julius II to authorize this marriage. If granted, this annulment would have left Henry free to marry another woman and produce more **heirs**. Pope Clement Ⅶ, however, did not want to **contradict** the decision of his **predecessor** Julius Ⅱ, nor did he dare to offend Emperor Charles Ⅴ, the nephew of Catherine, because the latter's imperial armies dominated Italy. He refused to grant Henry the annulment.

annul *v.* 宣布无效
heir *n.* 继承人
contradict *v.* 与……相抵触
predecessor *n.* 前任

When long **negotiations** with the Church failed to give Henry what he wanted, he decided to challenge the doctrines of the Catholic Church. By 1529, Henry had decided to start his own church. Thus the Church of England was formed, and his divorce was granted in 1533. Henry made Ann his Queen. But after giving birth to a girl, Elizabeth, Ann soon fell out of favor and was **beheaded**. Henry went on to marry four other women. He had only one son from his third wife: Edward. All three of Mary, Elizabeth, and Edward were to rule England at various points after Henry's death.

negotiation *n.* 谈判
behead *v.* 砍头

Successors of Henry Ⅷ. From left to right: Edward Ⅵ (rule **1547—1553**), Queen Mary Ⅰ (rue **1553—1558**), Queen Elizabeth Ⅰ (**1558—1603**).

① 在中世纪欧洲，天主教教义禁止离婚，只有在教会宣布婚姻无效的情况下，婚约方可解除。西欧主要天主教国家（西班牙、意大利、葡萄牙和爱尔兰）于1971年至1996年期间先后通过法律允许离婚。

The English Parliament passed a series of laws to put the church under the king's control and to weaken the link with Rome. The final break with Rome came in 1534 when the English Parliament passed the **Supremacy Act**, which declared the king to be "the Protector and only Supreme Head of the Church and the Clergy of England." The law placed the king above the church and the pope. Anyone who refused to swear an oath to Henry as head of the church was declared a **traitor**. Refusing to obey, Sir Thomas More was executed in 1535. Tens of thousands of Catholic monks and nuns were expelled from England. Monasteries were closed. Church property was confiscated. No one, either clergy or ordinary people, was allowed to send money to the pope in Rome.

the Supremacy Act《至尊法案》

traitor *n.* 叛国者

Although the church was brought fully under state control, England was not yet a Protestant country. The reasons for Henry's reform in England were mainly personal and political, not religious. Little had changed in religious matters such as doctrine, theology, and ceremony. While the Protestant influence in the country was growing, Catholic forces remained strong. More **substantial** changes in the English church were to be made by Henry's children.

substantial *adj.* 重大的

4.2.2 From Edward VI to Mary: the Rise and Fall of the English Reformation

When Henry died in 1547, his nine-year-old son Edward VI took the throne. Henry had named a large **council of regents** to rule England until Edward was old enough to be king. The council was composed of eight Catholics and eight Reformers. In reality, the politics of England were dominated by reform-minded Thomas Cranmer (the Archbishop of Canterbury) and Edward Seymour (uncle of Edward VI). The two men worked together to reform the church further. English instead of Latin was used in worship. Priests were permitted to marry. Catholic symbols and images were removed from churches. Cranmer's ***Book of Common Prayer*** was used as the service book in all Anglican churches. Young Edward was enthusiastic about reform as well. He was raised by Protestants. Renaissance ideas had dominated his education. Protestantism reached its highest point in English history.

council of regents 摄政会

Book of Common Prayer《公祷书》

However, Edward was a sickly child. In 1553, he died of lung disease. After his death, his **half-sister** Mary became queen of England. An abrupt change ensued. Raised as a Catholic, Mary used her position as the head of the English church to immediately restore the Catholic faith. She started by resuming use of the Latin Mass. Then she

half-sister *n.* 同父异母的姐妹

recognized the authority of the pope in England. Many people supported Mary's restoration of the Catholic faith as they believed that the reformers had gone too far. Most of the reforms undertaken by Henry and Edward were destroyed.

Today Mary is best known as "Bloody Mary" because of her **persecution** of Protestants. During her five-year reign nearly three hundred people were burned at the stake. Many who refused to reject Protestant beliefs continued to worship in underground churches or fled to other countries. Some Protestant leaders tried to replace Mary with her half-sister, Elizabeth. Mary had Elizabeth arrested and imprisoned in the Tower of London. Although she married Philip of Spain (soon to be King Philip Ⅱ), Mary died childless in 1558. As the English Parliament had forbidden Philip from taking the English throne, Mary had no choice, before her death, but to name Elizabeth her successor.

persecution *n.* 迫害

4.2.3 Elizabeth Ⅰ *and the Elizabethan Compromise*

Elizabethan Compromise 伊丽莎白的妥协政策

Elizabeth (reigned 1558—1603) was the daughter of Henry and Anne Boleyn. The reign of Elizabeth was one of the most successful in English history. Upon coming to the throne, Elizabeth moved quickly to resolve the difficult religious divide. A new Act of Supremacy was passed and re-established her position as the head of both church and state. The Church of England thus again rejected the authority of the pope. Intelligent, cautious, and self-confident, Elizabeth chose a **moderate** path while restoring Protestantism in England. Her middle way condemned Catholic teachings and practices, but it also forbade extreme Protestantism. This middle way came to be called the Elizabethan Compromise.

moderate *adj.* 温和的

In compiling a new *Book of Common Prayer*, Elizabeth included such a wide range of influences that all Protestant groups could accept it. While displaying some Lutheran and Calvinist features, the Anglican Church kept many aspects of Catholic worship and church organization. Elizabeth also revised part of the Protestant church service which had been adopted during Edward's reign to make it more acceptable to Catholics. Personally, Elizabeth preferred some of the older habits. She liked the use of the **crucifix** in church services. She disliked married clergy. Protestants had hoped for a complete victory, but the "Elizabethan Settlement" was considerably less than that. The Anglican Church under Elizabeth was clearly becoming Protestant, but it was a new brand of Protestantism. Its moderation and inclusiveness kept most people satisfied. With a mixture of compromise and tight

crucifix *n.* 有耶稣苦相的十字架

control, Elizabeth skillfully kept religion's destructive force in check and restored order in England.

Abroad, however, she faced an increasing threat of invasion by Catholic countries. Now that England under Elizabeth was again a Protestant country, it was drawn into the conflict between Protestant and Catholic states on the continent. Spain, the champion of Catholicism, thus appeared to Englishmen as their national enemy. And religion was far from the only matter to divide the two countries. One of the most powerful European states, Spain was expanding overseas and trying to prevent England from sharing the wealth of the New World. English seamen, often encouraged and backed by the Queen, raided Spanish merchant shipping and attacked Spanish **colonies.**

colony *n.* 殖民地
Invincible Armada 无敌舰队
fleet *n.* 舰队
boost *v.* 鼓舞
decline *n.* 衰败
near-monopoly *n.* 几乎完全的垄断
textile *n.* 纺织
lusty *adj.* 精力充沛
optimism *n.* 乐观主义

In 1588, King Philip Ⅱ of Spain decided to send his "**Invincible Armada**" to conquer England. Its surprise defeat by the English **fleet** was a turning point in history. In England it greatly **boosted** national pride which helped to unite Protestants and Catholics to some extent. In international politics, it marked the beginning of the gradual **decline** of Spain. England rose as a great sea power and continued to challenge the Spanish **near-monopoly** over the New World.

During Elizabeth's long reign of nearly fifty years, England enjoyed a remarkable period of growth and prosperity. The **textile** industry flourished and found new markets on the European continent. Companies were formed to trade with Russia, Africa, and the Near East. With support from the Queen, new industries were founded.① New colonies were founded. England in the Elizabethan era was young and **lusty**. All felt a sense of growth, expansion, and **optimism.**

5. The Catholic Counter-Reformation

counter-Reformation 反宗教改革运动

At the same time as the Protestant Reformation was reshaping religion and politics in 16th-century Western Europe, a reform movement also took place within the Roman Catholic Church. The movement is known as the **Counter-Reformation** because its changes were mainly a reaction to Protestantism, but in fact many Catholics had long been troubled by internal church corruption and had been seeking change for

① 例如，为了支持渔业发展，议会通过法令命令人们每周五必须吃鱼。

years already. Nevertheless, before the rise of Protestantism, few had directly called for reform. The success of the Protestant Reformation resulted in Catholic **self-criticism** and stirred up a Church-wide call for reform. The popes were not the main driver behind this reform, as they had led the push to **suppress** Protestantism during the early Reformation; instead it was the Holy Roman Emperor Charles V who finally pushed for reforms in the Church. It was he who pressured Pope Paul Ⅲ (reigned 1534—1549) to call the **Council of Trent**.

self-criticism *n.* 自我批评

suppress *v.* 镇压

Council of Trent 特伦托大公会议

5.1 The Council of Trent

Charles V appeared to have the upper hand after launching military attacks against the German Protestant princes in 1541. He planned to follow up with a religious meeting to win back the Protestants, and requested Pope Paul Ⅲ to call a council to deal with the criticisms they had raised. Strong **conservative hardliners** within the Church stopped him from doing this until 1545. Over the next eighteen years (1545—1563) Catholic leaders met on and off at Trent in Italy to deal with issues raised by Protestants as well as Catholic reformers. In many ways the Council of Trent marks the beginning of the modern Catholic Church.

conservative *adj.* 保守的

hardliner *n.* 强硬分子

In response to the extensive criticisms raised by Protestants, the council examined much of the church's theology and practices. Efforts were made to **eliminate** corruption and preserve morality in church administration. The Church **imposed** stricter **discipline** on its members. The council **condemned** the **scandals** arising from the sale of indulgences and ruled that indulgences were **under no circumstances** to be issued for money. The sale of church offices was forbidden. Bishops and priests were forbidden to hold more than one position **concurrently**. **Seminaries** were to be established for the education and training of priests.① While Latin remained as the official language of the church and the language of the Mass, priests were encouraged to give their **sermons** in the local, vernacular tongues.

eliminate *v.* 消除

impose *v.* 推行

discipline *n.* 纪律

condemn *v.* 谴责

scandal *n.* 丑闻

under no circumstances 无论任何情况都不得……

concurrently *adv.* 同时

seminary *n.* 神学院

sermon *n.* 布道

The council however responded **negatively** to almost all of the main **objections** of the Protestants. In response to the widely held Protestant belief that salvation came through faith alone, the council declared that faith had to be supported by good works. Good works were as necessary for salvation as faith. The council put Catholic tradition on the same level as the Bible as a source of truth and authority. The church

negatively *adv.* 否定地

objection *n.* 反对意见

---

① 在此之前教会对神职人员的教育并无任何具体要求。

Latin Vulgate edition 拉丁文的武加大圣经译本

recognized the **Latin Vulgate edition** compiled by St. Jerome in the late 4th century as the only authorized version of the Bible. The Protestant reformers' versions of the Bible were rejected. The council further insisted that only the Catholic Church has the right to interpret the Bible. The council also rejected Protestant positions on the **sacraments**. Steps were taken, too, to **check** the spread of Protestant teachings. The Council of Trent began work on a list of **subversive** books which all Catholics were forbidden to read, unless they enjoyed special permission.

sacraments *n.* 圣礼
check *v.* 限制
subversive *adj.* 反动的

After the Council of Trent, the Catholic Counter-Reformation became mainly **preoccupied** with **enforcing** its principles and requirements. The reforms of the council were far-reaching. Their enforcement was probably the most thoroughgoing reform in the history of the church. By the end of the 16th century, most of the abuses criticized by the Protestant reformers had been wiped out and the Roman Catholic Church had won back many of its followers in Europe.

be preoccupied with 全神贯注
enforce *v.* 执行

order *n.* 修会，修道团体
Jesuit *n.* 耶稣会

5.2 New Religious Orders: The Jesuits

In addition to the Council of Trent, another major factor which strengthened the Counter-Reformation was the foundation of several new religious orders. The largest and most famous of these new orders was the Society of Jesus, whose members are commonly known as Jesuits. The society was founded a **Spaniard**, **Ignatius Loyola** (1491—1556) in 1534 and formally approved by Pope Paul III six years later.

Spaniard *n.* 西班牙人
Ignatius Loyola 依纳爵·罗耀拉

In his younger days Loyola had been a soldier and had fought bravely against the French in the armies of the Emperor Charles Ⅴ. After he was wounded on the battlefield, he had to give up his military career. Lying on his hospital bed, he read a life of Christ and biographies of several saints and decided to be a knight for Christ. This happened in the very same year (1521) when Luther stood up against the Catholic Church at Worms. Loyola's remarkable career would make him a champion of Catholicism.

Over a period of twelve years, Loyola prepared for his life's mission through prayer, pilgrimages, and education. In 1528, he went to the University of Paris, the centre of Catholic learning in Europe at the time. There he met six pious and scholarly men who became the first members of the Society of Jesus. Loyola also wrote a small but powerful book, ***The Spiritual Exercises***. Published in 1541, this book gave practical advice on how to master one's will and serve God by a systematic program of **meditations** on sin and the life of Christ. Loyola

The Spiritual Exercises 《神操》
meditation *n.* 冥思
obedience *n.* 顺从

emphasized the importance of **obedience**. He encouraged his followers to understand their own attitudes, beliefs, and even lives as less important than the papacy and the Roman church. Loyola's *Spiritual Exercises* were a great influence on numerous Catholics. They became the basic handbook for all Jesuits.

Realizing the importance of education, the Jesuits made it one of their primary duties to **enlighten** and train the young. As schoolmasters, they soon had no equals in Europe. In Catholic countries, Jesuits became the **principal** teachers in universities, and their schools and colleges provided the best education. The work of the Jesuits spread literacy in Catholic countries. As Francis Bacon later said of Jesuit teaching, "Nothing better has been put into practice."

enlighten *v.* 启蒙

principal *adj.* 主要的

In Europe, the Jesuits won popular respect through the purity of their lives as well as their learning. Their political influence was considerable in France, Portugal, Spain, and Austria during the 16th and 17th centuries. They helped to stop the spread of Lutheranism into south Germany. They also assisted in the hunting down of the Huguenots in France. They also enjoyed spectacular success in missionary work beyond Europe, carrying Catholicism to India, Japan, China, South America, the St. Lawrence and Mississippi valleys in North America, Mexico, and California.

For devout Catholics, the greatest achievement of the Counter-Reformation was the defense and **revitalization** of their faith. It led to an extraordinary renewal of the Catholic faith in Europe. During the Middle Ages, especially in the Late Middle Ages, most Catholics had taken their religion as a matter of habit and ritual. The events of the 16th century forced Catholics to defend their beliefs and re-examine their lives, their actions, and their individual relationships to their faith. This renewal of devotion led to the formation of new religious orders and the construction of many churches, schools and charitable organizations. After the Counter-Reformation, Protestantism was unable to gain much new territory. Europe's current geographical division into predominantly Catholic and Protestant areas remains more or less as it was by the end of the 16th century.

revitalization *n.* 复兴

6. General Effects of the Reformation

It is difficult to gain a clear picture of the effects of the religious events of the 16th century on other aspects of life. Certain changes, at least, seem to be a direct or indirect consequence. The first effect of the religious **upheaval** was undoubtedly the increase in the power of princes and kings. Throughout the Middle Ages, relations between church and state had never been smooth, as religious and political leaders had different views on the power and status of the church. By supporting the Protestants, many **ambitious** rulers gained the upper hand in their power struggle against the Catholic Church in Rome. The Protestant Reformation could not have succeeded without the political and military support of powerful rulers in the Lutheran states of Germany and Scandinavia, in England, and even in Switzerland and Holland. The rulers of these territories ended up with much more **absolute** power than before. In Catholic states, too, rulers took advantage of the Church's difficulties to gain greater power over church matters. After the Reformation, the state gradually replaced the church as the main source of authority and focus of loyalty.

upheaval *n.* 动荡

ambitious *adj.* 野心勃勃的

absolute *adj.* 绝对的

Closely connected with this increase in monarchical power, Western Europe became more and more **secularized**. In the Middle Ages, numerous affairs such as education, charity, and justice were still controlled by the Church. When the power of the Church was broken and its lands and wealth seized in Protestant countries, governments stepped in to replace the Church's role in these areas: they established schools, cared for the poor and the sick, and made laws on marriage and the family. The role of the Church decreased in most areas of daily life. This secular trend was further strengthened by the rise of **rationalism**, modern science and technology in the post-Reformation era.

secularized *adj.* 去宗教化

rationalism *n.* 理性主义

In a less direct way, the Reformation may have led to an increase in **individualism**. The Church of Rome had always stressed unity of doctrine, and salvation through the organized church. Most of the reformers, however, tended to emphasize the relationship of each individual to God. They encouraged their followers to go directly to God, and follow the teachings of the Bible, i. e. the words of God, instead of directives from the Church of Rome. Each man could and should read the Bible and interpret it for himself. Such an emphasis on the value of the individual is part of the **democratic** faith. Indeed, many

individualism *n.* 个人主义

democratic *adj.* 民主的

radical Protestant reformers organized their movements in a democratic fashion. It can therefore also be argued that the Reformation had some influence on the rise of modern democracy.

However, the most immediate effect of the religious events of the 16th century was an **outburst** of religious **intolerance**. In 1500 almost all the **inhabitants** of western and central Europe were Catholic Christians and religious **violence** was almost unheard of. Sixty years later, Europe was divided into Catholics, Lutherans, Calvinists, and a dozen other **sects**. These religious groups were constantly fighting against each other, persecuting, and being persecuted. In Catholic countries, the church courts, spies, police, and the army were employed to wipe out heretics. Protestants were often tortured and burnt at the stake. Meanwhile in Protestant lands Catholics were driven out, put to death, or had their property confiscated. Unable to find peaceful ways to agree on the meaning of the Bible, Christians resorted to violence and brute force. The ensuing conflicts and wars proved how destructive religious fervor can be.

radical *adj.* 激进的

outburst *n.* 迸发

intolerance *n.* 不宽容，褊狭

inhabitant *n.* 居民

violence *n.* 暴力

sect *n.* 派别

7. Conclusion

The Protestant Reformation was one of the most important and wide-ranging movements in human history. Many argue that it was one of history's turning points. Most obviously, it changed the way people thought about religion. It opened up and widened the divisions within Christianity that were being felt in Europe in the 15th and 16th centuries. It diluted the power and influence of the Church of Rome. The Protestant Reformation destroyed the medieval ideal of a united Christian community. Western Christianity has been divided ever since. The Roman Catholic Counter-Reformation, a reaction to the Protestant Reformation in the middle of the century, decided many features of the Roman Catholic Church which still exist today. The church lost its authority to settle all disputes among Christians.

Besides its transformative impact on religion, the Reformation also had profound political and cultural effects. Some historians claim that the Reformation led to the rise of nationalism and the modern nation-state. Others argue that the Reformation gave birth to the modern notions of individualism and secularism. All in all, the Reformation reshaped the political map and cultural landscape of Europe. In many ways Christianity and European society would never be the same again.

Exercises

Ⅰ. Terminology: choose the suitable terms to fill in the blanks.

A. protestants B. Elizabetharian Settlement C. faith
D. Jesuits E. Ninety-Five Theses F. predestination
G. indulgence H. simony I. Anglicanism
J. the Supremacy Act

• Luther argued that salvation came only through __1__. The pope had no power to forgive sins. He could only confirm what God already had done.

• Calvin developed a strong doctrine of __2__, which means the future of man, from birth, is fixed by God for salvation or damnation. The chosen ones, or the elect, will go to heaven; the others will go to hell regardless of their deeds or their manner of life.

• The three major groupings within the Christian community are Roman Catholics, Orthodox, and __3__.

• The document that marked the beginning of the Reformation was __4__ written by Martin Luther.

• In the English Reformation, the Parliament passed an important law known as __5__ which established the monarch as the supreme head of both the state and the church.

• Since the reign of Queen Elizabeth I, __6__ became the official religion in England.

• In the Counter-Reformation launched by the Roman Catholics, the __7__ played a key role in revitalizing Roman Catholicism through their missionary works and educational activities.

• Within the Church of Rome many clergymen earned their positions not by merits but by money. This practice was known as __8__.

• Elizabeth chose a moderate path while restoring Protestantism in England. Her middle way condemned Catholic teachings and practices, but it also forbade extreme Protestantism. This middle way came to be called the __9__.

• In the medieval Europe, many Christians bought a special kind of coupon from the Church in order to reduce their sins. This coupon is called __10__.

Ⅱ. Decide whether the following statements are true (T) or false (F).

1. It was only in the 16th century that the Church of Rome's monopoly began to meet the challenge for religious reform. ( )

2. In the Middle Ages, Christians in Western Europe only needed to pay one tenth of their annual income to the he Church of Rome. ( )

3. By the 15th century the Pope had become powerful in both the secular life of the Europeans as well as in their religious life. ( )

4. The sales of Church offices led to low religious and personal standards of the clergymen. ( )

5. To allow a person to buy God's forgiveness and ransom his way out of hell, the Church developed the sale of indulgences. (   )

6. Martin Luther first expressed his idea of reforming the Church by criticizing the sale of indulgences. (   )

7. Reading of the Bible and his theological teaching made clearer Luther's idea about the malpractices of the Church. (   )

8. According to Luther, the Bible was the only source of political and religious authority. (   )

9. The Holy Roman Emperor Charles V helped the Pope in the movement of Catholic Counter-Reformation. (   )

10. Due to the Protestant Reformation and the Catholic Counter-Reformation, the Church of Rome lost its authority to settle all disputes among Christians. (   )

Ⅲ. Multiple choices: choose the answer that best completes the statement or answers the question.

1. Which of the following facts is NOT true with the situation in the Church of Rome before the Reformation?

A. The sale of Church offices to wealthy families.

B. The sale of indulgences to individual believers.

C. Some clegymen held several positions at the same time.

D. Clergymen must meet strict moral and educational standards.

2. Which of the following statements is NOT true with the text?

A. Martin Luther was a German missionary.

B. Martin was declared an outlaw in the Empire.

C. The Pope condemned Martin Luther's beliefs.

D. The Pope ordered Luther to change his beliefs.

3. Three of the following statements are true with the early experience of Luther. Which one is the exception?

A. Luther lived up to his father and became a priest.

B. Luther had a horrible experience in a thunderstorm.

C. He tried his best to get rid of his sin to satisfy God.

D. He damaged his health by eating and sleeping less.

4. Which of the following is true about Luther's discovery from reading the Bible?

A. His own individual faith would guarantee his salvation.

B. Saint Peter's guidance would guarantee his salvation.

C. Saint Paul's instructions would guarantee his salvation.

D. Jesus Christ's teachings would guarantee his salvation.

5. Which of the following is true about the central argument of the *Ninety-Five Theses*?

A. The *Ninety-Five Theses* marks the beginning of the Reformation.

B. It was an effort to draw attention to the corruption of the Church.

C. Repentance has the same power of the pope to forgive sins.

D. The sale of indulgences went against the true spirit of Christianity.

6. Luther called on the German princes to reject the foreign pope's authority and establish a reformed German church in ________.

A. *The Liberty of the Christian Man*

B. *Address to the Nobility of the German Nation*

C. *The Babylonian Captivity of the Church*

D. *the Ninety-Five Theses*

7. Luther attacked the belief that the sacramental system was the only means to salvation and called for the reform of monasticism in ________.

A. *The Liberty of the Christian Man*

B. *Address to the Nobility of the German Nation*

C. *The Babylonian Captivity of the Church*

D. *the Ninety-Five Theses*

8. Luther further explained his doctrine of faith and justification in ________.

A. *The Liberty of the Christian Man*

B. *Address to the Nobility of the German Nation*

C. *The Babylonian Captivity of the Church*

D. *the Ninety-Five Theses*

9. Luther made the first attempt to draw attention to the corruption of the Church in ________.

A. *The Liberty of the Christian Man*

B. *Address to the Nobility of the German Nation*

C. *The Babylonian Captivity of the Church*

D. *the Ninety-Five Theses*

10. Three of the following statements are true with Luther's teachings. Which one is the exception?

A. A priest of the Church never helps.

B. A priest of the Church is only the teacher.

C. The truth is only to be found in the Bible.

D. Every believer is a priest of his own.

11. The successful spread of Lutheranism in the Holy Roman Empire is due to three of the following facts. Which one is the exception?

A. The unstable political situation in the Holy Roman Empire.

B. Public discontent caused by high papal taxes on Germans.

C. Extreme anger in Germany against the power of the pope.

D. Luther's intention to extend his doctrine of social equality.

12. Like Luther, Calvin ________.

A. believed man, from birth, is predestined by God for salvation or damnation

B. believed that the order and discipline of the early church should be restored

C. regarded the Bible as the only source of truth and spiritual authority

D. regarded the church as a place to be with God by reading the Bible

13. Three of the following statements are true with Henry VIII. Which one is the exception?

A. He married his brother's widow against Roman Catholic rules.

B. He married his brother's widow with the Pope's authorization.

C. He was eager to divorce the queen to end the poor marriage.

D. He was eager to have a new marriage to bring him a male heir.

14. The reasons for Henry's reform in England were mainly ________.

A. religious　　B. personal　　C. political　　D. both B and C

15. Three of the following statements are true with England after the death of Henry VIII. Which one is the exception?

A. The council of regents to rule England was dominated by reformers.

B. Edward Ⅵ was enthusiastic about reform as Henry Ⅷ had been.

C. Edward Ⅵ was raised by Protestants rich with Renaissance ideas.

D. Mary succeeded Edward Ⅵ and began to restore the Catholic faith.

16. Three of the following statements are true with the Elizabethan Compromise. Which one is the exception?

A. The Church of England again rejected the authority of the pope.

B. The Church of England began to compromise with the Papacy.

C. Elizabeth again condemned Catholic teachings and practices.

D. Elizabeth, as a protestant, also forbade extreme Protestantism.

17. Three of the following statements are true with the Catholic Counter-Reformation. Which one is the exception?

A. It was in nature a reaction to Protestantism.

B. It was the result of Catholic self-criticism.

C. It resulted from the Protestant Reformation.

D. It resulted from a Church-wide call for reform.

18. Three of the following statements are true with the Council of Trent. Which one is the exception?

A. It was first a religious meeting called to win back the Protestants.

B. It condemned the scandals arising from the sale of indulgences.

C. It insisted on Catholic tradition as the mere source of authority.

D. It marks the beginning of the history of modern Catholic Church.

19. Three of the following statements are true with the Jesuits. Which one is the exception?

A. They were highly respected for their learning and the purity of their lives.

B. They became the principal university teachers in all European countries.

C. They helped to stop the spread of Lutheranism into south Germany.

D. They helped to spread Catholicism to the countries beyond Europe.

20. The most immediate effect of the Reformation was ________.

A. the increase in the power of princes and kings

B. the more and more secularized western Europe

C. the outburst of fighting among religious groups

D. the more emphasis on the value of the individual

参考文献

英文文献

1. BEATTY J L, JOHNSON O A, REISBORD J. Heritage of Western Civilization. Beijing: Pearson edu. Asia Ltd. & Beijing University Press, 2004.
2. BOARDMAN J, GRIFFIN J, MURRAY O. The Roman World. Oxford: Oxford University Press, 1989.
3. BOUCHARD C. Life and Society in the West: Antiquity and the Middle Ages. San Diego: Harcourt Brace Jovanovich Inc, 1988.
4. BUDIN S L. The Ancient Greeks: New Perspectives. California: ABC-CLIO, Inc, 2004.
5. BUIKER W J, JACKSON J S. The Essential World History. 3rd ed. Thomson Wadsworth, 2008.
6. BUIKER W J, JACKSON J S. World History, Volume 1: To 1800. 6th ed. Wadsworth, Cengage Learning, 2010.
7. BURKE P. The Renaissance. London: MacMillan Education, 1987.
8. BURKERT W. Die Orientalisierende Epoche in der Griechischen Religion und Literatur. Heidelberg: Carl Winter, 1984.
9. BURKERT W. The Orientalizing Revolution: Near Eastern Influence on Greek Culture in the Early Archaic Age, trans. Margaret E. Pinder & Walter Burkert, President and Fellows of Harvard College, 1992.
10. BREYER M. Ancient Greece. Westminster: Teacher Created Resources, Inc, 2004.
11. CAIRNS T. The Romans and Their Empire. London: Cambridge University Press, 1970.
12. CANTOR N, WERTHMAN M. Renaissance, Reformation, and Absolutism: 1450—1650. 2nd ed. New York: Thomas Y. Crowell Company, Inc, 1972.
13. CASSIUS D C. Dio's Roman History. With an English translation by Earnest Cary ; on the basis of the version of Herbert Baldwin Foster. Cambridge, Mass. Harvard University Press, 1914.
14. CHAMBER M, et al. Western Experience. 7th ed. McGraw-Hill Company, 1999.
15. CHRISTOPHER K. The Roman Empire : A Very Short Introduction. New York : Oxford University Press, 2006.
16. COFFIN J G, STACEY R C. Western Civilizations. New York: W. W. Norton & Company, Inc, 2005.
17. CRAWFORD M. The Roman republic. 2nd ed. London: Fontana Press, 1992.
18. SIDWELL D. A Survey of European Culture. Beijing: Foreign Language Teaching and

Research Press, 2008.

19. FACAROS D, LINDA T. Greece. New Holland Publishers, 2003.
20. GOMBRICH E H. A Little History of the World. New Haven and London: Yale University Press, 2008.
21. HAYES CALTON J H, BALDWIN M W, COLE C W. History of Europe. Rev. ed. New York: MacMillan Company, 1956.
22. JACKSON J S. Western History: A Brief History. Thomson Asia Pte Led and Peking University Press, 2005.
23. JOHNSON J E, JOHNSON D J. The Human Drama. World History: from 500 to 1450 C. E.. Princeton: Markus Wiener Publishers, 2002.
24. JORDAN W C. The Middle Ages: An Encyclopedia for Students. New York: Charles Scribner's Sons, 1996.
25. JUDITH M B, HOLLISTER C W. Medieval Europe: A Short History. McGraw-Hill Companies, Inc, 2006.
26. KEBRIC R B. Roman People. 4th ed. Boston: McGraw-Hill Companies, 2005.
27. KISHLANSKY M A, GEARY P, O'BREIN P. Civilization in the West, 3rd ed. New York: Addison Wesley Longman, Inc, 1998.
28. KISHLANSKY M A, GEARY P, O'BREIN P. A Brief History of Western Civilization: The Unfinished Legacy. 5th ed. New York: Pearson Education, Inc, 2007.
29. KOENIGSBERGER H G. Medieval Europe 400—1500. New York: Longman Inc, 1987.
30. LE GLAY M, VOISIN J L, LE BOHEC Y. A History of Rome. Translated by Antonia Nevill. Oxford: Blackwell Publishing, 2000.
31. LERNER R, MEACHAM S, BURNS E M. Western Civilizations: Their History and Their Culture. 12th ed. New York: W. W. Norton & Company, Inc, 1993.
32. LIBERATI A M, BOURBON F. Ancient Rome : History of a Civilization that Ruled the World. Vercelli, Italy : White Star, 2006.
33. LOTHERINGTON J. Years of Renewal: European History 1470—1600. London: Holder & Stoughton, 1988.
34. MCKAY J H, HILL B D, BUCKLER J. A History of Western Society. 3rd edition. Boston: Houoghton Mifflin Company, 1987.
35. MOORE R. Voices of Christianity: A Global Introduction. New York: McGraw-Hill, 2005.
36. MOSS H St L B. The Birth of the Middle Ages 395—814. London: Oxford University Press, 1969
37. NOBLE T, et al. Western Civilization beyond Boundaries. 5th ed. Boston & New York: Houghton Mifflin Company, 2009.
38. Oikonomidès, Nicolas. Silk Trade and Production in Byzantium the Sixth to the Ninth Century: The Seals of Kommerkiarioi. Dumbarton Oaks Paper, vol. 40: 33 – 53, 1986.
39. PETERSON R D. The Concise History of Christianity. Beijing: Beijing University Press, 2002
40. PLATO. Dialogues. Jowett tranlation. N. Y. : Pocket Books, 1950.

41. RENFREW C. The Emergence of Civilisation: The Cyclades and the Aegean in the Third Millennium B. C. London: Methuen and Co Ltd, 1972.
42. ROGERS P M. Aspects of Western Civiliztion. Pearson Edu. Inc, 2008.
43. ROSENWEIN B H. A Short History of the Middle Ages. Peterborough, Ontario: Broadview Press, 2002.
44. SAARI P, SAARI A. Renaissance and Reformation: Almanac. Farmington Hills, MI: Thomson Learning, Inc, 2002.
45. SHERMAN D. Western Civilization: Sources, Images, and Interpretations. 7th ed. New York: McGraw-Hill Company, 2008.
46. SHOTTER D. The Fall of the Roman Republic. New York & London: Routledge, 1994.
47. STEFFENS B. The Fall of the Roman Empire. San Diego: Greenhaven Press Inc, 1994.
48. WAITES B. Europe and the Wider World. London: Routledge, 1993.
49. WARRIOR V M. Roman Religion. Cambridge: Cambridge University Press, 2006.
50. WEBER E. The Western Tradition. Vol. From the Ancient World to Louis XIV. 4th ed. Lexington & Toronto: D. C. Heath & Company, 1990.
51. WILSON K, VAN DER DUSSEN J. The History of the Idea of Europe. N. Y. & London: Routledge, 1995.

中文文献

1. (法) 阿尔德伯特，等. 欧洲史. 蔡鸿滨，等，译. 海口：海南出版社，2000.
2. (英) 阿克罗伊德. 古代罗马. 冷杉，杨立新，译. 北京：生活·读书·新知三联书店，2007.
3. (英) 阿姆斯特朗. 神话简史. 重庆：重庆出版社，2005.
4. (古罗马) 奥勒. 沉思录. 长春：吉林大学出版社，2005.
5. (美) 巴尔赞. 从黎明到衰落：西方文化生活五百年. 林华，译. 北京：世界知识出版社，2002.
6. (英) 巴克豪斯. 西方经济学史. 莫竹苓，袁野，译. 海口：海南出版社，2007.
7. (英) 鲍克. 神之简史. 高师宁，等，译. 北京：三联书店，2007.
8. 曹卫东，张广海，等. 文化与文明. 桂林：广西师范大学出版社，2005.
9. (美) 昌达. 绑在一起. 刘波，译. 北京：中信出版社，2008.
10. 陈衡哲. 西洋史. 北京：东方出版社，2007.
11. (奥) 茨威格. 蒙田. 舒昌善，译. 北京：三联书店，2008.
12. (奥) 茨威格. 人类的群星闪耀时. 舒昌善，译. 北京：三联书店，2009.
13. 俄罗斯艺术科学院美术理论与美术史研究所. 文艺复兴欧洲艺术. 平野，译. 石家庄：河北教育出版社，2002.
14. 方汉文. 西方文化概论. 北京：中国人民大学出版社，2006.
15. (美) 房龙. 西方美术简史　欧洲印刷史话. 李丽，李丽娜，译. 北京：北京出版社，2001.

16. 冯承柏，等. 西方文化精义. 武汉：华中科技大学出版社，1998.
17. （美）哈斯金斯. 大学的兴起. 王建妮，译. 上海：上海人民出版社，2007.
18. （荷兰）赫伊津哈. 伊拉斯谟传. 何道宽，译. 桂林：广西师范大学出版社，2008.
19. （美）基恩. 基督教概况. 张之璐，译. 北京：北京大学出版社，2005.
20. （美）卡宁汉姆，赖希. 世界人文简史——文化与价值. 毛保诠，译. 北京：中国青年出版社，2005.
21. 来鲁宁. 欧洲概况. 北京：北京大学出版社，2004.
22. （法）赖那克. 阿波罗艺术史. 李朴园，译. 上海：上海书店出版社，2004.
23. 李安修. 宗教简史. 北京：中国友谊出版公司，2008.
24. 李世安，等. 世界文明史. 北京：中国人民大学出版社，2002.
25. （美）路威. 文明与野蛮. 吕叔湘，译. 北京：三联书店，2005.
26. （美）罗伦培登. 这是我的立场——马丁-路德传记. 陆中石，古乐人，译. 南京：译林出版社，1995.
27. 马克垚. 世界文明史. 北京：北京大学出版社，2004.
28. （英）麦格拉斯. 天堂简史. 高明贵，陈晓霞，译. 北京：北京大学出版社，2006.
29. （美）麦克里兰. 西方政治思想史. 彭淮栋，译. 海口：海南出版社，2007.
30. （英）佩特. 文艺复兴. 张岩冰，译. 桂林：广西师范大学出版社，2000.
31. （美）齐格勒. 新全球史. 魏凤莲，张颖，白玉广，译. 北京：北京大学出版社，2007.
32. （美）琼斯. 现代政治思想史. 张明贵，译. 台北：五南图书出版公司，2005.
33. （法）瑟利耶. 西欧人文图志. 吕艳霞，王恬，译. 北京：中国人民大学出版社，2008.
34. 司徒双，等. 欧洲文化入门. 2版. 北京：外语教学与研究出版社，1997.
35. （德）斯宾格勒. 西方的没落. 吴琼，译. 上海：三联书店，2006.
36. （英）斯蒂文森. 彩色欧洲史. 北京：中国友谊出版公司，2007.
37. （美）斯塔夫里阿诺斯. 全球通史. 吴象婴，梁赤民，译. 上海社会科学园出版社，1999.
38. 陶洁，等. 希腊罗马神话一百篇. 香港：中国对外翻译出版公司，1989.
39. 王曾才. 西方文化要义. 南京：江苏教育出版社，2006.
40. 王佐良，等. 欧洲文化入门. 北京：外语教学与研究出版社，1992.
41. （德）韦伯. 世界经济史纲. 胡长明，译. 北京：人民日报出版社，2007.
42. 姚介厚，李鹏程，杨深. 西欧文明. 福州：福建教育出版社，2008.
43. 叶胜年. 西方文化导论. 上海：上海外语教育出版社，2005.
44. 张桂林. 西方政治哲学. 北京：中国政法大学出版社，1999.
45. 周启迪. 世界上古史. 北京：北京师范大学出版社，2004.

参考网站

http://www.bbc.co.uk/history/
http://www.wikipedia.org

http://www.ideafinder.com/history/

http://weuropeanhistory.suite101.com/

http://images.google.com/images?source=ig&hl=en&rlz=&q=italian+Renaissance+painting&um=1&ie=UTF-8&ei=SjV-S62DJo_s7APFusjkCw&sa=X&oi=image_result_group&ct=title&resnum=1&ved=0CBMQsAQwAA

http://www.iep.utm.edu/

http://www.crandallu.ca/courses/grphil/IndexGrPh.htm

http://www.thebigview.com/greeks/navigator.html

http://www.historyworld.net/

http://www.greeklandscapes.com/

http://www.ancient-greece.org/

http://www.greek-thesaurus.gr/index.html

http://www.ancientgreece.com/

http://www.mesopotamia.co.uk/menu.html

http://www.bbc.co.uk/schools/

http://hypermedia.educ.psu.edu/k-12/edpgs/su96/meso/mesopotamia.html#terms

http://www.wadsworth.com/cgi-wadsworth/course_products_wp.pl?fid=M20b&flag=student&product_isbn_issn=9780495502852&discipline_number=21

http://en.wikibooks.org/w/index.php?title=Wikijunior_Ancient_Civilizations/Print_version&printable=yes

http://www.historylearningsite.co.uk/Martin_Luther_95_Theses.htm

http://www.schoolhistory.co.uk/

http://www.allfreeessays.com/topics/fall-of-roman-empire/0

http://www.flowofhistory.com/

http://www.crystalinks.com/mesopotamia.html

http://www.woodlands-junior.kent.sch.uk/Homework/history.html

Keys to Exercises

Chapter 1

Ⅰ. 1. C 2. A 3. B 4. H 5. I 6. D 7. J 8. F 9. E 10. G

Ⅱ. 1. F 2. T 3. T 4. T 5. F 6. F 7. T 8. F 9. F 10. F

Ⅲ. 1. C 2. B 3. B 4. D 5. B 6. D 7. B 8. C 9. C 10. C 11. B 12. C 13. D 14. C 15. C 16. A 17. B 18. B 19. C 20. B

Chapter 2

Ⅰ. 1. H 2. G 3. A 4. I 5. J 6. F 7. B 8. C 9. D 10. E

Ⅱ. 1. T 2. T 3. T 4. F 5. F 6. T 7. F 8. T 9. F 10. T

Ⅲ. 1. C 2. C 3. B 4. C 5. D 6. D 7. B 8. B 9. B 10. D 11. B 12. A 13. D 14. C 15. C 16. B 17. D 18. A 19. A 20. C

Chapter 3

Ⅰ. 1. E 2. G 3. D 4. H 5. I 6. J 7. C 8. A 9. B 10. F 11. K

Ⅱ. 1. T 2. F 3. T 4. F 5. T 6. T 7. F 8. T 9. T 10. F 11. T

Ⅲ. 1. D 2. B 3. B 4. C 5. A 6. B 7. D 8. C 9. A 10. B 11. B 12. D 13. C 14. B 15. C 16. D 17. B 18. B 19. B 20. A

Chapter 4

Ⅰ. 1. C 2. D 3. J 4. K 5. E 6. G 7. H 8. L 9. F 10. A 11. I 12. B

Ⅱ. 1. F 2. T 3. F 4. F 5. T 6. F 7. T 8. T 9. F 10. T 11. F 12. T 13. T

Ⅲ. 1. B 2. C 3. B 4. B 5. B 6. A 7. B 8. C 9. B 10. C 11. C 12. B 13. D 14. D 15. C 16. B 17. A 18. B 19. C 20. B 21. C 22. A 23. A

Chapter 5

Ⅰ. 1. F 2. B 3. G 4. J 5. E 6. A 7. C 8. H 9. D 10. I

Ⅱ. 1. F 2. T 3. T 4. F 5. F 6. T 7. T 8. T 9. F 10. F

Ⅲ. 1. C 2. A 3. D 4. D 5. A 6. B 7. B 8. C 9. A 10. D 11. B 12. D 13. D 14. D 15. A 16. C 17. B 18. C 19. B 20. C

Chapter 6

Ⅰ. 1. G 2. D 3. A 4. H 5. J 6. I 7. B 8. F 9. C 10. E 11. L 12. K

Ⅱ. 1. F 2. T 3. T 4. T 5. F 6. T 7. T 8. T 9. T 10. F

Ⅲ. 1. D 2. D 3. B 4. C 5. D 6. D 7. C 8. D 9. A 10. C 11. A 12. D 13. C 14. D 15. C 16. D 17. C 18. C 19. D 20. B

Chapter 7

Ⅰ. 1. C 2. E 3. J 4. A 5. B 6. F 7. G 8. H 9. I 10. D

Ⅱ. 1. T 2. F 3. T 4. T 5. T 6. F 7. F 8. T 9. F 10. F

Ⅲ. 1. C 2. C 3. D 4. A 5. A 6. C 7. A 8. D 9. A 10. B 11. D 12. B 13. D 14. C 15. D 16. C 17. C 18. C 19. B 20. D

Chapter 8

Ⅰ. 1. D 2. B 3. F 4. H 5. G 6. C 7. I 8. J 9. A 10. E

Ⅱ. 1. F 2. F 3. F 4. T 5. T 6. F 7. F 8. T 9. T 10. T

Ⅲ. 1. C 2. C 3. B 4. D 5. A 6. C 7. D 8. B 9. A 10. D 11. C 12. D 13. C 14. A 15. D 16. D 17. A 18. D 19. B 20. D

Chapter 9

Ⅰ. 1. C 2. F 3. A 4. E 5. J 6. I 7. D 8. H 9. B 10. G

Ⅱ. 1. F 2. F 3. T 4. T 5. T 6. T 7. T 8. T 9. F 10. T

Ⅲ. 1. D 2. D 3. A 4. A 5. D 6. B 7. C 8. A 9. D 10. A 11. D 12. C 13. C 14. D 15. B 16. B 17. B 18. C 19. B 20. C